Preface

The *Uniform Code for Building Conservation* establishes life-safety requirements for all existing buildings that undergo alteration or a change in use. Its provisions offer alternative methods of achieving safety so that the inventory of existing buildings can be preserved.

This code provides the jurisdiction with tools to effectively implement the provisions of *Uniform Building Code*™ Section 3403 and the exception to Section 3405. This is accomplished by identifying a minimum level of safety or performance for all existing buildings. The baseline is determined by the *Uniform Code for the Abatement of Dangerous Buildings*™ and the *Uniform Housing Code*™. The expression "less hazardous, based on life and fire risk" contained in *Uniform Building Code* Section 3405 covering change in use is given a more specific meaning by this code. Historic buildings are given certain exceptions and alternatives within the intent of *Uniform Building Code* Section 3403.5.

Also included for the purpose of assisting in the evaluation of existing buildings and the determination of acceptable alternates are five guidelines developed as a part of the United States Department of Housing and Urban Development's (HUD) Rehabilitation Guidelines Program. These guidelines cover archaic materials and assemblies and include a discussion of exit systems. These documents are copies of the HUD publications, and the contents have not been verified by the International Conference of Building Officials. The Conference assumes no responsibility for the information contained therein or its application and interpretation.

Vertical lines in margins indicate a change in the requirements from the 1994 publication. An analysis of changes between editions is published by the Conference.

Deletion indicators (◗) are provided in the margin where a paragraph or item listing has been deleted if the deletion resulted in a change in requirements.

CODES AND RELATED PUBLICATIONS

The International Conference of Building Officials (ICBO) publishes a family of codes, each correlated with the *Uniform Building Code*™ to provide jurisdictions with a complete set of building-related regulations for adoption. Some of these codes are published in affiliation with other organizations such as the International Fire Code Institute (IFCI) and the International Code Council (ICC). Reference materials and related codes also are available to improve knowledge of code enforcement and administration of building inspection programs. Publications and products are continually being added, so inquiries should be directed to Conference headquarters for a listing of available products. Many codes and references are also available on CD-ROM or floppy disk. These are denoted by (*). The following publications and products are available from ICBO:

CODES

*Uniform Building Code, Volumes 1, 2 and 3. The most widely adopted model building code in the United States, the performance-based *Uniform Building Code* is a proven document, meeting the needs of government units charged with the enforcement of building regulations. Volume 1 contains administrative, fire- and life-safety and field inspection provisions; Volume 2 contains structural engineering design provisions; and Volume 3 contains material, testing and installation standards.

*Uniform Mechanical Code™. Provides a complete set of requirements for the design, construction, installation and maintenance of heating, ventilating, cooling and refrigeration systems; incinerators and other heat-producing appliances.

International Plumbing Code™. Provides consistent and technically advanced requirements that can be used across the country to provide comprehensive regulations of modern plumbing systems. Setting minimum regulations for plumbing facilities in terms of performance objectives, the IPC provides for the acceptance of new and innovative products, materials and systems.

International Private Sewage Disposal Code™. Provides flexibility in the development of safety and sanitary individual sewage disposal systems and includes detailed provisions for all aspects of design, installation and inspection of private sewage disposal systems.

International Mechanical Code™. Establishes minimum regulations for mechanical systems using prescriptive and performance-related provisions. It is founded on broad-based principles that make possible the use of new materials and new mechanical designs.

Uniform Zoning Code™. This code is dedicated to intelligent community development and to the benefit of the public welfare by providing a means of promoting uniformity in zoning laws and enforcement.

*Uniform Fire Code™, Volumes 1 and 2. The premier model fire code in the United States, the *Uniform Fire Code* sets forth provisions necessary for fire prevention and fire protection. Published by the International Fire Code Institute, the *Uniform Fire Code* is endorsed by the Western Fire Chiefs Association, the International Association of Fire Chiefs and ICBO. Volume 1 contains code provisions compatible with the *Uniform Building Code*, and Volume 2 contains standards referenced from the code provisions.

*Urban-Wildland Interface Code™. Promulgated by IFCI, this code regulates both land use and the built environment in designated urban-wildland interface areas. This newly developed code is the only model code that bases construction requirements on the fire-hazard severity exposed to the structure. Developed under a grant from the Federal Emergency Management Agency, this code is the direct result of hazard mitigation meetings held after devastating wildfires.

Uniform Housing Code™. Provides complete requirements affecting conservation and rehabilitation of housing. Its regulations are compatible with the *Uniform Building Code.*

Uniform Code for the Abatement of Dangerous Buildings™. A code compatible with the *Uniform Building Code* and the *Uniform Housing Code* which provides equitable remedies consistent with other laws for the repair, vacation or demolition of dangerous buildings.

Uniform Sign Code™. Dedicated to the development of better sign regulation, its requirements pertain to all signs and sign construction attached to buildings.

Uniform Administrative Code™. This code covers administrative areas in connection with adoption of the *Uniform Building Code,* *Uniform Mechanical Code* and related codes. It contains provisions which relate to site preparation, construction, alteration, moving, repair and use and occupancies of buildings or structures and building service equipment, including plumbing, electrical and mechanical regulations. The code is compatible with the administrative provisions of all codes published by the Conference.

Uniform Building Security Code™. This code establishes minimum standards to make dwelling units resistant to unlawful entry. It regulates swinging doors, sliding doors, windows and hardware in connection with dwelling units of apartment houses or one- and two-family dwellings. The code gives consideration to the concerns of police, fire and building officials in establishing requirements for resistance to burglary which are compatible with fire and life safety.

Uniform Code for Building Conservation™. A building conservation guideline presented in code format which will provide a community with the means to preserve its existing buildings while achieving appropriate levels of safety. It is formatted in the same manner as the *Uniform Building Code,* is compatible with other Uniform Codes, and may be adopted as a code or used as a guideline.

Dwelling Construction under the Uniform Building Code™. Designed primarily for use in home building and apprentice training, this book contains requirements applicable to the construction of one- and two-story dwellings based on the requirements of the *Uniform Building Code.* Available in English or Spanish.

Dwelling Construction under the Uniform Mechanical Code™. This publication is for the convenience of the homeowner or contractor interested in installing mechanical equipment in a one- or two-family dwelling in conformance with the *Uniform Mechanical Code.*

Supplements to UBC and related codes. Published in the years between editions, the Supplements contain all approved changes, plus an analysis of those changes.

Uniform Building Code—1927 Edition. A special 60th anniversary printing of the first published *Uniform Building Code.*

One and Two Family Dwelling Code. Promulgated by ICC, this code eliminates conflicts and duplications among the model codes to achieve national uniformity. Covers mechanical and plumbing requirements as well as construction and occupancy.

Application and Commentary on the One and Two Family Dwelling Code. An interpretative commentary on the *One and Two Family Dwelling Code* intended to enhance uniformity of interpretation and application of the code nationwide. Developed by the three model code organizations, this document includes numerous illustrations of code requirements and the rationale for individual provisions.

Model Energy Code. This code includes minimum requirements for effective use of energy in the design of new buildings and structures and additions to existing buildings. It is based on American Society of Heating, Refrigeration and Air-conditioning Engineers Standard 90A-1980 and was originally developed jointly by ICBO, BOCA, SBCCI and the National Conference of States on Building Codes and Standards under a contract funded by the United States Department of Energy. The code is now maintained by ICC and is adopted by reference in the *Uniform Building Code.*

National Electrical Code®. The electrical code used throughout the United States. Published by the National Fire Protection Association, it is an indispensable aid to every electrician, contractor, architect, builder, inspector and anyone who must specify or certify electrical installations.

TECHNICAL REFERENCES AND EDUCATIONAL MATERIALS

Analysis of Revisions to the Uniform Codes™. An analysis of changes between the previous and new editions of the Uniform Codes is provided. Changes between code editions are noted either at the beginning of chapters or in the margins of the code text.

*Handbook to the Uniform Building Code. The handbook is a completely detailed and illustrated commentary on the *Uniform Building Code,* tracing historical background and rationale of the codes through the current edition. Also included are numerous drawings and figures clarifying the application and intent of the code provisions. Also available in electronic format.

*Handbook to the Uniform Mechanical Code. An indispensable tool for understanding the provisions of the current UMC, the handbook traces the historical background and rationale behind the UMC provisions, includes 160 figures which clarify the intent and application of the code, and provides a chapter-by-chapter analysis of the UMC.

*Uniform Building Code Application Manual. This manual discusses sections of the *Uniform Building Code* with a question-and-answer format, providing a comprehensive analysis of the intent of the code sections. Most sections include illustrative examples. The manual is in loose-leaf format so that code applications published in *Building Standards* magazine may be inserted. Also available in electronic format.

*Uniform Mechanical Code Application Manual. As a companion document to the *Uniform Mechanical Code,* this manual provides a comprehensive analysis of the intent of a number of code sections in an easy-to-use question-and-answer format. The manual is available in a loose-leaf format and includes illustrative examples for many code sections.

*Uniform Fire Code Applications Manual. This newly developed manual provides questions and answers regarding UFC provisions. A comprehensive analysis of the intent of numerous code sections, the manual is in a loose-leaf format for easy insertion of code applications published in IFCI's *Fire Code Journal.*

Quick-Reference Guide to the Occupancy Requirements of the 1997 UBC. Code requirements are compiled in this publication by occupancy groups for quick access. These tabulations assemble requirements for each occupancy classification in the code. Provisions, such as fire-resistive ratings for occupancy separations in Table 3-B, exterior wall and opening protection requirements in Table 5-A-1, and fire-resistive ratings for types of construction in Table 6-A, are tabulated for quick reference and comparison.

Plan Review Manual. A practical text that will assist and guide both the field inspector and plan reviewer in applying the code requirements. This manual covers the nonstructural and basic structural aspects of plan review.

Field Inspection Manual. An important fundamental text for courses of study at the community college and trade or technical school level. It is an effective text for those studying building construction or architecture and includes sample forms and checklists for use in the field.

Building Department Administration. An excellent guide for improvement of skills in departmental management and in the enforcement and application of the Building Code and other regulations administered by a building inspection department. This textbook will also be a valuable aid to instructors, students and those in related professional fields.

Building Department Guide to Disaster Mitigation. This new, expanded guide is designed to assist building departments in developing or updating disaster mitigation plans. Subjects covered include guidelines for damage mitigation, disaster-response management, immediate response, mutual aid and inspections, working with the media, repair and recovery policies, and public information bulletins. This publication is a must for those involved in preparing for and responding to disaster.

Building Official Management Manual. This manual addresses the unique nature of code administration and the managerial duties of the building official. A supplementary insert addresses the budgetary and financial aspects of a building department. It is also an ideal resource for those preparing for the management module of the CABO Building Official Certification Examination.

Legal Aspects of Code Administration. A manual developed by the three model code organizations to inform the building official on the legal aspects of the profession. The text is written in a logical sequence with explanation of legal terminology. It is designed to serve as a refresher for those preparing to take the legal module of the CABO Building Official Certification Examination.

Illustrated Guide to Conventional Construction Provisions of the UBC. This comprehensive guide and commentary provides detailed explanations of the conventional construction provisions in the UBC, including descriptive discussions and illustrated drawings to convey the prescriptive provisions related to wood-frame construction.

Introduction to the Uniform Building Code. A workbook that provides an overview of the basics of the UBC.

Uniform Building Code Update Workbook. This manual addresses many of the changes to the administrative, fire- and life-safety, and inspection provisions appearing in the UBC.

UMC Workbook. Designed for independent study or use with instructor-led programs based on the *Uniform Mechanical Code,* this comprehensive study guide consists of 16 learning sessions, with the first two sessions reviewing the purpose, scope, definitions and administrative provisions and the remaining 14 sessions progressively exploring the requirements for installing, inspecting and maintaining heating, ventilating, cooling and refrigeration systems.

UBC Field Inspection Workbook. A comprehensive workbook for studying the provisions of the UBC. Divided into 12 sessions, this workbook focuses on the UBC combustible construction requirements for the inspection of wood-framed construction.

Concrete Manual. A publication for individuals seeking an understanding of the fundamentals of concrete field technology and inspection practices. Of particular interest to concrete construction inspectors, it will also benefit employees of concrete producers, contractors, testing and inspection laboratories and material suppliers.

Reinforced Concrete Masonry Construction Inspector's Handbook. A comprehensive information source written especially for masonry inspection covering terminology, technology, materials, quality control, inspection and standards. Published jointly by ICBO and the Masonry Institute of America.

You Can Build It! Sponsored by ICBO in cooperation with CABO, this booklet contains information and advice to aid "do-it-yourselfers" with building projects. Provides guidance in necessary procedures such as permit requirements, codes, plans, cost estimation, etc.

Guidelines for Manufactured Housing Installations. A guideline in code form implementing the *Uniform Building Code* and its companion code documents to regulate the permanent installation of a manufactured home on a privately owned, nonrental site. A commentary is included to explain specific provisions, and codes applying to each component part are defined.

Accessibility Reference Guide. This guide is a valuable resource for architects, interior designers, plan reviewers and others who design and enforce accessibility provisions. Features include accessibility requirements, along with detailed commentary and graphics to clarify the provisions; cross-references to other applicable sections of the UBC and the Americans with Disabilities Act Accessibility Guidelines; a checklist of UBC provisions on access and usability requirements; and many other useful references.

Educational and Technical Reference Materials. The Conference has been a leader in the development of texts and course material to assist in the educational process. These materials include vital information necessary for the building official and subordinates in carrying out their responsibilities and have proven to be excellent references in connection with community college curricula and higher-level courses in the field of building construction technology and inspection and in the administration of building departments. Included are plan review checklists for structural, nonstructural, mechanical and fire-safety provisions and a full line of videotapes and automated products.

1997

UNIFORM CODE FOR BUILDING CONSERVATION™

First Printing

Publication date: May 1997

ISBN 1-884590-97-7

by

International Conference of Building Officials

5360 WORKMAN MILL ROAD
WHITTIER, CALIFORNIA 90601-2298
(800) 284-4406 • (562) 699-0541

PRINTED IN THE U.S.A.

TABLE OF CONTENTS

Chapter 1
TITLE AND SCOPE

SECTION 101 — TITLE

These regulations shall be known as the *Uniform Code for Building Conservation,* may be cited as such, and will be referred to herein as "this code."

SECTION 102 — PURPOSE

The purpose of this code is to encourage the continued use or reuse of legally existing buildings and structures.

SECTION 103 — SCOPE

The provisions of this code shall constitute the minimum standards for change of occupancy, alteration or repair of existing buildings and structures. Whenever reference is made to the appendix in this code, the provisions of the appendix shall not apply unless specifically adopted.

SECTION 104 — NONCONFORMING RIGHTS

Buildings in existence at the time of the adoption of this code may have their existing use or occupancy continued if such use or occupancy was legal at the time of the adoption of this code, provided such continued use is not dangerous to life and that subsequently adopted regulations specifically applicable to existing buildings or structures are satisfied.

Nothing in this code shall be construed to allow the degradation of those systems, devices and equipment required by the code under which the building was constructed.

SECTION 105 — ADDITIONS, ALTERATIONS AND REPAIRS

Buildings and structures to which additions, alterations or repairs are made shall comply with all the requirements of the Building Code for new construction except as specifically provided in this code. Additions, alterations or repairs may be made to any building or structure without requiring the existing building or structure to comply with all the requirements of the Building Code, provided:

1. Additions shall conform to requirements for a new building or structure.

2. Additions, alterations or repairs shall not cause an existing building or structure to become unsafe or overloaded.

3. Any building plus new additions shall not exceed the height, number of stories and area specified for new buildings.

4. Alterations or repairs to an existing building or structure that are nonstructural and do not adversely affect any structural member or any part of the building or structure having required fire resistance may be made with the same materials of which the building or structure is constructed. See Chapter 4 of this code for requirements for installation or replacement of glass. See Chapter 7 of this code for provisions requiring installation of smoke detectors in existing Group R Occupancies.

SECTION 106 — CHANGE OF OCCUPANCY

Any change in the use or occupancy of an existing building or structure shall comply with the provisions of this code. Any building that involves a change in use or occupancy shall not exceed the height, number of stories and area permitted for new buildings, except as permitted in this code.

SECTION 107 — MAINTENANCE

All buildings and structures and all parts thereof shall be maintained in a safe and sanitary condition. All systems, devices or safeguards that were required by the code under which the building was constructed shall be maintained in conformance with the requirements of that code. The owner or the owner's designated agent shall be responsible for the maintenance of buildings and structures. To determine compliance with this section, the building official may cause any structure to be reinspected.

SECTION 108 — ALTERNATE MATERIALS, ALTERNATE DESIGN AND METHODS OF CONSTRUCTION

The provisions of this code are not intended to prevent the use of any material, alternate design or method of construction not specifically prescribed by this code, provided any alternate has been approved and its use authorized by the building official.

The building official may approve any such alternate, provided the building official finds that the proposed design is satisfactory and complies with the provisions of this code and that the material, method or work offered is, for the purpose intended, at least the equivalent of that prescribed in this code in suitability, strength, effectiveness, fire resistance, durability, safety and sanitation.

The building official shall require that sufficient evidence or proof be submitted to substantiate any claims that may be made regarding its use. The details of any action granting approval of an alternate shall be recorded and entered in the files of the code enforcement agency.

SECTION 109 — MODIFICATIONS

When there are practical difficulties involved in carrying out the provisions of this code, the building official may accept compliance alternatives or grant modifications for individual cases. The building official shall first find that a special individual reason makes the strict letter of this code impractical and that the compliance alternative or modification is in conformance with the intent and purpose of this code and that such compliance alternative or modification does not lessen health, life and the intent of any fire-safety requirements or any degree of structural integrity. The details of any action granting modifications or the acceptance of a compliance alternative shall be recorded and entered in the files of the code enforcement agency.

SECTION 110 — TESTS

Whenever there is insufficient evidence of compliance with any of the provisions of this code or evidence that any material or construction does not conform to the requirements of this code, the building official may require tests as proof of compliance to be made at no expense to this jurisdiction.

Test methods shall be as specified by this code, the Building Code or by other recognized test standards. If there are no recognized and accepted test methods for the proposed alternate, the building official shall determine test procedures.

All tests shall be made by an approved agency. Reports of such tests shall be retained by the building official for the period required for the retention of public records.

Chapter 2
ENFORCEMENT AND PERMITS

SECTION 201 — ADMINISTRATION

The building official is hereby authorized to enforce the provisions of this code. The building official shall have the power to render interpretations of this code and to adopt and enforce rules and regulations supplemental to this code as deemed necessary in order to clarify the application of the provisions of this code. Such interpretations, rules and regulations shall be in conformity with the intent and purpose of this code.

SECTION 202 — PERMITS REQUIRED

Buildings or structures regulated by this code shall not be enlarged, altered, repaired, improved or converted unless a separate permit for each building or structure has first been obtained from the building official in accordance with and in the manner prescribed in the Building Code.

SECTION 203 — INSPECTION OF WORK

All buildings or structures within the scope of this code and all construction or work for which a permit is required shall be subject to inspection by the building official in accordance with and in the manner prescribed in this code and the Building Code.

SECTION 204 — RIGHT OF ENTRY

When it is necessary to make an inspection to enforce the provisions of this code, or when the building official has reasonable cause to believe that there exists in a building or upon a premises a condition that is contrary to or in violation of this code, which makes the building or premises unsafe, dangerous or hazardous, the building official may enter the building or premises at reasonable times to inspect or to perform the duties imposed by this code, provided that if such building or premises be occupied that credentials be presented to the occupant and entry requested. If such building or premises be unoccupied, the building official shall first make a reasonable effort to locate the owner or other person having charge or control of the building or premises and request entry. If entry is refused, the building official shall have recourse to the remedies provided by law to secure entry.

SECTION 205 — LIABILITY

The building official charged with the enforcement of this code, acting in good faith and without malice in the discharge of the duties required by this code or other pertinent law or ordinance shall not thereby be rendered personally liable for damages that may accrue to persons or property as a result of an act or by reason of an act or omission in the discharge of such duties. A suit brought against the building official or employee because of such act or omission performed by the building official or employee in the enforcement of any provision of such codes or other pertinent laws or ordinances implemented through the enforcement of this code or enforced by the code enforcement agency shall be defended by this jurisdiction until final termination of such proceedings, and any judgment resulting therefrom shall be assumed by this jurisdiction.

This code shall not be construed to relieve from or lessen the responsibility of any person owning, operating or controlling any building or structure for any damages to persons or property caused by defects, nor shall the code enforcement agency or its parent jurisdiction be held as assuming any such liability by reason of the inspections authorized by this code or any permits or certificates issued under this code.

SECTION 206 — UNSAFE BUILDINGS OR STRUCTURES

All buildings or structures regulated by this code that are structurally unsafe or not provided with adequate egress, or which constitute a fire hazard, or are otherwise dangerous to human life are, for the purpose of this section, unsafe.

Building service equipment regulated by codes adopted by this jurisdiction, which constitutes a fire, electrical or health hazard, or insanitary condition, or is otherwise dangerous to human life is, for the purpose of this section, unsafe. Any use of buildings, structures or building service equipment constituting a hazard to safety, health or public welfare by reason of inadequate maintenance, dilapidation, obsolescence, fire hazard, disaster, damage or abandonment is, for the purpose of this section, an unsafe use.

Parapet walls, cornices, spires, towers, tanks, statuary and other appendages or structural members that are supported by, attached to, or a part of a building and that are in deteriorated condition or otherwise unable to sustain the design loads that are specified in this code are hereby designated as unsafe building appendages.

All such unsafe buildings, structures or appendages and building service equipment are hereby declared to be public nuisances and shall be abated by repair, rehabilitation, demolition or removal in accordance with the procedures set forth in the Dangerous Buildings Code or such alternate procedures as may have been or as may be adopted by this jurisdiction. As an alternative, the building official, or other employee or official of this jurisdiction as designated by the governing body, may institute any other appropriate action to prevent, restrain, correct or abate the violation.

SECTION 207 — BUILDING CONSERVATION ADVISORY AND APPEALS BOARD

In order to provide for final interpretation of the provisions of this code and to hear appeals provided for hereunder, there is hereby established a building conservation advisory and appeals board consisting of five members who are not employees of the jurisdiction. The building official shall be an ex officio member of and shall act as secretary to said board. The board shall be appointed by the governing body and shall hold office at its pleasure. The board shall adopt reasonable rules of procedure for conducting its business and shall render all decisions and findings in writing to the appellant with a copy to the building official. Copies of all rules of procedure adopted by the board shall be delivered to the building official, who shall make them freely accessible to the public.

Chapter 3
DEFINITIONS

SECTION 301 — DEFINITIONS

For the purpose of this code, certain terms, phrases, words and their derivatives shall be construed as specified in this chapter. Words used in the singular include the plural and the plural the singular. Words used in the masculine gender include the feminine and the feminine the masculine.

Where terms are not defined, they shall have their ordinary accepted meanings within the context in which they are used. *Webster's Third New International Dictionary of the English Language, Unabridged,* copyright 1986, shall be considered as providing ordinarily accepted meanings.

ADDITION is an extension or increase in floor area or height of a building or structure.

ALTER or ALTERATION is any change, addition or modification in construction or occupancy.

APPROVED AGENCY is an established and recognized agency regularly engaged in conducting tests or furnishing inspection services, when such agency has been approved by the building official.

BUILDING CODE is the *Uniform Building Code* promulgated by the International Conference of Building Officials, as adopted by this jurisdiction.

BUILDING OFFICIAL is the officer or other designated authority charged with the administration and enforcement of this code, or duly authorized representative.

BUILDING SERVICE EQUIPMENT refers to the plumbing, mechanical, electrical and elevator equipment including piping, wiring, fixtures and other accessories that provide sanitation, lighting, heating, ventilation, cooling, refrigeration, firefighting and transportation facilities essential for the habitable occupancy of the building or structure for its designated use and occupancy.

COMPLIANCE ALTERNATIVE is conformance with the intent of this code, using means, materials or design features that can be demonstrated to the satisfaction of the building official to perform in a manner equivalent to those specifically required by this code.

DANGEROUS BUILDING is any building or structure deemed to be dangerous by Section 302 of the *Uniform Code for the Abatement of Dangerous Buildings* or such alternate procedures as may have been adopted by this jurisdiction.

DANGEROUS BUILDINGS CODE is the *Uniform Code for the Abatement of Dangerous Buildings* promulgated by the International Conference of Building Officials, as adopted by this jurisdiction.

ELECTRICAL CODE is the *National Electrical Code* promulgated by the National Fire Protection Association, as adopted by this jurisdiction.

EQUIVALENCY is meeting the intent of this code by means other than those detailed in specific code provisions.

EXISTING BUILDING is a building or structure erected prior to the adoption of the current Building Code of the jurisdiction and has been issued a certificate of occupancy or has been legally occupied.

HISTORIC BUILDING is a building or structure that has been designated by official action of the legally constituted authority of this jurisdiction as having special historical or architectural significance.

IMMINENT HAZARD is a condition that could cause serious or life-threatening injury or death at any time.

OCCUPANCY is the purpose for which a building, or part thereof, is used or intended to be used.

REHABILITATE is to return a building or structure to a state of utility through additions, alterations or repairs. As applied to historic structures, it includes the preservation of those portions or features that are of historical, architectural and cultural value.

REPAIR is the reconstruction or renewal of any part of an existing building.

SUBSTANDARD BUILDING is any residential building defined as substandard by the adopted housing code of the jurisdiction.

Chapter 4
MINIMUM STANDARDS FOR EXISTING BUILDINGS

SECTION 401 — GENERAL

401.1 General. Existing buildings or structures within the scope of this code shall meet the minimum standards set forth in this chapter, as well as any specific occupancy requirements set forth in this code. Buildings and structures undergoing a change of occupancy or a change in the character of their use shall also meet the requirements of Chapter 5. Historic buildings and structures shall meet the requirements of Chapter 6 and the provisions of this chapter where applicable. Buildings or structures shall meet the minimum level of performance specified in this chapter through compliance with the specific provisions of this code.

401.2 Heights and Areas. The heights and areas of existing buildings or structures shall be acceptable, provided the requirements of this chapter are satisfied. Requirements for buildings and structures undergoing a change of occupancy shall be as provided in Chapter 5.

SECTION 402 — LIFE SAFETY

402.1 General. Safety to life in existing buildings and structures shall meet the intent of the Building Code. The provisions of this section shall be deemed as meeting the intent of the Building Code for existing buildings, provided that none of the life-safety features required by the code under which the building was constructed will be reduced below the level established by that code or equivalent provisions of the currently adopted Building Code. Means of egress system capacity and the arrangement of exits shall comply with the requirements of the Building Code. Means of egress systems complying with Sections 402.2 through 402.4 shall be deemed as meeting the intent of the Building Code for existing buildings, provided that an exit system evaluated under the provisions of this code is judged by the building official to be at least equivalent to the exit system that was required by the code under which the building was constructed or equivalent provisions of the currently adopted Building Code.

402.2 Means of Egress. All elements of the means of egress system shall be of sufficient size, width and arrangement to provide safe and adequate means of egress. Every required means of egress shall have access to a public way, directly or through yards, courts or similar spaces, and such access shall be permanently maintained clear of any obstruction that would impede egress.

402.3 Number of Means of Egress. Occupants of every floor above the first story and basements shall have access to at least two separate means of egress. When approved by the building official, one of the means of egress may be an exterior fire escape complying with Section 402.5. A fire escape shall not be substituted for a stairway that was required by the code under which the building was constructed.

> **EXCEPTIONS:** 1. In all occupancies, second stories with an occupant load of less than 10 may have one means of egress.
>
> 2. Only one means of egress need be provided from the second story within an individual dwelling unit that has an occupant load of less than 10.
>
> 3. Two or more dwelling units on the second story may have access to only one common means of egress when the total occupant load does not exceed 10.
>
> 4. Floors and basements used exclusively for service of the building may have one means of egress. For the purposes of this exception, storage rooms, laundry rooms, maintenance offices and similar uses shall not be considered as providing service to the building.
>
> 5. Basements within an individual dwelling unit having an occupant load of less than 10 may have one means of egress.
>
> 6. Occupied roofs on Group R, Division 3 Occupancies may have one means of egress if such occupied areas are less than 500 square feet (46.45 m^2) located no higher than immediately above the second story.

402.4 Corridors. Corridors serving as a part of the means of egress system that have an occupant load of 30 or more in a Group A, B, E, F, I, H, M or S Occupancy or an occupant load of 10 or more in a Group R, Division 1 Occupancy shall have walls and ceilings of not less than one-hour fire-resistive construction. Existing walls and ceilings surfaced with wood lath and plaster or $1/_2$-inch-thick (12.7 mm) gypsum wallboard may be permitted in lieu of one-hour fire-resistive construction, provided the surfaces are in good condition.

Door openings into such corridors shall be protected by a tightfitting smoke- and draft-control assembly having a fire-protection rating of not less than 20 minutes when such opening protection was required by the code under which the building was constructed. Door-closing devices, door gaskets and other requirements imposed by the code under which the building was constructed shall be maintained. When the building was constructed under a code that did not require 20-minute smoke- and draft-control assemblies, doorway openings shall be protected by doors having a fire-protection rating of not less than 20 minutes or by a minimum $1^3/_8$-inch-thick (34.9 mm) solid-bonded wood-core door or an equivalent insulated steel door. In such case, the frames need not have a fire-resistive time period. Doors shall be maintained self-closing or shall be automatic closing by activation of a smoke detector.

Transoms and openings other than doors from corridors to rooms shall be protected as required by the Building Code. When the code under which the building was constructed permitted unprotected transoms or other unprotected openings, other than doors, such transoms or openings shall be covered with a minimum of $3/_4$-inch-thick (19.1 mm) wood structural panel or $1/_2$-inch-thick (12.7 mm) gypsum wallboard or equivalent material on the room side. Openings with fixed wired glass set in steel frames are permitted in corridor walls and ceilings.

> **EXCEPTION:** Existing corridor walls, ceilings and opening protection not in compliance with the above may be continued when the building is protected with an approved automatic sprinkler system throughout. Such sprinkler system may be supplied from the domestic water-supply system, provided the system is of adequate pressure, capacity and sizing for the combined domestic and sprinkler requirements.

402.5 Fire Escapes. Existing fire escapes complying with this section may be accepted by the building official as one of the required means of egress. The fire escape shall not be the primary or the only means of egress. Fire escapes shall not take the place of stairways required by the codes under which the building was constructed. Fire escapes shall be subject to reinspection as required by the building official. The building official may require documentation to show compliance with the requirements of this section.

Fire escapes shall comply with the following:

1. Access from a corridor shall not be through an intervening room.

EXCEPTION: Access through an intervening room may be permitted if the intervening door is not lockable and an exit sign is installed above the door that will direct occupants to the fire escape.

2. All openings in an exterior wall below or within 10 feet (3048 mm), measured horizontally, of an existing fire escape serving a building over two stories in height shall be protected by a self-closing fire assembly having a three-fourths-hour fire-protection rating. When located within a recess or vestibule, adjacent enclosure walls shall be not less than one-hour fire-resistive construction.

3. Egress from the building shall be by an opening having a minimum clear width and height of not less than 29 inches (737 mm). Such openings shall be openable from the inside without the use of a key or special knowledge or effort. The sill of an opening giving access to the fire escape shall be not more than 30 inches (762 mm) above the floor of the building or balcony.

4. Fire escape stairways and their ba[...] dead load plus a live load of not less [...] foot (4788 Pa) or concentrated load o[...] placed anywhere on the balcony or stairway to produce the maximum stress conditions. The stairway shall have a slope not to exceed 60 degrees from the horizontal and shall have a minimum width of 18 inches (457 mm). The stairway shall be provided with a top and intermediate railing on each side. Treads shall be not less than 4 inches (102 mm) in width and the rise between treads shall not exceed 10 inches (254 mm). All stairway and balcony railings shall support a horizontally applied force of not less than 50 pounds per lineal foot (218.9 N/m) of railing or a concentrated load of 200 pounds (890 N) placed anywhere on the railing to produce the maximum stress conditions.

5. Fire escape balconies shall be not less than 44 inches (1118 mm) in width with no floor opening greater than $^5/_8$ inch (15.9 mm) in width except the stairway opening. Stairway openings in such balconies shall be not less than 22 inches by 44 inches (559 mm by 1118 mm). The guardrail of each balcony shall be not less than 36 inches (914 mm) high with not more than 9 inches (229 mm) between intermediate rails.

6. Fire escapes shall extend to the roof or provide an approved gooseneck ladder between the top floor landing and the roof when serving buildings four or more stories in height having roofs with a slope not exceeding 4 units vertical in 12 units horizontal (33.3% slope). Such ladders shall be designed and connected to the building to withstand a horizontal force of 100 pounds per lineal foot (1459 N/m); each rung shall support a concentrated load of 500 pounds (2224 N) placed anywhere on the rung to produce the maximum stress conditions. All ladders shall be at least 15 inches (381 mm) in clear width, be located within 12 inches (305 mm) of the building and shall be placed flatwise relative to the face of the building. Ladder rungs shall be $^3/_4$ inch (19.1 mm) in diameter and shall be located 10 inches to 12 inches (254 mm to 305 mm) on center. Openings for roof access ladders through cornices and similar projections shall have minimum dimensions of 30 inches by 33 inches (762 mm by 838 mm).

7. The lowest balcony shall be not more than 18 feet (5486 mm) from the ground. Fire escapes shall extend to the ground or be provided with counterbalanced stairs reaching to the ground.

8. Fire escapes shall be kept clear and unobstructed at all times and maintained in good working order.

9. The fire escape shall have a clearance from electrical service conductors as required by the Electrical Code.

402.6 Stairways. Existing winding or spiral stairways may serve as one means of egress from a building, provided that a complying handrail is located at the stair's outside perimeter. (Also see

Section 405.) A winding or spiral stairway may not be the principal means of egress when used in conjunction with a fire escape as a second means of egress. Means of egress width shall comply with the Building Code. Circular stairways complying with the Building Code shall be acceptable as a means of egress.

SECTION 403 — STRUCTURAL SAFETY

A building or structure or its individual structural members that exceed the limits established by the Dangerous Buildings Code shall be replaced or strengthened in order that the building, structure or individual structural members will comply with the requirements of the Building Code for new construction. Roofs, floors, walls, foundations and all stuctural components of such buildings or structures shall be capable of resisting the forces and loads specified in Chapter 16 of the Building Code.

Unreinforced masonry buildings undergoing structural alterations and located in Seismic Zone 4 shall be strengthened in accordance with the requirements of Appendix Chapter 1.

EXCEPTION: Buildings undergoing minor alterations or repairs as provided in Section 3403 of the Building Code.

Unreinforced masonry buildings located in Seismic Zones 3 and 4 shall have parapet bracing and wall anchors installed at the roof line whenever a reroofing permit is issued. Such parapet braces and wall anchors shall be designed in accordance with Appendix Chapter 1.

EXCEPTION: Group R, Division 1 and Group R, Division 3 Occupancies containing not more than five dwelling units or guest rooms and used solely for residential purposes.

SECTION 404 — WEATHER PROTECTION

404.1 General. Every building shall be weather protected to provide shelter for the occupants against the elements and to exclude dampness.

404.2 Roofs. The roof of every building or structure shall provide weather protection for the building. All devices that were provided or are required to prevent ponding or flooding or to convey the roof water shall be capable of fulfilling that purpose.

404.3 Other Enclosing Elements. All weather-exposed surfaces of every existing building or structure shall provide weather protection.

SECTION 405 — OTHER SAFETY FEATURES

405.1 Stairs.

405.1.1 Rise and run. The largest tread run within any flight of stairs shall not exceed the smallest by more than $^3/_8$ inch (9.5 mm). The greatest riser height within any flight of stairs shall not exceed the smallest by more than $^3/_8$ inch (9.5 mm).

405.1.2 Handrails. Every stairway shall have at least one handrail.

EXCEPTION: A handrail is not required for existing stairs having less than four risers.

Spiral and winding stairways shall have a handrail on the outside perimeter.

405.2 Guardrails. All unenclosed floor and roof openings, open and glazed sides of stairways, landings and ramps, balconies or porches that are more than 30 inches (762 mm) above grade or floor below, and roofs used for other than service of the building shall be protected by a guardrail.

EXCEPTION: Guardrails need not be provided at the following locations:

1. On the loading side of loading docks.
2. On the auditorium side of a stage or enclosed platform.
3. On private stairways 30 inches (762 mm) or less in height.

Existing guardrails, other than guardrails located on the open side of a stairway, which are at least 36 inches (914 mm) in height, shall be permitted to remain. Guardrails lower than 36 inches (914 mm) in height shall be augmented or corrected to raise their effective height to 36 inches (914 mm). Guardrails for stairways, exclusive of their landings, may have a height that is not less than 30 inches (762 mm) measured above the nosing of treads. When approved by the building official, the spacing between existing intermediate railings or openings in existing ornamental patterns may be accepted. See Section 608 for existing guardrails in historical structures.

405.3 Glazing. The installation or replacement of glass shall be as required for new construction by the Building Code.

405.4 Electrical. The electrical service, lines, switches, outlets, fixtures and fixture coverings, and supports in every building or structure shall be in good repair. Broken, loose, frayed, inoperative, defective or missing portions shall be repaired or replaced. All unsafe conditions shall be corrected.

405.5 Plumbing. Leaking drain or supply lines shall be repaired or replaced. All unsafe conditions shall be corrected. Any cross connections or siphonage between fixtures shall be corrected.

405.6 Mechanical. Mechanical systems shall have any unsafe conditions corrected.

Chapter 5
MINIMUM PROVISIONS FOR CHANGE OF OCCUPANCY

SECTION 501 — GENERAL

501.1 Change of Occupancy. The character of the occupancy of existing buildings and structures may be changed, provided the building or structure meets the requirements of this chapter and the requirements of Chapter 4. Where no specific requirements are included herein, the building or structure shall comply with the Building Code.

Every change of occupancy to one classified in a different group or a different division of the same group shall require a new certificate of occupancy regardless of whether any alterations to the building are required by this code.

If the building or portion thereof does not conform to the requirements of this code for the proposed occupancy group or division, the building or portion thereof shall be made to conform to the Building Code except as specified in this code. The building official may issue a new certificate occupancy stating that the building complies with this code.

501.2 Hazard Category Classifications. The relative degree of hazard between different occupancy groups or between divisions of the same group shall be as set forth in the hazard category classifications, Tables 5-A through 5-E. An existing building may have its occupancy changed to an occupancy within the same hazard group or to an occupancy in a lesser hazard group without complying to all the provisions of this chapter. An existing building shall comply with the requirements of the Building Code, except as specified in this chapter, when a change in occupancy will place it in a higher hazard group or when the occupancy is changed to Group A, Division 1 or 2; or Group E, H or I.

SECTION 502 — HEIGHTS AND AREAS

Heights and areas of buildings and structures shall meet the requirements of the Building Code for the new occupancy.

> **EXCEPTION:** Existing buildings exceeding the maximum allowable heights and areas permitted for new buildings may undergo a change of occupancy if the hazard level of the new occupancy is equal to or less than the existing hazard group as shown in Table 5-A.

SECTION 503 — FIRESAFETY

503.1 General. When a change of occupancy is made to a higher hazard group as shown in Table 5-B, all elements of the exit system shall comply with the requirements of the Building Code.

> **EXCEPTIONS:** 1. Existing corridors and stairways meeting the requirements of Chapter 4 may be used.
>
> 2. Means of egress elements may meet the compliance alternatives contained in the UCBC Guidelines.

503.2 Existing Means of Egress Systems. Existing means of egress systems complying with Chapter 4 shall be accepted if the occupancy change is to an equal or lesser hazard group when evaluated in accordance with Table 5-B.

503.3 Separation of Occupancies. When a change of occupancy is made to a higher hazard group as shown in Table 5-C, occupancy separations shall be provided as specified in the Building Code. When approved by the building official, existing wood lath and plaster in good condition or $^1/_2$-inch-thick (12.7 mm) gypsum wallboard may be accepted where a one-hour occupancy separation is required.

503.4 Enclosure of Vertical Shafts.

503.4.1 General. Vertical shafts may be designed to meet the requirements of atria as required by the Building Code or the requirements of this section.

503.4.2 Stairways. Interior stairways shall be enclosed as required by the Building Code when a change of occupancy is made to a higher hazard group as shown in Table 5-B.

> **EXCEPTIONS:** 1. In other than Group I Occupancies, an enclosure will not be required for openings serving only one adjacent floor and not connected with corridors or stairways serving other floors.
>
> 2. Existing stairways not enclosed need not be enclosed in a continuous vertical shaft if each story is separated from other stories by one-hour fire-resistive construction or approved wired glass set in steel frames and all exit corridors are sprinklered. The openings between the corridor and occupant space shall have at least one sprinkler head above the openings on the tenant side. The sprinkler system may be supplied from the domestic water-supply system, provided the system is of adequate pressure, capacity and sizing for the combined domestic and sprinkler requirements.

503.4.3 Other vertical shafts. Interior vertical shafts, including, but not limited to, elevator hoistways, service and utility shafts, shall be enclosed with a minimum of one-hour fire-resistive construction.

> **EXCEPTIONS:** 1. Vertical openings, other than stairways, need not be enclosed if the entire building is provided with an approved automatic sprinkler system.
>
> 2. Where one-hour fire-resistive floor construction is required, vertical shafts need not be enclosed when such shafts are blocked at every floor level by the installation of not less than 2 full inches (51 mm) of solid wood or equivalent construction.

503.4.4 Openings into vertical enclosures. All openings into such shafts shall be protected by fire assemblies having a fire-protection rating of not less than one hour and shall be maintained self-closing or shall be automatic closing by actuation of a smoke detector. All other openings shall be fire protected in an approved manner. Existing fusible link-type automatic door-closing devices may be permitted if the fusible link rating does not exceed 135°F (57°C).

SECTION 504 — PROPERTY PROTECTION

504.1 Fire Resistance of Walls. Exterior walls shall have fire resistance and opening protection as set forth in the Building Code. This provision shall not apply to walls at right angles to the property line.

> **EXCEPTIONS:** 1. Where a fire-resistive rating greater than two hours is required for a building of any type of construction, existing noncombustible exterior walls having a fire-resistive rating equivalent to two hours as determined by UCBC Guideline 2 may be accepted, provided:
>
> 1.1 The building is classified as a Group A, Division 3; Group B; Group F; Group M; and Group S, Divisions 1, 2, 3 and 4, and
>
> 1.2 The building does not exceed three stories in height.
>
> 2. Existing exterior walls shall be accepted if the occupancy is changed to a hazard group, which is equal to or less than the existing occupancy as defined in Table 5-D.

504.2 Opening Protection. Openings in exterior walls shall be protected as required by the Building Code. When openings in the exterior walls are required to be protected due to distance from the property line, the sum of the area of such openings shall not exceed 50 percent of the total area of the wall in each story.

EXCEPTIONS: 1. Protected openings shall not be required for Group R, Division 1 Occupancies that do not exceed three stories in height and that are located not less than 3 feet (914 mm) from the property line.

2. Where opening protection is required, an automatic fire-extinguishing system throughout may be substituted for opening protection.

3. Opening protection may be omitted when the change of occupancy is to an equal or lower hazard classification in accordance with Table 5-D.

SECTION 505 — STRUCTURAL SAFETY

505.1 Vertical Loads. Buildings and structures shall comply with the requirements of the Building Code for vertical load.

EXCEPTIONS: 1. Analysis and test methods for evaluation of existing materials may use the methods specified in the code under which the building was constructed, or other standards as approved by the building official.

2. Existing roofs may be retained provided any unsafe or overloaded conditions are corrected and where the roof dead load is not increased by use, reroofing or added equipment.

505.2 Earthquake Loads. Buildings undergoing a change of occupancy shall meet the earthquake regulations of the Building Code for the new occupancy.

EXCEPTIONS: 1. A building of Type I-F.R. or Type II-F.R. construction shall be individually evaluated for safety.

2. Existing buildings may undergo a change of occupancy if the hazard group is equal to or less than the existing occupancy as shown in Table 5-E.

3. Unreinforced masonry bearing wall buildings may be strengthened in accordance with Appendix Chapter 1.

505.3 Wind Loads. Buildings shall not be considered as dangerous buildings when subjected to the requirements of the Building Code.

SECTION 506 — LIGHT AND VENTILATION

Light and ventilation shall comply with the requirements of the Building Code.

TABLE 5-A—HAZARD CATEGORIES AND CLASSIFICATIONS HEIGHTS AND AREAS

RELATIVE HAZARD	OCCUPANCY CLASSIFICATION
1.	A-1, H, I-3 (highest hazard group)
2.	A-2, A-2.1, I-1.1, I-1.2, I-2
3.	A-3, A-4, B, E, F, M, R-1, S
4.	R-3, U (lowest hazard group)

TABLE 5-B—HAZARD CATEGORIES AND CLASSIFICATIONS LIFE SAFETY AND EXITS

RELATIVE HAZARD	OCCUPANCY CLASSIFICATION
1.	A-1, A-2, A-2.1, E, I, H-1, H-2 (highest hazard group)
2.	A-3, A-4
3.	R-1, R-3, B dining and drinking establishments
4.	B all others, F, H other than H-1 and H-2, M, S-1, S-2
5.	S-3, S-4, S-5
6.	U (lowest hazard group)

TABLE 5-C—HAZARD CATEGORIES AND CLASSIFICATIONS OCCUPANCY SEPARATIONS

RELATIVE HAZARD	OCCUPANCY CLASSIFICATION
1.	H, I, S-3, S-4 (highest hazard group)
2.	A, B, F, M, S-1, S-2, S-5
3.	E
4.	R-1, U
5.	R-3 (lowest hazard group)

TABLE 5-D—HAZARD CATEGORIES AND CLASSIFICATIONS EXPOSURE OF EXTERIOR WALLS AND STAIRWAY ENCLOSURES

RELATIVE HAZARD	OCCUPANCY CLASSIFICATION
1.	H (highest hazard group)
2.	M, S-1, S-2
3.	A, E, I
4.	B, F-1, R, S-3, S-4, S-5
5.	F-2, U (lowest hazard group)

TABLE 5-E—HAZARD CATEGORIES AND CLASSIFICATIONS EARTHQUAKE SAFETY

RELATIVE HAZARD	OCCUPANCY CLASSIFICATION
1.	A, E, I (highest hazard group)
2.	R-1
3.	F-2, H, S-5
4.	B, F-1, M, S-1, S-2, S-3, S-4
5.	R-3, U (lowest hazard group)

Chapter 6
HISTORIC STRUCTURES

SECTION 601 — PURPOSE

It is the intent of this chapter to provide means for the preservation of historic buildings.

SECTION 602 — GENERAL

Historic buildings and structures shall meet the minimum standards specified in this chapter.

> **EXCEPTION:** Compliance alternatives approved by the building official are allowed when the following criteria are met:
>
> 1. Conformance with the general intent of this code.
>
> 2. Compliance with the minimum standards required by Chapter 4 and the specific occupancy requirements of this code.
>
> 3. Conformance with the requirements of Chapter 5 when a change of occupancy occurs, except as modified in this chapter.
>
> 4. All unsafe and substandard conditions described in this code are corrected.
>
> 5. The restored building or structure shall be no more hazardous, based on life safety, firesafety and sanitation, than the building was before renovation.

SECTION 603 — REPAIRS

Repairs to any portion of a historic building or structure may be made with original materials and original methods of construction, subject to provisions of this chapter.

SECTION 604 — RELOCATED BUILDINGS

Foundations of relocated historic buildings and structures shall comply with the Building Code. Relocated historic buildings shall otherwise be considered a historic building for the purposes of this code. Relocated historic buildings and structures shall be so sited that exterior wall and opening requirements comply with the Building Code or the compliance alternatives of this code.

SECTION 605 — FIRESAFETY

605.1 General. Every historic building that does not conform to the construction requirements specified in this code for the occupancy or use and that constitutes a distinct fire hazard as defined herein shall be provided with an approved automatic fire-extinguishing system as determined appropriate by the building official. However, an automatic fire-extinguishing system shall not be used to substitute for, or act as an alternate to, the required number of exits from any facility.

605.2 Means of Egress. Existing door openings and corridor and stairway widths of less than that specified elsewhere in this code may be approved, provided that in the opinion of the building official there is sufficient width and height for a person to pass through the opening or traverse the means of egress.

When approved by the building official, the front or main exit doors need not swing in the direction of the path of exit travel, provided other approved means of egress having sufficient capacity to serve the total occupant load are provided.

605.3 Fire-resistive Requirements. One-hour fire-resistive construction throughout need not be required regardless of construction or occupancy.

605.4 Transoms. Existing transoms may be maintained if fixed in the closed position. Fixed wired glass set in a steel frame shall be installed on one side of the transom.

SECTION 606 — STRUCTURAL SAFETY

606.1 Vertical Loads. Historic buildings shall comply with the requirements of the Building Code for floor live loads.

> **EXCEPTION:** The building official may accept existing floors and approve operational controls that limit the live load on any floor.

606.2 Earthquake Loads. Unreinforced masonry buildings may be exempted from seismic strengthening required elsewhere in this code if the occupancy or character of use is such that the hazard is low.

SECTION 607 — SPECIAL CHANGE OF OCCUPANCY PROVISIONS

Historic structures undergoing a change of occupancy shall comply with Chapter 5. Historic structures may comply with the following alternatives:

1. Where finish materials are required to have a flame-spread classification of Class III or better, existing nonconforming materials shall be surfaced with an approved fire-retardant paint or finish.

> **EXCEPTION:** Existing nonconforming materials need not be surfaced with an approved fire-retardant paint or finish when an automatic fire-extinguishing system is installed throughout and the nonconforming materials can be substantiated as historic in character.

2. Regardless of occupancy group, roof-covering materials not less than Class C shall be permitted where a fire-retardant roof covering is required. Nonrated materials may be acceptable only where approved by the building official.

SECTION 608 — GUARDRAILS

608.1 Height. Existing guardrails shall comply with the requirements of Section 405.2.

608.2 Guardrail Openings. The spacing between existing intermediate railings or openings in existing ornamental patterns shall be accepted. Missing elements or members of a guardrail may be replaced in a manner that will preserve the historic appearance of the building or structure.

Chapter 7
REQUIREMENTS FOR GROUP R OCCUPANCIES

SECTION 701 — MINIMUM STANDARDS FOR ALL RESIDENTIAL BUILDINGS

701.1 Smoke Detectors.

701.1.1 General. Dwelling units and hotel or lodging house guest rooms that are used for sleeping purposes shall be provided with approved smoke detectors. Detectors shall be installed in accordance with the approved manufacturer's instructions.

701.1.2 Power source. Smoke detectors may be battery operated or may receive their primary power from the building wiring when such wiring is served from a commercial source. Wiring shall be permanent and without a disconnecting switch other than those required for overcurrent protection.

701.1.3 Location within dwelling units. In dwelling units, detectors shall be mounted on the ceiling or wall at a point centrally located in the corridor or area giving access to each separate sleeping area. Where sleeping rooms are on an upper level, the detector shall be placed at the center of the ceiling directly above the stairway. Detectors shall also be installed in the basement of dwelling units having a stairway that opens from the basement into the dwelling. Detectors shall sound an alarm audible in all sleeping areas of the dwelling unit in which they are located.

701.1.4 Location in efficiency dwelling units and hotels. In efficiency dwelling units, hotel suites and in hotel sleeping rooms, detectors shall be located on the ceiling or wall of the main room or hotel sleeping room. When sleeping rooms within an efficiency dwelling unit or hotel suite are on an upper level, the detector shall be placed at the center of the ceiling directly above the stairway. When actuated, the detector shall sound an alarm audible within the sleeping area of the dwelling unit, hotel suite or sleeping room in which it is located.

701.2 Means of Egress. Every dwelling unit or guest room shall have access directly to the outside or to a public corridor or exit balcony. All buildings or portions thereof shall be provided with means of egress and appurtenances as required by Chapter 4 of this code.

701.3 Light and Ventilation. All guest rooms, dormitories and habitable rooms within a dwelling unit shall be provided with natural light by means of exterior glazed openings. Such openings shall be openable to permit the flow of natural ventilation, or spaces shall be equipped with mechanical ventilation. Where mechanical ventilation is used, it shall meet the requirements of the Building Code.

701.4 Heating. Dwelling units and guest rooms shall be provided with heating facilities capable of maintaining a room temperature of 70°F (21°C) at a point 3 feet (914 mm) above the floor in all habitable rooms.

701.5 Sanitation. Every dwelling unit and every lodging house shall be provided with a bathroom with a water closet.

701.6 Plumbing. All plumbing fixtures shall be connected to a sanitary sewer or to an approved private sewage disposal system. All plumbing fixtures shall be connected to an approved system of water supply and provided with hot and cold running water necessary for its normal operation. All plumbing fixtures shall be of an approved glazed earthenware type or of a similarly nonabsorbent material.

701.7 Room Separations. Every water closet, bathtub or shower shall be installed in a room that will afford privacy to the occupant.

SECTION 702 — CHANGE OF OCCUPANCY

Buildings that are changed into a Group R Occupancy shall meet all the requirements specified in the Building Code for that occupancy group. Buildings meeting the requirements of Chapter 5 of this code are acceptable.

Appendix Chapter 1
SEISMIC STRENGTHENING PROVISIONS FOR UNREINFORCED MASONRY BEARING WALL BUILDINGS

SECTION A101 — PURPOSE

The purpose of this chapter is to promote public safety and welfare by reducing the risk of death or injury that may result from the effects of earthquakes on existing unreinforced masonry bearing wall buildings.

The provisions of this chapter are intended as minimum standards for structural seismic resistance, and established primarily to reduce the risk of life loss or injury. Compliance with these provisions will not necessarily prevent loss of life or injury, or prevent earthquake damage to rehabilitated buildings.

SECTION A102 — SCOPE

A102.1 General. The provisions of this chapter shall apply to all existing buildings having at least one unreinforced masonry bearing wall. The elements regulated by this chapter shall be determined in accordance with Table A-1-A. Except as provided herein, other structural provisions of the Building Code shall apply. This chapter does not require alteration of existing electrical, plumbing, mechanical or firesafety systems.

A102.2 Essential and Hazardous Facilities. The provisions of this chapter are not intended to apply to the strengthening of buildings or structures in Occupancy Categories 1 and 2 of Table 16-K of the Building Code when located in Seismic Zones 2B, 3 and 4. Such buildings or structures shall be strengthened to meet the requirements of the Building Code for new buildings of the same occupancy category or to such other criteria as have been established by the jurisdiction.

SECTION A103 — DEFINITIONS

For the purpose of this chapter, the applicable definitions in the Building Code shall also apply.

ARCHAIC MASONRY MATERIALS include adobe, unburned clay and rubble and cut stone masonry. These materials shall comply with the requirements of Section A114.

COLLAR JOINT is the vertical space between adjacent wythes and may contain mortar.

CROSSWALL is a new or existing wall that meets the requirements of Section A111.3. A crosswall is not a shear wall.

CROSSWALL SHEAR CAPACITY is the allowable shear value times the length of the crosswall, v_cL_o.

DIAPHRAGM EDGE is the intersection of the horizontal diaphragm and a shear wall.

DIAPHRAGM SHEAR CAPACITY is the allowable shear value times the depth of the diaphragm, v_uD.

ESSENTIAL FACILITY is any building or structure classified in Occupancy Category 1 of Table 16-K of the Building Code.

HAZARDOUS FACILITY is any building or structure classified in Occupancy Category 2 of Table 16-K of the Building Code.

NORMAL WALL is a wall perpendicular to the direction of seismic forces.

OPEN FRONT is an exterior building wall line, without vertical elements of the lateral-force-resisting system in one or more stories.

POINTING is the partial reconstruction of the bed joints of an unreinforced masonry wall as defined in UBC Standard 21-8.

UNREINFORCED MASONRY includes adobe, burned clay, concrete or sand-lime brick, hollow clay or concrete block, plain concrete, hollow clay tile, rubble and cut stone and unburned clay masonry. These materials shall comply with the requirements of Section A106 or Section A114 as applicable.

UNREINFORCED MASONRY BEARING WALL is a URM wall that provides the vertical support for the reaction of floor or roof-framing members.

UNREINFORCED MASONRY (URM) WALL is a masonry wall in which the area of reinforcing steel is less than 25 percent of the minimum steel ratios required by the Building Code for reinforced masonry.

YIELD STORY DRIFT is the lateral displacement of one level relative to the level above or below at which yield stress is first developed in a frame member.

SECTION A104 — SYMBOLS AND NOTATIONS

For the purpose of this chapter, the applicable symbols and notations in the Building Code shall apply.

A = cross-sectional area of unreinforced masonry pier or wall, square inches (10^{-6} m^2).

A_b = total area of the bed joints above and below the test specimen for each in-place shear test, square inches (10^{-6} m^2).

C_p = numerical coefficient as specified in Table A-1-C for special procedure diaphragm shear transfer.

D = in-plane width dimension of pier, inches (10^{-3} m), or depth of diaphragm, feet (m).

DCR = demand-capacity ratio specified in Section A111.4.2.

F_{wx} = force applied to a wall at level x, pounds (N).

H = least clear height of opening on either side of a pier, inches (10^{-3} m).

h/t = height-to-thickness ratio of URM wall. Height, h, is measured between wall anchorage levels and/or slab-on-grade.

L = span of diaphragm between shear walls, or span between shear wall and open front, feet (m).

L_o = length of crosswall, feet (m).

L_i = effective span for an open-front building specified in Section A111.8, feet (m).

P_D = superimposed dead load at the location under consideration, pounds (kN). For determination of the rocking shear capacity, dead load at the top of the pier under consideration shall be used.

p_{D+L} = stress resulting from the dead plus actual live load in place at the time of testing, pounds per square inch (psi) (kPa).

Pw = weight of wall, pounds (N).

V_a = $v_a A$, the allowable shear in any URM pier, pounds (N).

v_a = allowable shear stress for unreinforced masonry, psi (kPa).

v_c = allowable shear value for a crosswall sheathed with any of the materials given in Table A-1-D or A-1-E, pounds per foot (N/m).

V_{ca} = total shear capacity of crosswalls in the direction of analysis immediately above the diaphragm level being investigated, $v_c L_o$, pounds (N).

V_{cb} = total shear capacity of crosswalls in the direction of analysis immediately below the diaphragm level being investigated, $v_c L_o$, pounds (N).

V_p = shear force assigned to a pier on the basis of its relative shear rigidity, pounds (N).

V_r = pier rocking shear capacity of any URM wall or wall pier, pounds (N).

v_t = mortar shear strength as specified in Section A106.3.3.4, psi (kPa).

V_{test} = load at incipient cracking for each in-place shear test per UBC Standard 21-6, pounds (kN).

vt_o = mortar shear test values as specified in Section A106.3.3.4, psi (kPa).

v_u = allowable shear value for a diaphragm sheathed with any of the materials given in Table A-1-D or A-1-E, pounds per foot (N/m).

V_{wx} = total shear force resisted by a shear wall at the level under consideration, pounds (N).

W = total seismic dead load as defined in Chapter 16 of the Building Code, pounds (N).

W_d = total dead load tributary to a diaphragm, pounds (N).

W_w = total dead load of an unreinforced masonry wall above the level under consideration or above an open-front building, pounds (N).

W_{wx} = dead load of a URM wall assigned to Level X halfway above and below the level under consideration, pounds (N).

Z = seismic zone factor given in Table 16-I of the Building Code.

$\Sigma v_u D$ = sum of diaphragm shear capacities of both ends of the diaphragm, pounds (N).

$\Sigma\Sigma v_u D$ = for diaphragms coupled with crosswalls, $v_u D$ includes the sum of shear capacities of both ends of diaphragms coupled at and above the level under consideration, pounds (N).

ΣW_d = total dead load to all the diaphragms at and above the level under consideration, pounds (N).

SECTION A105 — GENERAL REQUIREMENTS

A105.1 General. Buildings shall have a seismic-resisting system conforming with Chapter 16 of the Building Code, except as modified by this chapter.

A105.2 Alterations and Repairs. Alterations and repairs required to meet the provisions of this chapter shall comply with applicable structural requirements of the Building Code unless specifically provided for in this chapter.

A105.3 Requirements for Plans. The following construction information shall be included in the plans required by this chapter:

1. Dimensioned floor and roof plans showing existing walls and the size and spacing of floor and roof-framing members and sheathing materials. The plans shall indicate all existing and new crosswalls and shear walls and their materials of construction. The location of these walls and their openings shall be fully dimensioned and drawn to scale on the plans.

2. Dimensioned wall elevations showing openings, piers, wall classes as defined in Section A106.3.3.6, thickness, heights, wall shear test locations, and cracks or damaged portions requiring repairs, the general condition of the mortar joints, and if and where pointing is required. Where the exterior face is veneer, the type of veneer, its thickness and its bonding and/or ties to the structural wall masonry shall also be noted.

3. The type of interior wall and ceiling materials and framing.

4. The extent and type of existing wall anchorage to floors and roof when used in the design.

5. The extent and type of parapet corrections that were previously performed, if any.

6. Repair details, if any, of cracked or damaged unreinforced masonry walls required to resist forces specified in this chapter.

7. All other plans, sections and details necessary to delineate required retrofit construction.

8. The design procedure used shall be stated on both the plans and the permit application.

9. Details of the anchor prequalification program required by UBC Standard 21-7, if utilized, including location and results of all tests.

A105.4 Structural Observation. Structural observation shall be provided in Seismic Zones 3 and 4 for all structures regulated by this chapter. The owner shall employ the engineer or architect responsible for the structural design, or another engineer or architect designated by the engineer or architect responsible for the structural designs, to perform structural observation as defined in Section 220 of the UBC. Observed deficiencies shall be reported in writing to the owner's representative, special inspector, contractor and the building official. The structural observer shall submit to the building official a written statement that the site visits have been made and identify any reported deficiencies that, to the best of the structural observer's knowledge, have not been resolved.

SECTION A106 — MATERIALS REQUIREMENTS

A106.1 General. Materials permitted by this chapter, including their appropriate allowable design values and those existing configurations of materials specified herein, may be utilized to meet the requirements of this chapter.

A106.2 Existing Materials. Existing materials utilized as part of the required vertical-load-carrying or lateral-force-resisting system shall be in sound condition or shall be repaired or removed and replaced with new materials. Archaic masonry materials shall comply with Section A114. All other unreinforced masonry materials shall comply with the following requirements:

1. The lay-up of the masonry units complies with Section A106.3.2 and the quality of bond between the units has been verified to the satisfaction of the building official;

2. Concrete masonry units are verified to be load-bearing units complying with UBC Standard 21-4 or such other standard as is acceptable to the building official; and

3. The compressive strength of plain concrete walls shall be determined based on cores taken from each class of concrete wall. The location and number of tests shall be the same as prescribed for strength tests in Sections A106.3.3.2 and A106.3.3.3.

The use of archaic and other materials not specified in this code shall be based on substantiating research data or engineering judgment with the approval of the building official.

A106.3 Existing Unreinforced Masonry.

A106.3.1 General. Unreinforced masonry walls utilized to carry vertical loads or seismic forces parallel and perpendicular to the wall plane shall be tested as specified in this section. All masonry that does not meet the minimum standards established by this chapter shall be removed and replaced with new materials or alternatively shall have its structural functions replaced with new materials and shall be anchored to supporting elements.

A106.3.2 Lay-up of walls.

A106.3.2.1 Multiwythe solid brick. The facing and backing shall be bonded so that not less than 10 percent of the exposed face area is composed of solid headers extending not less than 4 inches (102 mm) into the backing. The clear distance between adjacent full-length headers shall not exceed 24 inches (610 mm) vertically or horizontally. Where the backing consists of two or more wythes, the headers shall extend not less than 4 inches (102 mm) into the most distant wythe or the backing wythes shall be bonded together with separate headers whose area and spacing conform to the foregoing. Wythes of walls not bonded as described above shall be considered as veneer. Veneer wythes shall not be included in the effective thickness used in calculating the height to thickness and the shear capacity of the wall.

> **EXCEPTION:** In other than Seismic Zone 4, veneer wythes anchored as specified by the Building Code and made composite with backup masonry can be used for calculation of the effective thickness.

A106.3.2.2 Grouted or ungrouted hollow concrete or clay block, structural hollow clay tile and adobe. Grouted or ungrouted hollow concrete or clay block, structural hollow clay tile and adobe shall be laid in a running bond pattern.

A106.3.2.3 Rubble and stone masonry. Rubble and stone masonry may be laid up randomly. Other lay-up patterns are allowed if their performance can be justified as being at least equal to those specified above.

A106.3.2.4 Other lay-up patterns. Lay-up patterns other than those specified in Sections A106.3.2.1, A106.3.2.2 and A106.3.2.3 above are allowed if their performance can be justified.

A106.3.3 Mortar.

A106.3.3.1 Tests. The quality of mortar in all masonry walls shall be determined by performing in-place shear tests in accordance with UBC Standard 21-6. Alternative methods of testing may be approved by the building official for masonry walls other than brick.

A106.3.3.2 Location of tests. The shear tests shall be taken at locations representative of the mortar conditions throughout the entire building, taking into account variations in workmanship at different building height levels, variations in weathering of the exterior surfaces, and variations in the condition of the interior surfaces due to deterioration caused by leaks and condensation of water and/or by the deleterious effects of other substances contained within the building. The exact test locations shall be determined at the building site by the engineer or architect in responsible charge of the structural design work. An accurate record of all such tests and their location in the building shall be recorded and these results shall be submitted to the building department for approval as part of the structural analysis.

A106.3.3.3 Number of tests. The minimum number of tests per class shall be as follows:

1. At each of both the first and top stories, not less than two tests per wall or line of wall elements providing a common line of resistance to lateral forces.

2. At each of all other stories, not less than one test per wall or line of wall elements providing a common line of resistance to lateral forces.

3. In any case, not less than one test per 1,500 square feet (139.4 m²) of wall surface and not less than a total of eight tests.

A106.3.3.4 Minimum quality of mortar.

1. Mortar shear test values, v_{to}, in psi (kPa) shall be obtained for each in-place shear test in accordance with the following equation:

$$v_{to} = (V_{\text{test}}/A_b) - p_{D+L} \qquad (A6\text{-}1)$$

2. Individual unreinforced masonry walls with v_{to} consistently less than 30 psi (207 kPa) shall be entirely pointed or removed.

3. The mortar shear strength, v_t, is the value in psi (kPa) that is exceeded by 80 percent of the mortar shear test values, v_{to}.

4. Unreinforced masonry with mortar shear strength, v_t, less than 30 psi (207 kPa) shall be removed, pointed and retested or have its structural function replaced and shall be anchored to supporting elements in accordance with Sections A106.3.1 and A113.8. When existing mortar in any wythe is pointed to increase its shear strength and retested, the condition of the mortar in the adjacent bed joints of the inner wythe or wythes and the opposite outer wythe shall be examined for extent of deterioration. The shear strength of any wall class shall be no greater than that of the weakest wythe of that class.

A106.3.3.5 Collar joints. The collar joints shall be inspected at the test locations during each in-place shear test, and estimates of the percentage of the surfaces of adjacent wythes that are covered with mortar shall be reported along with the results of the in-place shear tests.

A106.3.3.6 Unreinforced masonry classes. Existing unreinforced masonry shall be categorized into one or more classes based on shear strength, quality of construction, state of repair, deterioration and weathering. A class shall be characterized by the allowable masonry shear stress determined in accordance with Section A108.2. Classes shall be defined for whole walls, not for small areas of masonry within a wall.

A106.3.3.7 Pointing. Deteriorated mortar joints in unreinforced masonry walls shall be pointed according to UBC Standard 21-8. Nothing shall prevent pointing of any deteriorated masonry wall joints before the tests are made, except as required in Section A107.1.

SECTION A107 — QUALITY CONTROL

A107.1 Pointing. Preparation and mortar pointing shall be performed with special inspection.

> **EXCEPTION:** At the discretion of the building official, incidental pointing may be performed without special inspection.

A107.2 Masonry Shear Tests. In-place shear tests shall comply with UBC Standard 21-6.

A107.3 Existing Wall Anchors. Existing wall anchors utilized as all or part of the required tension anchors shall be tested in pull-out according to UBC Standard 21-7. The minimum number of anchors tested shall be four per floor, with two tests at walls with joists framing into the wall and two tests at walls with joists parallel to the wall, but not less than 10 percent of the total number of existing tension anchors at each level.

A107.4 New Bolts. Twenty-five percent of all new embedded bolts resisting only shear forces in unreinforced masonry walls shall be tested using a calibrated torque wrench in accordance with UBC Standard 21-7.

> **EXCEPTION:** Special inspection in accordance with the Building Code may be provided during installation in lieu of testing.

All new embedded bolts resisting tension forces or a combination of tension and shear forces shall be subject to periodic special inspection in accordance with Section 1701 of the Building Code prior to placement of the bolt and grout or adhesive in the drilled hole. Five percent of all bolts resisting tension forces shall be subject to a direct-tension test and an additional 20 percent shall be tested using a calibrated torque wrench. Testing shall be performed in accordance with UBC Standard 21-7.

New through bolts need not be tested.

SECTION A108 — ALLOWABLE DESIGN VALUES

A108.1 Allowable Values.

1. Allowable values for existing materials are given in Table A-1-D, and for new materials in Table A-1-E.

2. Allowable values not specified in this chapter shall be as specified elsewhere in the Building Code.

A108.2 Masonry Shear. The allowable unreinforced masonry shear stress, v_a, shall be determined for each masonry class from the following equation:

$$v_a = 0.1v_t + 0.15P_D/A \qquad \text{(A8-1)}$$

The mortar shear test value, v_t, shall be determined in accordance with Section A106.3.3, and shall not exceed 100 psi (690 kPa) for the determination of v_a.

The one-third increase in allowable values of the Building Code is not allowed for v_a.

A108.3 Masonry Compression. Where any increase in dead plus live compression stress occurs, the allowable compression stress in unreinforced masonry shall not exceed 100 psi (690 kPa). The one-third increase in allowable stress of the Building Code is allowed.

A108.4 Masonry Tension. Unreinforced masonry shall be assumed as having no tensile capacity.

A108.5 Unreinforced Masonry Materials Other than Solid Masonry Units. The provisions of this chapter are primarily intended for solid masonry unit construction, but are also applicable to other unreinforced masonry materials when the following conditions are satisfied:

1. The building does not exceed two stories in height,

2. The shear stress of hollow-unit masonry is limited to that permitted by Formulas (A6-1) and (A8-1) based on the net area in contact through the bed joints, but not more than that calculated using a mortar shear strength, v_t, of 100 psi (690 kPa).

3. In the case of plain concrete, the compressive strength (f'_c) shall not be less than 900 psi (6206 kPa) and the allowable shear strength is limited to not more than $0.02f'_c$.

4. In the case of all other unreinforced masonry materials, the shear stress is limited to 3 psi (20.7 kPa) based on the net area in contact through the bed joint.

5. The special procedure of Section A111 shall not be used for buildings constructed of archaic masonry materials.

Unreinforced masonry not meeting the above criteria shall have its structural function replaced and shall be resupported, if required, in accordance with Section A113.7.

A108.6 Existing Tension Anchors. The allowable resistance values of the existing anchors shall be 40 percent of the average of the tension tests of existing anchors having the same wall thickness and joist orientation. The one-third increase in allowable value of the Building Code is not allowed for existing tension anchors.

A108.7 Foundations. For existing foundations, new total dead loads may be increased over existing dead load by 25 percent. New total dead load plus live load plus seismic forces may be increased over existing dead load plus live load by 50 percent. Higher values may be justified only in conjunction with a geotechnical investigation.

SECTION A109 — ANALYSIS AND DESIGN PROCEDURE

A109.1 General. Except as modified herein, the analysis and design relating to the structural alteration of existing buildings shall be in accordance with the Building Code.

A109.2 Selection of Procedure. All buildings shall be analyzed by either the general procedure of Section A110, which is based on Chapter 16 of the Building Code, or when applicable, buildings may be analyzed by the special procedure of Section A111.

SECTION A110 — GENERAL PROCEDURE

A110.1 Minimum Design Lateral Forces. Buildings shall be analyzed to resist minimum lateral forces assumed to act nonconcurrently in the direction of each of the main axes of the structure in accordance with the following:

$$V = 0.33 ZW \qquad \text{(A10-1-1)}$$

for buildings with an occupant load of 100 or more as determined by Table 10-A of the Building Code and without crosswalls complying with Section A111.3 or

$$V = 0.25 ZW \qquad \text{(A10-1-2)}$$

for all other buildings.

For buildings more than one story in height, the total force shall be distributed over the height of the building in accordance with the procedures of Chapter 16 of the Building Code.

For the purpose of this chapter, a dynamic analysis need not be performed for those buildings with irregularities, as defined in Tables 16-L and 16-M of the Building Code, which would otherwise require such analysis. All other design and analysis requirements of these tables shall apply.

A110.2 Lateral Forces on Elements of Structures. Parts of structures shall be analyzed and designed as required in Chapter 16 of the Building Code.

> **EXCEPTIONS:** 1. Unreinforced masonry walls for which height-to-thickness ratios do not exceed ratios set forth in Table A-1-B need not be analyzed for out-of-plane loading. Unreinforced masonry walls which exceed the allowable h/t ratios of Table A-1-B shall be braced according to Section A113.5.
>
> 2. Parapets complying with Section A113.6 need not be analyzed for out-of-plane loading.

A110.3 Shear Walls (In-plane Loading). Shear walls shall comply with Section A112.

SECTION A111 — SPECIAL PROCEDURE

A111.1 Limits. The special procedures of this section may be applied only to buildings with the following characteristics:

1. The building is not an essential or hazardous facility.

2. Flexible diaphragms at all levels above the base of structure.

3. A maximum of six stories above the base of the building.

4. Except for single-story buildings with an open front on one side only, a minimum of two lines of vertical elements of the lateral-force-resisting system complying with Section A112 parallel to each axis. At least one line in each direction shall be a masonry or concrete shear wall. Requirements for open-front buildings are contained in Section A111.8.

A111.2 Lateral Forces on Elements of Structures. With the exception of the diaphragm provisions in Section A111.4, elements of structures shall comply with Section A110.2.

A111.3 Crosswalls. Crosswalls when used shall meet the requirements of this section.

A111.3.1 Crosswall definition. A crosswall is a wood-framed wall sheathed with any of the materials described in Table A-1-D or A-1-E or other system as defined in Section A111.3.5. Spacing of crosswalls shall not exceed 40 feet (12 192 mm) on center measured perpendicular to the direction of consideration, and shall be placed in each story of the building. Crosswalls shall extend the full story height between diaphragms.

> **EXCEPTIONS:** 1. Crosswalls need not be provided at all levels in accordance with Section A111.4.2, Item 4.
>
> 2. Existing crosswalls need not be continuous below a wood diaphragm at or within 4 feet (1219 mm) of grade provided:
>
> 2.1 Shear connections and anchorage requirements, Section A111.5 are satisfied at all edges of the diaphragm.
>
> 2.2 Crosswalls with total shear capacity of $0.20Z\Sigma Wd$ interconnect the diaphragm to the foundation.
>
> 2.3 The demand/capacity ratio of the diaphragm between the crosswalls that are continuous to their foundations shall be calculated as:
>
> $$DCR = (0.83ZW_d + V_{ca}) / 2v_uD \qquad \text{(A11-1)}$$
>
> and DCR shall not exceed 2.5.

A111.3.2 Crosswall shear capacity. Within any 40 feet (12 192 mm) measured along the span of the diaphragm, the sum of the crosswall shear capacities shall be at least 30 percent of the diaphragm shear capacity of the strongest diaphragm at or above the level under consideration.

A111.3.3 Existing crosswalls. Existing crosswalls shall have a maximum height-to-length ratio between openings of 1.5 to 1. Existing crosswall connections to diaphragms need not be investigated as long as the crosswall extends to the framing of the diaphragm above and below.

A111.3.4 New crosswalls. New crosswall connections to the diaphragm shall develop the crosswall shear capacity. New crosswalls shall have the capacity to resist an overturning moment equal to the crosswall shear capacity times the story height. Crosswall overturning moments need not be cumulative over more than two stories.

A111.3.5 Other crosswall systems. Other systems, such as moment-resisting frames, may be used as crosswalls provided that the yield story drift does not exceed 1 inch (25.4 mm) in any story.

A111.4 Wood Diaphragms.

A111.4.1 Acceptable diaphragm span. A diaphragm is acceptable if the point (L,DCR) on Figure A-1-1 falls within Region 1, 2 or 3.

A111.4.2 Demand-capacity ratios. Demand-capacity ratios shall be calculated for the diaphragm at any level according to the following formulas:

1. For a diaphragm without qualifying crosswalls at levels immediately above or below:

$$DCR = 0.83ZW_d/\Sigma v_uD \qquad \text{(A11-2)}$$

2. For a diaphragm in a single-story building with qualifying crosswalls:

$$DCR = 0.83ZW_d/(\Sigma v_uD + V_{cb}) \qquad \text{(A11-3)}$$

3. For diaphragms in a multistory building with qualifying crosswalls in all levels:

$$DCR = 0.83Z\Sigma W_d/(\Sigma\Sigma v_uD + V_{cb}) \qquad \text{(A11-4)}$$

DCR shall be calculated at each level for the set of diaphragms at and above the level under consideration. In addition, the roof diaphragm shall also meet the requirements of Formula (A11-3).

4. For a roof diaphragm and the diaphragm directly below if coupled by crosswalls:

$$DCR = 0.83Z\Sigma W_d/\Sigma\Sigma v_uD \qquad \text{(A11-5)}$$

A111.4.3 Chords. An analysis for diaphragm flexure need not be made and chords need not be provided.

A111.4.4 Collectors. An analysis of diaphragm collector forces shall be made for the transfer of diaphragm edge shears into vertical elements of the lateral-force-resisting system. Collector forces may be resisted by new or existing elements.

A111.4.5 Diaphragm openings.

1. Diaphragm forces at corners of openings shall be investigated and shall be developed into the diaphragm by new or existing materials.

2. In addition to the demand-capacity ratios of Section A111.4.2, the demand-capacity ratio of the portion of the diaphragm adjacent to an opening shall be calculated using the opening dimension as the span.

3. Where an opening occurs in the end quarter of the diaphragm span v_uD for the demand-capacity ratio, calculation shall be based on the net depth of the diaphragm.

A111.5 Diaphragm Shear Transfer. Diaphragms shall be connected to shear walls with connections capable of developing a minimum force given by the lesser of the following formulas:

$$V = {}^1\!/_2\, Z\, C_p\, W_d \qquad \text{(A11-6)}$$

using the C_p values in Table A-1-C, or

$$V = v_uD \qquad \text{(A11-7)}$$

A111.6 Shear Walls (In-plane Loading).

A111.6.1 Wall story force. The wall story force distributed to a shear wall at any diaphragm level shall be the lesser value calculated as:

1. For buildings without crosswalls,

$$F_{wx} = 0.33Z(W_{wx} + W_d/2) \qquad \text{(A11-8)}$$

but need not exceed

$$F_{wx} = 0.33ZW_{wx} + v_uD \qquad \text{(A11-9)}$$

2. For buildings with crosswalls in all levels:

$$F_{wx} = 0.25Z(W_{wx} + W_d/2) \qquad \text{(A11-10)}$$

but need not exceed

$$F_{wx} = 0.25Z \left[W_{wx} + \Sigma W_d (v_u D / \Sigma \Sigma v_u D) \right] \quad \text{(A11-11)}$$

but need not exceed

$$F_{wx} = 0.25Z W_{wx} + v_u D \quad \text{(A11-12)}$$

A111.6.2 Wall story shear. The wall story shear shall be the sum of the wall story forces at and above the level of consideration.

$$V_{wx} = \Sigma F_{wx} \quad \text{(A11-13)}$$

A111.6.3 Shear wall analysis. Shear walls shall comply with Section A112.

A111.6.4 Moment frames. Moment frames used in place of shear walls shall be designed as required in Chapter 16 of the Building Code, except that the forces shall be as specified in Section A111.6.1 and the story drift ratio shall be limited to 0.005, except as further limited by Section A112.4.2.

A111.7 Out-of-plane Forces—Unreinforced Masonry Walls.

A111.7.1 Allowable unreinforced masonry wall height-to-thickness ratios. The provisions of Section A110.2 are applicable except the allowable height-to-thickness ratios given in Table A-1-C shall be determined from Figure A-1-1 as follows:

1. In Region 1, height-to-thickness ratios for buildings with crosswalls may be used if qualifying crosswalls are present in all stories.

2. In Region 2, height-to-thickness ratios for buildings with crosswalls may be used whether or not qualifying crosswalls are present.

3. In Region 3, height-to-thickness ratios for "all other buildings" shall be used whether or not qualifying crosswalls are present.

A111.7.2 Walls with diaphragms in different regions. When diaphragms above and below the wall under consideration have demand-capacity ratios in different regions of Figure A-1-1, the lesser height-to-thickness ratio shall be used.

A111.8 Open-Front Design Procedure. A single-story building with an open front on one side and crosswalls parallel to the open front may be designed by the following procedure:

1. Effective diaphragm span, L_i, for use in Figure A-1-1 shall be determined in accordance with the following formula:

$$L_i = 2 \left[(W_w / W_d) L + L \right] \quad \text{(A11-14)}$$

2. Diaphragm demand-capacity ratio shall be calculated as:

$$DCR = 0.83Z(W_d + W_w) / [(v_u D) + V_{cb}] \quad \text{(A11-15)}$$

SECTION A112 — ANALYSIS AND DESIGN

A112.1 General. The following requirements are applicable to both the general procedure and special procedure for analysis of vertical elements of the lateral-force-resisting system.

A112.2 Existing Unreinforced Masonry Walls.

A112.2.1 Flexural rigidity. Flexural components of deflection may be neglected in determining the rigidity of an unreinforced masonry wall.

A112.2.2 Shear walls with openings. Wall piers shall be analyzed according to the following procedure, which is diagramed in Figure A-1-2. The calculated length of the pier, D, shall be reduced by one half the embedded length of any steel lintels in the pier.

1. For any pier,
   1.1 The pier shear capacity shall be calculated as:

$$V_a = v_a A \quad \text{(A12-1)}$$

   1.2 The pier rocking shear capacity shall be calculated as:

$$V_r = 0.5 P_D D / H \quad \text{(A12-2)}$$

2. The wall piers at any level are acceptable if they comply with one of the following modes of behavior:

   2.1 **Rocking controlled mode.** When the pier rocking shear capacity is less than the pier shear capacity, i.e., $V_r < V_a$ for each pier in a level, forces in the wall at that level, V_{wx}, shall be distributed to each pier, in proportion to $P_D D / H$.

   For the wall at that level:

$$V_{wx} < \Sigma V_r \quad \text{(A12-3)}$$

   2.2 **Shear controlled mode.** Where the pier shear capacity is less than the pier rocking capacity, i.e., $V_a < V_r$ in at least one pier in a level, forces in the wall at the level, V_{wx}, shall be distributed to each pier in proportion to D/H.

   For each pier at that level:

$$V_p < V_a \quad \text{(A12-4)}$$

   and

$$V_p < V_r \quad \text{(A12-5)}$$

   If $V_p < V_a$ for each pier and $V_p > V_r$ for one or more piers, such piers shall be omitted from the analysis, and the procedure shall be repeated for the remaining piers, unless the wall is strengthened and reanalyzed.

3. **Masonry pier tension stress.** Unreinforced masonry wall piers need not be analyzed for tension stress.

A112.2.3 Shear walls without openings. Shear walls without openings shall be analyzed as for walls with openings except that V_r shall be calculated as follows:

$$V_r = (0.50 P_D + 0.25 P_w) D / H \quad \text{(A12-6)}$$

A112.3 Plywood Sheathed Shear Walls. Plywood sheathed shear walls may be used to resist lateral forces for buildings with flexible diaphragms analyzed according to provisions of Section A110. Plywood sheathed shear walls may not be used to share lateral forces with other materials along the same line of resistance.

A112.4 Combinations of Vertical Elements.

A112.4.1 Lateral-force distribution. Lateral forces shall be distributed among the vertical-resisting elements in proportion to their relative rigidities except that moment frames shall comply with Section A112.4.2.

A112.4.2 Moment-resisting frames. A moment frame shall not be used with an unreinforced masonry wall in a single line of resistance unless the wall has piers that are capable of sustaining rocking in accordance with Section A112.2.2 and the frames are designed to carry 100 percent of the lateral forces, and the story drift ratio shall be limited to 0.0025.

SECTION A113 — DETAILED SYSTEM DESIGN REQUIREMENTS

A113.1 Wall Anchorage.

A113.1.1 Anchor locations. Unreinforced masonry walls shall be anchored at the roof and floor levels as required in Section A110.2. Ceilings of plaster or similar materials, when not attached directly to roof or floor framing, and abutting masonry walls, shall be anchored to the walls at a maximum spacing of 6 feet (1829 mm) or removed.

A113.1.2 Anchor requirements. Anchors shall consist of bolts installed through the wall as specified in Table A-1-E, or by an approved equivalent at a maximum anchor spacing of 6 feet (1829 mm). All wall anchors shall be secured to the joists to develop the required forces.

A113.1.3 Minimum wall anchorage. Anchorage of masonry walls to each floor or roof shall resist a minimum force determined in accordance with Chapter 16 of the Building Code or 200 pounds per linear foot (2920 N/m), whichever is greater, acting normal to the wall at the level of the floor or roof. Existing wall anchors, if used, must meet the requirements of this chapter or must be upgraded.

A113.1.4 Anchors at corners. At the roof and floor levels, both shear and tension anchors shall be provided within 2 feet (610 mm) horizontally from the inside of the corners of the walls.

A113.2 Diaphragm Shear Transfer. Bolts transmitting shear forces shall have a maximum bolt spacing of 6 feet (1829 mm) and shall have nuts installed over malleable iron or plate washers when bearing on wood, and heavy-cut washers when bearing on steel.

A113.3 Collectors. Collector elements shall be provided that are capable of transferring the seismic forces originating in other portions of the building to the element providing the resistance to those forces.

A113.4 Ties and Continuity. Ties and continuity shall conform to Chapter 16 of the Building Code.

A113.5 Wall Bracing.

A113.5.1 General. Where a wall height-to-thickness ratio exceeds the specified limits, the wall may be laterally supported by vertical bracing members per Section A113.5.2 or by reducing the wall height by bracing per Section A113.5.3.

A113.5.2 Vertical bracing members. Vertical bracing members shall be attached to floor and roof construction for their design loads independently of required wall anchors. Horizontal spacing of vertical bracing members shall not exceed one half the unsupported height of the wall or 10 feet (3048 mm). Deflection of such bracing members at design loads shall not exceed one tenth of the wall thickness.

A113.5.3 Intermediate wall bracing. The wall height may be reduced by bracing elements connected to the floor or roof. Horizontal spacing of the bracing elements and wall anchors shall be as required by design, but shall not exceed 6 feet (1829 mm) on center. Bracing elements shall be detailed to minimize the horizontal displacement of the wall by the vertical displacement of the floor or roof.

A113.6 Parapets. Parapets and exterior wall appendages not conforming to this chapter shall be removed, or stabilized or braced to ensure that the parapets and appendages remain in their original position.

The maximum height of an unbraced unreinforced masonry parapet above the lower of either the level of tension anchors or roof sheathing shall not exceed the height-to-thickness ratio shown in Table A-1-F. If the required parapet height exceeds this maximum height, a bracing system designed for the forces determined in accordance with Chapter 16 of the Building Code shall support the top of the parapet. Parapet corrective work must be

performed in conjunction with the installation of tension roof anchors.

The minimum height of a parapet above any wall anchor shall be 12 inches (305 mm).

> **EXCEPTION:** If a reinforced concrete beam is provided at the top of the wall, the minimum height above the wall anchor may be 6 inches (152 mm).

A113.7 Veneer.

1. Veneer shall be anchored with approved anchor ties conforming to the required design capacity specified in the Building Code and placed at a maximum spacing of 24 inches (610 mm) with a maximum supported area of 4 square feet (0.372 m^2).

> **EXCEPTION:** Existing anchor ties for attaching brick veneer to brick backing may be acceptable provided the ties are in good condition and conform to the following minimum size and material requirements.
>
> Existing veneer anchor ties may be considered adequate if they are of corrugated galvanized iron strips not less than 1 inch (25.4 mm) in width, 8 inches (203 mm) in length and $1/16$ inch (1.6 mm) in thickness or equal.

2. The location and condition of existing veneer anchor ties shall be verified as follows:

2.1 An approved testing laboratory shall verify the location and spacing of the ties and shall submit a report to the building official for approval as part of the structural analysis.

2.2 The veneer in a selected area shall be removed to expose a representative sample of ties (not less than four) for inspection by the building official.

A113.8 Nonstructural Masonry Walls. Unreinforced masonry walls that carry no design vertical or lateral loads and are not required by the design to be part of the lateral-force-resisting system shall be adequately anchored to new or existing supporting elements. The anchors and elements shall be designed for the out-of-plane forces specified in Chapter 16 of the Building Code. The height- or length-to-thickness ratio between such supporting elements for such walls shall not exceed 9.

A113.9 Truss and Beam Supports. Where trusses and beams, other than rafters or joists, are supported on masonry, independent secondary columns shall be installed to support vertical loads of the roof or floor members.

> **EXCEPTION:** Secondary supports are not required in Seismic Zones 1, 2A and 2B.

A113.10 Adjacent Buildings. Where elements of adjacent buildings do not have a separation of at least 5 inches (127 mm), the allowable height-to-thickness ratios for "all other buildings" per Table A-1-B shall be used in the direction of consideration.

SECTION A114 — BUILDINGS OF ARCHAIC UNREINFORCED MASONRY

A114.1 General. A building or structure of archaic unreinforced masonry shall comply with the provisions set forth in this chapter and Chapter 6 of this code if the building is considered historic.

A114.2 Unburned Clay Masonry or Adobe and Stone. Existing or reerected walls of adobe construction shall conform to the following:

1. Exterior bearing walls of unreinforced adobe or stone masonry shall not exceed a height- or length-to-thickness ratio specified in Table A-1-G. Such walls shall be provided with a reinforced concrete bond beam at the top that interconnects all

walls. The bond beam shall have a minimum depth of 6 inches (152 mm). The bond beam may have a width equal to the width of the wall less 8 inches (203 mm), provided the resulting width is not less than 8 inches (203 mm). Bond beams of other materials may be used with the approval of the building official.

Exterior-bearing walls shall have a minimum wall thickness of 18 inches (457 mm) in Seismic Zones 3 and 4, and 12 inches (305 mm) in other seismic zones. Interior adobe partitions shall be a minimum of 10 inches (254 mm) in thickness. No adobe or stone structure shall exceed one story in height unless the historic evidence, satisfactory to the building official, indicates a two-story height. Bond beams shall be provided at the roof and second-floor levels.

2. Foundations shall be reinforced concrete under newly reconstructed walls and shall be 50 percent wider than the wall above, soil conditions permitting, except that the foundation wall may be 4 inches (102 mm) less in width than the wall if a rock,

burned brick or stabilized adobe facing is necessary to provide authenticity.

3. New or existing unstabilized brick and adobe brick masonry shall test to 75 percent of the compressive strength required by the Building Code for new material. Unstabilized brick may be used where existing bricks are unstabilized and where the building is not susceptible to flooding conditions or direct exposure. Adobe may be allowed a maximum value of 3 pounds per square inch (20.7 kPa) for shear with no increase of lateral forces.

4. Mortar may be of the same soil composition and stabilization as the brick in lieu of cement mortar.

5. Nominal tension stresses due to seismic forces normal to the wall may be neglected if the wall meets thickness requirements and shear values allowed by this subsection.

A114.3 Archaic Materials. Allowable stresses for archaic materials not specified in this code shall be based on substantiating research data or engineering judgment with the approval of the building official.

TABLE A-1-A—ELEMENTS REGULATED BY THIS CHAPTER

BUILDING ELEMENTS	SEISMIC ZONE			
	2A	2B	3	4
Parapets	X	X	X	X
Walls, anchorage	X	X	X	X
Walls, h/t ratios			X	X	X
Walls, in-plane shear		X	X	X
Diaphragms[1]			X	X
Diaphragms, shear transfer[2]		X	X	X
Diaphragms, demand-capacity ratios[2]			X	X

[1]Applies only to buildings designed according to the general procedures of Section A110.
[2]Applies only to buildings designed according to the special procedures of Section A111.

TABLE A-1-B—ALLOWABLE VALUE OF HEIGHT-TO-THICKNESS RATIO OF UNREINFORCED MASONRY WALLS

WALL TYPES	SEISMIC ZONE 2B BUILDINGS	SEISMIC ZONE 3 BUILDINGS	SEISMIC ZONE 4 BUILDINGS WITH CROSSWALLS[1]	SEISMIC ZONE 4 ALL OTHER BUILDINGS
Walls of one-story buildings	20	16	16[2, 3]	13
First-story wall of multistory building	20	18	16	15
Walls in top story of multistory building	14	14	14[2, 3]	9
All other walls	20	16	16	13

[1]Applies to the special procedures of Section A111 only. See Section A111.7 for other restrictions.
[2]This value of height-to-thickness ratio may be used only where mortar shear tests establish a tested mortar shear strength, v_t, of not less than 100 psi (690 kPa). This value may also be used where the tested mortar shear strength is not less than 60 psi (414 kPa) and a visual examination of the collar joint indicates not less than 50 percent mortar coverage.
[3]Where a visual examination of the collar joint indicates not less than 50 percent mortar coverage, and the tested mortar shear strength, v_t, is greater than 30 psi (207 kPa) but less than 60 psi (414 kPa), the allowable height-to-thickness ratio may be determined by linear interpolation between the larger and smaller ratios in direct proportion to the tested mortar shear strength.

TABLE A-1-C—HORIZONTAL FORCE FACTOR, C_p[1]

CONFIGURATION OF MATERIALS	C_p
Roofs with straight or diagonal sheathing and roofing applied directly to the sheathing, or floors with straight tongue-and-groove sheathing	0.50
Diaphragms with double or multiple layers of boards with edges offset, and blocked plywood systems	0.75

[1]Applicable to the special procedures of Section A111 only.

TABLE A-1-D—ALLOWABLE VALUES FOR EXISTING MATERIALS

EXISTING MATERIALS OR CONFIGURATIONS OF MATERIALS[1]	ALLOWABLE VALUES
	× 14.594 for N/m
1. Horizontal diaphragms[2]	
1.1 Roofs with straight sheathing and roofing applied directly to the sheathing	100 lbs. per foot for seismic shear
1.2 Roofs with diagonal sheathing and roofing applied directly to the sheathing	250 lbs. per foot for seismic shear
1.3 Floors with straight tongue-and-groove sheathing	100 lbs. per foot for seismic shear
1.4 Floors with straight sheathing and finished wood flooring with board edges offset or perpendicular	500 lbs. per foot for seismic shear
1.5 Floors with diagonal sheathing and finished wood flooring	600 lbs. per foot for seismic shear
2. Crosswalls[2,3]	
2.1 Plaster on wood or metal lath	Per side: 200 lbs. per foot for seismic shear
2.2 Plaster on gypsum lath	175 lbs. per foot for seismic shear
2.3 Gypsum wallboard, unblocked edges	75 lbs. per foot for seismic shear
2.4 Gypsum wallboard, blocked edges	125 lbs. per foot for seismic shear
3. Existing footings, wood framing, structural steel and reinforced steel	
3.1 Plain concrete footings	f'_c = 1,500 psi (10.34 MPa) unless otherwise shown by tests[4]
3.2 Douglas fir wood	Allowable stress same as D.F. No. 1[4]
3.3 Reinforcing steel	f_t = 18,000 lbs. per square inch (124.1 N/mm^2) maximum[4]
3.4 Structural steel	f_t = 20,000 lbs. per square inch (137.9 N/mm^2) maximum[4]

[1]Material must be sound and in good condition.

[2]A one-third increase in allowable stress is not allowed.

[3]Shear values of these materials may be combined, except the total combined value shall not exceed 300 pounds per foot (4380 N/m).

[4]Stresses given may be increased for combinations of loads as specified in the Building Code.

**TABLE A-1-E—ALLOWABLE VALUES OF NEW MATERIALS USED
IN CONJUNCTION WITH EXISTING CONSTRUCTION**

NEW MATERIALS OR CONFIGURATIONS OF MATERIALS	ALLOWABLE VALUES[1]
1. Horizontal diaphragms[2]	
1.1 Plywood sheathing nailed directly over existing straight sheathing with ends of plywood sheets bearing on joists or rafters and edges of plywood located on center of individual sheathing boards	225 lbs. per foot (3283 N/m)
1.2 Plywood sheathing nailed directly over existing diagonal sheathing with ends of plywood sheets bearing on joists or rafters	375 lbs. per foot (5473 N/m)
1.3 Plywood sheathing nailed directly over existing straight or diagonal sheathing with ends of plywood sheets bearing on joists or rafters with edges of plywood located over new blocking and nailed to provide a minimum nail penetration into framing and blocking of $1^5/_8$ inches (41 mm)	75 percent of the values specified in Chapter 23 of the Building Code
2. Shear walls: (general procedure) Plywood sheathing applied directly over wood studs. No value shall be given to plywood applied over existing plaster or wood sheathing	100 percent of the value specified in Chapter 23 of the Building Code for shear walls
3. Crosswalls: (special procedure only)	
3.1 Plywood sheathing applied directly over wood studs. No value shall be given to plywood applied over existing plaster or wood sheathing	133 percent of the value specified in Chapter 23 of the Building Code for shear walls
3.2 Drywall or plaster applied directly over wood studs	100 percent of the values in Table 25-I of the Building Code
3.3 Drywall or plaster applied to sheathing over existing wood studs	The values specified in Table 25-I of the Building Code reduced as noted in Footnote 1 of that table.
4. Tension bolts	
4.1 Bolts extending entirely through unreinforced masonry walls secured with bearing plates on far side of a three-wythe-minimum wall with at least 30 square inches (19 355 mm[2]) of area[4,5]	1,800 lbs. (8006 N) per bolt[6] 900 lbs. (4003 N) per bolt for two-wythe walls[6]
4.2 Bolts extending to the exterior face of the wall with a $2^1/_2$-inch (63.5 mm) round plate under the head and drilled at an angle of $22^1/_2$ degrees to the horizontal, installed as specified for shear bolts[4,5,7]	1,200 lbs. (5338 N) per bolt
5. Shear bolts Bolts embedded a minimum of 8 inches (203 mm) into unreinforced masonry walls and centered in a $2^1/_2$-inch-diameter (63.5 mm) hole filled with dry-pack or nonshrink grout. Through bolts with first 8 inches (203 mm) as noted above and embedded bolts as noted in Item 4.2[5, 7]	$^1/_2$ inch (12.7 mm) diameter = 350 lbs. (1557 N)[6] $^5/_8$ inch (15.9 mm) diameter = 500 lbs. (2224 N)[6] $^3/_4$ inch (19 mm) diameter = 750 lbs. (3336 N)[6]
6. Infilled walls Reinforced masonry infilled openings in existing unreinforced masonry walls. Provide keys or dowels to match reinforcing	Same as values specified for unreinforced masonry walls
7. Reinforced masonry Masonry piers and walls reinforced per Chapter 21 of the Building Code	Same as values specified in Chapter 21 of the Building Code[8]
8. Reinforced concrete Concrete footings, walls and piers reinforced as specified in Chapter 19 of the Building Code and designed for tributary loads	Same values as specified in Chapter 19 of the Building Code[8]

[1]A one-third increase in allowable stress is not allowed, except as noted.

[2]Values and limitations are for nailed plywood. Higher values may be used for other fastening systems such as wood screws or staples when approved by the building official.

[3]In addition to existing sheathing value.

[4]Bolts to be $^1/_2$-inch (12.7 mm) minimum in diameter.

[5]Drilling for bolts and dowels shall be done with an electric rotary drill. Impact tools shall not be used for drilling holes or tightening anchors and shear bolt nuts.

[6]Other bolt sizes, values and installation methods may be used provided a testing program is conducted in accordance with UBC Standard 21-7. Bolt spacing shall not exceed 6 feet (1829 mm) on center and shall not be less than 12 inches (305 mm) on center.

[7]Embedded bolts to be tested as specified in Section A107.

[8]Stresses given may be increased for combinations of loads as specified in the Building Code.

TABLE A-1-F—MAXIMUM ALLOWABLE HEIGHT-TO-THICKNESS RATIOS FOR PARAPETS

	SEISMIC ZONE			
	2A	2B	3	4
Maximum allowable height-to-thickness ratio	2.5	2.5	1.5	1.5

TABLE A-1-G—MAXIMUM HEIGHT-TO-THICKNESS RATIOS FOR ADOBE OR STONE WALLS

	SEISMIC ZONE		
	2B	3	4
One-story buildings	12	10	8
Two-story buildings			
First story	14	11	9
Second story	12	10	8

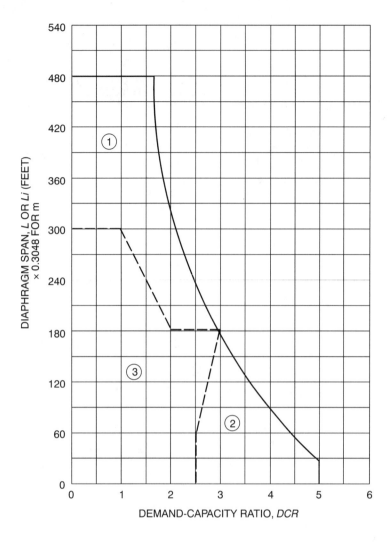

1. Region of demand/capacity ratios where crosswalls may be used to increase *h/t* ratios.
2. Region of demand/capacity ratios where *h/t* ratios of "with crosswalls" may be used.
3. Region of demand/capacity ratios where *h/t* ratios of "all other buildings" shall be used.

FIGURE A-1-1—ACCEPTABLE DIAPHRAGM SPAN

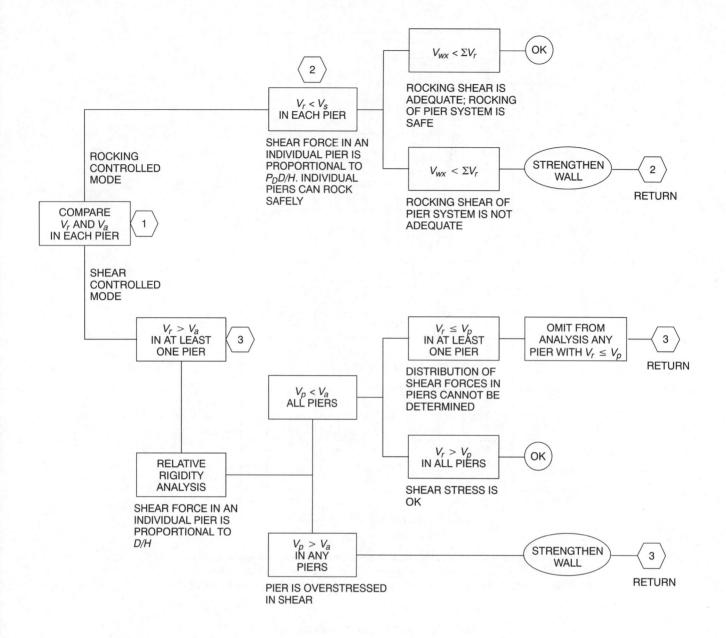

V_a = allowable shear strength of a pier.
V_p = shear force assigned to a pier on the basis of a relative shear rigidity analysis.
V_r = rocking shear capacity of pier.
V_{wx} = total shear force resisted by the wall.
ΣV_r = rocking shear capacity of all piers in the wall.

FIGURE A-1-2 —ANALYSIS OF URM WALL IN-PLANE SHEAR FORCES

Appendix Chapter 2
LIFE-SAFETY REQUIREMENTS FOR
EXISTING HIGH-RISE BUILDINGS

SECTION A201 — SCOPE

These provisions apply to existing high-rise buildings constructed prior to the adoption of this chapter and that house Group B offices or Group R, Division 1 Occupancies, each having floors used for human occupancy located more than 75 feet (22 860 mm) above the lowest level of fire department vehicle access.

SECTION A202 — GENERAL

Existing high-rise buildings as specified in Section A201 shall be modified to conform with not less than the minimum provisions specified in Table A-2-A and as further enumerated within this chapter.

The provisions of this chapter shall not be construed to allow the elimination of fire-protection systems or a reduction in the level of firesafety provided in buildings constructed in conformance with previously adopted codes.

SECTION A203 — COMPLIANCE DATA

After adoption of this chapter, the building official shall duly notify the owners whose buildings are subject to the provisions of this chapter. Upon receipt of such notice, the owner shall, subject to the following time limits, take necessary actions to comply with the provisions of this chapter.

Plans and specifications for the necessary alterations shall be filed with the building official within the time period established by the jurisdiction after the date of owner notification. Work on the required alterations to the building shall commence within 30 months of the date of owner notification and such work shall be completed within five years from the date of owner notification.

The building official shall grant necessary extensions of time when it can be shown that the specified time periods are not physically practical or pose an undue hardship. The granting of an extension of time for compliance shall be based on the showing of good cause and subject to the filing of an acceptable systematic progressive plan of correction with the building official.

SECTION A204 — AUTHORITY OF THE BUILDING OFFICIAL

For the purpose of applying the provisions of this chapter, the building official shall have the authority to consider alternative approaches and grant necessary deviations from this chapter as follows:

1. Allow alternate materials or methods of compliance if such alternate materials or methods of compliance will provide levels of fire and life safety equal to or greater than those specifically set forth in this chapter.

2. Waive specific individual requirements if it can be shown that such requirements are not physically possible or practical and that a practical alternative cannot be provided.

SECTION A205 — BUILDING CONSERVATION ADVISORY AND APPEALS BOARD

Appeals of the determinations of the building official in applying the provisions of this code may be made by an appeal directed to the building conservation advisory and appeals board as established by Section 207 of this code.

SECTION A206 — SPECIFIC PROVISIONS AND ALTERNATES

A206.1 Specific Provisions. The following provisions shall apply when required by Table A-2-A.

A206.1.1 Type of construction. Buildings classified as Type II-N, III-N or V-N construction shall be equipped with an approved automatic sprinkler system installed in accordance with UBC Standard 9-1.

> **EXCEPTION:** Installation of meters or backflow preventers for the connection to the water works system need not be provided unless required by other regulations of the authority having jurisdiction.

A206.1.2 Automatic sprinklers. All required exit corridors, stairwells, elevator lobbies, public assembly areas occupied by 100 or more persons and commercial kitchens shall be protected by an approved automatic sprinkler system meeting the design criteria of UBC Standard 9-1. A minimum of one sprinkler shall be provided on the room side of every corridor opening.

> **EXCEPTION:** Sprinklers may be omitted in stairwells of noncombustible construction.

A206.1.3 Fire department communication system. When it is determined by test that the portable fire department communication equipment is ineffective, a communication system acceptable to the fire department shall be installed within the existing high-rise building to permit emergency communication between fire-suppression personnel.

A206.1.4 Single-station smoke detectors. Single-station smoke detectors shall be installed within all dwelling units or guest rooms in accordance with the manufacturer's installation instructions. In dwelling units, the detector shall be mounted on the ceiling or wall at a point centrally located in the corridor or area giving access to each separate sleeping area. When sleeping rooms are located on an upper level, the detector shall be installed at the center of the ceiling directly above the stairway within the unit. In efficiency dwelling units, hotel suites and in hotel guest rooms, detectors shall be located on the ceiling or wall of the main room or hotel sleeping room. When actuated, the detector shall provide an audible alarm in the sleeping area of the dwelling unit, hotel suite or guest room in which it is located.

Such detectors may be battery operated.

A206.1.5 Manual fire alarm system. An approved manual fire alarm system connected to a central, proprietary or remote station service, or an approved manual fire alarm system that will provide an audible signal at a constantly attended location, shall be provided.

A206.1.6 Occupant voice notification system. An approved occupant voice notification system shall be provided. Such system shall provide communication from a location acceptable to the fire department and shall permit voice notification to at least all normally occupied areas of the building.

The occupant voice notification system may be combined with a fire alarm system, provided the combined system has been approved and listed for such use. The sounding of a fire alarm signal in any given area or floor shall not prohibit voice communication to other areas or floors. Combination systems shall be designed to permit voice transmission to override the fire alarm signal, but the fire alarm shall not terminate in less than three minutes.

A206.1.7 Vertical shaft enclosures. Openings through two or more floors except mezzanine floors, which contain a stairway or elevator, shall be provided with vertical shaft enclosure protection as specified herein. Such floor openings, when not enclosed by existing shaft enclosure construction, shall be protected by one-hour fire-resistive-rated shaft enclosure construction. For floor openings that are enclosed by existing shaft enclosure construction having fire-resistive capabilities similar to wood lath and plaster in good condition, $^1/_2$-inch (12.7 mm) gypsum wallboard or approved $^1/_4$-inch-thick (6.4 mm) wired glass is acceptable. Wired glass set in a steel frame may be installed in existing shaft enclosure walls but shall be rendered inoperative and fixed in a closed position.

Openings through two or more floors for other than stairways or elevators, such as openings provided for piping, ducts, gas vents, dumbwaiters, and rubbish and linen chutes, shall be provided with vertical shaft enclosure protection as specified for stairways and elevators.

> **EXCEPTION:** Openings for piping, ducts, gas vents, dumbwaiters and rubbish and linen chutes of copper or ferrous construction are permitted without a shaft enclosure, provided the floor openings are effectively firestopped at each floor level.

A206.1.8 Shaft enclosure opening protection. Openings other than those provided for elevator doors in new vertical shaft enclosures constructed of one-hour fire-resistive construction shall be equipped with approved fire assemblies having a fire-protection rating of not less than one hour. Openings other than those provided for elevator doors in existing vertical shaft enclosures shall be equipped with approved 20-minute-rated fire assemblies, $1^3/_4$-inch (44.5 mm) solid wood doors or the equivalent thereto. Doors shall be either self-closing or automatic closing and automatic latching.

All elevators on all floors shall open into elevator lobbies that are separated from the remainder of the building as is required for corridor construction in the Building Code, unless the building is protected throughout by a sprinkler system.

A206.1.9 Manual shutoff of heating, ventilating and air-conditioning (HVAC) systems. Heating, ventilating and air-conditioning systems shall be equipped with manual shutoff controls installed at an approved location when required by the fire department.

A206.1.10 Automatic elevator recall system. Elevators shall be equipped with an approved automatic recall system as required by Section 403.7, Item 2, of the Building Code.

A206.1.11 Unlocked stairway doors. Exit doors into exit stairway enclosures shall be maintained unlocked from the stairway side on at least every fifth floor level. All unlocked doors shall bear a sign stating ACCESS ONTO FLOOR THIS LEVEL.

Stairway doors may be locked, subject to the following conditions:

1. Stairway doors that are to be locked from the stairway side shall have the capability of being unlocked simultaneously without unlatching upon a signal from an approved location.

2. A telephone or other two-way communications system connected to an approved emergency service that operates continuously shall be provided at not less than every fifth floor in each required stairway.

A206.1.12 Stair shaft ventilation. Stair shaft enclosures that extend to the roof shall be provided with an approved manually openable hatch to the exterior having an area not less than 16 square feet (1.5 m^2) with a minimum dimension of 2 feet (610 mm).

> **EXCEPTIONS:** 1. Stair shaft enclosures complying with the requirements for smokeproof enclosures.
> 2. Stair shaft enclosures pressurized as required for mechanically operated smokeproof enclosures to a minimum of 0.15-inch (37 Pa) and a maximum of 0.50-inch water column (124 Pa).

A206.1.13 Elevator shaft ventilation. Elevator shaft enclosures that extend to the roof shall be vented to the outside with vents whose area shall not be less than $3^1/_2$ percent of the area of the elevator shaft, with a minimum of 3 square feet (0.28 m^2) per elevator.

> **EXCEPTION:** Where energy conservation or hoistway pressurization requires that the vents be normally closed, automatic venting by actuation of an elevator lobby detector or power failure may be accepted.

A206.1.14 Posting of elevators. A permanent sign shall be installed in each elevator cab adjacent to the floor status indicator and at each elevator call station on each floor reading IN FIRE EMERGENCY, DO NOT USE ELEVATOR—USE EXIT STAIRS, or similar verbiage approved by the building official.

> **EXCEPTION:** Sign may be omitted at the main entrance floor-level call station.

A206.1.15 Exit stairways. All high-rise buildings shall have a minimum of two approved exit stairways.

A206.1.16 Corridor construction. Corridors serving as a means of egress for an occupant load of 30 or more shall have walls and ceilings of not less than one-hour fire-resistive construction as required by this code. Existing walls may be surfaced with wood lath and plaster in good condition or $^1/_2$-inch (12.7 mm) gypsum wallboard for corridor walls and ceilings and occupancy separations when approved.

A206.1.17 Corridor openings. Openings in corridor walls and ceilings shall be protected by not less than $1^3/_8$-inch (34.9 mm) solid-bonded wood-core doors, approved $^1/_4$-inch-thick (6.4 mm) wired glass, approved fire dampers conforming to approved recognized standards, or by equivalent protection in lieu of any of these items. See UBC Chapter 35, Part IV. Transoms shall be fixed closed and covered with $^1/_2$-inch (12.7 mm) Type X gypsum wallboard or equivalent material installed on both sides of the opening.

A206.1.18 Corridor door closers. Exit-access doors into corridors shall be equipped with self-closing devices or shall be automatic closing by actuation of a smoke detector. When spring hinges are used as the closing device, not less than two such hinges shall be installed on each door leaf.

A206.1.19 Corridor dead ends. The length of dead end corridors serving an occupant load of more than 30 shall not exceed 20 feet (6096 mm).

A206.1.20 Interior finish. The interior finish in corridors, exit stairways and extensions thereof shall conform to the provisions of Chapter 8 of the Building Code.

A206.1.21 Stairway illumination. When the building is occupied, stairways shall be illuminated with lights having an intensity of not less than 1 footcandle (10.8 lx) at the floor level. Such lighting shall be equipped with an independent alternate source of power such as a battery pack or on-site generator.

A206.1.22 Corridor illumination. When the building is occupied, corridors shall be illuminated with lights having an intensity of not less than 1 footcandle (10.8 lx) at the floor level. Such lighting shall be equipped with an independent alternate source of power such as a battery pack or on-site generator.

A206.1.23 Stairway exit signs. The location of stairways shall be clearly indicated by illuminated exit signs. Such exit signs shall be equipped with an independent alternate source of power such as a battery pack or on-site generator or shall be of an approved self-illuminating type.

A206.1.24 Exit signs. Illuminated exit signs shall be provided in all exits and exit-access doorways and located in such a manner as to clearly indicate the direction of egress. Such exit signs shall be equipped with an independent alternate source of power such as a battery pack or on-site generator or shall be of an approved self-illuminating type.

A206.1.25 Emergency plan. The management for all buildings shall establish and maintain a written fire- and life-safety emergency plan that has been approved by the chief. The chief shall develop written criteria and guidelines on which all plans shall be based.

A206.1.26 Posting of emergency plan and exiting plans. Copies of the emergency plan and exiting plans (including elevator and stairway placarding) shall be posted in locations approved by the chief.

A206.1.27 Fire drills. The management of all buildings shall conduct fire drills for their staff and employees at least every 120 days. The fire department must be advised of such drills at least 24 hours in advance. A written record of each drill shall be maintained in the building management office and made available to the fire department for review.

A206.2 Sprinkler Alternatives. The requirements of Table A-2-A may be modified as specified by the following for existing high-rise buildings of Type I, II-F.R., II One-hour, III One-hour, IV or V One-hour construction when an approved automatic sprinkler system is installed throughout the building in accordance with UBC Standard 9-1:

Item 5—Manual fire-warning system shall not be required.

Item 6—Occupant voice notification system shall not be required; however, if the building is equipped with a public address system, the public address system shall be available for use as an occupant voice notification system.

Item 7—Vertical shaft enclosures may be of nonrated construction for required stairway enclosures. Vertical shaft enclosures of openings in floors provided for elevators, escalators and supplemental stairways shall not be required, provided such openings are protected by an approved curtain board and water curtain system.

Item 8—Protection of openings in vertical shaft enclosures may be nonrated but shall not be less than a $1^3/_4$-inch (44.5 mm) solid-wood door or the equivalent thereto. Closing and latching hardware shall be provided.

Item 10—An automatic elevator recall system shall not be required.

Item 12—Stair shaft ventilation shall not be required.

Item 16—Existing corridor construction need not be altered.

Item 17—Door openings into corridors may be protected by assemblies other than those specified in Section A206.1, provided an effective smoke barrier is maintained. Closing and latching hardware shall be provided. Protection of duct penetrations is not required.

Item 19—The length of existing corridor dead ends shall not be limited.

Item 20—Interior finish in corridors, stairways and extensions thereof may be reduced by one classification but shall not be less than Class III.

Installation of meters or backflow preventers for the connection to the water works system need not be provided unless required by other regulations of the authority having jurisdiction.

TABLE A-2-A—OCCUPANCY CLASSIFICATION AND USE[1]

ITEM REQUIRED	GROUP R, DIVISION 1						GROUP B		
	Apartment			Hotel			Office		
	Height Zones[2]								
	1	2	3	1	2	3	1	2	3
1. Automatic sprinklers in buildings of Type II-N, III-N or V-N construction. See Section A206.1.1.	R	R	—	R	R	—	R	R	—
2. Automatic sprinklers in corridors, stairways, elevator lobbies, public assembly areas, kitchens and at door openings to corridors. See Section A206.1.2.	R	R	R	R	R	R	R	R	R
3. Fire department communication system or radios. See Section A206.1.3.	R	R	R	R	R	R	R	R	R
4. Single-station smoke detectors. See Section A206.1.4.	R	R	R	R	R	R	NR	NR	NR
5. Manual fire warning system. See Section A206.1.5.	R	R	R	R	R	R	R	R	R
6. Occupant voice notification system. See Section A206.1.6.	NR	R	R	NR	R	R	NR	NR	NR
7. Vertical shaft enclosure walls of one-hour fire resistance. See Section A206.1.7.	R	R	R	R	R	R	R	R	R
8. Protection of openings in vertical shaft enclosures by 20-minute-rated assemblies. See Section A206.1.8.	R	R	R	R	R	R	R	R	R
9. Manual shutoff of HVAC systems. See Section A206.1.9.	R	R	R	R	R	R	R	R	R
10. Automatic elevator recall system. See Section A206.1.10.	R	R	R	R	R	R	R	R	R
11. Unlocked stairway doors every fifth floor. See Section A206.1.11.	R	R	R	R	R	R	NR	R	R
12. Stair shaft ventilation. See Section A206.1.12.	R	R	R	R	R	R	R	R	R
13. Elevator shaft ventilation. See Section A206.1.13.	R	R	R	R	R	R	R	R	R
14. Posting of elevators as not intended for exiting purposes. See Section A206.1.14.	R	R	R	R	R	R	R	R	R
15. Minimum of two exits from each floor, of which one may be a fire escape. See Section A206.1.15.	R	R	R	R	R	R	R	R	R
16. Corridor wall construction. See Section A206.1.16.	R	R	R	R	R	R	R	R	R
17. Protected corridor openings with 20-minute-rated assemblies or $1^3/_4$-inch (44.5 mm) solid wood door. See Section A206.1.17.	R	R	R	R	R	R	NR	NR	NR
18. Corridor doors equipped with self-closing devices. See Section A206.1.18.	R	R	R	R	R	R	NR	NR	NR
19. Corridor dead ends limited to 35 feet (10 668 mm) maximum. See Section A206.1.19.	R	R	R	R	R	R	NR	NR	NR
20. Interior finish controlled in corridors, stairways and extensions thereof. See Section A206.1.20.	R	R	R	R	R	R	R	R	R
21. Stairway illumination. See Section A206.1.21.	R	R	R	R	R	R	R	R	R
22. Corridor illumination. See Section A206.1.22.	R	R	R	R	R	R	NR	NR	NR
23. Stairway exit signs. See Section A206.1.23.	R	R	R	R	R	R	R	R	R
24. Exit and exit-access doorway exit signs. See Section A206.1.24.	R	R	R	R	R	R	R	R	R
25. Emergency planning. See Section A206.1.25.	R	R	R	R	R	R	R	R	R
26. Posting of emergency instructions. See Section A206.1.26.	R	R	R	R	R	R	R	R	R
27. Fire drills. See Section A206.1.27.	NR	NR	NR	R	R	R	NR	NR	NR

[1]R indicates provisions are required.

NR indicates provisions are not required.

[2]Height zones are established based on a building having a floor as measured to the top of the floor surface used for human occupancy located within the ranges of heights above the lowest level of fire department vehicle access in accordance with the following:

Height Zone 1: More than 75 feet (22 860 mm), but not in excess of 149 feet (45 415 mm).

Height Zone 2: More than 149 feet (45 415 mm), but not in excess of 399 feet (121 615 mm).

Height Zone 3: More than 399 feet (121 615 mm).

Appendix Chapter 3
ACCESSIBILITY

SECTION A301 — SCOPE

The provisions of this appendix apply to renovation, alteration and additions to existing buildings including those identified as historic buildings. This chapter identifies minimum standards for removing architectural barriers, and providing and maintaining accessibility to existing buildings and their related facilities.

SECTION A302 — DEFINITIONS

For the purpose of this chapter, certain terms are defined as follows:

ALTERATION is any change, addition, or modification in construction or occupancy.

ALTERATION, SUBSTANTIAL, is any alteration where the total cost of all alterations (including, but not limited to, electrical, mechanical, plumbing and structural changes) for a building or facility within any 12-month period amounts to 50 percent or more of the assessed value.

STRUCTURALLY IMPRACTICAL describes alterations that require changes to load-bearing structural members other than conventional light-frame construction.

SECTION A303 — ADDITIONS

A303.1 General. New additions may be made to existing buildings without making the entire building comply, provided the new additions conform to the provisions of Chapter 11 of the Building Code and applicable sections of CABO/ANSI A117.1. Unless structurally impractical, existing buildings to which additions are attached shall comply with this section.

A303.2 Entrances. When a new addition to a building or facility does not have an accessible entrance, then at least one entrance in the existing building or facility shall be accessible.

A303.3 Accessible Route. When the only accessible entrance to the addition is located in the existing building or facility, at least one accessible route of travel shall be provided through the existing building or facility to all rooms, elements and spaces in the new addition that are required to be accessible.

A303.4 Toilet and Bathing Facilities. When there are no toilet rooms and bathing facilities in the addition and these facilities are provided in the existing building, then at least one toilet and bathing facility in the existing building shall comply with Chapter 11 of the Building Code or with Section A304.3.6 of this appendix.

SECTION A304 — ALTERATIONS

A304.1 General. Unless it is structurally impractical, alterations to existing buildings or facilities shall comply with the following:

1. When existing elements, spaces, essential features or common areas are altered, then each such altered element, space, feature or area shall comply with the applicable provisions of Chapter 11 of the Building Code and applicable provisions of CABO/ANSI A117.1.

2. When an escalator or new stairway is planned or installed requiring major structural changes, then a means of vertical transportation shall be installed in accordance with CABO/ANSI A117.1.

3. Where alterations of single elements, when considered together, provide access to an area of a building or facility, the entire area or space shall be accessible.

4. Alteration of an existing element, space or area of a building shall not impose a requirement for greater accessibility than that which would be required for new construction.

5. When the alteration work is limited solely to the electrical, mechanical or plumbing systems and does not involve the alteration, structural or otherwise, of any elements and spaces required to be accessible under these standards, this appendix and Chapter 11 of the Building Code do not apply.

A304.2 Substantial Alterations. Where substantial alteration occurs to a building or facility, each element or space that is altered or added shall comply with the applicable provisions of Chapter 11 of the Building Code and CABO/ANSI A117.1 or this appendix, except when it is structurally impractical. The altered building or facility shall contain:

1. At least one accessible route.

2. At least one accessible entrance, preferably the main entrance. When additional entrances are altered, they shall comply.

3. The following toilet facilities, whichever is greater:

3.1 At least one toilet facility for each sex in the altered building.

3.2 At least one toilet facility for each sex on each substantially altered floor, where such facilities are provided.

A304.3 Modifications.

A304.3.1 General. The modifications set forth in this section may be used for compliance when the required standard is structurally impractical or when providing access to historic buildings.

A304.3.2 Ramps. Curb ramps and ramps constructed on existing sites, or in existing buildings or facilities, may have slopes and rises as specified for existing facilities in CABO/ANSI A117.1, when space limitations preclude the use of a slope of 1 unit vertical in 12 units horizontal (8.33% slope) or less.

A304.3.3 Stairs. Full extension of stair handrails is not required when such extension would be hazardous or impossible due to plan configuration. When an accessible elevator is provided, existing stairs need not be made accessible.

A304.3.4 Elevators. If a safety door edge is provided on existing automatic elevators, the automatic door reopening devices as specified in CABO/ANSI A117.1 may be omitted.

When existing hoistway shaft or structural elements prohibit strict compliance with CABO/ANSI A117.1, the minimum floor area dimensions may be reduced, but in no case shall they be less than 48 inches by 48 inches (1219 mm by 1219 mm).

A304.3.5 Doors.

A304.3.5.1 Clearance. When existing elements prohibit strict compliance with the clearance requirements, a projection of $5/8$-inch (15.9 mm) maximum is permitted for the latch side door stop.

A304.3.5.2 Thresholds. Existing thresholds measuring $3/4$ inch (19.1 mm) high or less that are modified to provide a beveled edge on each side may be retained.

A304.3.6 Toilet rooms.

A304.3.6.1 Shared facilities. The addition of one unisex toilet facility accessible to all occupants on the floor may be provided in lieu of making existing toilet facilities accessible when it is structurally impractical to comply with this appendix and Chapter 11 of the Building Code.

A304.3.6.2 Stall size. In alterations when provision of a standard stall is structurally impractical or when Plumbing Code requirements prevent combining existing stalls to provide an accessible stall, an alternate stall as described in CABO/ANSI A117.1 may be provided in lieu of a standard stall.

A304.3.7 Assembly areas. Seating shall adjoin an accessible route of travel that also serves as a means of emergency egress or route to an area for evacuation assistance.

SECTION A305 — HISTORIC PRESERVATION

A305.1 General. Generally, the accessibility provisions of this appendix shall be applied to historic buildings and facilities as defined in Section 3403.5 of the Building Code.

The building official shall determine whether provisions required by this appendix for accessible routes of travel (interior or exterior), ramps, entrances, toilets, parking or signage would threaten or destroy the historic significance of the building or facility.

If it is determined that any of the accessibility requirements listed above would threaten or destroy the historic significance of a building or facility, the modifications of Section A304.3 for that feature may be utilized.

A305.2 Special Provisions. When removing architectural barriers or providing accessibility would threaten or destroy the historic significance of a building or facility, the following special provisions may be used:

1. At least one accessible route from a site access point to an accessible route shall be provided.

2. At least one accessible entrance that is used by the public shall be provided.

> **EXCEPTION:** When it is determined by the building official that no entrance used by the public can comply, access at any entrance that is unlocked during business hours may be used provided directional signs are located at the main entry. The route of travel for the accessible entry shall not pass through hazardous areas, storage rooms, closets, kitchens or spaces used for similar purposes.

3. Where toilet facilities are provided, at least one toilet facility complying with Section A303 or A304 shall be provided along an accessible route. Such toilet facility shall be a shared facility available to both sexes.

4. Accessible routes from an accessible entrance to all publicly used spaces, on at least the level of accessible entrance, shall be provided. Access shall be provided to all levels of a building or facility when practical.

SECTION A306 — APPEAL

A306.1 Request for Appeal. An appeal from the standards for accessibility for existing buildings may be filed with the building official when:

1. Existing structural elements or physical constraints of the site prevent full compliance or would threaten or destroy the historical significance of a historic building, or

2. The cost of compliance with this chapter would exceed 25 percent of the total project cost, inclusive of the cost of eliminating barriers, within a 12-month period.

A306.2 Review. Review of appeal requests shall include consideration of alternative methods that may provide partial access.

Appendix Chapter 4
ENERGY CONSERVATION

SECTION A401 — ADDITIONS TO EXISTING BUILDINGS

Additions may be made to existing buildings or structures without making the entire building or structure comply with the energy conservation requirements of the jurisdiction. The new addition shall conform to the provisions of the jurisdiction's energy conservation regulations as they relate to new construction only.

SECTION A402 — CHANGE OF OCCUPANCY

A change in the occupancy or use of an existing building or structure constructed under an energy conservation code that would require an increase in demand for either fossil fuel or electrical energy supply shall not be permitted unless such building or structure is made to comply with the requirements of the jurisdiction's energy conservation regulations.

Appendix Chapter 5
EARTHQUAKE HAZARD REDUCTION IN EXISTING TILT-UP CONCRETE WALL BUILDINGS
Note: This is a new appendix chapter.

SECTION A501 — PURPOSE

The purpose of this chapter is to promote public safety and welfare by reducing the risk of death or injury that may result from the effects of earthquakes on tilt-up concrete wall buildings. Buildings have been categorized, based on past earthquakes, as being potentially hazardous and prone to significant damage, including possible collapse, in a moderate to major earthquake. The provisions of this chapter are minimum standards for structural seismic resistance established primarily to reduce the risk of life loss or injury on both subject and adjacent properties and will not necessarily prevent loss of life or injury or prevent earthquake damage to an existing building that complies with these standards.

SECTION A502 — SCOPE

The provisions of this chapter shall apply to all buildings in Seismic Zones 2B, 3 and 4, but designed under building codes in effect prior to the adoption of the 1976 edition of the *Uniform Building Code,* which have tilt-up concrete walls and flexible diaphragms as defined herein.

SECTION A503 — DEFINITIONS

For purposes of this chapter, the applicable definitions in Chapters 16, 19 and 23 of the Building Code and the following shall apply:

FLEXIBLE DIAPHRAGMS are roofs and floors including, but not limited to, those sheathed with plywood, wood decking (1x or 2x) or metal decks without concrete topping slabs.

TILT-UP CONCRETE WALL is a form of precast concrete wall panel construction, either cast in the horizontal position at the site and, after curing, lifted and moved into place in a vertical position, or cast off-site in a fabricator's shop.

SECTION A504 — SYMBOLS AND NOTATIONS

For the purpose of this chapter, the applicable symbols and notations in the Building Code shall apply.

SECTION A505 — GENERAL REQUIREMENTS

A505.1 General. Buildings shall have a seismic-resisting system conforming to Chapter 16 of the Building Code, except as modified by this chapter.

A505.2 Alterations and Repairs. Alterations and repairs required to meet the provisions of this chapter shall comply with applicable structural requirements of the Building Code unless specifically provided in this chapter.

A505.3 Requirements for Plans. The plans shall accurately reflect the results of the engineering investigation and design and show all pertinent dimensions and sizes for plan review and construction. The following shall be provided:

1. Floor plans and roof plans shall show existing framing construction, diaphragm construction, proposed wall anchors, crossties and collectors. Existing nailing, anchors, ties and collectors shall also be shown on the plans if these are part of the design.

2. At elevations where there are alterations or damage, details shall show roof and floor heights, dimensions of openings, location and extent of existing damage, and proposed repair.

3. Typical wall panel details and sections with panel thickness, height, pilasters and location of anchors shall be provided.

4. Details shall include existing and new anchors and the method of development of anchor forces into the diaphragm framing, existing and/or new crossties, existing and/or new or improved support of roof and floor girders at pilasters or walls.

5. The basis for design and design code shall be stated on the plans.

A505.4 Structural Observation. Structural observation shall be provided in Seismic Zones 3 and 4 for all structures regulated by this chapter. The owner shall employ the engineer or architect responsible for the structural design, or another engineer or architect designated by the engineer or architect responsible for the structural designs, to perform structural observations as defined in Section 220 of the UBC. Observed deficiencies shall be reported in writing to the owner's representative, special inspector, contractor and the building official. The structural observer shall submit to the building official a written statement that the site visits have been made and identify any reported deficiencies that, to the best of the structural observer's knowledge, have not been resolved.

SECTION A506 — ANALYSIS AND DESIGN

A506.1 Wall Panel Anchorage. Concrete walls shall be anchored to all floors and roofs that provide lateral support for the wall. The anchorage shall provide a positive direct connection between the wall and floor or roof construction capable of resisting the horizontal forces specified in the following formula:

$$F_p = ZIC_p W_p \qquad \text{(A6-1)}$$

WHERE:

$C_p = 0.75.$

Z and I shall be those used for the building or a minimum force of 250 pounds per linear foot (3.65 kN/m) of wall, whichever is greater. The required anchorage shall be based on the tributary wall panel assuming simple supports at floors and roof.

> **EXCEPTION:** Alternate designs may be approved by the building official when justified by rational analysis.

A506.2 Special Requirements for Wall Anchors and Continuity Ties. The steel elements of the wall anchorage system and continuity ties shall be designed in accordance with the Building Code. When the allowable stress design method is used, the load factor shall be 1.7. The one-third stress increase permitted by Chapter 16 shall not be permitted for materials using allowable stress design methods.

Design of embedments in concrete shall be in accordance with Chapter 19 of the Building Code and shall use a load factor of 2.0 in lieu of the 1.4 for earthquake loading.

Wall anchors shall be provided to resist out-of-plane forces, independent of existing shear anchors.

> **EXCEPTION:** Existing cast-in-place shear anchors may be used as wall anchors if the tie element can be readily attached to the anchors

and if the engineer or architect can establish tension values for the existing anchors through the use of approved as-built plans or testing, and through analysis showing that the bolts are capable of resisting the total shear load (including dead load) while being acted upon by the maximum tension force due to earthquake. Criteria for analysis and testing shall be determined by the building official.

Expansion anchors are only allowed with special inspection and approved testing for seismic loading. Attaching the edge of plywood sheathing to steel ledgers is not considered as complying with the positive anchoring requirements of this chapter. Attaching the edge of steel decks to steel ledgers is not considered as providing the positive anchorage of this chapter unless testing and/or analysis are performed that establish shear values for the attachment perpendicular to the edge of the deck. Any installation shall be subject to special inspection.

A506.3 Development of Anchor Loads into the Diaphragm. Development of anchor loads into roof and floor diaphragms shall comply with Chapter 16 of the Building Code.

> **EXCEPTION:** If continuously tied girders are present, the maximum spacing of the continuity ties is the greater of the girder spacing or 24 feet (7315 mm).

In wood diaphragms, anchorage shall not be accomplished by use of toenails or nails subject to withdrawal, and wood ledgers, top plates or framing shall not be used in cross-grain bending or cross-grain tension. The continuous ties required in Chapter 16 of the Building Code shall be in addition to the diaphragm sheathing.

Lengths of development of anchor loads in wood diaphragms shall be based on existing field nailing of the sheathing unless existing edge nailing is positively identified on the original construction plans or at the site.

At re-entrant corners where continuity collectors do not exist, they shall be provided. New collectors shall be designed to the capacity required to develop into the diaphragm of a force equal to the lesser of the rocking or shear capacity of the re-entrant wall, or the tributary shear. The capacity of the collector need not exceed the capacity of the diaphragm. Shear anchors for the re-entrant wall shall be provided to transfer the full collector force (load). If a truss or beam other than rafters or purlins is supported by the re-entrant wall or by a column integral with the re-entrant wall, an independent secondary column is required to support the roof or floor members whenever rocking or shear capacity of the re-entrant wall is less than the tributary shear.

A506.4 Anchorage at Pilasters. Anchorage at pilasters shall be designed for the tributary wall anchoring load per Section A506.1, considering the wall as a two-way slab. The pilasters or the walls immediately adjacent to the pilasters shall be anchored directly to the roof framing such that the existing vertical anchor bolts at the top of the pilasters are by-passed without permitting tension or shear failure at the top of the pilasters.

> **EXCEPTION:** If existing vertical anchor bolts at the top of the pilasters are used for the anchorage, additional exterior confinement shall be provided.

The minimum anchorage force at a floor or roof between the pilasters shall be that specified in Section A506.1.

A506.5 Symmetry. Symmetry of wall anchorage and continuity connectors about the minor axis of the framing member is required.

> **EXCEPTION:** Eccentricity may be allowed when it can be shown that all components of forces are positively resisted. The resistance must be supported by calculations or tests.

A506.6 Minimum Roof Member Size. Wood members used to develop anchorage forces to the diaphragm must be at least 3-inch (76 mm) nominal for new construction and replacement. All such members must be checked for gravity and earthquake loading as part of the wall anchorage system. For existing buildings, the member check shall be without the one-third stress increase per Section A506.2.

> **EXCEPTION:** Existing 2x members may be doubled and internailed to meet the strength requirement.

A506.7 Combination of Anchor Types. Anchors used in combination shall be of compatible behavior and stiffness.

A506.8 Miscellaneous. Existing mezzanines relying on tilt-up walls for vertical and/or lateral support shall be anchored to the walls for the tributary mezzanine load. Walls depending on the mezzanine for lateral support shall be anchored per Sections A506.1, A506.2 and A506.3.

> **EXCEPTION:** Existing mezzanines that have independent lateral and vertical support need not be anchored to the walls.

Existing interior masonry or concrete walls that extend to the floor above or to the roof diaphragm shall also be anchored for out-of-plane forces per Sections A506.1 and A506.3. Walls extending through the roof diaphragm shall be anchored for out-of-plane forces on both sides to provide diaphragm continuity. In the in-plane direction, the walls may be isolated or shall be developed into the diaphragm for a lateral force equal to the lesser of the rocking or shear capacity of the wall, or the tributary shear, but need not exceed the diaphragm capacity.

SECTION A507 — MATERIALS OF CONSTRUCTION

All materials permitted by the Building Code, including their appropriate allowable stresses and those existing configurations of materials specified in Appendix Chapter 1 of this code, may be utilized to meet the requirements of this appendix chapter.

Appendix Chapter 6

PRESCRIPTIVE PROVISIONS FOR SEISMIC STRENGTHENING OF CRIPPLE WALLS AND SILL PLATE ANCHORAGE OF LIGHT, WOOD-FRAMED, RESIDENTIAL BUILDINGS

Note: This is a new appendix chapter.

SECTION A601 — GENERAL

A601.1 Purpose. The provisions of this chapter are intended to promote public safety and welfare by reducing the risk of earthquake-induced damage to existing wood-framed residential buildings. The requirements contained in this chapter are prescriptive minimum standards intended to improve the seismic performance of residential buildings, but will not necessarily prevent earthquake damage.

This chapter sets standards for strengthening that may be approved by the building official without requiring plans or calculations prepared by an architect or an engineer. The provisions of this chapter are not intended to prevent the use of any material or method of construction not prescribed herein. The building official may require that construction documents for strengthening using alternate material or methods be prepared by an architect or engineer.

A601.2 Scope. The provisions of this chapter apply to light, wood-frame Group R, Division 3 and Group R, Division 1 Occupancies located in Seismic Zones 3 and 4, containing one or more of the structural weaknesses specified in Section A603.

> **EXCEPTION:** The provisions of this chapter do not apply to the buildings or elements thereof, listed below. These buildings or elements require analysis by an engineer or architect in accordance with Section A601.3 to determine appropriate strengthening.
>
> 1. Group R, Division 1 Occupancies with more than four dwelling units.
>
> 2. Buildings with a lateral force-resisting system using poles or columns embedded in the ground.
>
> 3. Cripple walls that exceed 4 feet (1219 mm) in height.
>
> 4. Buildings exceeding three stories in height and any three-story building with cripple wall studs exceeding 14 inches (356 mm) in height.
>
> 5. Buildings where the building official determines that conditions exist that are beyond the scope of the prescriptive requirements of this chapter.

The provisions of this chapter do not apply to structures, or portions thereof, constructed on a concrete slab on grade.

The details and prescriptive provisions herein are not intended to be the only acceptable strengthening methods permitted. Alternate details and methods may be used when approved by the building official. Approval of alternates shall be based on test data showing that the method or material used is at least equivalent in terms of strength, deflection and capacity as provided by the prescriptive methods and materials. See Table A-6-C for the capacities provided by the prescriptive elements and connections.

The provisions of this chapter may be used to strengthen historic structures provided they are not in conflict with other related provisions and requirements that may apply.

A601.3 Alternative Design Procedures. When analysis by an engineer or architect is required in accordance with Section A601.2, such analysis shall be in accordance with all requirements of the Building Code, except that the base shear may be determined in accordance with the following:

$$V = 0.33ZW \qquad (A1\text{-}1)$$

SECTION A602 — DEFINITIONS

For the purpose of this chapter, in addition to the applicable definitions in the Building Code, certain additional terms are defined as follows:

CHEMICAL ANCHOR is an assembly consisting of a threaded rod, washer, nut and chemical adhesive approved by the building official for installation in existing concrete or masonry.

COMPOSITE PANEL is a wood structural panel product composed of a combination of wood veneer and wood-based material and bonded with waterproof adhesive.

CRIPPLE WALL is a wood-framed stud wall extending from the top of the foundation to the underside of the lowest floor framing.

EXPANSION BOLT is a single assembly approved by the building official for installation in existing concrete or masonry. For the purpose of this chapter, expansion bolts shall contain a base designed to expand when properly set, wedging the bolt in the predrilled hole. Assembly shall also include appropriate washer and nut.

ORIENTED STRAND BOARD (OSB) is a mat-formed wood structural panel product composed of thin rectangular wood strands or wafers arranged in oriented layers and bonded with waterproof adhesive.

PERIMETER FOUNDATION is a foundation system that is located under the exterior walls of a building.

PLYWOOD is a wood structural panel product composed of sheets of wood veneer bonded together with the grain of adjacent layers oriented at right angles to one another.

SNUG-TIGHT is as tight as an individual can torque a nut on a bolt by hand using a wrench with a 10-inch (254 mm) long handle and the point at which the full surface of the plate washer is contacting the wood member and slightly indents the wood surface.

WAFERBOARD is a mat-formed wood structural panel product composed of thin rectangular wood wafers arranged in random layers and bonded with waterproof adhesive.

WOOD STRUCTURAL PANEL is a structural panel product composed primarily of wood and meeting the requirements of United States Voluntary Product Standard PS 1 and United States Voluntary Product Standard PS 2. Wood structural panels include all-veneer plywood, composite panels containing a combination of veneer and wood-based material, and mat-formed panels such as oriented strand board and waferboard.

SECTION A603 — STRUCTURAL WEAKNESSES

For the purpose of this chapter, structural weaknesses shall be as specified below.

1. Sill plates or floor framing that are supported directly on the ground without an approved foundation system.

2. A perimeter foundation system that is constructed only of wood posts supported on isolated pad footings.

3. Perimeter foundation systems that are not continuous.

> **EXCEPTIONS:** 1. Existing single-story exterior walls not exceeding 10 feet (3048 mm) in length forming an extension of floor area beyond the line of an existing continuous perimeter foundation.
>
> 2. Porches, storage rooms and similar spaces not containing fuel-burning appliances.

4. A perimeter foundation system that is constructed of unreinforced masonry.

5. Sill plates that are not connected to the foundation or are connected with less than what is required by the Building Code.

> **EXCEPTION:** When approved by the building official, connections of a sill plate to the foundation made with other than sill bolts may be accepted if the capacity of the connection is equivalent to that required by the Building Code.

6. Cripple walls that are not braced in accordance with the requirements of Section A604.4 and Table A-6-A or cripple walls not braced with diagonal sheathing or wood structural panels in accordance with the Building Code.

SECTION A604 — STRENGTHENING REQUIREMENTS

A604.1 General.

A604.1.1 Scope. The structural weaknesses noted in Section A603 shall be strengthened in accordance with the requirements of this section. Strengthening work may include both new construction and alteration of existing construction. Except as provided herein, all strengthening work and materials shall comply with the applicable provisions of the Building Code. Alternate methods of strengthening may be used provided such systems are designed by an engineer or architect and approved by the building official.

A604.1.2 Condition of existing wood materials. All existing wood materials that will be a part of the strengthening work (sills, studs, sheathing, etc.) shall be in a sound condition and free from defects that substantially reduce the capacity of the member. Any wood material found to contain fungus infection shall be removed and replaced with new material. Any wood material found to be infested with insects or to have been infested with insects shall be strengthened or replaced with new materials to provide a net dimension of sound wood at least equal to its undamaged original dimension.

A604.1.3 Floor joists not parallel to foundations. Floor joists framed perpendicular or at an angle to perimeter foundations shall be restrained by either an existing nominal 2-inch (51 mm) wide continuous rim joist or by nominal 2-inch (51 mm) wide full depth blocking between alternate joists in one- and two-story buildings, and between each joist in three-story buildings. Existing blocking for multistory buildings must occur at each joist space above a braced cripple wall panel.

Existing connections at the top and bottom edge of an existing rim joist or blocking need not be verified in one-story buildings. In multistory buildings the existing top edge connection need not be verified; however, bottom edge connection to either the foundation sill plate or top plate of a cripple wall shall be verified. The minimum existing bottom edge connection shall consist of 8d toe nails spaced 6 inches (152 mm) apart for a continuous rim joist or three 8d toenails per block. When this minimum bottom edge con-

nection is not present, or cannot be verified, a supplemental connection installed as shown in Figure A-6-8 shall be provided.

Where an existing continuous rim joist or the minimum existing blocking does not occur, new $^3/_4$-inch (19 mm) wood structural panel blocking installed tightly between floor joists and nailed as shown in Figure A-6-8 shall be provided at the inside face of the cripple wall and nailed as shown in Figure A-6-8. In lieu of $^3/_4$-inch (19 mm) wood structural panel blocking, tightfitting, full depth 2 × (51 mm) blocking, may be used. New blocking may be omitted where it will interfere with vents or plumbing that penetrates the wall.

A604.1.4 Floor joists parallel to foundations. Where existing floor joists are parallel to the perimeter foundations, the end joist shall be located over the foundation and, except for required ventilation openings, shall be continuous and in continuous contact with the foundation sill plate or top plate of the cripple wall. Existing connections at the top and bottom edge of the end joist need not be verified in one-story buildings. In multistory buildings, the existing top edge connection of the end joist need not be verified; however, the bottom edge connection to either the foundation sill plate or the top plate of a cripple wall shall be verified. The minimum bottom edge connection shall be 8d toenails spaced 6 inches (152 mm) apart. If this minimum bottom edge connection is not present, or cannot be verified, a supplemental connection installed as shown in Figure A-6-9 shall be provided.

A604.2 Foundations.

A604.2.1 New perimeter foundations. New perimeter foundations shall be provided for structures with the structural weaknesses noted in Items 1 and 2 of Section A603. Soil investigations or geotechnical studies are not required for this work unless the building is located in a special study zone as designated by the jurisdiction or other public agency.

A604.2.2 Foundation evaluation by engineer or architect. Partial perimeter foundations or unreinforced masonry foundations shall be evaluated by an engineer or architect for the force levels noted in Formula (A1-1). Test reports or other substantiating data to determine existing foundation material strengths shall be submitted for review. When approved by the building official, these foundation systems may be strengthened in accordance with the recommendations included with the evaluation in lieu of being replaced.

> **EXCEPTION:** In lieu of testing existing foundations to determine material strengths and when approved by the building official, a new nonperimeter foundation system, designed for the forces noted in Formula (A1-1), may be used to resist all exterior wall lateral forces.

A604.2.3 Details for new perimeter foundations. All new perimeter foundations shall be continuous and constructed according to one of the details shown in Figure A-6-1 or A-6-2.

> **EXCEPTIONS:** 1. When approved by the building official, the existing clearance between existing floor joists or girders and existing grade below the floor need not comply with the Building Code.
>
> 2. When approved by the building official, and when designed by an engineer or architect, partial perimeter foundations may be used in lieu of a continuous perimeter foundation.

A604.2.4 Required compressive strength. New concrete foundations shall have a minimum compressive strength of 2,500 psi (17.24 MPa) at 28 days.

A604.2.5 New hollow-unit masonry foundations. New hollow-unit masonry foundations shall be solidly grouted. Mortar shall be Type M or S, and the grout and masonry units shall comply with the Building Code.

A604.2.6 Reinforcing steel. Reinforcing steel shall comply with the requirements of the Building Code.

A604.3 Foundation Sill Plate Anchorage.

A604.3.1 Existing perimeter foundations. When the building has an existing continuous perimeter foundation, all perimeter wall sill plates shall be bolted to the foundation with chemical anchors or expansion bolts in accordance with Table A-6-A.

Anchors or bolts shall be installed in accordance with Figure A-6-3 with the plate washer installed between the nut and the sill plate. The nut shall be tightened to a snug-tight condition after curing is complete for chemical anchors and after expansion wedge engagement for expansion bolts. The installation of nuts on all bolts shall be subject to verification by the building official. Where existing conditions prevent anchor or bolt installation through the sill plate, this connection may be made in accordance with Figure A-6-4A, A-6-4B or A-6-4C. The spacing of these alternate connections shall comply with the maximum spacing requirements of Table A-6-A. Expansion bolts shall not be used when the installation causes surface cracking of the foundation wall at the location of the bolt.

A604.3.2 Placement of chemical anchors and expansion bolts. Chemical anchors or expansion bolts shall be placed within 12 inches (305 mm), but not less than 9 inches (229 mm), from the ends of sill plates and shall be placed in the center of the stud space closest to the required spacing. New sill plates may be installed in pieces when necessary because of existing conditions. For lengths of sill plate greater than 12 feet (3658 mm), anchors or bolts shall be spaced along the sill plate as noted in Table A-6-A. For other lengths of sill plate, see Table A-6-B. For lengths of sill plates less than 30 inches (762 mm), a minimum of one anchor or bolt shall be installed.

> **EXCEPTION:** Where physical obstructions such as fireplaces, plumbing or heating ducts interfere with the placement of an anchor or bolt, the anchor or bolt shall be placed as close to the obstruction as possible, but not less than 9 inches (229 mm) from the end of the plate. Center-to-center spacing of the anchors or bolts shall be reduced as necessary to provide the minimum total number of anchors required based on the full length of the wall. Center-to-center spacing shall not be less than 12 inches (305 mm).

A604.3.3 New perimeter foundations. Sill plates for new perimeter foundations shall be bolted as required by Table A-6-A and as shown in Figure A-6-1 or A-6-2.

A604.4 Cripple Wall Bracing.

A604.4.1 General. Exterior cripple walls, not exceeding 4 feet (1219 mm) in height, shall use the prescriptive bracing method listed below. Cripple walls over 4 feet (1219 mm) in height require analysis by an engineer or architect in accordance with Section A601.3.

A604.4.1.1 Sheathing installation requirements. Wood structural panel sheathing shall not be less than $^{15}/_{32}$-inch (12 mm) thick and installed in accordance with either Figure A-6-5 or A-6-6. All individual pieces of wood structural panels shall be nailed with 8d common nails spaced 4 inches (102 mm) on center at all edges and at 12 inches (305 mm) on center at each intermediate support with not less than two nails for each stud. Nails shall be driven so that their heads on crowns are flush with the surface of the sheathing and shall penetrate the supporting member a minimum of $1^1/_2$ inches (38 mm). When a nail fractures the surface, it shall be left in place and not counted as part of the required nailing. A new 8d nail shall be located within 2 inches (51 mm) of the discounted nail and hand driven flush with the sheathing surface. All horizontal joints must occur over nominal 2-inch-by-4-inch (51 mm by 102 mm) blocking installed with the nominal 4-inch (102 mm) dimension against the face of the plywood.

Vertical joints at adjoining pieces of wood structural panels shall be centered on existing studs such that there is a minimum $^1/_8$ inch (3.2 mm) between the panels and the nails are placed a minimum of $^1/_2$ inch (12.7 mm) from the edges of the existing stud. Where such edge distances cannot be maintained because of the width of the existing stud, a new stud shall be added adjacent to the existing studs and connected in accordance with Figure A-6-7.

A604.4.2 Distribution and amount of bracing. See Table A-6-A and Figure A-6-10 for the distribution and amount of bracing required. Each braced panel must be at least two times the height of the cripple stud wall but not less than 48 inches (1219 mm) in length or width. Where the minimum amount of bracing prescribed in Table A-6-A cannot be installed along any walls, the bracing must be designed in accordance with Section A601.3.

> **EXCEPTION:** Where physical obstructions such as fireplaces, plumbing or heating ducts interfere with the placement of cripple wall bracing, the bracing shall then be placed as close to the obstruction as possible. Total amount of bracing required shall not be reduced because of obstructions.

A604.4.3 Stud space ventilation. When bracing materials are installed on the interior face of studs forming an enclosed space between the new bracing and existing exterior finish, each braced stud space must be ventilated. Adequate ventilation and access for future inspection shall be provided by drilling one 2-inch to 3-inch (51 mm to 76 mm) diameter round hole through the sheathing nearly centered between each stud at the top and bottom of the cripple wall. Such holes should be spaced a minimum of 1-inch (25 mm) clear from the sill or top plates. In stud spaces containing sill bolts, the hole shall be located on the center line of the sill bolt but not closer than 1-inch (25 mm) clear from the nailing edge of the sheathing. When existing blocking occurs within the stud space, additional ventilation holes shall be placed above and below the blocking or the existing block shall be removed and a new nominal 2-inch by 4-inch (51 mm by 102 mm) block installed with the nominal 4-inch (102 mm) dimension against the face of the plywood. For stud heights less than 18 inches (457 mm), only one ventilation hole will be provided.

A604.4.4 Existing underfloor ventilation. Existing underfloor ventilation shall not be reduced without providing equivalent new ventilation as close to the existing as possible. Braced panels may include underfloor ventilation openings when the height of the opening, measured from the top of the foundation wall to the top of the opening, does not exceed 25 percent of the height of the cripple stud wall; however, the length of the panel shall be increased a distance equal to the length of the opening or one stud space minimum. Where an opening exceeds 25 percent of the cripple wall height, braced panels shall not be located where the opening occurs. See Figure A-6-7.

> **EXCEPTION:** For homes with a post and pier foundation system where a new continuous perimeter foundation system is being installed, new ventilation shall be provided in accordance with the Building Code.

A604.5 Quality Control. All work shall be subject to inspection by the building official including, but not limited to:

1. Placement and installation of new chemical anchors or expansion bolts installed in existing foundations. Special inspection is not required for chemical anchors installed in existing foundations regulated by the prescriptive provisions of this chapter.

2. Installation and nailing of new cripple wall bracing.

3. Any work may be subject to special inspection when required by the building official in accordance with the Building Code.

A604.6 Phasing of the Strengthening Work. When approved by the building official, the strengthening work contained in this chapter may be completed in phases. The strengthening work in any phase shall be performed on two parallel sides of the structure at the same time.

TABLE A-6-A—SILL PLATE ANCHORAGE AND CRIPPLE WALL BRACING

NUMBER OF STORIES ABOVE CRIPPLE WALLS	MINIMUM SILL PLATE CONNECTION AND MAXIMUM SPACING[1,2]	AMOUNT OF BRACING[3,4,5]	
		A Combination of Exterior Walls Finished with Portland Cement Plaster and Roofing Using Clay Tile or Concrete Tile Weighing More than 6 psf (287 N/m²)	All Other Conditions
One story	$1/2$-inch (12.7 mm) spaced 6 feet-0 inch (1829 mm) center to center with washer plate	Each end and not less than 50 percent of the wall length	Each end and not less than 40 percent of the wall length
Two stories	$1/2$-inch (12.7 mm) spaced 4 feet-0 inch (1219 mm) center to center with washer plate; or $5/8$-inch (15.9 mm) spaced 6 feet-0 inch (1829 mm) center to center with washer plate	Each end and not less than 70 percent of the wall length	Each end and not less than 50 percent of the wall length
Three stories	$5/8$-inch (15.9 mm) spaced 4 feet-0 inch (1219 mm) center to center with washer plate	100 percent of the wall length[6]	Each end and not less than 80 percent of the wall length[6]

[1]Sill plate anchors shall be chemical anchors or expansion bolts in accordance with Section A604.3.1.
[2]All washer plates shall be 2 inches by 2 inches by $3/16$ inch (51 mm by 51 mm by 4.8 mm) minimum.
[3]See Figure A-6-10 for braced panel layout.
[4]Braced panels at ends of walls shall be located as near the end as possible.
[5]All panels along a wall shall be nearly equal in length and shall be nearly equally spaced along the length of the wall.
[6]The minimum required underfloor ventilation openings are permitted in accordance with Section A604.4.4.

TABLE A-6-B—SILL PLATE ANCHORAGE FOR VARIOUS LENGTHS OF SILL PLATE[1,2]

NUMBER OF STORIES	LENGTHS OF SILL PLATE		
	Less than 12 Feet (3658 mm) to 6 Feet (1829 mm)	Less than 6 Feet (1829 mm) to 30 Inches (762 mm)	Less Than 30 Inches (762 mm)[3]
One story	Three connections	Two connections	One connection
Two stories	Four connections for $1/2$-inch (12.7 mm) anchors or bolts or Three connections for $5/8$-inch (15.9 mm) anchors or bolts	Two connections	One connection
Three stories	Four connections	Two connections	One connection

[1]Connections shall be either chemical anchors or expansion bolts.
[2]See Section A604.3.2 for minimum end distances.
[3]Connection shall be placed as near the center of the length of plate as possible.

TABLE A-6-C—CAPACITIES OF PRESCRIPTIVE BRACING ELEMENTS AND CONNECTIONS FOR COMPARISON WITH ALTERNATIVE MATERIALS OR PRODUCTS

CONNECTION OR ELEMENT	SEISMIC LOAD ADJUSTED SHEAR VALUE
1. For cripple wall bracing 8d common nails 4'-0" (1219 mm) long braced panel	104 pounds (463 N) each nail 1,520 pounds (6761 N) each panel
2. For foundation sill connections $1/2$" (12.7 mm) bolt in 2x (51 mm) sill plate $5/8$" (15.9 mm) bolt in 2x (51 mm) sill plate	840 pounds (3736 N) each bolt 1,260 pounds (5604 N) each bolt
3. For shear transfer between end joist, rim joist, or floor edge block to foundation sill or top plate of cripple wall 8d common toenail	86 pounds (383 N) each nail

MINIMUM FOUNDATION DIMENSIONS						MINIMUM FOUNDATION REINFORCING	
NUMBER OF STORIES	W	F	D[1,2]	T	H	VERTICAL REINFORCING	
						Single pour wall and footing	Footing poured separate from wall
1	12 inches (305 mm)	6 inches (152 mm)	12 inches (305 mm)	6 inches (152 mm)			
2	15 inches (381 mm)	7 inches (178 mm)	18 inches (457 mm)	8 inches (203 mm)	≤ 36 inches (914 mm)	#4 @ 48 inches (1219 mm) on center	#4 @ 32 inches (813 mm) on center
3	18 inches (457 mm)	8 inches (203 mm)	24 inches (610 mm)	10 inches (254 mm)	≥ 36 inches (914 mm)	#4 @ 48 inches (1219 mm) on center	#4 @ 18 inches (457 mm) on center

[1]Where frost conditions occur, the minimum depth shall extend below the frost line.
[2]The ground surface along the interior side of the foundation may be excavated to the elevation of the top of the footing.

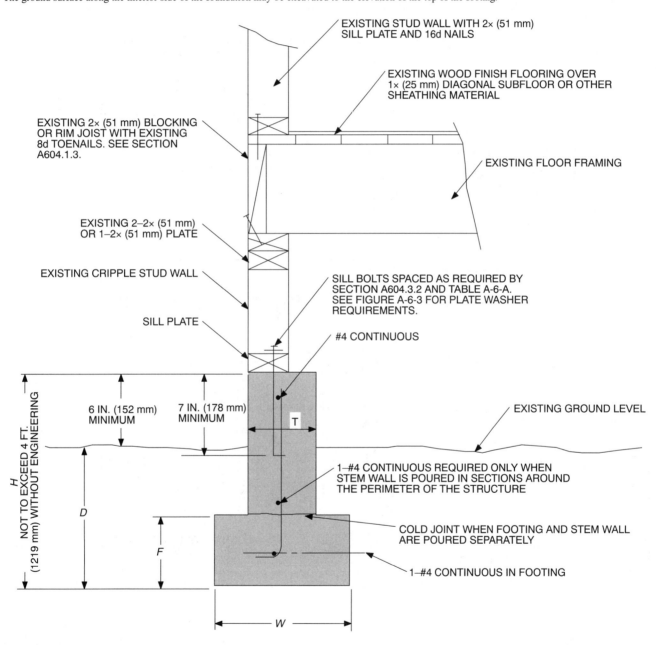

NOTE: See Figure A-6-5 or A-6-6 for cripple wall bracing.

FIGURE A-6-1—NEW REINFORCED CONCRETE FOUNDATION SYSTEM

MINIMUM FOUNDATION DIMENSIONS   MINIMUM FOUNDATION REINFORCING

NO. OF STORIES	W	F	$D^{1,2}$	T	H	VERTICAL REINFORCING	HORIZONTAL REINFORCING
1	12 inches (305 mm)	6 inches (152 mm)	12 inches (305 mm)	6 inches (152 mm)	≤ 24 inches (610 mm)	#4 @ 24 inches (610 mm) on center	#4 continuous at top of stem wall
2	15 inches (381 mm)	7 inches (178 mm)	18 inches (457 mm)	8 inches (203 mm)	≥ 24 inches (610 mm)	#4 @ 24 inches (610 mm) on center	#4 @ 16 inches (406 mm) on center
3	18 inches (457 mm)	8 inches (203 mm)	24 inches (610 mm)	10 inches (254 mm)			

[1]Where frost conditions occur, the minimum depth shall extend below the frost line.
[2]The ground surface along the interior side of the foundation may be excavated to the elevation of the top of the footing.

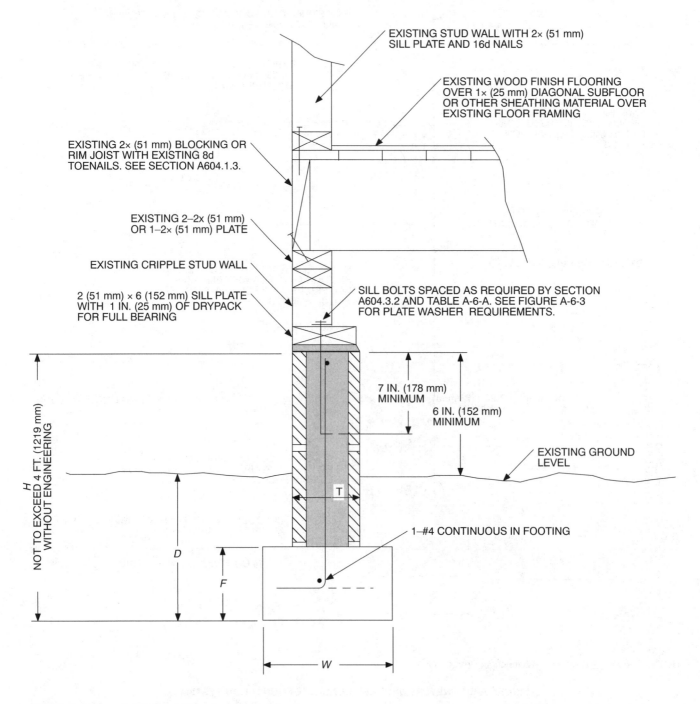

NOTE: See Figure A-6-5 or A-6-6 for cripple wall bracing.

FIGURE A-6-2—NEW HOLLOW-MASONRY UNIT FOUNDATION WALL

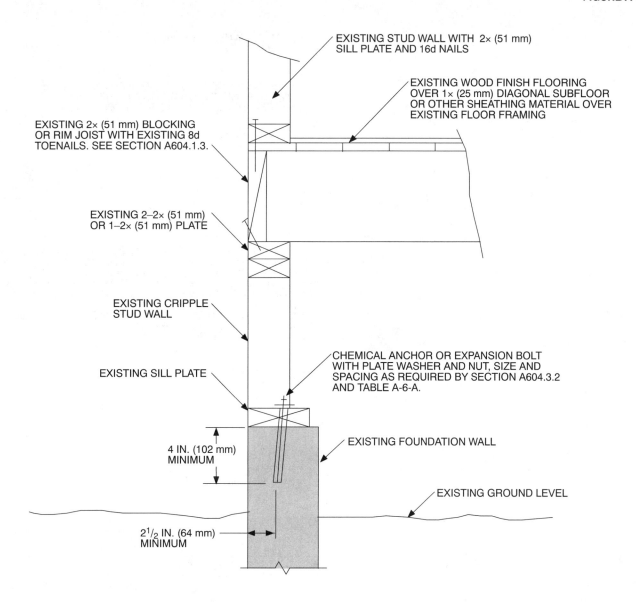

EXISTING STUD WALL WITH 2× (51 mm) SILL PLATE AND 16d NAILS

EXISTING WOOD FINISH FLOORING OVER 1× (25 mm) DIAGONAL SUBFLOOR OR OTHER SHEATHING MATERIAL OVER EXISTING FLOOR FRAMING

EXISTING 2× (51 mm) BLOCKING OR RIM JOIST WITH EXISTING 8d TOENAILS. SEE SECTION A604.1.3.

EXISTING 2–2× (51 mm) OR 1–2× (51 mm) PLATE

EXISTING CRIPPLE STUD WALL

CHEMICAL ANCHOR OR EXPANSION BOLT WITH PLATE WASHER AND NUT, SIZE AND SPACING AS REQUIRED BY SECTION A604.3.2 AND TABLE A-6-A.

EXISTING SILL PLATE

EXISTING FOUNDATION WALL

4 IN. (102 mm) MINIMUM

EXISTING GROUND LEVEL

$2^1/_2$ IN. (64 mm) MINIMUM

NOTES:
1. Plate washers shall comply with the following:
   $^1/_2$ in. (12.7 mm) anchor or bolt – 2 in. (51 mm) × 2 in. (51 mm) × $^3/_{16}$ in. (4.8 mm).
   $^5/_8$ in. (15.9 mm) anchor or bolt – 2 in. (51 mm) × 2 in. (51 mm) × $^3/_{16}$ in. (4.8 mm).
2. See Figure A-6-5 or A-6-6 for cripple wall bracing.

FIGURE A-6-3—SILL PLATE BOLTING TO EXISTING FOUNDATION

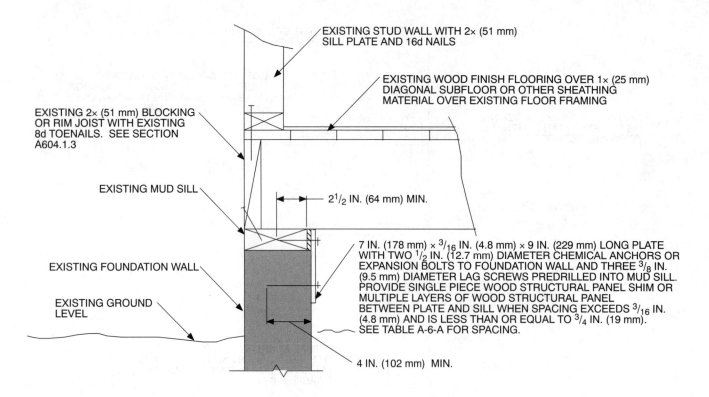

EXISTING STUD WALL WITH 2× (51 mm) SILL PLATE AND 16d NAILS

EXISTING WOOD FINISH FLOORING OVER 1× (25 mm) DIAGONAL SUBFLOOR OR OTHER SHEATHING MATERIAL OVER EXISTING FLOOR FRAMING

EXISTING 2× (51 mm) BLOCKING OR RIM JOIST WITH EXISTING 8d TOENAILS. SEE SECTION A604.1.3

EXISTING MUD SILL

2¹/₂ IN. (64 mm) MIN.

EXISTING FOUNDATION WALL

7 IN. (178 mm) × ³/₁₆ IN. (4.8 mm) × 9 IN. (229 mm) LONG PLATE WITH TWO ¹/₂ IN. (12.7 mm) DIAMETER CHEMICAL ANCHORS OR EXPANSION BOLTS TO FOUNDATION WALL AND THREE ³/₈ IN. (9.5 mm) DIAMETER LAG SCREWS PREDRILLED INTO MUD SILL. PROVIDE SINGLE PIECE WOOD STRUCTURAL PANEL SHIM OR MULTIPLE LAYERS OF WOOD STRUCTURAL PANEL BETWEEN PLATE AND SILL WHEN SPACING EXCEEDS ³/₁₆ IN. (4.8 mm) AND IS LESS THAN OR EQUAL TO ³/₄ IN. (19 mm). SEE TABLE A-6-A FOR SPACING.

EXISTING GROUND LEVEL

4 IN. (102 mm) MIN.

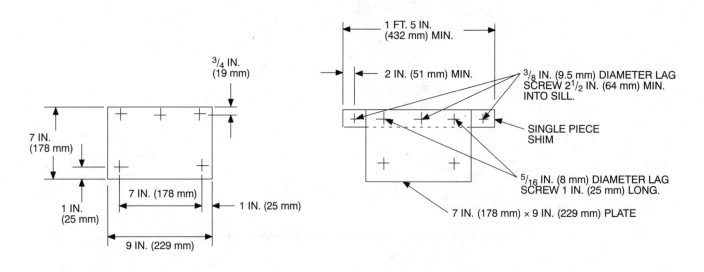

³/₄ IN. (19 mm)

7 IN. (178 mm)

7 IN. (178 mm)

1 IN. (25 mm)

1 IN. (25 mm)

9 IN. (229 mm)

HOLE DIAMETER SHALL NOT EXCEED ¹/₁₆ IN. (1.6 mm) LARGER THAN CONNECTOR DIAMETER

1 FT. 5 IN. (432 mm) MIN.

2 IN. (51 mm) MIN.

³/₈ IN. (9.5 mm) DIAMETER LAG SCREW 2¹/₂ IN. (64 mm) MIN. INTO SILL.

SINGLE PIECE SHIM

⁵/₁₆ IN. (8 mm) DIAMETER LAG SCREW 1 IN. (25 mm) LONG.

7 IN. (178 mm) × 9 IN. (229 mm) PLATE

CONNECTION WHEN SHIM SPACE EXCEEDS ³/₄ IN. (19 mm) IN WIDTH TO 2¹/₂ IN. (64 mm)

NOTE: If shim space exceeds 2¹/₂ in. (64 mm), alternate details will be required.

FIGURE A-6-4A—SILL PLATE BOLTING IN EXISTING FOUNDATION—ALTERNATE

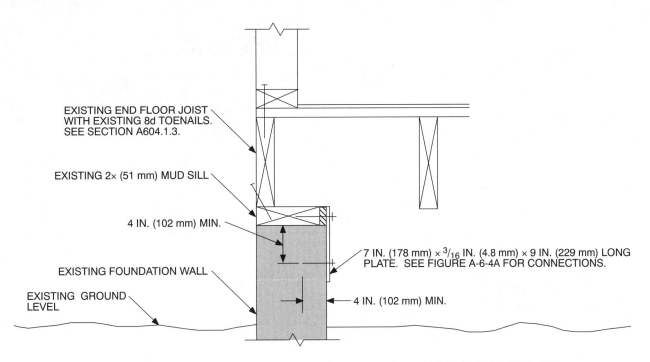

EXISTING END FLOOR JOIST WITH EXISTING 8d TOENAILS. SEE SECTION A604.1.3.

EXISTING 2× (51 mm) MUD SILL

4 IN. (102 mm) MIN.

EXISTING FOUNDATION WALL

EXISTING GROUND LEVEL

7 IN. (178 mm) × $^3/_{16}$ IN. (4.8 mm) × 9 IN. (229 mm) LONG PLATE. SEE FIGURE A-6-4A FOR CONNECTIONS.

4 IN. (102 mm) MIN.

FIGURE A-6-4B—SILL BOLTING EXISTING FOUNDATION WITHOUT CRIPPLE WALL AND FRAMING PARALLEL FOUNDATION WALL

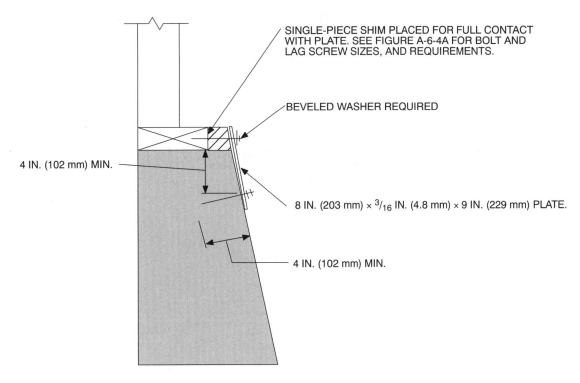

SINGLE-PIECE SHIM PLACED FOR FULL CONTACT WITH PLATE. SEE FIGURE A-6-4A FOR BOLT AND LAG SCREW SIZES, AND REQUIREMENTS.

BEVELED WASHER REQUIRED

4 IN. (102 mm) MIN.

8 IN. (203 mm) × $^3/_{16}$ IN. (4.8 mm) × 9 IN. (229 mm) PLATE.

4 IN. (102 mm) MIN.

ALTERNATE CONNECTION FOR BATTERED FOOTING

FIGURE A-6-4C—SILL PLATE BOLTING IN EXISTING FOUNDATION—ALTERNATE

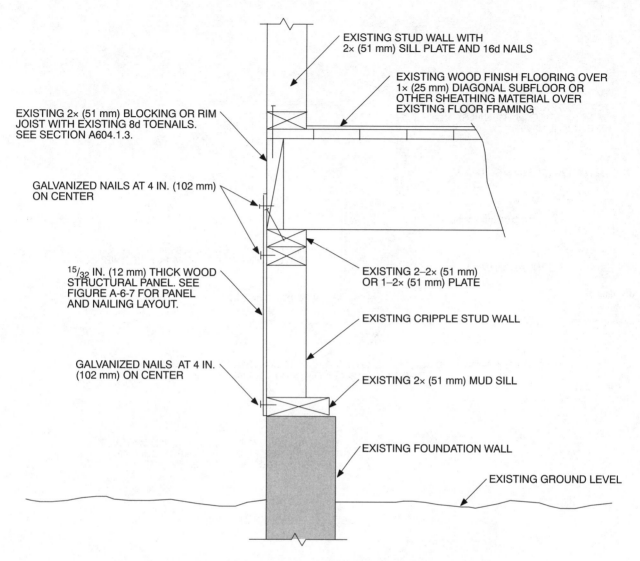

EXISTING STUD WALL WITH
2× (51 mm) SILL PLATE AND 16d NAILS

EXISTING WOOD FINISH FLOORING OVER
1× (25 mm) DIAGONAL SUBFLOOR OR
OTHER SHEATHING MATERIAL OVER
EXISTING FLOOR FRAMING

EXISTING 2× (51 mm) BLOCKING OR RIM
JOIST WITH EXISTING 8d TOENAILS.
SEE SECTION A604.1.3.

GALVANIZED NAILS AT 4 IN. (102 mm)
ON CENTER

$^{15}/_{32}$ IN. (12 mm) THICK WOOD
STRUCTURAL PANEL. SEE
FIGURE A-6-7 FOR PANEL
AND NAILING LAYOUT.

EXISTING 2–2× (51 mm)
OR 1–2× (51 mm) PLATE

EXISTING CRIPPLE STUD WALL

GALVANIZED NAILS AT 4 IN.
(102 mm) ON CENTER

EXISTING 2× (51 mm) MUD SILL

EXISTING FOUNDATION WALL

EXISTING GROUND LEVEL

**FIGURE A-6-5—CRIPPLE WALL BRACING WITH WOOD STRUCTURAL PANEL
ON EXTERIOR FACE OF CRIPPLE STUDS**

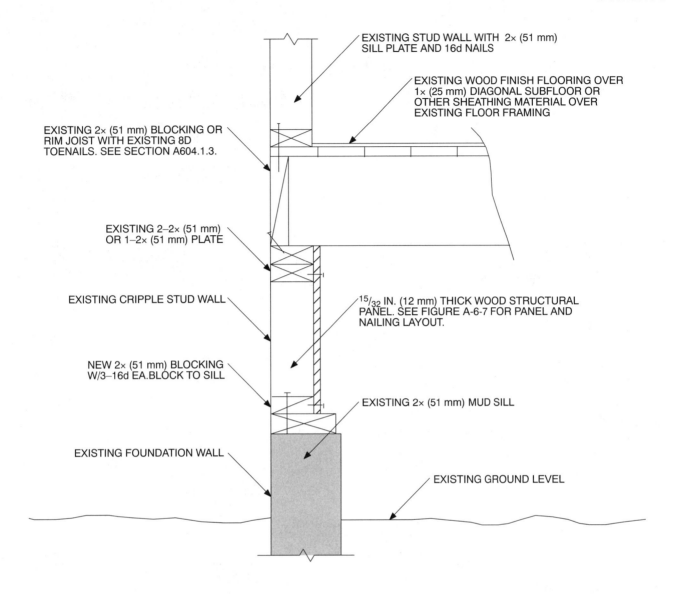

EXISTING STUD WALL WITH 2× (51 mm) SILL PLATE AND 16d NAILS

EXISTING WOOD FINISH FLOORING OVER 1× (25 mm) DIAGONAL SUBFLOOR OR OTHER SHEATHING MATERIAL OVER EXISTING FLOOR FRAMING

EXISTING 2× (51 mm) BLOCKING OR RIM JOIST WITH EXISTING 8D TOENAILS. SEE SECTION A604.1.3.

EXISTING 2–2× (51 mm) OR 1–2× (51 mm) PLATE

EXISTING CRIPPLE STUD WALL

$^{15}/_{32}$ IN. (12 mm) THICK WOOD STRUCTURAL PANEL. SEE FIGURE A-6-7 FOR PANEL AND NAILING LAYOUT.

NEW 2× (51 mm) BLOCKING W/3–16d EA.BLOCK TO SILL

EXISTING 2× (51 mm) MUD SILL

EXISTING FOUNDATION WALL

EXISTING GROUND LEVEL

NOTE: See Figure A-6-3 or A-6-4A for sill plate bolting.

FIGURE A-6-6—CRIPPLE WALL BRACING WITH WOOD STRUCTURAL PANEL ON INTERIOR FACE OF CRIPPLE STUDS

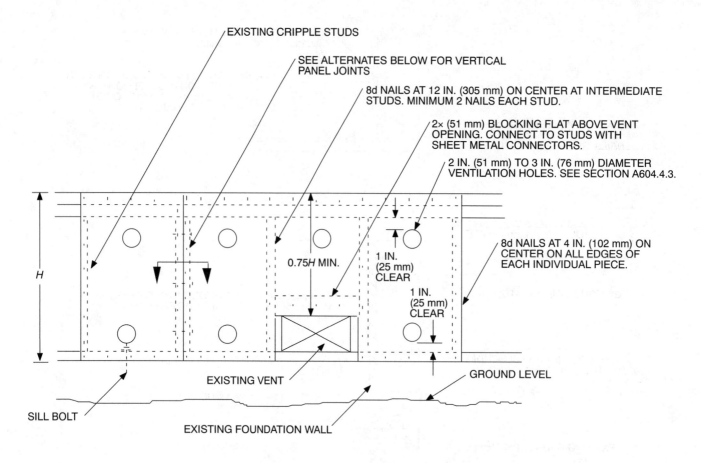

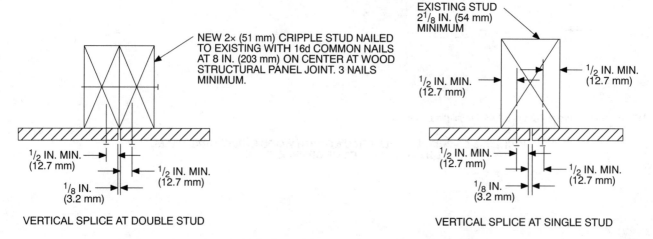

VERTICAL SPLICE AT DOUBLE STUD   VERTICAL SPLICE AT SINGLE STUD

FIGURE A-6-7—PARTIAL CRIPPLE STUD WALL ELEVATION

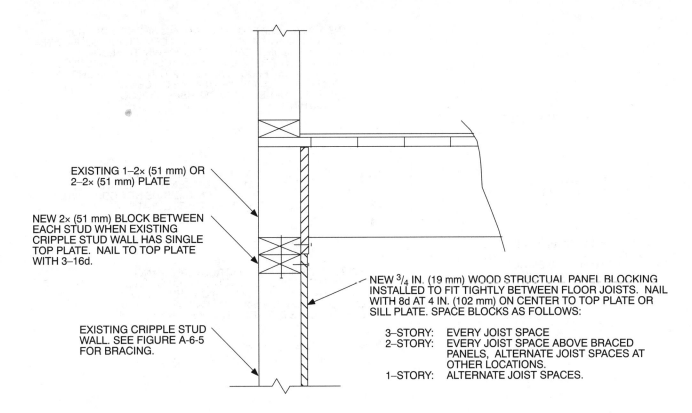

EXISTING 1–2× (51 mm) OR 2–2× (51 mm) PLATE

NEW 2× (51 mm) BLOCK BETWEEN EACH STUD WHEN EXISTING CRIPPLE STUD WALL HAS SINGLE TOP PLATE. NAIL TO TOP PLATE WITH 3–16d.

EXISTING CRIPPLE STUD WALL. SEE FIGURE A-6-5 FOR BRACING.

NEW 3/4 IN. (19 mm) WOOD STRUCTURAL PANEL BLOCKING INSTALLED TO FIT TIGHTLY BETWEEN FLOOR JOISTS. NAIL WITH 8d AT 4 IN. (102 mm) ON CENTER TO TOP PLATE OR SILL PLATE. SPACE BLOCKS AS FOLLOWS:

3–STORY: EVERY JOIST SPACE
2–STORY: EVERY JOIST SPACE ABOVE BRACED PANELS, ALTERNATE JOIST SPACES AT OTHER LOCATIONS.
1–STORY: ALTERNATE JOIST SPACES.

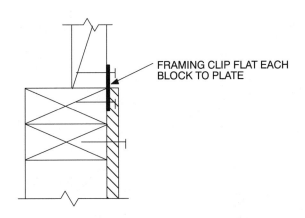

FRAMING CLIP FLAT EACH BLOCK TO PLATE

FIGURE A-6-8—ALTERNATE BLOCKING WHERE RIM JOIST OR BLOCKING HAS BEEN OMITTED

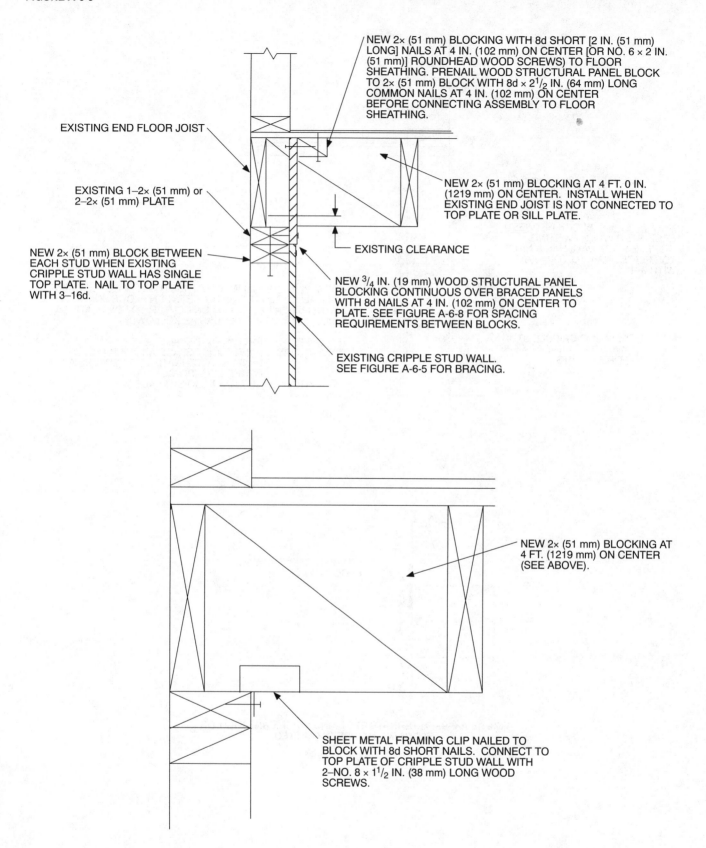

NEW 2× (51 mm) BLOCKING WITH 8d SHORT [2 IN. (51 mm) LONG] NAILS AT 4 IN. (102 mm) ON CENTER [OR NO. 6 × 2 IN. (51 mm)] ROUNDHEAD WOOD SCREWS) TO FLOOR SHEATHING. PRENAIL WOOD STRUCTURAL PANEL BLOCK TO 2× (51 mm) BLOCK WITH 8d × 2^1/$_2$ IN. (64 mm) LONG COMMON NAILS AT 4 IN. (102 mm) ON CENTER BEFORE CONNECTING ASSEMBLY TO FLOOR SHEATHING.

EXISTING END FLOOR JOIST

EXISTING 1–2× (51 mm) OR 2–2× (51 mm) PLATE

NEW 2× (51 mm) BLOCK BETWEEN EACH STUD WHEN EXISTING CRIPPLE STUD WALL HAS SINGLE TOP PLATE. NAIL TO TOP PLATE WITH 3–16d.

NEW 2× (51 mm) BLOCKING AT 4 FT. 0 IN. (1219 mm) ON CENTER. INSTALL WHEN EXISTING END JOIST IS NOT CONNECTED TO TOP PLATE OR SILL PLATE.

EXISTING CLEARANCE

NEW ^{3}/$_4$ IN. (19 mm) WOOD STRUCTURAL PANEL BLOCKING CONTINUOUS OVER BRACED PANELS WITH 8d NAILS AT 4 IN. (102 mm) ON CENTER TO PLATE. SEE FIGURE A-6-8 FOR SPACING REQUIREMENTS BETWEEN BLOCKS.

EXISTING CRIPPLE STUD WALL. SEE FIGURE A-6-5 FOR BRACING.

NEW 2× (51 mm) BLOCKING AT 4 FT. (1219 mm) ON CENTER (SEE ABOVE).

SHEET METAL FRAMING CLIP NAILED TO BLOCK WITH 8d SHORT NAILS. CONNECT TO TOP PLATE OF CRIPPLE STUD WALL WITH 2–NO. 8 × 1^1/$_2$ IN. (38 mm) LONG WOOD SCREWS.

FIGURE A-6-9—CONNECTION CRIPPLE WALL TO FLOOR SHEATHING WHEN FLOOR FRAMING IS PARALLEL TO WALL

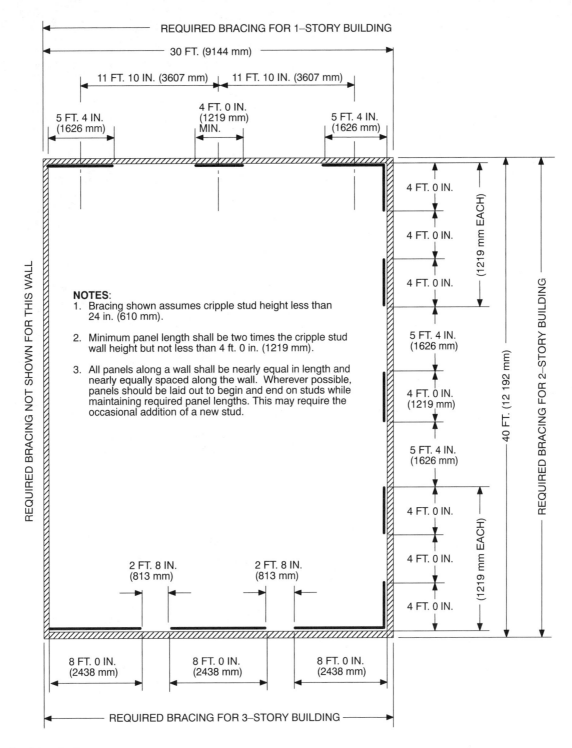

NOTES:
1. Bracing shown assumes cripple stud height less than 24 in. (610 mm).

2. Minimum panel length shall be two times the cripple stud wall height but not less than 4 ft. 0 in. (1219 mm).

3. All panels along a wall shall be nearly equal in length and nearly equally spaced along the wall. Wherever possible, panels should be laid out to begin and end on studs while maintaining required panel lengths. This may require the occasional addition of a new stud.

Bracing determination:

1–story building – each end and not less than 40% of wall length.[1]
Transverse wall – 30 ft. (9144 mm) × 0.40 = 12 ft. (3658 mm) minimum panel length = 4 ft. 0 in. (1219 mm)

2–story building – each end and not less than 50% of wall length.[1]
Longitudinal wall – 40 ft. (12 192 mm) × 0.50 = 20 ft. 0 in. (6096 mm) min. of bracing.

3–story building – each end and not less than 80% of wall length.[1]
Transverse wall – 30 ft. (9144 mm) × 0.80 = 24 ft. 0 in. (7315 mm) min. of bracing.

[1]See Table A-6-A for buildings with both plaster walls and roofing exceeding 6 psf (287 N/m²).

FIGURE A-6-10—FLOOR PLAN—CRIPPLE WALL BRACING LAYOUT

GUIDELINES

Preface

The following guidelines are intended to provide additional technical information to the building official in evaluating compliance alternatives. They provide examples of alternate solutions to some common conditions in rehabilitating and regulating older buildings. Although the guidelines were initially intended for use with residential occupancies, the material portions can also be effectively used with other occupancy groups.

The guidelines were developed in 1979 and reflect the codes as published at that time. In using the guidelines, one must double-check to ensure that the most current information from current editions is used. Definitions may differ between the model codes. Before using the information from another code, the definitions must be checked.

The guidelines were developed for the United States Department of Housing and Urban Development (HUD). The National Institute of Building Sciences (NIBS) was project director. Subcontractors included the Council of American Building Officials and the model code groups, technical institutions, professional associations and practicing architects and engineers.

The International Conference of Building Officials has not verified the information contained in the guidelines and assumes no responsibility for its application and interpretation.

Acknowledgments

The material herein was prepared by the National Institute of Building Sciences on the basis of research performed by Building Technology, Inc. Technical reviewers for the Institute included John Behrens, John Degenkolb, Harold Cutler, Alfred Goldberg, Harold Nelson, Richard Bletzacker and Paul Heilstedt. The guideline was written and arranged by Howard Markman.

Overall management and production of the *Rehabilitation Guidelines* was directed by William Brenner of the Institute, with David Hattis of Building Technology, Inc. the principal technical consultant. Guideline cover graphics and layouts were designed by the Design Communication Collaborative.

INTRODUCTION

Code requirements for egress can create a great number of technical problems and constraints during building rehabilitation. Existing exits which appear to be adequate will often not comply with the highly specific requirements for new building construction. Adding new exits or upgrading existing ones to meet new construction standards can require the removal or alteration of otherwise sound structural elements such as walls, floors, hallway partitions, and doors.

This guideline applies to one- and two-family dwellings and apartment houses less than 75 feet in height. Dormitories, lodging or boarding houses, and residential hotels meeting the general assumptions noted below could also be within the scope of this guideline. The guideline is not a code, but like a building or fire prevention code, it is intended for use by persons knowledgeable about fire prevention and building construction. Its use should facilitate the maximal re-use of existing egress elements in circumstances where, for some reason, building code requirements for new construction are being applied. In general, there are two such circumstances:

* Repair and improvement of existing residential buildings, when compliance with the code requirements for new construction is triggered by a 25-50% Rule or similar rule which is in effect in the jurisdiction.

* Change of use or occupancy into a residential occupancy (e.g., from one- and two-family dwelling to apartment house, from office building to apartment house), when compliance with the code requirements for new construction is triggered by the provisions of the building code in effect or some other provision.

For rehabilitation involving a change of use or occupancy, this guideline applies when egress elements are already in place or where other building elements (structural or non-structural) make literal code compliance impractical. By contrast, for example, this guideline does not apply to a warehouse that will be completely gutted during conversion to an apartment house. Such a conversion can, in most instances, be designed to meet new code requirements for egress without hardship.

This guideline is an endeavor to suggest solutions which will establish an approximately equivalent overall level of fire safety without attempting to obtain literal code compliance. It is not a criticism of new construction requirements and does not imply that the suggested solutions are equivalent. Where compliance with new construction requirements does not present serious difficulty and is otherwise feasible, this guideline should not be the sole justification for noncompliance.

In communities where new construction requirements would not normally be applied to a rehabilitation project (e.g., the community has enacted its own building rehabilitation code), there may still be use for selected portions of this guideline. There may be other instances, though, where the solutions suggested below are more stringent or restrictive than those already permitted or intended by the community. In such cases, the community must accept the responsibility to devise solutions that respond to unique local needs. The *Guideline for Setting and Adopting Standards for Building Rehabilitation* outlines a procedure to meet this task. Each community must assess its resources and its needs, and then define and set forth the codes, standards, or regulations necessary to meet the common good.

BASIC FIRE PROTECTION AND EGRESS PRINCIPLES

A safe means of escape from fire is fundamental to fire protection. But total evacuation of a building is not the only way to provide life safety from fire, and it is not always the most efficient: fire officials would need hours to totally evacuate a very tall building. Different building types will often pose different egress problems. Code requirements for egress must be responsive to the qualities and needs of the people to be protected and the hazards that they face.

The differing requirements of the three model building codes (Basic, Standard, Uniform) and the *Life Safety Code* illustrate that there is no single correct solution. The codes reflect the differences in opinion and philosophy that exist whenever professional judgment must be exercised. The issue is not which approach is most correct, but which is most appropriate once the character of the building and the occupants are known.

Given that a fire ignition has occurred, there are two basic approaches to solving the life safety problem: protect the people or control the fire. The people could either be evacuated from the building or protected in place until the fire is extinguished and the danger passes. The fire could be controlled by suppression (e.g., automatic sprinklers) and/or compartmentation (e.g., fire resistive construction, protection of horizontal/vertical openings).

Smoke control systems attempt to prevent smoke and other fire gases from spreading throughout a burning building. Exits free of smoke can be used more safely and efficiently; the protection of occupants becomes more feasible because life-threatening combustion products are removed from the building. No specific recommendations have been included in this guideline concerning the use of smoke control systems, but the potential of this rapidly improving technology must be recognized.

In low and mid-rise residential buildings, the simplest and most direct solution is to evacuate the occupants. This may avoid the need to upgrade the fire resistance of major structural elements such as walls, floor/ceiling assemblies, and doors. Such major renovation is counter to the goal of decreasing the cost and complexity of building rehabilitation, particularly when alternatives are usually available.

A building's evacuation system consists of three interrelated component parts:

* Fire detection and alarm;

* A path of escape or means of egress; and

* A safe destination.

For a one- and two-family dwelling "fire detection and alarm" is a smoke detector; the "means of egress" is the front door or escape window; the "safe destination" is the outside. This concept is equally applicable to apartment houses, though the problems and requirements become more complex. Fire detection and alarm is more difficult because a single station smoke detector will only warn the occupants of that apartment unit, not the entire building. Two or more exits, instead of a single exit, are generally required. The door from an apartment unit normally opens onto a corridor, rather than directly to the outside.

The approach taken by the guideline is quite basic: identify what is required under the code, isolate the deficiencies, and then devise solutions to correct or compensate for each problem area. To correct a deficiency is to comply with the code; to compensate for a deficiency is to meet the spirit and general intent of the code. Note again the stated goal of this guideline: "an approximately equivalent overall level of fire safety."

There exists no exact method for determining whether one set of corrective measures exactly equals another. But it is possible, with reason and professional judgment, to articulate the intent and purpose of code requirements, and then to select among the available fire protection techniques, systems, and materials to devise a solution which is responsive to the code. The benefit of this approach is that it provides needed flexibility by taking advantage of the different approaches and interrelationships noted above: fire control vs. evacuation, improved detection and alarm vs. upgrading of the escape path, etc.

The task is also made easier because some fire protection measures have more than one impact. For example, a suppression system can potentially control the fire, provide an emergency alarm to building occupants, summon the fire department, and increase the time for safe escape by confining the fire to its compartment of origin and protecting the egress path. Smoke detectors allow more time for escape while the fire is still in its incipient, least threatening stage and may permit early extinguishment.

The problems discussed and solutions presented should by no means be considered exhaustive. There is no intent to limit the types of solutions that may be developed or considered effective. The guideline recognizes this, for the problems and solutions which have been included are headed "Selected Problems and Representative Solutions." Each building will present specific problems that will require specific treatment. Once the intent of the code requirement and the impact of the deficiency are understood, it may be possible to fashion an alternative solution. But the most important consideration will always be the character and status of the occupants and the use and arrangement of the building.

GENERAL ASSUMPTIONS

The following assumptions have been made in developing this guideline, and may impact upon its applicability.

The rehabilitated structure must be intended for general residential use and the resident population representative of the population at large, which may include elderly and handicapped persons. However, housing that is *primarily* directed towards elderly or handicapped persons is not within the scope of this guideline. The inability or increased difficulty of these persons to react quickly and properly, without assistance, to an alarm of danger requires an analysis and degree of safety that is beyond the generalized scope of this guideline.

It has been assumed that the occupants are familiar with their surroundings, particularly the location of exits. This assumption makes the guideline inapplicable to hotels/motels or other occupancies with a transient resident population.

The population density has been assumed to be small enough such that there would be no problem of queuing at the exits. That is, all residents should be able to move continuously towards the exits without having to wait in line. Queuing can be a problem in dormitories, boarding houses, and group residences. Therefore, the number and capacity of exits in these residential buildings must be given special attention.

Building codes contain a number of highly specific provisions controlling the quality of exits such as exit signage, illumination, emergency lighting, handrails, etc. It is assumed that both existing exits and any new exits that may be called for under this guideline will comply fully with these requirements.

It is assumed that the building is not deficient in too many areas. The concept of compensating for one deficiency by relying upon or providing other positive features becomes either too difficult or too tenuous if there are too many problems. For just as a single fire protection feature can provide several positive benefits, a single deficiency can have several negative impacts, and multiple deficiencies simply compound the problem further.

As used in this guideline, "means of egress" includes those elements of an egress system which are permitted under building codes for new construction (e.g., enclosed interior stairs, smokeproof towers, horizontal exits). "Means of escape" includes all "means of egress" as well as any other elements of an egress system not normally permitted for new construction or considered as a primary egress path (e.g., fire escapes, escape windows, escape ladders).

ARRANGEMENT OF THE GUIDELINE

The various sections of the guideline have been placed in a sequence that parallels the review procedure normally followed by local enforcing officials. They have been arranged as follows:

The occupant load (see discussion below), the physical characteristics of the building (e.g., height, area), and the use (e.g., apartment) determine the *minimum* number of exits that are required. Section 1: NUMBER OF EXITS addresses this area.

Once the required minimum number of exits is known, the number of available exits is counted. The concern is that the exits be of the proper type and that minimum fire resistive enclosure requirements, if any, are met. For example, some codes place limits on the use or number of horizontal exits. Generally, codes require stairs to be enclosed by fire resistive construction. Guidelines have not been developed for every acceptable exit element, but Sections 2-5: HORIZONTAL EXITS; INTERIOR STAIRS/ ENCLOSURES; EXTERIOR EXIT STAIRS; and FIRE ESCAPE STAIRS apply here.

The location and layout of the qualifying exits is then examined. See Section 6: ARRANGEMENT OF EXITS. Improper arrangement may require that additional exits be provided.

Access to these exits must also be evaluated and corrective measures taken as needed. Section 7: TRAVEL DISTANCE; Section 8: DEAD-END TRAVEL; and Section 9: CORRIDORS AND EXTERIOR EXIT BALCONIES should be applied at this time. As above, additional exits may be required if conditions are too severe.

Once the number of required exits has been provided and their arrangement and access is satisfactory, the capacity of the exits and minimum width dimensions must be considered. Section 10: EXIT CAPACITY/WIDTHS applies here.

Finally, the specific construction details of the egress elements must be evaluated. See Section 11: CONSTRUCTION DETAILS AND SPECIFICATIONS.

Each of the eleven sections is separated into three major parts. First, there is a summary of the code requirements and their intent, including a discussion of the respective requirements of the *Basic Building Code*, published by the Building Officials and Code Administrators International; the *Standard Building Code*, published by the Southern Building Code Congress International; and the *Uniform Building Code*, published by the International Conference of Building Officials. The *Life Safety Code*, published by the National Fire Protection Association, is not a building code, but it has been included because it deals at length with egress and has been used in a regulatory context.* Second, there is a discussion of how to identify conditions in a building to determine whether a problem exists. Third, there is a discussion of selected problems, some representative solutions, and a general narrative relating the two.

References to the applicable sections of the model codes have been included throughout the guideline. The codes have been abbreviated as follows:

BOCA   *Basic Building Code* (1978 Edition)
NFPA   *NFPA Life Safety Code* (1976 Edition)
SBCC   *Standard Building Code* (1979 Edition)
UBC   *Uniform Building Code* (1979 Edition)

GENERAL REQUIREMENTS

SMOKE DETECTORS

Smoke detectors cannot control the growth or spread of a fire. But early detection and alarm allows more time for safe escape and possibly control or extinguishment at a time when the fire is still developing. This is particularly important in residential occupancies when all the occupants are asleep. Of course, all detectors must be properly installed, located, and maintained.

Therefore, the installation of a single station smoke detector for each sleeping area of every dwelling unit is hereby required before allowing any significant deviation from the requirements for new construction.

The model codes referenced in the guideline already require the installation of smoke detectors in every dwelling unit.** However, not all local communities have adopted one of the model codes, an earlier edition of a code without the smoke detector requirement may still be in effect, or a community may have deleted the smoke detector requirement.

The net effect of some of the solutions discussed below is to meet the requirements for new construction. In such cases, the requirement for smoke detectors does not apply because there is no significant deviation from the code. Smoke detectors must still be installed if otherwise required under a local code. But when a community has chosen not to adopt such a general provision, this guideline has no basis for imposing a requirement for smoke detectors once a particular deficiency has been corrected to comply

with the code. The affected sections of the guideline are noted accordingly.

HEIGHT AND AREA LIMITATIONS

Building codes usually limit the allowable height and area of a building as a function of its occupancy and type of construction. For rehabilitation involving a change of occupancy into a residential occupancy, compliance with the new construction height and area limitations of the code is hereby required before the solutions recommended in this guideline may be applied. Any allowances for increased height and/or area permitted by the code may still be applied.

OCCUPANT LOAD

The occupant load is the number of people that can be expected to be present in a building. The occupant load is used to calculate the number of exits and the capacity or width of these exits.

For the purpose of specifying the number and capacity of exits, the occupant load may not be reduced below a minimum specified in the code, regardless of the number of people actually expected. However, the actual occupant loading is used whenever it exceeds the minimum specified in the code.

Though each code specifies how the occupant load is to be calculated, the general method is to divide the total gross floor area by a minimum design density of 200 sq. ft. per person. The only exception is 300 sq. ft. per person in one- and two-family dwellings and 50 sq. ft. per person in dormitories under the *Uniform Building Code*. The occupant load for each floor must also be computed though the method may vary somewhat. (BOCA: 606.0; UBC: 3301(d), Table 33-A; SBCC: 1105.1; NFPA: 5-3.1, 11-1.5).

Given the low population density of most residential use buildings, occupant loading will rarely present a problem. More often, it is the minimum dimension requirement for an exit element, rather than the number of persons who must rely upon that exit element, that is the source of difficulty. In residential rehabilitation, it is usually the size and configuration of the building and the arrangement and quality of the existing exits, not the number of building occupants, that will control the number of exits that must be provided.

---

* There are literally thousands of different building codes being enforced throughout the United States. The model building codes were selected because they are nationally known and have been adopted, either in whole or in part, by many communities.

** The *Life Safety Code* does not require smoke detectors in dormitories and only "on each floor level" of lodging houses. (11-5.3.2.1)

1
NUMBER OF EXITS

SUMMARY OF CODE REQUIREMENTS AND INTENT

The codes specify the minimum number of exits that must be provided. The exits must be adequate for each floor as well as for the building as a whole. Other considerations such as travel distance, remoteness, or capacity of existing exits may require additional exits to be provided. These issues are discussed separately and, therefore, are not considered here.

Code Intent

Requirements for a minimum number of exits are established to increase the reliability of the means of egress system. The intent is that for any single fire ignition that prohibits travel to one exit, there will be an alternate exit that can be used. This does not address multiple fire ignitions, as may be likely with fires that are incendiary (intentionally set).

Having a minimum of two means of egress is one of the most fundamental principles of life safety from fire. The codes do allow certain residential configurations to have only a single exit, but every one of these special cases must also comply with the separate, general requirement for operable windows of specified minimum dimensions. These windows allow for escape, provide a source of fresh air if it is necessary to await rescue, and allow for rescue of building occupants by fire service personnel. Therefore, even these buildings could be considered to have two means of escape. All rehabilitated buildings should have escape windows whenever feasible.

Code Analysis

Basic Building Code - 1978

Not less than two exitways serving every story, except in one- and two-family dwellings, with the following exceptions where one exitway is accepted (609.2, 609.3):

- On the first story of buildings 2000 sq. ft. or less with an occupancy load less than 50 on the first story;
- Residential multi-family buildings, two stories or less, with four or less dwelling units per floor, maximum exitway access travel of 50 ft., minimum 1 hour fire resistance rating of exitway enclosure, and minimum 1 hour opening protection.

The 1980 Supplement added to Section 609.2 the requirement that a minimum of three exits are needed if the occupant load is between 501 and 1000 persons, and a minimum of four exits must be provided for occupant loads in excess of 1000.

Uniform Building Code - 1979

Every building or usable portion thereof must have at least one exit, except if there are over 10 occupants, there must be two exits. Floors above the first story having an occupant load of more than 10 shall have not less than two exits, subject to the following two exceptions:

- Unless the number of occupants exceeds 10, only one exit shall be required from a second floor area within an individual dwelling unit;
- Two or more dwelling units on the second floor may have access to only one common exit when the total occupant load does not exceed 10.

The requirement for two exits is applied to individual dwelling units as well: a single apartment unit larger than 2000 sq. ft. (10 occupants × 200 sq. ft. per occupant) would require two exits from the private unit onto the public exitway; a similar requirement applies to an individual unit of a one- and two-family dwelling larger than 3000 sq. ft. (10 occupants × 300 sq. ft per occupant), even if it were a one story building.

Regardless of the occupant loading, floors above the second story and basements require not less than two exits, except when such floors or basements are used exclusively for the service of the building; only one exit is required from a basement within an individual dwelling unit. As noted above, individual units and basements with an occupant load greater than 10 must have two exits as well. Every story or portion thereof having an occupant load of 501 to 1000 must have not less than three exits; four exits are required when the occupant load exceeds 1000. (3302(a), Table 33-A, A-1215(b,d)).

Standard Building Code - 1979

Not less than two independent exits except for one- and two-family dwellings and other exceptions noted below.

MINIMUM NUMBER OF EXITS	OCCUPANT LOAD
2	50-500
3	501-1000
4	more than 1000

Residential occupancies having not more than four dwelling units per floor, less than 3500 sq. ft. per floor, and less than three stories in height may be served by one common exit. The travel distance from the entrance door of any living unit to the single exit cannot exceed 30 ft. (1103.2).

NFPA Life Safety Code - 1976

Two separate exits are required with the following exceptions:

- One- and two-family dwellings;
- A unit with direct exit to the street at ground level, by an outside stairway, or by a 1 hour rated enclosed stair serving only that apartment;
- Any height building with four or less units per floor with direct access to a smokeproof tower or outside stair (20 ft. maximum travel distance);
- A building three stories or less with 1 hour exit and protected openings, corridors with 1 hour fire resistance rating, 20 ft. maximum travel distance (11-3.2.4).

Summary

A minimum of two exits is generally required, although some residential occupancies need have only one if certain requirements are met. The codes are not consistent as to when only one exit will be allowed.

IDENTIFYING EXISTING CONDITIONS

Determine the required number of exits by considering (depending on the particular code in force):

- Occupancy (one- and two-family vs. apartment house);
- Area (for computation of occupant load);
- Number of dwelling units;
- Number of stories;
- Arrangement of spaces (service rooms, two story dwelling units, etc).

Determine the number of apparent exits for each floor in the proposed building by counting the number of separate paths that discharge to a public way or protected area of refuge. The exits, or exit elements, either alone or in combination, are:

- Interior stairway;
- Exterior stairway;
- Horizontal exit;
- Smokeproof tower;
- Fire escape;
- Ramp;
- Exit passageway;
- Lobby or vestibule;
- Exterior exit door.

The number of exits is "apparent" because an exit or exit element may be found to violate some other code provisions addressed later in the guideline.

Particularly in larger buildings, several required stairways and passageways often combine at a later point and discharge through a single exit passageway, lobby, or vestibule. The codes impose limits upon exits that may combine at a later point and care must be taken that this limit is not violated.

SELECTED PROBLEMS AND REPRESENTATIVE SOLUTIONS

1.1

Problem: Less exits are available than required.

Solution: Consider the use of means of escape, such as fire escapes (see Section 5 below), ladders, fire balconies, etc., which are not normally accepted by codes as exit elements for new construction, in order to provide the required number of exits. At least one exit should be a means of egress in substantial compliance with code requirements (i.e., two means of escape should not be accepted). This exit should preferably follow the path normally used by the building occupants. In an emergency situation, it is common for people to exit from a building the same way they entered and to travel the path most familiar.*

Discussion: In accepting this solution, an analysis should be made which takes into account the public acceptability (e.g., would tenants share a common balcony or accept unlocked doors to create an area of refuge), the climate (e.g., accumulations of snow or ice), the ability of fire service personnel to effect rescue or gain access to the building to fight the fire, and the degree of mobility or agility necessary for safe escape.

1.2

Problem: One exit available in a building with three occupiable floors when two exits are required.

Solution: A single exit could be accepted if each floor arrangement meets the special conditions for a single exit for two story buildings (e.g., number of occupants or dwelling units, limitations on exitway access travel), the stairway is well designed (dimensions as required by code, handrails, illumination, etc.), and the requirement for operable windows is met. The exitway must either be enclosed with construction having a minimum 1 hour fire resistance or the apartments must be separated from the exit with construction having a similar rating. Existing wood lath and

plaster in good condition may remain. Doors to the exit enclosure or apartment doors opening directly onto stairs must have a minimum 1 hour fire resistance. Existing doors, if substantial (e.g., minimum 1³/₄ inch bonded solid core door), may remain if equipped with self-closing devices. Lesser doors must be protected on both sides by automatic sprinkler protection. These sprinklers may be connected to the domestic water supply and need not be equipped to sound a building alarm. The following figure illustrates the conditions for allowing a single exit.

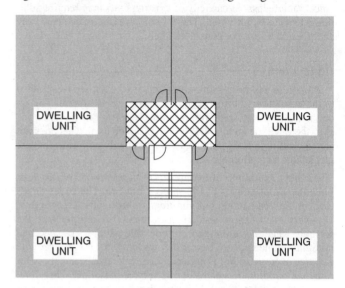

NOTES:
- Not more than 4 units, maximum floor area, or 10 occupants, as per code.
- Also, travel distance limitations per code.

Discussion: A single exit is allowed by the codes for the specified arrangements up to two stories because the building is low, an escape window is required, the exit access travel distance is limited, compartmentation or an exit enclosure is required, and the number of occupants is small. The requirement for smoke detectors and a high quality exit, coupled with escape windows, the limited number of occupants, and compartmentation, is the basis for extending the exception for a single exit to include buildings with three occupiable floors.

1.3

Problem: One exit available in a building over three stories.

Solution: A code complying smokeproof tower or exterior stair could be accepted as the single exit. The building must comply with the height and area requirements for new construction. The arrangement of each floor must meet the special conditions for a single exit for two story buildings and the stairway must be well designed and protected against the elements. Access to the exterior stair or smokeproof tower must either be open to the outside or by a protected corridor. Doors opening onto an enclosed corridor must be substantial (e.g., minimum 1³/₄ inch bonded solid core door) and equipped with self-closing devices. Lesser doors must be protected on both sides by automatic sprinkler protection. These sprinklers may be connected to the domestic water supply and need not be equipped to sound a building alarm. Doors to a smokeproof tower must comply with the code.

---

* This does not mean that elevators should be accepted as a means of escape. In such a case, it is the exit that most closely follows the normal path of entrance.

Discussion: The *Life Safety Code* accepts a smokeproof tower or exterior stair as the sole exit for any height building with four or less units per floor with direct access to the exit (20 ft. maximum travel distance). It is also the traditional design method in Europe and much of the world. The added requirement for smoke detectors, compliance with height and area requirements, and an open air exit access or protected corridor increases the reliability of the single exit. The ability of the fire service to effect rescue or gain access to the building to fight the fire must also be considered.

2
HORIZONTAL EXITS

SUMMARY OF CODE REQUIREMENTS AND INTENT

Code Intent

The code intent is to create an area of refuge within a building by providing a continuous barrier that will resist the passage of heat, smoke, and other fire gases. A horizontal exit is a passage from one building area to another. The areas must be separated by fire resistant construction with the appropriate opening protection (self-closing or automatic closing fire doors). A horizontal exit does not have to be limited to one building, and can be a bridge or protected passageway from one building to another.

Code Analysis and Summary

A horizontal exit is a way of passage from a building to a protected area of refuge, on approximately the same level, within the same or another building. The area of refuge must afford safety from fire and smoke.

Walls or partitions forming the separation through which the horizontal exits provide passage must provide 2 hours fire resistance. Opening protection (e.g., fire doors, fire dampers) must have $1^1/_2$ hours fire resistance. Fire doors in horizontal exits must be either self-closing or automatically close upon activation of an associated smoke detector, except that only automatic doors are allowed under the Uniform Code.* Doors must swing in the direction of exit travel, except that the occupant load must be 50 or more under the Uniform and Standard Codes before this requirement is imposed.

The Standard and Life Safety Codes provide that horizontal exits cannot comprise more than $1/_2$ the required number of exits. The Uniform, Standard, and Life Safety Codes require that the area of refuge into which the horizontal exit leads have an enclosed stair, door, or other "standard" exit that leads directly to the exterior. The Basic Code requires one interior stairway or smokeproof enclosure on each side of the horizontal exit in multi-story buildings.

The area of refuge must be of sufficient area to be occupied by the total occupant load of the connected areas based upon 3 sq. ft. per person (net). The codes contain various other prescriptive requirements relating to dimensions, materials, and hardware. (BOCA: 614.0 and reported code amendment; UBC: 3307, 3303(b); SBCC: 1119; NFPA: 5-2.4)

IDENTIFYING EXISTING CONDITIONS

Determine the fire resistance of the wall or partition assembly and protection of openings by reference to the code in effect, current or past listings, labels, or the *Guideline on Fire Ratings of Archaic Materials and Assemblies.*

SELECTED PROBLEMS AND REPRESENTATIVE SOLUTIONS

2.1

Problem: The fire resistance of the wall or partition, as determined above, is below that required by code.

Solution: Upgrade the wall or partition construction to meet code requirements.

Discussion: The fire resistance of the wall or partition should be improved by repairing the existing construction or adding a new layer(s) of fire resistive materials. See the *Guideline on Fire Ratings of Archaic Materials and Assemblies.* If the fire resistance is upgraded to code requirements, single station smoke detectors need not be installed, unless otherwise locally required.

-or-

Solution: Accept a wall or partition of 1 hour fire resistance. Doors must provide 1 hour fire resistance and close automatically upon activation of a smoke detector. The wall or partition should be carefully inspected to insure that all penetrations, particularly ducts or other utility services, are properly protected and the existing materials are intact and structurally sound.**

Discussion: The single station smoke detector will provide added time for escape. Additionally, the expected severity of fires in residential occupancies should be contained by 1 hour fire resistive construction.

2.2

Problem: Fire resistance of the opening protection, as determined above, is below that required by code.

Solution: One hour doors may be accepted in a wall assembly having 2 hours fire resistance if protected on both sides by automatic sprinkler protection. These sprinklers may be connected to the domestic water supply and need not be equipped to sound a building alarm. Otherwise, the door must be upgraded to meet the code requirements or replaced.

Discussion: The water spray from the local sprinkler will compensate for the reduced fire resistance.

2.3

Problem: The only exit from an area of refuge is another horizontal exit, in violation of the code.

Solution: Accept such an arrangement (i.e., one intermediate compartment) if the fire resistance of all walls or partitions separating the compartments, and of the protection of all openings in the walls or partitions, fully complies with the code requirements. The following figure illustrates this solution.

---

* A current change to the Basic Code only accepts automatic closing doors.

** The area of refuge to which the horizontal exit leads must have either a complying exit stair or exterior exit door.

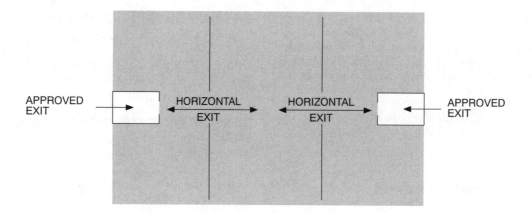

Discussion: As shown above, the area of refuge reached after passing through the intermediate compartment must have a complying stair or exterior exit door.

3
INTERIOR STAIRS/ENCLOSURES

SUMMARY OF CODE REQUIREMENTS AND INTENT

Enclosed stairs are recognized as an exit by all codes if they are properly designed and constructed. In multi-story buildings they are the most likely type of exit to be encountered. They provide a protected means for evacuation of a building by its occupants. By their nature as a vertical shaft through a building, stairs also provide a potential path for the spread of fire from floor to floor.

Code Intent

Requirements for a fire resistive enclosure of stairs are established in order to achieve the following objectives:

- To provide a protected way from any story of a building to a public way or to an area of refuge;
- To limit the spread of fire from floor to floor;
- To provide a protected access for fire service personnel.

Code Analysis

Basic Building Code - 1978

Required interior exitway stairs must have an enclosure of 1 hour fire resistance in buildings three stories or less, 2 hour fire resistance rating in buildings four stories or more. Stairs within a single dwelling unit are excepted. Also excepted, when automatic sprinkler protection is provided, are stairs between no more than three communicating floors close to street level which serve no more than $^1/_2$ the required occupant load and which have adequate capacity for all occupants of all the communicating levels.

Stairway doors must be self-closing and have 1 hour fire resistance in 1 hour construction and $1^1/_2$ hours fire resistance in 2 hour construction. Labeled fire doors shall have a maximum transmitted temperature end point of not more than 450°F above ambient at the end of 30 minutes of standard fire test exposure. Other openings are limited in area and must be protected. (616.6.3, 616.9.2, Table 214)

Uniform Building Code - 1979

For new construction, interior stairways are required to be enclosed, with the following exception: stairways in one- and two-family dwellings and within individual apartment units. Enclosure walls must be a minimum of 2 hour fire resistive construction in buildings more than four stories in height and not less than 1 hour fire resistive construction elsewhere. All exit doors in an exit enclosure must be protected by a fire assembly having a fire resistance of not less than 1 hour where 1 hour shaft construction is permitted and $1^1/_2$ hours where 2 hour shaft construction is required. Doors must be maintained self-closing or automatic closing by actuation of a smoke detector. The maximum transmitted temperature end point shall not exceed 450°F above ambient at the end of 30 minutes of fire exposure. (3308(a)-(c), 4306(b))

Appendix Chapter 12 is a retroactive provision that establishes minimum requirements for all existing apartment buildings and hotels more than two stories in height. Because all such buildings in a community would be required to comply with these minimum safety regulations, Section 103 of the Uniform Code provides that a community must specifically adopt the Appendix for its provisions to apply.

Appendix Chapter 12 sets forth the following requirements. Every interior stairway must be enclosed with walls of at least 1 hour fire resistive construction. Wood lath and plaster in good condition is acceptable for this purpose. The stairway need not be enclosed in a continuous shaft if cut off at each story by 1 hour fire resistive construction. Enclosure is not required if an automatic sprinkler system is provided in all portions of the building except apartments. Stairway doors must be self-closing and equivalent to a solid wood door not less than $1^3/_4$ inches thick.

Standard Building Code - 1979

Required exit stairs must be enclosed in 1 hour fire resistive construction in buildings three or less stories in height; 2 hour fire resistive construction in buildings four or more stories in height. Exceptions are similar to those noted above for the *Basic Building Code*. (1106)

Doors in stairs must be $1^1/_2$ hour fire resistive assemblies for 2 hour walls, and 1 hour fire resistive assemblies for 1 hour walls. The maximum transmitted temperature end point shall not exceed 450°F above ambient after 30 minutes of standard fire test exposure.

NFPA Life Safety Code - 1976

Stairways must be protected as follows:

Fire resistance of walls in buildings of one-three stories shall be 1 hour; four or more stories, 2 hours. Fire resistance of doors in buildings of one-three stories shall be $^3/_4$ hour; four or more stories, $1^1/_2$ hours. In buildings provided with total automatic sprinkler protection, the fire resistance of walls in buildings of one-three stories may be reduced to $^3/_4$ hour; four or more stories,

1 hour. The fire resistance of doors in sprinklered buildings of any height shall be $^3/_4$ hour. (11-3.5.3.1.1, 11-3.8.3.1.1)

Exceptions, including the exception allowing unenclosed stairs as part of communicating floors, are similar to those noted above for the *Basic Building Code*. (6-1)

Summary

The Basic, Standard, and Life Safety Codes generally have identical provisions (2 hours with $1^1/_2$ hour door over three stories; 1 hour enclosure and door below four stories), except that the *Life Safety Code* only requires a $^3/_4$ hour door in a 1 hour stair enclosure. The Uniform Code differs in that buildings up to four stories, rather than three stories, only need a 1 hour enclosure. The Uniform Code, Appendix Chapter 12, contains much more lenient requirements for existing residential buildings.

IDENTIFYING EXISTING CONDITIONS

- Determine the location of all unenclosed stairs;

- Determine the fire resistance of stair enclosures and doors by reference to the code in effect, current listings, or the *Guideline on Fire Ratings of Archaic Materials and Assemblies.*

SELECTED PROBLEMS AND REPRESENTATIVE SOLUTIONS

3.1

Problem: The fire resistance of the stair enclosure, as determined above, is below that required by the code in effect.

Solution: The fire resistance of the stair enclosure should be improved by repairing the existing construction or adding a new layer(s) of fire resistant materials. See the *Guideline on Fire Ratings of Archaic Materials and Assemblies.*

Discussion: If the fire resistance is upgraded to code requirements, single station smoke detectors need not be installed, unless otherwise locally required.

3.2

Problem: A 2 hour enclosure is required and an unenclosed stair does not meet the applicable code exception for communicating floors.

Solution: The stair may be enclosed at each story by construction having 1 hour fire resistance. The walls forming this enclosure may be located on each story wherever convenient, but as close as possible to the stair. Walls should extend through any concealed or void spaces to the underside of the floor or roof above. Any area or section of a floor/ceiling assembly necessary to form a continuous enclosure from story to story must also have 1 hour fire resistance.

If necessary, a limited number of apartment doors may open directly onto the stair enclosure. These doors must provide 1 hour fire resistance, be self-closing, and meet all other code requirements for stairway doors. The following figure illustrates this solution.

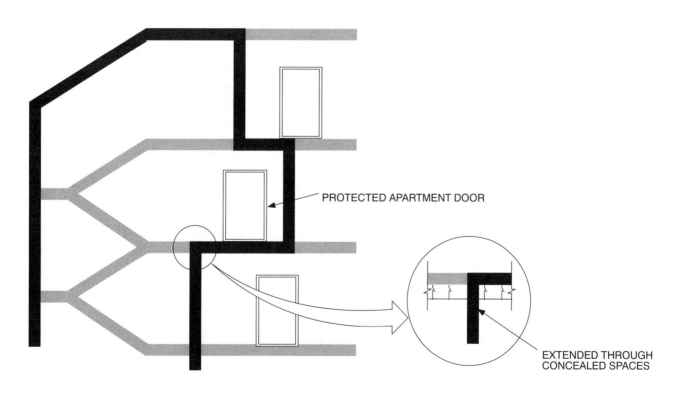

PROTECTED APARTMENT DOOR

EXTENDED THROUGH CONCEALED SPACES

Discussion: This solution provides a protected way of escape from any story while limiting the potential of fire spreading from floor to floor. The population density is low and the fire loading should not be excessive. Single station smoke detectors will allow more time for escape.

3.3

Problem: A l hour enclosure is required, and an unenclosed stair does not meet the applicable code exceptions for communicating floors.

Solution: The stair may be enclosed at each story by construction having a fire resistance of 45 minutes (e.g., $^1/_2$ inch type X gypsum wallboard). Up to 25% of the wall area on any given floor may be fire-rated wire glass in a steel frame. Substantial doors (e.g., minimum $1^3/_4$ inch solid bonded core door) may be used if equipped with self-closing devices.

Discussion: Reducing the required fire resistance from 1 hour to 45 minutes should still allow adequate time for safe escape given the smoke detectors and low occupant loading. The use of wired glass is often least objectionable from architectural and security considerations.

3.4

Problem: A 1 hour enclosure is required, and the stairway is enclosed with wood lath and plaster construction.

Solution: Accept the existing enclosure if it is in good condition and all penetrations and openings are either sealed or properly protected. A visual check should be made to insure the quality of the existing construction. There should be no other serious code deficiencies in the building.

Discussion: The presence of smoke detectors, the absence of any other serious code deficiencies, and the limited occupant loading make it reasonable to allow the existing enclosure to remain.

4
EXTERIOR EXIT STAIRS

SUMMARY OF CODE REQUIREMENTS AND INTENT

Code Intent

The code intent for exterior stairs is the same as for interior stairs. However, because the stairs are outside the building, they do not create a vertical shaft through which the fire could spread. An important consideration, though, is the proximity of an exterior stair to openings in the exterior walls: a fire inside of the building could break out windows or other openings and cause the stair to become impassable.

A visual enclosure is sometimes required for exterior or outside stairs so that acrophobia (fear of heights) will not impede travel or lead to panic.

Code Analysis

Basic Building Code - 1978

Exterior stairs are accepted in buildings not exceeding five stories or 65 feet in height and if at least one door from each tenant opens onto a roofed-over open porch or balcony served by at least two stairways. Only one stairway is required if the code only requires a single exit. Requirements for fire doors are not imposed,

though handrails and guards must be provided as for interior stairs. In buildings three or more stories in height, openings below and within 10 feet horizontally of the exterior stairs must be protected by "automatic opening protectives" of $^3/_4$ hour fire resistance. Exterior stairs must conform to the requirements for interior stairs in all other respects. (619.0)

Uniform Building Code - 1979

For new construction, exterior stairs must meet the requirements for inside stairs except for opening protection. In buildings three or more stories in height, openings below or within 10 feet measured horizontally must be protected by a self-closing fire assembly having $^3/_4$ hour fire resistance, except that openings may be unprotected when two separated exterior stairways serve an exterior exit balcony. (3305, 3305(1))

In existing buildings (Appendix Chapter 12, where specifically adopted), the only requirements are that exterior stairs must be noncombustible or of wood of not less than 2 inch nominal thickness with solid treads and risers. (Appendix Chapter 12, 1215(g))

Standard Building Code - 1979

Exterior stairs may be used in buildings not exceeding six stories or 75 feet in height if at least one door from each tenant opens onto a roofed-over open porch or balcony served by at least two stairways so located as to provide a choice of independent means of egress leading directly to grade. Openings below and within 10 feet horizontally of the exterior stair must be protected with $^3/_4$ hour fire resistive automatic opening protectives; opening protection is not required for buildings not more than three stories in height where all parts of the exterior stair are at least 6 feet from the building wall. Exterior stairs must conform to the requirements for interior stairs in all other respects. (1129)

NFPA Life Safety Code - 1976

Where interior stairs are required to be enclosed, exterior stairs must be separated from the interior of the building by fire resistive walls as required for interior stair enclosures; fire doors or fixed wire glass windows must protect any openings therein. Such protection is not required in buildings three stories or less in height where there is a remote second exit. Other openings within specified distances must be protected. A "visual" enclosure must be provided for the benefit of persons afraid of heights. Exterior stairs must conform to the requirements of interior stairs in all other respects. (5-2.5)

Summary

The codes differ as to both when an exterior stair may be allowed and the need for protection of openings. The Basic and Standard Codes only permit exterior stairs in pairs, though a single stairway is acceptable under the Basic Code if the building only requires a single exit. The Uniform Code does not require exterior stairs in pairs, but waives the requirement for opening protection if the second stair is provided. For existing buildings, the Uniform Code, Appendix Chapter 12, does not require the protection of openings for a single exterior stair. Only the *Life Safety Code* requires a "visual" enclosure for the benefit of persons afraid of heights.

IDENTIFYING EXISTING CONDITIONS

Determine the fire resistance of walls or opening protectives within or adjacent to the exterior stairs by reference to labels, the code in effect, current listings, or the *Guideline on Fire Ratings of Archaic Materials and Assemblies.*

SELECTED PROBLEMS AND REPRESENTATIVE SOLUTIONS

4.1

Problem: The fire resistance of the opening protection, as determined above, is below that required by the code in effect.

Solution: The openings need not be protected if there are a minimum of two exterior stairs located as to provide remote means of egress from an exterior exit balcony.

Discussion: This solution is recognized by the Uniform Code. It is unlikely that a fire would block the access to or the use of both exterior stairs. The requirement for single station smoke detectors is added justification.

4.2

Problem: Fire resistance of the opening protection, as determined above, is below that required, and there is only a single exterior stair.

Solution: Upgrade the fire resistance of the opening protection by repairing the existing construction or adding a new layer(s) of fire rated materials. See the *Guideline on Fire Ratings of Archaic Materials and Assemblies.* Windows must be wire glass in steel frames, either fixed or automatically closing, sealed, or otherwise made to comply with the code.

Discussion: If the fire resistance is upgraded to code requirements, single station smoke detectors need not be installed, unless otherwise locally required.

-or-

Solution: Install local sprinklers over opening protection. Such sprinklers may be connected to the domestic water supply and need not sound an alarm upon activation. Windows must be protected as above.

Discussion: The water spray on the exposed surface will compensate for the reduced fire resistance. The sprinklers should be located on the inside of the opening.

5
FIRE ESCAPE STAIRS

SUMMARY OF CODE REQUIREMENTS AND INTENT

Code Intent

The code intent is to regulate the quality of the required means of escape. Fire escapes are not favored because they are more difficult to traverse and afford less protection to occupants than other types of exits, such as enclosed interior stairs or exit passageways. However, properly designed and protected fire escapes can sometimes provide a practical solution when the existing number of exits or exit capacity is less than required.

Code Analysis

Basic Building Code - 1978

Fire escapes are permitted only on existing buildings, and then only when "more adequate exitway facilities cannot be provided." Fire escapes cannot provide more than 50% of the re-

quired exit capacity. Doors and windows "along the fire escape" must be protected with $3/4$ hour fire resistance rated opening protectives. (621.0).

Uniform Building Code - 1979

Fire escapes are not allowed for new construction.

Appendix Chapter 12, where specifically adopted, permits fire escapes to be used as one means of escape in existing buildings. Under specified conditions a "ladder device" may be used "in lieu of a fire escape." There are no requirements for protection of adjacent openings. (Appendix Chapter 12, 1215(h))

Standard Building Code - 1979

If "more adequate exit facilities cannot be provided," fire escapes can be used on existing buildings four stories or less in height. Fire escapes cannot provide more than 50% of the required exit capacity. All openings within 10 feet of fire escapes must be protected with approved opening protectives of at least $3/4$ hour fire resistance. (1116)

NFPA Life Safety Code - 1976

Fire escape stairs may be used only in existing buildings, but cannot constitute more than 50% of the required exit capacity. Openings within specified limits "shall be completely protected by approved fire doors or metal-frame wire glass windows." (5-2.9)

Summary

Fire escapes are not accepted as a means of egress for new construction. The Basic, Standard, and Life Safety Codes permit fire escapes in existing buildings, but only up to 50% of the required exit capacity. Appendix Chapter 12 of the Uniform Code, when adopted, allows a fire escape as "one means of egress" in "existing nonconforming . . . [apartments] more than two stories in height." All codes except Appendix Chapter 12 require adjacent openings to be protected, though the provisions are not consistent and there are exceptions. The codes all contain other highly specific construction specifications.

IDENTIFYING EXISTING CONDITIONS

- Determine that the soundness and structural serviceability of the fire escape is as required by code;
- Determine that access to fire escape(s) is as required by code;
- Determine the fire resistance of the protection of openings by reference to labels, the code in effect, current listings, or the *Guideline on Fire Ratings of Archaic Materials and Assemblies.*

SELECTED PROBLEMS AND REPRESENTATIVE SOLUTIONS

5.1

Problem: Fire resistance of the opening protection, as determined above, is below that required by the code in effect.

Solution: Upgrade the fire resistance of the opening protection by repairing the existing construction or adding a new layer(s) of fire rated materials. See the *Guideline on Fire Ratings of Archaic Materials and Assemblies.* Windows must be wire glass in steel frames, sealed, or otherwise made to comply with the code.

-or-

Solution: Install local sprinklers over opening protection. Such sprinklers may be connected to the domestic water supply and need not sound an alarm upon activation. Windows must be protected as above.

Discussion: The water spray on the exposed surface will compensate for the reduced fire resistance. The sprinklers should be located on the inside of the opening.

6
ARRANGEMENT OF EXITS

SUMMARY OF CODE REQUIREMENTS AND INTENT

Code Intent

The intent of providing exit remoteness, when two or more exits are required, is to minimize the probability that access to the exits will be blocked by any one fire. The term "remote" is subjective and frequently a matter of interpretation.

Exits which appear to be remote from each other sometimes converge at a distant point. Stairways discharging into a common lobby or passageway are examples. These exits are not truly remote because a blockage at the point of confluence renders both exits useless.

Code Analysis and Summary

Exits must be located so that they are discernible and have unobstructed access. They also must be arranged to lead directly to the street. When more than one exit is required, exits must be as remote from each other as practicable, and must be arranged to allow direct access in separate directions. Exits shall be arranged and constructed as to minimize any possibility that both may be blocked by any one fire or other emergency condition. (BOCA: 602.2, 602.3; SBCC: 1103.1; NFPA: 5-5)

The *Uniform Building Code* has a prescriptive technique for determining exit remoteness. If two exits are required, they must be placed a distance apart equal to not less than $1/2$ the length of the maximum overall diagonal dimension of the building or area to be served measured in a straight line between exits. An exception is made for exit enclosures interconnected by an approved corridor. Where three or more exits are required, they must be arranged a reasonable distance apart so that if one becomes blocked the others will be available. (UBC: 3302(c))

IDENTIFYING EXISTING CONDITIONS

Note the arrangement of the acceptable exit elements on the building plans or analyze by a visual inspection of the physical structure.

SELECTED PROBLEMS AND REPRESENTATIVE SOLUTIONS

6.1

Problem: The required exits are not remote from one another.

Solution: Separate the non-remote exits by smoke barriers located as to establish distinct and separate smoke zones.

Discussion: With certain building configurations it is possible to isolate non-remote exits from one another. By constructing

smoke barrier partitions, the requirement of direct access to the exits in separate directions can be met. Figure 1 illustrates this concept. No matter where the fire may originate, any occupant can safely pass from one zone into another. This approach would not work for the building in Figure 2 because these exits, though now in separate zones, cannot be reached by moving in separate directions: a fire blocking one exit would block the second.

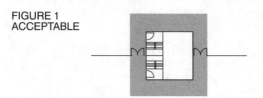

FIGURE 1
ACCEPTABLE

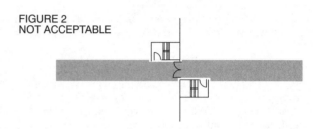

FIGURE 2
NOT ACCEPTABLE

The smoke partitions could be constructed of wire glass, gypsum or other suitable materials. Construction similar to the existing corridor walls is also acceptable. The barriers must extend from exterior wall to exterior wall and from the floor to the underside of the floor or roof above, through any concealed or void spaces. Existing walls and partitions can be used to help form this continuous barrier.

The doors need not swing in the direction of exit travel, but double-acting doors are not acceptable. Doors shall close automatically upon the activation of an associated smoke detector. Doors, when closed, must fit tightly and prevent the passage of smoke. Requirements for minimum corridor or hallway dimensions should be complied with as closely as possible. See Section 7: TRAVEL DISTANCE, if travel distance limitations are exceeded.

-or-

Solution: Provide additional exit(s) (e.g., stair, fire escape, fire balcony).

Discussion: If separation of the exit(s) as discussed above is not possible, then additional exit(s) must be provided so that all occupants will have remote access to the required number of exits. The quality of the additional exit(s) (e.g., interior stair vs. escape ladder) will depend upon the use and occupancy of the building. If a high quality remote exit is provided (e.g., interior stair), single station smoke detectors need not be provided, unless otherwise locally required.

7
TRAVEL DISTANCE

SUMMARY OF CODE REQUIREMENTS AND INTENT

Code Intent

The intent of requirements governing the maximum travel distance to an exit is to limit the time an occupant needs to reach an exit. When combined with the requirements for a minimum number of exits and for exit remoteness, the limitation on travel distance is intended to assure that even if one exit is blocked by a fire, an occupant will still be able to reach another exit or a location of refuge before the fire has spread in a manner as to prevent it. The actual time for escape implied by the maximum travel distance limitation is not explicitly stated.

Code Analysis

Basic Building Code - 1978

Tile maximum length of "exitway access travel" to "an approved exitway" (defined as "that portion of a means of egress which is separated from all other spaces of a building by construction or equipment as required in this code to provide a protected way of travel to the exitway discharge") is as follows:

Without Fire Suppression System	100 feet
With Fire Suppression System	150 feet

If the travel distance within a living unit is less than 50 feet, or 100 feet if sprinklered, the distance of travel is measured from the "exitway access entrance to the nearest exitway" (i.e., from the apartment door). (607.4)

Uniform Building Code - 1979

Maximum distance of travel "from any point to an exterior exit door, horizontal exit, exit passageway or an enclosed stairway" is as follows:

Without Automatic Sprinklers	150 feet
With Automatic Sprinklers	200 feet

These distances may be increased 100 feet when the last 150 feet is within a corridor that meets specific requirements as to width, height, obstructions, dead ends, and openings. (3302(d))

Standard Building Code - 1979

Maximum travel distance from any point to the "nearest exit" (defined as "that portion of a means of egress which is separated from the area of the building from which escape is to be made, by walls, floors, doors or other means which provide the protected path . . . to the exterior") is as follows:

Unsprinklered	150 feet
Sprinklered	200 feet

If the travel distance within a living unit is less than 50 feet, the distance of travel to an exit is measured from the corridor entrance. (1103.1)

NFPA Life Safety Code - 1976

The following are the requirements for travel distance (11-3.5, 11-3.6, 11-3.7, 11-3.8):

	TO THE "NEAREST EXIT" FROM AN APARTMENT ENTRANCE DOOR	TO A CORRIDOR DOOR FROM ANY ROOM DOOR
No Sprinklers or Detection	100 ft.	50 ft.
Automatic Detectors	150 ft.	75 ft.
Partial Sprinkler Protection	150 ft.	50 ft.
Total Sprinkler Protection	150 ft.	100 ft.

"Exit" is defined similarly to "exitway" in the Basic Code.

Summary

The codes have varying dimensional requirements for travel distance. All allow an increase in exit travel distance if there are automatic sprinklers. Only the *Life Safety Code* allows an increase with automatic detection. The Uniform Code differs from the other codes by specifying the four exit elements to which the travel distance is to be measured.

IDENTIFYING EXISTING CONDITIONS

Determine the distance from the most remote point on every story of a building or from the most remote apartment entrance door (depending on the local code in effect) to the nearest acceptable exit element. Measure the distance along the most direct natural path of travel.

SELECTED PROBLEMS AND REPRESENTATIVE SOLUTIONS

7.1

Problem: Measured travel distance exceeds the maximum travel distance required by the code in effect.

Six alternative solutions to this problem are suggested below. Some of these solutions may be combined for an additional increase in the allowable travel distance. A table showing suggested increases in travel distance for the different combinations follows the discussion of the individual solutions. The maximum cumulative increase should not exceed 125 feet.

Smoke Barrier

Solution: The allowable travel distance may be increased by up to 75 feet if the path is divided by a smoke barrier with smoke actuated automatic closing door. The smoke barrier could be constructed of wire glass, gypsum, or other suitable materials. The barrier must extend from exterior wall to exterior wall and from the floor to the underside of the floor or roof above, through any concealed or void spaces. The doors need not swing in the direction of exit travel, but double-acting doors are not acceptable. Doors, when closed, must fit tightly and prevent the passage of smoke. Requirements for minimum corridor or hallway dimensions should be complied with as closely as possible.

Discussion: The added compartmentation created by the smoke barrier reduces the chance that the entire path of travel would be blocked by heat or smoke after a given period of time, thereby compensating for the added escape time due to a longer travel distance. The single station smoke detectors will also provide added time for escape.

Automatic Alarm/Heat Detector

Solution: The allowable travel distance may be increased by up to 50 feet if the building is equipped with an automatic fire alarm system activated by heat detectors located inside every apartment within 6 feet of the corridor door. The alarm should notify all building occupants. Entrance doors to apartments must be equipped with self-closing devices.

Discussion: While the single station smoke detector will notify the occupants of that apartment, other building residents would not be made aware of the emergency. Interconnection of the individual smoke detectors, which are still required, is not realistic because of the large number of false alarms that may be expected. Heat detectors are less sensitive to the environmental causes of false alarms (e.g., burnt toast), but are still capable of providing an alarm before a fire could develop beyond the apartment of origin.

Manual Alarm

Solution: The allowable travel distance may be increased by up to 50 feet if a manual alarm system, not otherwise required by the code, is installed. The alarm should notify all building occupants. Entrance doors to apartments must be equipped with self-closing devices.

Discussion: The smoke detector within the apartment will allow the occupant to escape while the fire is still small. The other building residents could then be warned by the sounding of the manual alarm.

Automatic Sprinkler/No Alarm

Solution: The allowable travel distance may be increased by up to 50 feet if an automatic sprinkler system is installed in the corridor and an additional sprinkler head is located to protect the apartment side of every corridor door. Such sprinklers need not sound an alarm upon activation. Doors must be equipped with self-closing devices. Single station smoke detectors are still required.

Discussion: The automatic sprinklers and door closers should contain a fire within the apartment of origin and keep the corridor passable.

Automatic Sprinkler/Automatic Alarm

Solution: If the partial sprinkler system discussed above is equipped to sound an alarm to all building occupants, the allowable travel distance may be increased by up to 100 feet. Doors must still be equipped with self-closing devices.

Discussion: The sprinkler head inside the apartment door will perform a function similar to the heat detector in the Automatic Alarm/Heat Detector solution by initiating an alarm of a fire to the other building occupants. The sprinkler system will help contain the fire within the apartment of origin and keep the corridor passable. Single station smoke detectors are still required to warn the occupants within the apartment of origin.

Provide Additional Exit(s)

Solution: Provide additional exit(s) (e.g., stair, fire escape, fire balcony) located so that travel distance limitations are not exceeded.

Discussion: The quality of the additional exit(s) (e.g., interior stair vs. escape ladder) will depend upon the use and occupancy of the building. If a high quality exit is provided (e.g., interior stair), single station smoke detectors need not be provided, unless otherwise locally required.

Suggested Cumulative Increases

The following chart contains the suggested cumulative increases if more than one solution is implemented.

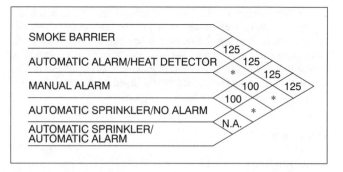

The combinations with an asterisk (*) show no specific increase in travel distance because they perform similar life safety functions of fire detection and/or alarm: the heat detector and sprinkler head inside the apartment door; the alarm sounded automatically by the heat detector or sprinkler head, or manually by an occupant. However, there is an increase in reliability: there is a second system present should the first device fail to operate. There are also different fire scenarios where one system would be more responsive or appropriate than the other. The increase in travel distance is best left to the informed judgment of the local official, applied to the particulars of a specific structure.

8
DEAD-END TRAVEL

SUMMARY OF CODE REQUIREMENTS AND INTENT

Code Intent

Dead-end corridors of any length are undesirable features in buildings for two reasons. People who must use a dead-end corridor as part of the exit access (no choice of travel to exits) could be trapped by a fire or smoke between them and the exits. The other reason is that people moving within the exit access could enter the dead-end, especially under smoky or low light conditions, and become trapped or confused. Some controversy exists as to which concern the codes are intended to address, if not both. The answer is important because the design solutions differ.

All the codes use the term "dead-end" but do not define it. The *Life Safety Code* also uses the phrase "maximum single path corridor length," which would indicate a concern for the availability of two remote exits. The model codes appear to focus upon the individual who may turn off onto a dead-end corridor or hallway.

Code Analysis and Summary

The Basic, Uniform, and Standard Codes impose a 20 foot maximum length for dead-ends (BOCA: 610.2; UBC: 3304(e); SBCC: 1104.3). The *Life Safety Code* imposes a maximum single path corridor length of 30 feet, except that lengths of 35 feet are acceptable in existing or totally sprinklered buildings. (11-3.5, 11-3.6, 11-3.7, 11-3.8, as changed by Tentative Interim Amendment)

IDENTIFYING EXISTING CONDITIONS

There are two approaches, illustrated in the figure below, to the identification of paths of dead-end travel. The result may not be the same in both instances.

From the perspective of an occupant in a corridor moving towards a proper exit (Perspective B), a dead-end is any path of travel onto which the occupant could mistakenly turn that does not lead to an exit. The length of the dead-end is the maximum distance that the occupant could travel before realizing the mistake, i.e., to the end of the dead-end path.

From the perspective of an occupant moving from an individual dwelling unit into the corridor (Perspective A), a dead-end is any path of travel for which no choice of exits exists, assuming that two or more exits are required. That is, an exit can be reached by traveling in a single direction only. The length of the dead-end is the maximum distance that an occupant entering onto the corridor at the most remote point of access would have to travel until alternate paths to remote exits become available. The corridor may extend beyond the most remote point of access from a dwelling unit to the corridor, e.g., to a window or janitor's closet. However, it is assumed that the occupants, familiar with their surroundings, would move towards, not away from, the nearest exit. Therefore, for this perspective only, the length of the dead-end does not include the length of the path that does not lead to an exit. It would be included under the approach in the previous paragraph.

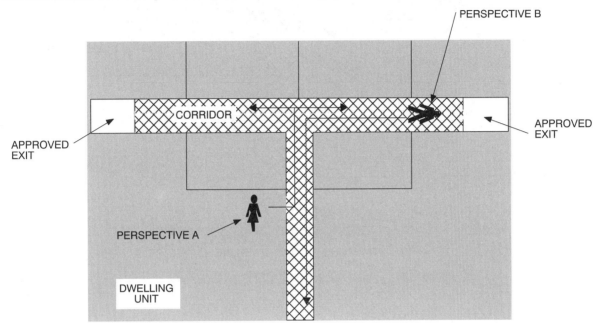

SELECTED PROBLEMS AND REPRESENTATIVE SOLUTIONS

8.1

<u>Problem</u>: Excessive lengths of dead-end travel.

<u>Solution</u>: Provide an additional exit to eliminate the dead-end.

<u>Discussion</u>: The most direct solution is to construct an exit at or near the end of the dead-end path. A person turning off the main corridor would still have access to an exit; a person leaving an individual dwelling unit would have a choice of two remote exits. This exit must be directly accessible from the corridor or hallway. Higher quality exit components such as interior or exterior stairs are preferred. Fire escapes or balconies could be accepted depending upon the nature and characteristics of the occupant loading, fire department capabilities, building height, etc. If high quality exits are provided, single station smoke detectors need not be provided, unless otherwise locally required.

-or-

<u>Solution</u>: Construct a physical partition limiting the path of dead-end travel.

<u>Discussion</u>: By constructing a physical partition, a person who mistakenly turns off the proper path onto a dead-end would be alerted to the mistake. The distance from the proper path to the partition must be within the limits for dead-ends specified within the respective codes, but should be less than that allowed whenever practicable. The partition need not have any fire resistance rating. Any doors may be kept in the open position provided they shall close automatically upon the activation of a local smoke detector. The partition shall be clearly marked to indicate the path is NOT AN EXIT.

This solution does not provide two remote exits for those occupants whose dwelling units access onto the dead-end path. While the codes are not clear on this issue, the following analysis has been used. The portion of the building served by an excessive dead-end path is analyzed as though it were the second story of a two story building. Then, the number of exits required for this portion is determined. The conditions for allowing a single exit are noted in Section 1: NUMBER OF EXITS. If only one exit is required, then the building is considered to be in compliance because the dead-end path still provides one path of escape. The *Uniform Building Code* provides that "every building or USABLE PORTION THEREOF shall have at least one exit." (3302(a)) (emphasis added) Two exits are required only when certain limits are exceeded.

Travel distances for the dwelling units in this portion of the building are computed as follows:

The regular travel distance limitations outlined in Section 7: TRAVEL DISTANCE must still be met. For example, the travel distance from the door of the most remote dwelling unit in that portion of the building to the nearest exit may not exceed 100 feet in a non-sprinklered building constructed under the Basic Code.

The special limitation on travel distance when a single exit is allowed must also be considered. The distance from the door of the most remote dwelling unit to the point where two remote exits become available must not exceed this limit. The *Uniform Building Code* has no such limitation. The allowable distances in the Basic and Standard Building Codes are 50 feet and 30 feet, respectively. Though the *Life Safety Code* allows dead-ends of 35 feet in existing buildings, the maximum travel distance when a single exit is allowable is only 20 feet.

The following figure illustrates the approach detailed above. Should the analysis reveal that the conditions for a single exit are not met by this portion of the building, then an additional exit must be provided.

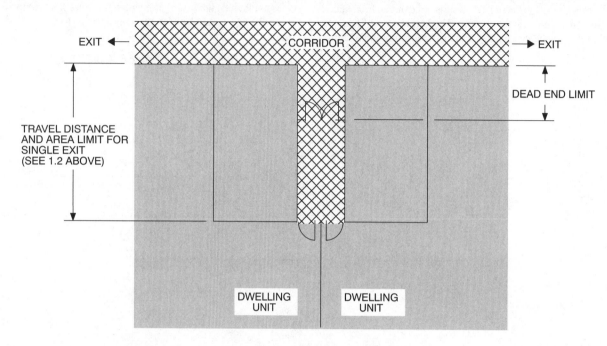

9
CORRIDORS AND EXTERIOR EXIT BALCONIES (SEPARATION AND FIRE RESISTANCE)

SUMMARY OF CODE REQUIREMENTS AND INTENT

Corridors in residential occupancies are the common and public spaces through which occupants travel from their apartments to an exit element. It is the length of corridors that is usually controlled by code provisions governing travel distance. The codes establish certain requirements for the separation of corridors from other building spaces. See also Section 10: EXIT CAPACITY/ WIDTHS for dimensional requirements for corridors.

Code Intent

Fire resistance requirements for corridor enclosures and doors are intended to maintain the integrity of the corridor and prevent flames and smoke from blocking the exit route. This will enable the occupants to safely travel through the corridors to the exits.

Code Analysis

Basic Building Code - 1978

A corridor is defined as "a hallway, passageway or other compartmented space providing the occupants with access to the required exitway of the building or floor area." (201.2)

Corridors serving more than 30 occupants (i.e., floor area greater than 6000 sq. ft.) must be enclosed by walls having 1 hour fire resistance. Corridor walls must extend from the floor to the ceiling (need not extend through space above suspended ceiling). Doors opening onto corridors serving over 30 occupants must be self-closing or automatic closing, with a 20 minute fire protection rating. (610.4)

Open porches or balconies leading to exterior exitway stairs must be separated on their interior side by construction having a fire resistance of 1 hour in buildings of three stories or less, and of 2 hours in all other buildings. Doors in such separations must be rated at $3/4$ hour and $1^1/2$ hours, respectively. Other openings must be protected and are limited in area. (619.1.1)

Uniform Building Code - 1979

A corridor is not specifically defined.

Walls of corridors and interior sides of exterior exit balconies serving an occupant load of 30 or more (i.e., floor area 6000 sq. ft. or more) must be of not less than 1 hour fire resistive construction. Ceilings of corridors must be at least that required for a 1 hour fire resistive floor/ceiling assembly.

Where corridor walls are required to be of 1 hour fire resistive construction, doors must be "tight-fitting smoke and draft control," self-closing or automatic closing assemblies with a 20 minute fire protection rating. Other openings in corridor walls must be fixed and protected by $1/4$ inch wired glass in steel frames and may not exceed 25% of the wall area separating any room and the corridor. Protection of openings in the interior walls of exterior exit balconies is not required. (3304)

Travel distance in an enclosed corridor may be increased (see Section 7: TRAVEL DISTANCE).

Standard Building Code - 1979

A corridor is not specifically defined.

All exit access corridors serving over 30 occupants (i.e., floor area greater than 6000 sq. ft.) must be enclosed by walls having a minimum of 1 hour fire resistance. An exterior balcony may serve as an exit access corridor if it complies with all the requirements for a corridor. Doors opening onto corridors serving over 30 occupants must be self-closing, tight fitting, smoke and draft assemblies with a 20 minute fire protection rating. (702.3, Table 700 and Notes, 1108)

NFPA Life Safety Code - 1976

A corridor is not specifically defined.

Walls enclosing exit access corridors must have 1 hour fire resistance. The fire resistance may be reduced to $^3/_4$ hour and $^1/_2$ hour for buildings with automatic detectors and automatic sprinklers, respectively; $^1/_2$ hour fire resistance is permitted in existing buildings. Access to an exit may be by means of an exterior balcony, porch, gallery, or roof, in which case the materials of construction are required to be "as permitted for the building served."

Doors opening onto exit access corridors must have a 20 minute fire protection rating, except that previously approved $1^3/_4$ inch rated bonded wood core doors and frames may remain in use. Doors between apartments and corridors must be self-closing. (5-5.4,11-3.2.8, 11-3.5.3.1.3 and Exception No. 2, 11-3.6.3.1.3, 11-3.7.3.1.3, 11-3.8.3.1.2)

Summary

The Basic and Standard Codes require a 1 hour enclosure and 20 minute doors for corridors serving over 30 occupants; the Uniform Code applies similar requirements when the occupant load is 30 or more. The *Life Safety Code* requires a similar corridor enclosure, irrespective of occupant loading, but allows reduction of the separation requirement as a function of automatic detection and extinguishment. Only the *Life Safety Code* accepts lower ratings for existing buildings. All codes require doors to have some form of door closing mechanism.

The three model codes disagree on the treatment of exterior exit balconies. The Uniform and Standard Codes treat them as corridors, though the Uniform Code does not require openings in interior walls of exterior exit balconies to be protected. The Basic Code seems to be stricter, treating them as part of the "exitway" rather than "exitway access."

IDENTIFYING EXISTING CONDITIONS

Determine the occupant load served by the corridor in question. If it is in excess of the code specified criteria of 30 occupants (or 6000 sq. ft. of area served), proceed with the following:

* Determine the fire resistance of the corridor wall assembly and doors by reference to the code in effect, current listings, or the *Guideline on Fire Ratings of Archaic Materials and Assemblies;*

* Identify all other openings in corridor walls, such as transoms, and determine their area and the design of their closing devices, if any;

* Determine the presence and operability of door closing devices.

SELECTED PROBLEMS AND REPRESENTATIVE SOLUTIONS

9.1

Problem: The fire resistance of the corridor enclosure, as determined above, is below that required by the code in effect.

Solution: If the existing corridor wall consists of wood lath and plaster in good condition, it should be accepted as having adequate fire resistance. If of lesser construction or in need of repair, the fire resistance of the corridor enclosure should be improved by repairing the existing construction or adding a new layer(s) of fire rated materials. See the *Guideline on Fire Ratings of Archaic Materials and Assemblies.*

Discussion: If the fire resistance is upgraded to code requirements, single station smoke detectors need not be installed, unless otherwise locally required.

-or-

Solution: A corridor enclosure of 30 minutes fire resistance should be accepted. Buildings with more than three occupiable floors must be equipped with an automatic fire alarm system activated by heat detectors located inside every apartment door that leads to the corridor. The alarm should notify all building occupants. Doors to apartments must be equipped with self-closing devices.

Discussion: The door closers, single station smoke detectors, and automatic fire alarm system (when required) will provide earlier detection and alarm and increase the reliability of the compartmentation. The corridor walls should be carefully inspected to insure that they extend from the floor to the underside of the floor or roof above, are properly firestopped, and that any pokethroughs or penetrations are properly protected. There should not be any other serious code deficiencies.

9.2

Problem: The fire resistance of corridor doors is lower than that required by the code in effect.

Solution: Unrated corridor doors should be accepted if they are protected by a local sprinkler which will spray the door in case of a fire on the room side of the corridor door. Such a sprinkler may be connected to the domestic water supply and need not sound an alarm upon activation. Doors must be equipped with self-closing devices.

Discussion: The water spray on the exposed surface will compensate for the reduced fire resistance.

-or-

Solution: Upgrade the existing corridor doors. See the *Guideline on Fire Ratings of Archaic Materials and Assemblies.*

9.3

Problem: The corridor walls have openings other than doors which are inadequately protected as required by the code in effect.

Solution: All transoms should be closed with plasterboard, fixed wire glass, or other like materials. Other openings should be improved by repairing the existing construction or adding a new layer(s) of fire rated materials.

Discussion: See the *Guideline on Fire Ratings of Archaic Materials and Assemblies* for guidance. If the fire resistance is upgraded to code requirements, single station smoke detectors need not be installed, unless otherwise locally required.

Where the sealing of transoms or the use of wire glass would seriously compromise the character of a building, flexibility should be shown. Partial sprinkler systems or alternate materials such as polycarbonate could be considered. Single station smoke detectors would still be required unless the fire performance of these materials or systems is documented as meeting code requirements.

10
EXIT CAPACITY/WIDTHS

SUMMARY OF CODE REQUIREMENTS AND INTENT

The codes regulate the capacity of exits by relating the required width of the various exit elements to the occupant load they serve, and by establishing minimum widths for each of the exit elements. Capacity is expressed as the number of building occupants that can be served by an exit element per unit of exit width.

Code Intent

It is the intent of the codes to provide an exit capacity large enough to move the total expected occupant load into the exits before the exit access becomes untenable.

Safe exiting time is implied in the codes only, and cannot yet be validly calculated. It was discussed, however, when the values for exit capacity were established by the NFPA Life Safety Code Committee. Doors and other level egress components were considered to have a rated capacity of 60 persons per minute per 22 inch unit of exit width, and stairs were rated at 45 persons per minute per unit of exit width. This is considered a standard 4:3 ratio for pedestrian movement. These values are based on the following studies: National Bureau of Standards, *Design and Construction of Building Exits,* Pub. No. M151, Washington, D.C., 1935; London Transport Board, *Second Report of the Operational Research Team on the Capacity of Footways,* Research Report No. 95, London, 1958. If stairs are sized to a capacity of 75 people per unit, a time of 100 seconds is implied (75 people/unit divided by 45 people/minute-unit). The same result is obtained for horizontal or level travel (100 people/unit divided by 60 people/minute-unit).

The 22 inch unit of exit width, which is used in all but the *Uniform Building Code,* represents the median width of the human body at shoulder height. Its origin is said to be in experience gained by the military. The Uniform Code's requirements imply an exit capacity of 100 people per 24 inches of exit width. Using the 22 inch exit unit system, this results in an exit capacity of about 92 people per exit unit.

Code Analysis

Basic Building Code - 1978

Exit capacity is based on a unit of egress width of 22 inches with 12 inches or more considered as $1/2$ unit in addition to one or more units (608.1), except that a 40 inch door is considered to have two units of egress width.

Exit capacity per unit of egress width (608.2):

	WITHOUT FIRE SUPPRESSION SYSTEM	WITH FIRE SUPPRESSION SYSTEM
Stairways	75	113
Doors, Ramps, Corridors	100	150

Minimum width:

Corridors, Ramps	44 inches; 36 inches in one- and two-family dwellings (610.3, 615.2.1)
Doors	32 inches; 28 inches in one- and two-family dwellings (612.3)
Stairways	44 inches; 36 inches for occupancy load 50 or less (616.2.1)
Fire escapes	22 inches (621.3.1)
Passageways	44 inches or $3/4$ of aggregate widths of all stairways and doorways leading thereto, whichever is greater (611.4)

Uniform Building Code - 1979

The total width of exits (measured in feet) cannot be less than the total occupant load served divided by 50, divided about equally among the separate exits. The total exit width for any story is based on the occupant load of that story, plus a percentage of the occupant load of other floors which exit through the story under consideration: 50 percent of the first adjacent story above (and below, if applicable), and 25 percent of the story immediately adjacent to the first adjacent story. (3302(b))

Minimum width:

Corridors, Exit Balconies, and Passageways	44 inches for occupant load of 10 or more; 36 inches within dwelling units (3304(b))
Doors	32 inches (3303(e))
Stairways and Ramps	44 inches for occupant load over 50; 36 inches for load of 50 or less; 30 inches for private stairway (3303(b))
Exit Courts	44 inches or tributary occupant load (3310(b))
Fire Escapes (existing buildings stairs only)	29 inches—clear access opening; 18 inches—(Appendix Chapter 12, 1215(h))

Standard Building Code - 1979

Exit capacity is based on a unit of egress width of 22 inches with 12 inches or more considered as $1/2$ unit in addition to one or more units. (1105.2)

Exit capacity per unit of exit width (1105.3):

Stairs	75 People
Level Travel (Doors, Ramps, Corridors)	100 People

Minimum width:

Any means of egress	36 inches (1105.3(e))
Exitway access, Corridors, Ramps	44 inches; 36 inches in one- and two-family dwellings (1105.3(g))
Stairs	44 inches; 36 inches for 50 or less occupants (1115.6(c))
Courts, Passageways	36 inches or aggregate capacity of all tributary means of egress (1112(c)); 44 inches or $3/4$ of aggregate tributary stair and door widths (1128.2)
Doors	32 inches (1117.1(b))
Fire Escapes	22 inches—stairs (1116(d))

NFPA Life Safety Code - 1976

Exit capacity is based on a unit of exit width of 22 inches with 12 inches or more considered as $1/2$ unit in addition to one or more units. (5-3.2)

Exit capacity per unit of exit width (11-1.6.1):

| Level egress Class A Ramps, Doors | 100 People |
| Stairways and other types of exits | 75 People (see Table 5-2.9.4 for fire escapes) |

Minimum width:

Any exit access, Doors	28 inches (currently being changed to 32 inches) (5-2.1.1.3.1)
Stairs	44 inches for occupant load of 50 or more; 36 inches for occupant load of less than 50 (5-2.2.1.2)
Fire Escapes	22 inches; 18 inches for 20 or less occupants (5-2.9.4)
Ramps	44 inches for Class A (5-2.6.1.2) 30 inches for Class B (5-2.6.1.2)
Exit Passageway	Aggregate of tributary capacities (5-2.7.3)
Street Floor Exit	Aggregate capacity of street floor and $3/4$ of exit units of stairs from other floors discharging through street floor (11-2.2.3.1)

Summary

Three of the codes use the 22 inch exit unit in computing required exit widths. The Uniform Code differs from the other three codes in the method used; however, the resulting widths are close. Only the Basic Code allows an increase in the capacity per unit of egress width if the building is sprinklered.

Minimum widths are generally similar for all the codes except that the *Life Safety Code*, as currently revised, accepts a minimum corridor width of 32 inches. The other codes require 44 inches in apartment buildings.

IDENTIFYING EXISTING CONDITIONS

- Determine the number of required exit units or feet of exit (depending on the code in effect) for each exit element identified in Section 1: NUMBER OF EXITS above; for each access corridor or hallway leading from any apartment to an exit; and for each grade level egress. Base the computation on the number of occupants served by the element in question, in accordance with the code in effect. When communicating stairs or other openings are present, attention must be given to the potential need for the simultaneous evacuation of multiple floors;

- Determine the required width of each exit element and corridor or hallway, based upon the number of exit units or feet of exit computed above and the minimum dimension requirements;

- Determine or measure the actual width of each exit element, corridor or hallway, and grade level egress identified above by field measurement or scaling dimensioned plans.

SELECTED PROBLEMS AND REPRESENTATIVE SOLUTIONS

10.1

Problem: The width of an existing exit element, or a new exit element constrained by structural or architectural features of the building, is less than the minimum width specified in the code in effect.

Solution: If the element is wide enough to provide the required exit capacity and is equal to or greater than some minimal dimen-

sion, though lower than that specified in the code, it should be accepted. This new minimum should be over 22 inches.

28 inches should be considered, as formerly specified for some elements by all four codes.

Discussion: In most cases, considerations of functionality (movement of furniture, etc.), appearance, marketability, and accessibility to the handicapped will result in minimum dimensions greater than those suggested above, and may, in fact, have been the reason for the higher minimums specified in current codes. For egress only, however, one unit of exit width should be adequate given the low occupant loading. A higher minimum than 22 inches is suggested, since that dimension represents only the median width of the human body at shoulder height.

11
CONSTRUCTION DETAILS AND SPECIFICATIONS

SUMMARY OF CODE REQUIREMENTS AND INTENT

Code Intent

The codes set out many other requirements for the component parts of the various exit elements that make up a building's egress system. Typical areas include: allowable materials, hand-rails, tread and riser design, landings, platforms, guards, door hardware, signage, lighting, alarms, and emergency lighting. The intent of these provisions is to ensure a quality design that will promote safe and easy passability. The individual code requirements have not been set out because they are too numerous and highly specific.

IDENTIFYING EXISTING CONDITIONS

Note the relevant features on the building plans or analyze by a visual inspection of the physical structure.

SELECTED PROBLEMS AND REPRESENTATIVE SOLUTIONS

Because these provisions tend to be highly specific and detailed, existing components of the egress system will often not be in compliance. However, the impact or effect of the deficiency must be realistically appraised in light of the number of occupants that will rely upon the exit element in question and their ability to safely use the exit element as it presently exists. If the numbers are small and the occupants are generally representative of the population at large, then minor deviations should be tolerated.

For additional guidance to understanding potential problems and solutions related to stairway design, refer to NBS Building Science Series, No. 108, "Safety on Stairs," November 1978, and Building Science Series, No. 120, "Guidelines for Stair Safety," May 1979, National Bureau of Standards, U.S. Department of Commerce.

Of the many potential problems, there are three that appear the most common and raise the greatest concern.

11.1

Problem: Existing winding and/or spiral stairs not permitted by the code in effect.

Solution: Allow their continued use if occupants are generally representative of the population at large (mobile, agile, and capable of rapid movement under emergency condition); upgrade stairs in all other respects, particularly handrails and lighting.

Discussion: Winding or spiral stairs are not favored because the uneven tread pattern and changes in direction can make passage difficult. The use of these stairs could be continued if the occupants can be expected to use them safely and the stairs complied in other respects (e.g., not excessively steep or narrow). Lighting should be improved if necessary; emergency lighting, handrails, etc. should be improved or provided.

11.2

Problem: Nonconforming tread and riser dimensions.

Solution: Accept stairs which are steeper than those permitted by the code in effect. Handrails should be provided on both sides, and stairs should be upgraded where necessary. See Section 10: EXIT CAPACITY/WIDTHS for stairs less than the required minimum.

Discussion: All codes contain minimum tread and maximum riser dimensions. Some codes use the mathematical formula that the sum of $[(2 \times rise) + run]$ must be between 24 and 25 inches. Such criteria may arbitrarily eliminate stairs which are otherwise quite passable. Rather than the absolute values of stair dimensions, it is the nonuniformity of tread or riser dimensions within a set of stairs which is a major cause of stairway accidents. Nonconform-

ing stairs may be considered for acceptance if they are uniform and the occupancy is such that those who may need the stairs in an emergency are familiar with their particular characteristics. As in 11.1 above, the stairs should be otherwise of high quality and passable. Lighting should be improved if necessary; emergency lighting, etc., should be improved or provided.

11.3

Problem: Ceiling heights for stairs, passageways, etc. are lower than the minimum specified by the code in effect.

Solution: Allow the continued use if passable by the occupants, provided the ceiling height is no less than the minimum door height specified by the code in effect.

Discussion: Low ceiling heights make an exit not only physically difficult to traverse, but can create an impression of closeness or of a closed space that may create a sense of apprehension, particularly if the path is also narrow or somewhat lengthy. If the number of occupants is low so that crowding would not be expected and the distance is not excessive, discretion should be exercised. The familiarity of the occupants with this exit element should also be considered. Lighting, particularly emergency lighting, is very important. A regular pattern of markings showing the direction of the ultimate exit to the outside can also be reassuring. Other aspects of the exit element should be improved or provided if missing.

UCBC–2 FIRE RATINGS OF
ARCHAIC MATERIALS

Acknowledgments

The material herein was prepared by the National Institute of Building Sciences on the basis of research conducted by Brady Williamson, principal author, and Cecile Grant, editor, of the J. Bradford Corporation; Joseph Zicherman, Fred Fisher, and Harry Hasegawa, of IFT, Inc., coauthors; and Herman Spaeth, Harriet Watson, Vytenis Babrauskas, and Norman Kornsand, consultants. Technical reviewers for the Institute included Harold Nelson, Richard Bletzacker, and Russel Parks. Final editing of the guideline was performed by Howard Markman, aided by Ruth Fidelman and Duncan Wilson.

Overall management and production of the Rehabilitation Guidelines was directed by William Brenner of the Institute, with David Hattis of Building Technology, Inc. the principal technical consultant. Guideline cover graphics and layouts were designed by the Design Communication Collaborative.

INTRODUCTION

The *Guideline on Fire Ratings of Archaic Materials and Assemblies* focuses upon the fire-related performance of archaic construction. "Archaic" encompasses construction typical of an earlier time, generally prior to 1950. "Fire-related performance" includes fire resistance, flame spread, smoke production, and degree of combustibility.

The purpose of this guideline is to update the information which was available at the time of original construction, for use by architects, engineers, and code officials when evaluating the fire safety of a rehabilitation project. In addition, information relevant to the evaluation of general classes of materials and types of construction is presented for those cases when documentation of the fire performance of a particular archaic material or assembly cannot be found.

It has been assumed that the building materials and their fastening, joining, and incorporation into the building structure are sound mechanically. Therefore, some determination must be made that the original manufacture, the original construction practice, and the rigors of aging and use have not weakened the building. This assessment can often be difficult because process and quality control was not good in many industries, and variations among locally available raw materials and manufacturing techniques often resulted in a product which varied widely in its strength and durability. The properties of iron and steel, for example, varied widely, depending on the mill and the process used.

There is nothing inherently inferior about archaic materials or construction techniques. The pressures that promote fundamental change are most often economic or technological—matters not necessarily related to concerns for safety. The high cost of labor made wood lath and plaster uneconomical. The high cost of land and the congestion of the cities provided the impetus for high-rise construction. Improved technology made it possible. The difficulty with archaic materials is not a question of suitability, but familiarity.

Code requirements for the fire performance of key building elements (e.g., walls, floor/ceiling assemblies, doors, shaft enclosures) are stated in performance terms: hours of fire resistance. It matters not whether these elements were built in 1908 or 1980, only that they provide the required degree of fire resistance. The level of performance will be defined by the local community, primarily through the enactment of a building or rehabilitation code. This guideline is only a tool to help evaluate the various building elements, regardless of what the level of performance is required to be.

The problem with archaic materials is simply that documentation of their fire performance is not readily available. The application of engineering judgment is more difficult because building officials may not be familiar with the materials or construction method involved. As a result, either a full-scale fire test is required or the archaic construction in question removed and replaced. Both alternatives are time consuming and wasteful.

This guideline and the accompanying Appendix are designed to help fill this information void. By providing the necessary documentation, there will be a firm basis for the continued acceptance of archaic materials and assemblies.

1
FIRE-RELATED PERFORMANCE OF ARCHAIC MATERIALS AND ASSEMBLIES

1.1
FIRE PERFORMANCE MEASURES

This guideline does not specify the level of performance required for the various building components. These requirements are controlled by the building occupancy and use and are set forth in the local building or rehabilitation code.

The fire resistance of a given building element is established by subjecting a sample of the assembly to a "standard" fire test which follows a "standard" time-temperature curve. This test method has changed little since the 1920's. The test results tabulated in the Appendix have been adjusted to reflect current test methods.

The current model building codes cite other fire-related properties not always tested for in earlier years: flame spread, smoke production, and degree of combustibility. However, they can generally be assumed to fall within well defined values because the principal combustible component of archaic materials is cellulose. Smoke production is more important today because of the increased use of plastics. However, the early flame spread tests, developed in the early 1940's, also included a test for smoke production.

"Plastics," one of the most important classes of contemporary materials, were not found in the review of archaic materials. If plastics are to be used in a rehabilitated building, they should be evaluated by contemporary standards. Information and documentation of their fire-related properties and performance is widely available.

Flame spread, smoke production and degree of combustibility are discussed in detail below. Test results for eight common species of lumber, published in an Underwriter's Laboratories' report (104), are noted in the following table:

TUNNEL TEST RESULTS FOR EIGHT SPECIES OF LUMBER

SPECIES OF LUMBER	FLAME SPREAD	FUEL CONTRIBUTED	SMOKE DEVELOPED
Western White Pine	75	50-60	50
Northern White Pine	120-215	120-140	60-65
Ponderosa Pine	80-215	120-135	100-110
Yellow Pine	180-190	130-145	275-305
Red Gum	140-155	125-175	40-60
Yellow Birch	105-110	100-105	45-65
Douglas Fir	65-100	50-80	10-100
Western Hemlock	60-75	40-65	40-120

Flame Spread

The flame spread of interior finishes is most often measured by the ASTM E-84 "tunnel test." This test measures how far and how fast the flames spread across the surface of the test sample. The resulting flame spread rating (FSR) is expressed as a number on a continuous scale where cement-asbestos board is 0 and red oak is 100. (Materials with a flame spread greater than red oak have an FSR greater than 100.) The scale is divided into distinct groups or classes. The most commonly used flame spread classifications are: Class I or A*, with a 0-25 FSR; Class II or B, with a 26-75 FSR; and Class III or C, with a 76-200 FSR. The *NFPA Life Safety*

---

* Some codes use Roman numerals, others use letters.

Code also has a Class D (201-500 FSR) and Class E (over 500 FSR) interior finish.

These classifications are typically used in modern building codes to restrict the rate of fire spread. Only the first three classifications are normally permitted, though not all classes of materials can be used in all places throughout a building. For example, the interior finish of building materials used in exits or in corridors leading to exits is more strictly regulated than materials used within private dwelling units.

In general, inorganic archaic materials (e.g., bricks or tile) can be expected to be in Class I. Materials of whole wood are mostly Class II. Whole wood is defined as wood used in the same form as sawn from the tree. This is in contrast to the contemporary reconstituted wood products such as plywood, fiberboard, hardboard, or particle board. If the organic archaic material is not whole wood, the flame spread classification could be well over 200 and thus would be particularly unsuited for use in exits and other critical locations in a building. Some plywoods and various wood fiberboards have flame spreads over 200. Although they can be treated with fire retardants to reduce their flame spread, it would be advisable to assume that all such products have a flame spread over 200 unless there is information to the contrary.

Smoke Production

The evaluation of smoke density is part of the ASTM E-84 tunnel test. For the eight species of lumber shown in the table above, the highest levels are 275-305 for Yellow Pine, but most of the others are less smoky than red oak which has an index of 100. The advent of plastics caused substantial increases in the smoke density values measured by the tunnel test. The ensuing limitation of the smoke production for wall and ceiling materials by the model building codes has been a reaction to the introduction of plastic materials. In general, cellulosic materials fall in the 50-300 range of smoke density which is below the general limitation of 450 adopted by many codes.

Degree of Combustibility

The model building codes tend to define "noncombustibility" on the basis of having passed ASTM E-136 or if the material is totally inorganic. The acceptance of gypsum wallboard as noncombustible is based on limiting paper thickness to not over $1/8$ inch and a 0-50 flame spread rating by ASTM E-84. At times there were provisions to define a Class I or A material (0-25 FSR) as noncombustible, but this is not currently recognized by most model building codes.

If there is any doubt whether or not an archaic material is noncombustible, it would be appropriate to send out samples for evaluation. If an archaic material is determined to be noncombustible according to ASTM E-136, it can be expected that it will not contribute fuel to the fire.

1.2
COMBUSTIBLE CONSTRUCTION TYPES

One of the earliest forms of timber construction used exterior load-bearing masonry walls with columns and/or wooden walls supporting wooden beams and floors in the interior of the building. This form of construction, often called "mill" or "heavy timber" construction, has approximately 1 hour fire resistance. The exterior walls will generally contain the fire within the building.

With the development of dimensional lumber, there was a switch from heavy timber to "balloon frame" construction. The balloon frame uses load-bearing exterior wooden walls which have long timbers often extending from foundation to roof. When longer lumber became scarce, another form of construction, "platform" framing, replaced the balloon framing. The difference between the two systems is significant because platform framing is automatically fire-blocked at every floor while balloon framing commonly has concealed spaces that extend unblocked from basement to attic. The architect, engineer, and code official must be alert to the details of construction and the ease with which fire can spread in concealed spaces.

2
BUILDING EVALUATION

A given rehabilitation project will most likely go through several stages. The preliminary evaluation process involves the designer in surveying the prospective building. The fire resistance of existing building materials and construction systems is identified; potential problems are noted for closer study. The final evaluation phase includes: developing design solutions to upgrade the fire resistance of building elements, if necessary; preparing working drawings and specifications; and the securing of the necessary code approvals.

2.1
PRELIMINARY EVALUATION

A preliminary evaluation should begin with a building survey to determine the existing materials, the general arrangement of the structure and the use of the occupied spaces, and the details of construction. The designer needs to know "what is there" before a decision can be reached about what to keep and what to remove during the rehabilitation process. This preliminary evaluation should be as detailed as necessary to make initial plans. The fire-related properties need to be determined from the applicable building or rehabilitation code, and the materials and assemblies existing in the building then need to be evaluated for these properties. Two work sheets are shown below to facilitate the preliminary evaluation.

Two possible sources of information helpful in the preliminary evaluation are the original building plans and the building code in effect at the time of original construction. Plans may be on file with the local building department or in the offices of the original designers (e.g., architect, engineer) or their successors. If plans are available, the investigator should verify that the building was actually constructed as called for in the plans, as well as incorporate any later alterations or changes to the building. Earlier editions of the local building code should be on file with the building official. The code in effect at the time of construction will contain fire performance criteria. While this is no guarantee that the required performance was actually provided, it does give the investigator some guidance as to the level of performance which may be expected. Under some code administration and enforcement systems, the code in effect at the time of construction also defines the level of performance that must be provided at the time of rehabilitation.

Figure 1 illustrates one method for organizing preliminary field notes. Space is provided for the materials, dimensions, and condition of the principal building elements. Each floor of the structure should be visited and the appropriate information obtained. In practice, there will often be identical materials and construction on every floor, but the exception may be of vital importance. A schematic diagram should be prepared of each floor showing the layout of exits and hallways and indicating where each element described in the field notes fits into the structure as a whole. The exact arrangement of interior walls within apartments is of secondary importance from a fire safety point of view and need not be shown on the drawings unless these walls are required by code to have a fire resistance rating.

The location of stairways and elevators should be clearly marked on the drawings. All exterior means of escape (e.g., fire escapes) should be identified.*

The following notes explain the entries in Figure 1.

Exterior Bearing Walls: Many old buildings utilize heavily constructed walls to support the floor/ceiling assemblies at the exterior of the building. There may be columns and/or interior bearing walls within the structure, but the exterior walls are an important factor in assessing the fire safety of a building.

The field investigator should note how the floor/ceiling assemblies are supported at the exterior of the building. If columns are incorporated in the exterior walls, the walls may be considered non-bearing.

Interior Bearing Walls: It may be difficult to determine whether or not an interior wall is load bearing, but the field investigator should attempt to make this determination. At a later stage of the rehabilitation process, this question will need to be determined exactly. Therefore, the field notes should be as accurate as possible.

Exterior Non-Bearing Walls: The fire resistance of the exterior walls is important for two reasons. These walls (both bearing and non-bearing) are depended upon to: a) contain a fire *within* the building of origin; or b) keep an exterior fire *outside* the building. It is therefore important to indicate on the drawings where any openings are located as well as the materials and construction of all doors or shutters. The drawings should indicate the presence of wired glass, its thickness and framing, and identify the materials used for windows and door frames. The protection of openings adjacent to exterior means of escape (e.g., exterior stairs, fire escapes) is particularly important. The ground floor drawing should locate the building on the property and indicate the precise distances to adjacent buildings.

Interior Non-Bearing Walls (Partitions): A partition is a "wall that extends from floor to ceiling and subdivides space within any story of a building." (48) Figure 1 has two categories (A & B) for Interior Non-Bearing Walls (Partitions) which can be used for different walls, such as hallway walls as compared to inter-apartment walls. Under some circumstances there may be only one type of wall construction; in others, three or more types of wall construction may occur.

FIGURE 1   PRELIMINARY EVALUATION FIELD NOTES

Building Element		Materials	Thickness	Condition	Notes
Exterior Bearing Walls					
Interior Bearing Walls					
Exterior Non-Bearing Walls					
Interior Non-Bearing Walls or Partitions:	A				
	B				
Structural Frame: Columns					
Beams					
Other					
Floor/Ceiling Structural System Spanning					
Roofs					
Doors (including frame and hardware): a) Enclosed vertical exitway					
b) Enclosed horizontal exitway					
c) Other					

---

* Problems providing adequate exiting are discussed at length in the *Egress Guideline for Residential Rehabilitation.*

The field investigator should be alert for differences in function as well as in materials and construction details. In general, the details within apartments are not as important as the major exit paths and stairwells. The preliminary field investigation should attempt to determine the thickness of all walls. A term introduced below called "thickness design" will depend on an accurate ($\pm$ $1/4$ inch) determination. Even though this initial field survey is called "preliminary," the data generated should be as accurate and complete as possible.

The field investigator should note the exact location from which observations are recorded. For instance, if a hole is found through a stairwell wall which allows a cataloguing of the construction details, the field investigation notes should reflect the location of the "find." At the preliminary stage it is not necessary to core every wall; the interior details of construction can usually be determined at some location.

Structural Frame: There may or may not be a complete skeletal frame, but usually there are columns, beams, trusses, or other like elements. The dimensions and spacing of the structural elements should be measured and indicated on the drawings. For instance, if there are ten inch square columns located on a thirty foot square grid throughout the building, this should be noted. The structural material and cover or protective materials should be identified wherever possible. The thickness of the cover materials should be determined to an accuracy of $\pm$ $1/4$ inch. As discussed above, the preliminary field survey usually relies on accidental openings in the cover materials rather than a systematic coring technique.

Floor/Ceiling Structural Systems: The span between supports should be measured. If possible, a sketch of the cross-section of the system should be made. If there is no location where accidental damage has opened the floor/ceiling construction to visual inspection, it is necessary to make such an opening. An evaluation of the fire resistance of a floor/ceiling assembly requires detailed knowledge of the materials and their arrangement. Special attention should be paid to the cover on structural steel elements and the condition of suspended ceilings and similar membranes.

Roofs: The preliminary field survey of the roof system is initially concerned with water-tightness. However, once it is apparent that the roof is sound for ordinary use and can be retained in the rehabilitated building, it becomes necessary to evaluate the fire performance. The field investigator must measure the thickness and identify the types of materials which have been used. Be aware that there may be several layers of roof materials.

Doors: Doors to stairways and hallways represent some of the most important fire elements to be considered within a building. The uses of the spaces separated largely controls the level of fire performance necessary. Walls and doors enclosing stairs or elevator shafts would normally require a higher level of performance than between a the bedroom and bath. The various uses are differentiated in Figure 1.

Careful measurements of the thickness of door panels must be made, and the type of core material within each door must be determined. It should be noted whether doors have self-closing devices; the general operation of the doors should be checked. The latch should engage and the door should fit tightly in the frame. The hinges should be in good condition. If glass is used in the doors, it should be identified as either plain glass or wired glass mounted in either a wood or steel frame.

Materials: The field investigator should be able to identify ordinary building materials. In situations where an unfamiliar material is found, a sample should be obtained. This sample should measure at least 10 cubic inches so that an ASTM E-136 fire test can be conducted to determine if it is combustible.

Thickness: The thickness of all materials should be measured accurately since, under certain circumstances, the level of fire resistance is very sensitive to the material thickness.

Condition: The method of attaching the various layers and facings to one another or to the supporting structural element should be noted under the appropriate building element. The "secureness" of the attachmnent and the general condition of the layers and facings should be noted here.

Notes: The "Notes" column can be used for many purposes, but it might be a good idea to make specific references to other field notes or drawings.

After the building survey is completed, the data collected must be analyzed. A suggested work sheet for organizing this information is given below as Figure 2.

The required fire resistance and flame spread for each building element are normally established by the local building or rehabilitation code. The fire performance of the existing materials and assemblies should then be estimated, using one of the techniques described below. If the fire performance of the existing building element(s) is equal to or greater than that required, the materials and assemblies may remain. If the fire performance is less than required, then corrective measures must be taken.

The most common methods of upgrading the level of protection are to either remove and replace the existing building element(s) or to repair and upgrade the existing materials and assemblies. Other fire protection measures, such as automatic sprinklers or detection and alarm systems, also could be considered, though they are beyond the scope of this guideline. If the upgraded protection is still less than that required or deemed to be acceptable, additional corrective measures must be taken. This process must continue until an acceptable level of performance is obtained.

FIGURE 2   **PRELIMINARY EVALUATION WORKSHEET**

Building Element		Required Fire Resistance	Required Flame Spread	Estimated Fire Resistance	Estimated Flame Spread	Method of Upgrading	Estimated Upgraded Protection	Notes
Exterior Bearing Walls								
Interior Bearing Walls								
Exterior Non-Bearing Walls								
Interior Non-Bearing Walls or Partitions	A							
	B							
Structural Frame: Columns								
Beams								
Other								
Floor/Ceiling Structural System Spanning								
Roofs								
Doors (including frame and hardware): a) Enclosed vertical exitway								
b) Enclosed horizontal exitway								
c) Others								

2.2 FIRE RESISTANCE OF EXISTING BUILDING ELEMENTS

The fire resistance of the existing building elements can be estimated from the tables and histograms contained in the Appendix. The Appendix is organized first by type of building element: walls, columns, floor/ceiling assemblies, beams, and doors. Within each building element, the tables are organized by type of construction (e.g., masonry, metal, wood frame), and then further divided by minimum dimensions or thickness of the building element.

A histogram precedes every table that has 10 or more entries. The X-axis measures fire resistance in hours; the Y-axis shows the number of entries in that table having a given level of fire resistance. The histograms also contain the location of each entry within that table for easy cross-referencing.

The histograms, because they are keyed to the tables, can speed the preliminary investigation. For example, Table 1.3.2, *Wood Frame Walls 4" to Less Than 6" Thick,* contains 96 entries. Rather than study each table entry, the histogram shows that every wall assembly listed in that table has a fire resistance of less than 2 hours. If the building code required the wall to have 2 hours fire resistance, the designer, with a minimum of effort, is made aware of a problem that requires closer study.

Suppose the code had only required a wall of 1 hour fire resistance. The histogram shows far fewer complying elements (19) than noncomplying ones (77). If the existing assembly is not one of the 19 complying entries, there is a strong possibility the existing assembly is deficient. The histograms can also be used in the converse situation. If the existing assembly is not one of the smaller number of entries with a lower than required fire resistance, there is a strong possibility the existing assembly will be acceptable.

At some point, the existing building component or assembly must be located within the tables. Otherwise, the fire resistance must be determined through one of the other techniques presented in the guideline. Locating the building component in the Appendix Tables not only guarantees the accuracy of the fire resistance rating, but also provides a source of documentation for the building official.

2.3 EFFECTS OF PENETRATIONS IN FIRE RESISTANT ASSEMBLIES

There are often many features in existing walls or floor/ceiling assemblies which were not included in the original certification or fire testing. The most common examples are pipes and utility wires passed through holes poked through an assembly. During the life of the building, many penetrations are added, and by the time a building is ready for rehabilitation it is not sufficient to just consider the fire resistance of the assembly as originally constructed. It is necessary to consider all penetrations and their relative impact upon fire performance. For instance, the fire resistance of the corridor wall may be less important than the effect of plain glass doors or transoms. In fact, doors are the most important single class of penetrations.

A fully developed fire generates substantial quantities of heat and excess gaseous fuel capable of penetrating any holes which might be present in the walls or ceiling of the fire compartment. In general, this leads to a severe degradation of the fire resistance of those building elements and to a greater potential for fire spread. This is particularly applicable to penetrations located high in a compartment where the positive pressure of the fire can force the unburned gases through the penetration.

Penetrations in a floor/ceiling assembly will generally completely negate the barrier qualities of the assembly and will lead to rapid spread of fire to the space above. It will not be a problem, however, if the penetrations are filled with noncombustible materials strongly fastened to the structure. The upper half of walls are similar to the floor/ceiling assembly in that a positive pressure can reasonably be expected in the top of the room, and this will push hot and/or burning gases through the penetration unless it is completely sealed.

Building codes require doors installed in fire resistive walls to resist the passage of fire for a specified period of time. If the door to a fully involved room is not closed, a large plume of fire will typically escape through the doorway, preventing anyone from using the space outside the door while allowing the fire to spread. This is why door closers are so important. Glass in doors and transoms can be expected to rapidly shatter unless constructed of listed or approved wire glass in a steel frame. As with other building elements, penetrations or non-rated portions of doors and transoms must be upgraded or otherwise protected.

Table 5.1 in Section V of the Appendix contains 41 entries of doors mounted in sound tightfitting frames. Part 3.4 below outlines one procedure for evaluating and possibly upgrading existing doors.

3
FINAL EVALUATION AND DESIGN SOLUTION

The final evaluation begins after the rehabilitation project has reached the final design stage and the choices made to keep certain archaic materials and assemblies in the rehabilitated building. The final evaluation process is essentially a more refined and detailed version of the preliminary evaluation. The specific fire resistance and flame spread requirements are determined for the project. This may involve local building and fire officials reviewing the preliminary evaluation as depicted in Figures 1 and 2 and the field drawings and notes. When necessary, provisions must be made to upgrade existing building elements to provide the required level of fire performance.

There are several approaches to design solutions that can make possible the continued use of archaic materials and assemblies in the rehabilitated structure. The simplest case occurs when the materials and assembly in question are found within the Appendix Tables and the fire performance properties satisfy code requirements. Other approaches must be used, though, if the assembly cannot be found within the Appendix or the fire performance

needs to be upgraded. These approaches have been grouped into two classes: experimental and theoretical.

3.1
THE EXPERIMENTAL APPROACH

If a material or assembly found in a building is not listed in the Appendix Tables, there are several other ways to evaluate fire performance. One approach is to conduct the appropriate fire test(s) and thereby determine the fire-related properties directly. There are a number of laboratories in the United States which routinely conduct the various fire tests. A current list can be obtained by writing the Center for Fire Research, National Bureau of Standards, Washington, D.C. 20234.

The contract with any of these testing laboratories should require their observation of specimen preparation as well as the testing of the specimen. A complete description of where and how the specimen was obtained from the building, the transportation of the specimen, and its preparation for testing should be noted in detail so that the building official can be satisfied that the fire test is representative of the actual use.

The test report should describe the fire test procedure and the response of the material or assembly. The laboratory usually submits a cover letter with the report to describe the provisions of the fire test that were satisfied by the material or assembly under investigation. A building official will generally require this cover letter, but will also read the report to confirm that the material or assembly complies with the code requirements. Local code officials should be involved in all phases of the testing process.

The experimental approach can be costly and time consuming because specimens must be taken from the building and transported to the testing laboratory. When a load bearing assembly has continuous reinforcement, the test specimen must be removed from the building, transported, and tested in one piece. However, when the fire performance cannot be determined by other means, there may be no alternative to a full-scale test.

A "non-standard" small-scale test can be used in special cases. Sample sizes need only be 10-25 square feet, while full-scale tests require test samples of either 100 or 180 square feet in size. This small-scale test is best suited for testing non-load bearing assemblies against thermal transmission only.

3.2
THE THEORETICAL APPROACH

There will be instances when materials and assemblies in a building undergoing rehabilitation cannot be found in the Appendix Tables. Even where test results are available for more or less similar construction, the proper classification may not be immediately apparent. Variations in dimensions, loading conditions, materials, or workmanship may markedly affect the performance of the individual building elements, and the extent of such a possible effect cannot be evaluated from the tables.

Theoretical methods being developed offer an alternative to the full-scale fire tests discussed above. For example, Section 4302(b) of the 1979 edition of the *Uniform Building Code* specifically allows an engineering design for fire resistance in lieu of conducting full-scale tests. These techniques draw upon computer simulation and mathematical modeling, thermodynamics, heat-flow analysis, and materials science to predict the fire performance of building materials and assemblies.

One theoretical method, known as the "Ten Rules of Fire Endurance Ratings," was published by T. Z. Harmathy in the May,

1965 edition of *Fire Technology*. (35) Harmathy's Rules provide a foundation for extending the data within the Appendix Tables to analyze or upgrade current as well as archaic building materials or assemblies.

HARMATHY'S TEN RULES

Rule 1: The "thermal"* fire endurance of a construction consisting of a number of parallel layers is greater than the sum of the "thermal" fire endurances characteristic of the individual layers when exposed separately to fire.

The minimum performance of an untested assembly can be estimated if the fire endurance of the individual components is known. Though the exact rating of the assembly cannot be stated, the endurance of the assembly is greater than the sum of the endurance of the components.

When a building assembly or component is found to be deficient, the fire endurance can be upgraded by providing a protective membrane. This membrane could be a new layer of brick, plaster, or drywall. The fire endurance of this membrane is called the "finish rating." Appendix Tables 1.5.1 and 1.5.2 contain the finish ratings for the most commonly employed materials. (See also the notes to Rule 2).

The test criteria for the finish rating is the same as for the thermal fire endurance of the total assembly: average temperature increases of 250°F above ambient or 325°F above ambient at any one place with the membrane being exposed to the fire. The temperature is measured at the interface of the assembly and the protective membrane.

Rule 2: The fire endurance of a construction does not decrease with the addition of further layers.

Harmathy notes that this rule is a consequence of the previous rule. Its validity follows from the fact that the additional layers increase both the resistance to heat flow and the heat capacity of the construction. This, in turn, reduces the rate of temperature rise at the unexposed surface.

This rule is not just restricted to "thermal" performance but affects the other fire test criteria: direct flame passage, cotton waste ignition, and load bearing performance. This means that certain restrictions must be imposed on the materials to be added and on the loading conditions. One restriction is that a new layer, if applied to the exposed surface, must not produce additional thermal stresses in the construction, i.e., its thermal expansion characteristics must be similar to those of the adjacent layer. Each new layer must also be capable of contributing enough additional strength to the assembly to sustain the added dead load. If this requirement is not fulfilled, the allowable live load must be reduced by an amount equal to the weight of the new layer. Because of these limitations, this rule should not be applied without careful consideration.

Particular care must be taken if the material added is a good thermal insulator. Properly located, the added insulation could improve the "thermal" performance of the assembly. Improperly located, the insulation could block necessary thermal transmission through the assembly, thereby subjecting the structural elements to greater temperatures for longer periods of time, and could cause premature structural failure of the supporting members.

Rule 3: The fire endurance of constructions containing continuous air gaps or cavities is greater than the fire endurance of similar constructions of the same weight, but containing no air gaps or cavities.

By providing for voids in a construction, additional resistances are produced in the path of heat flow. Numerical heat flow analyses indicate that a 10 to 15 percent increase in fire endurance can be achieved by creating an air gap at the midplane of a brick wall. Since the gross volume is also increased by the presence of voids, the air gaps and cavities have a beneficial effect on stability as well. However, constructions containing combustible materials within an air gap may be regarded as exceptions to this rule because of the possible development of burning in the gap.

There are numerous examples of this rule in the tables. For instance:

Table 1.1.4; Item W-8-M-82: Cored concrete masonry, nominal 8 inch thick wall with one unit in wall thickness and with 62% minimum of solid material in each unit, load bearing (80 PSI). Fire endurance: $2^1/_2$ hours.

Table 1.1.5; Item W-10-M-11: Cored concrete mansonry, nominal 10 inch thick wall with two units in wall thickness and a 2 inch air space, load bearing (80 PSI). The units are essentially the same as item W-8-M-82. Fire endurance: $3^1/_2$ hours.

These walls show 1 hour greater fire endurance by the addition of the 2 inch air space.

Rule 4: The farther an air gap or cavity is located from the exposed surface, the more beneficial is its effect on the fire endurance.

Radiation dominates the heat transfer across an air gap or cavity, and it is markedly higher where the temperature is higher. The air gap or cavity is thus a poor insulator if it is located in a region which attains high temperatures during fire exposure.

Some of the clay tile designs take advantage of these factors. The double cell design, for instance, ensures that there is a cavity near the unexposed face. Some floor/ceiling assemblies have air gaps or cavities near the top surface and these enhance their thermal performance.

Rule 5: The fire endurance of a construction cannot be increased by increasing the thickness of a completely enclosed air layer.

Harmathy notes that there is evidence that if the thickness of the air layer is larger than about $1/_2$ inch, the heat transfer through the air layer depends only on the temperature of the bounding surfaces, and is practically independent of the distance between them. This rule is not applicable if the air layer is not completely enclosed, i.e., if there is a possibility of fresh air entering the gap at an appreciable rate.

Rule 6: Layers of materials of low thermal conductivity are better utilized on that side of the construction on which fire is more likely to happen.

As in Rule 4, the reason lies in the heat transfer process, though the conductivity of the solid is much less dependent on the ambient temperature of the materials. The low thermal conductor creates a substantial temperature differential to be established across its thickness under transient heat flow conditions. This rule may not be applicable to materials undergoing physico-chemical changes accompanied by significant heat absorption or heat evolution.

---

* The "thermal" fire endurance is the time at which the average temperature on the unexposed side of a construction exceeds its initial value by 250° when the other side is exposed to the "standard" fire specified by ASTM Test Method E-19.

Rule 7: The fire endurance of asymmetrical constructions depends on the direction of heat flow.

This rule is a consequence of Rules 4 and 6 as well as other factors. This rule is useful in determining the relative protection of corridors and stairwells from the surrounding spaces. In addition, there are often situations where a fire is more likely, or potentially more severe, from one side or the other.

Rule 8: The presence of moisture, if it does not result in explosive spalling, increases the fire endurance.

The flow of heat into an assembly is greatly hindered by the release and evaporation of the moisture found within cementitious materials such as gypsum, portland cement, or magnesium oxychloride. Harmathy has shown that the gain in fire endurance may be as high as 8 percent for each percent (by volume) of moisture in the construction. It is the moisture chemically bound within the construction material at the time of manufacture or processing that leads to increased fire endurance. There is no direct relationship between the relative humidity of the air in the pores of the material and the increase in fire endurance.

Under certain conditions there may be explosive spalling of low permeability cementitious materials such as dense concrete. In general, one can assume that extremely old concrete has developed enough minor cracking that this factor should not be significant.

Rule 9: Load-supporting elements, such as beams, girders and joists, yield higher fire endurances when subjected to fire endurance tests as parts of floor, roof, or ceiling assemblies than they would when tested separately.

One of the fire endurance test criteria is the ability of a load-supporting element to carry its design load. The element will be deemed to have failed when the load can no longer be supported.

Failure usually results for two reasons. Some materials, particularly steel and other metals, lose much of their structural strength at elevated temperatures. Physical deflection of the supporting element, due to decreased strength or thermal expansion, causes a redistribution of the load forces and stresses throughout the element. Structural failure often results because the supporting element is not designed to carry the redistributed load.

Roof, floor, and ceiling assemblies have primary (e.g., beams) and secondary (e.g., floor joists) structural members. Since the primary load-supporting elements span the largest distances, their deflection becomes significant at a stage when the strength of the secondary members (including the roof or floor surface) is hardly affected by the heat. As the secondary members follow the deflection of the primary load-supporting element, an increasingly larger portion of the load is transferred to the secondary members.

When load-supporting elements are tested separately, the imposed load is constant and equal to the design load throughout the test. By definition, no distribution of the load is possible because the element is being tested by itself. Without any other structural members to which the load could be transferred, the individual elements cannot yield a higher fire endurance than they do when tested as parts of a floor, roof or ceiling assembly.

Rule 10: The load-supporting elements (beams, girders, joists, etc.) of a floor, roof, or ceiling assembly can be replaced by such other load-supporting elements which, when tested separately, yielded fire endurances not less than that of the assembly.

This rule depends on Rule 9 for its validity. A beam or girder, if capable of yielding a certain performance when tested separately, will yield an equally good or better performance when it forms a part of a floor, roof, or ceiling assembly. It must be emphasized that the supporting element of one assembly must not be replaced by the supporting element of another assembly if the performance of this latter element is not known from a separate (beam) test. Because of the load-reducing effect of the secondary elements that results from a test performed on an assembly, the performance of the supporting element alone cannot be evaluated by simple arithmetic. This rule also indicates the advantage of performing separate fire tests on primary load-supporting elements.

ILLUSTRATION OF HARMATHY'S RULES

Harmathy provided one schematic figure which illustrated his Rules.* It should be useful as a quick reference to assist in applying his Rules.

---

* Reproduced from the May 1965 *Fire Technology* (Vol. 1, No. 2). Copyright National Fire Protection Association, Boston. Reproduced by permission.

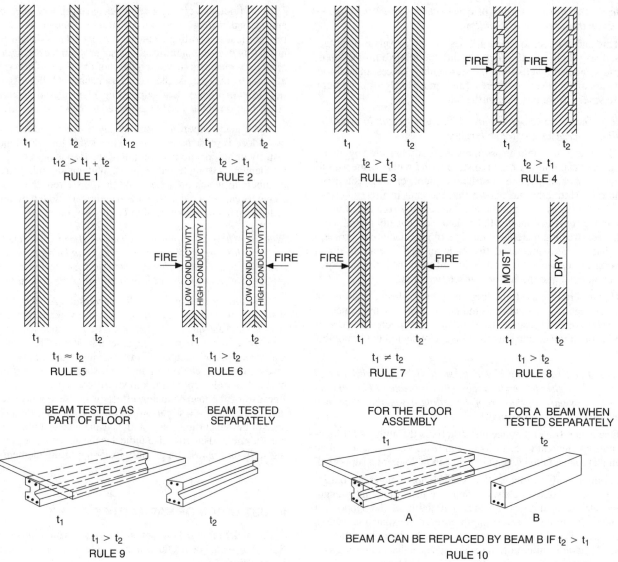

Diagrammatic illustration of ten rules.

t = fire endurance

EXAMPLE APPLICATION OF HARMATHY'S RULES

The following examples, based in whole or in part upon those presented in Harmathy's paper (35), show how the Rules can be applied to practical cases.

Example 1

Problem

A contractor would like to keep a partition which consists of a $3\frac{3}{4}$ inch thick layer of red clay brick, a $1\frac{1}{4}$ inch thick layer of plywood, and a $\frac{3}{8}$ inch thick layer of gypsum wallboard, at a location where 2 hour fire endurance is required. Is this assembly capable of providing a 2 hour protection?

Solution

(1) This partition does not appear in the Appendix Tables.

(2) Bricks of this thickness yield fire endurances of approximately 75 minutes (Table 1.1.2, Item W-4-M-2).

(3) The $1\frac{1}{4}$ inch thick plywood has a finish rating of 30 minutes.

(4) The $\frac{3}{8}$ inch gypsum wallboard has a finish rating of 10 minutes.

(5) Using the recommended values from the tables and applying Rule 1, the fire endurance (FI) of the assembly is larger than the sum of the individual layers, or

$$FI > 75 + 30 + 10 = 115 \text{ minutes}$$

Discussion

This example illustrates how the Appendix Tables can be utilized to determine the fire resistance of assemblies not explicitly listed.

Example 2

Problem

(1) A number of buildings to be rehabilitated have the same type of roof slab which is supported with different structural elements.

(2) The designer and contractor would like to determine whether or not this roof slab is capable of yielding a 2 hour fire endurance. According to a rigorous interpretation of ASTM E-119, however, only the roof assembly, including the roof slab as well as the cover

and the supporting elements, can be subjected to a fire test. Therefore, a fire endurance classification cannot be issued for the slabs separately.

(3) The designer and contractor believe this slab will yield a 2 hour fire endurance even without the cover, and any beam of at least 2 hour fire endurance will provide satisfactory support. Is it possible to obtain a classification for the slab separately?

Solution

(1) The answer to the question is yes.

(2) According to Rule 10 it is not contrary to common sense to test and classify roofs and supporting elements separately. Furthermore, according to Rule 2, if the roof slabs actually yield a 2 hour fire endurance, the endurance of an assembly, including the slabs, cannot be less than 2 hours.

(3) The recommended procedure would be to review the tables to see if the slab appears as part of any tested roof or floor/ceiling assembly. The supporting system can be regarded as separate from the slab specimen, and the fire endurance of the assembly listed in the table is at least the fire endurance of the slab. There would have to be an adjustment for the weight of the roof cover in the allowable load if the test specimen did not contain a cover.

(4) The supporting structure or element would have to have at least a 2 hour fire endurance when tested separately.

Discussion

If the tables did not include tests on assemblies which contained the slab, one procedure would be to assemble the roof slabs on any convenient supporting system (not regarded as part of the specimen) and to subject them to a load which, besides the usually required superimposed load, includes some allowances for the weight of the cover.

Example 3

Problem

A steel-joisted floor and ceiling assembly is known to have yielded a fire endurance of 1 hour and 35 minutes. At a certain location, a 2 hour endurance is required. What is the most economical way of increasing the fire endurance by at least 25 minutes?

Solution

(1) The most effective technique would be to increase the ceiling plaster thickness. Existing coats of paint would have to be removed and the surface properly prepared before the new plaster could be applied. Other materials (e.g., gypsum wallboard) could also be considered.

(2) There may be other techniques based on other principles, but an examination of the drawings would be necessary.

Discussion

(1) The additional plaster has at least three effects:

   a) The layer of plaster is increased and thus there is a gain of fire endurance (Rule 1).

   b) There is a gain due to shifting the air gap farther from the exposed surface (Rule 4).

   c) There is more moisture in the path of heat flow to the structural elements (Rules 7 and 8).

(2) The increase in fire endurance would be at least as large as that of the finish rating for the added thickness of plaster. The combined effects in (1) above would further increase this by a factor of 2 or more, depending upon the geometry of the assembly.

Example 4

Problem

The fire endurance of item W-l0-M-l in Table 1.1.5 is 4 hours. This wall consists of two $3^3/_4$ inch thick layers of structural tiles separated by a 2 inch air gap and $^3/_4$ inch portland cement plaster or stucco on both sides. If the actual wall in the building is identical to item W-10-M-1 except that it has a 4 inch air gap, can the fire endurance be estimated at 5 hours?

Solution

The answer to the question is no for the reasons contained in Rule 5.

Example 5

Problem

In order to increase the insulating value of its precast roof slabs, a company has decided to use two layers of different concretes. The lower layer of the slabs, where the strength of the concrete is immaterial (all the tensile load is carried by the steel reinforcement), would be made with a concrete of low strength but good insulating value. The upper layer, where the concrete is supposed to carry the compressive load, would remain the original high strength, high thermal conductivity concrete. How will the fire endurance of the slabs be affected by the change?

Solution

The effect on the thermal fire endurance is beneficial:

(1) The total resistance to heat flow of the new slabs has been increased due to the replacement of a layer of high thermal conductivity by one of low conductivity.

(2) The layer of low conductivity is on the side more likely to be exposed to fire, where it is more effectively utilized according to Rule 6. The layer of low thermal conductivity also provides better protection for the steel reinforcement, thereby extending the time before reaching the temperature at which the creep of steel becomes significant.

3.3
"THICKNESS DESIGN" STRATEGY

The "thickness design" strategy is based upon Harmathy's Rules 1 and 2. This design approach can be used when the construction materials have been identified and measured, but the specific assembly cannot be located within the tables. The tables should be surveyed again for thinner walls of like material and construction detail that have yielded the desired or greater fire endurance. If such an assembly can be found, then the thicker walls in the building have more than enough fire resistance. The thickness of the walls thus becomes the principal concern.

This approach can also be used for floor/ceiling assemblies, except that the thickness of the cover* and the slab become the central concern. The fire resistance of the untested assembly will be at least the fire resistance of an assembly listed in the table having a similar design but with less cover and/or thinner slabs. For other structural elements (e.g., beams and columns), the element listed in the table must also be of a similar design but with less cover thickness.

3.4
EVALUATION OF DOORS

A separate section on doors has been included because the process for evaluation presented below differs from those suggested previously for other building elements. The impact of unprotected openings or penetrations in fire resistant assemblies has been detailed in Part 2.3 above. It is sufficient to note here that openings left unprotected will likely lead to failure of the barrier under actual fire conditions.

For other types of building elements (e.g., beams, columns), the Appendix Tables can be used to establish a minimum level of fire performance. The benefit to rehabilitation is that the need for a full-scale fire test is then eliminated. For doors, however, this cannot be done. The data contained in Appendix Table 5.1, *Resistance of Doors to Fire Exposure*, can only provide guidance as to whether a successful fire test is even feasible.

For example, a door required to have 1 hour fire resistance is noted in the tables as providing only 5 minutes. The likelihood of achieving the required 1 hour, even if the door is upgraded, is remote. The ultimate need for replacement of the doors is reasonably clear, and the expense and time needed for testing can be saved. However, if the performance documented in the table is near or in excess of what is being required, then a fire test should be conducted. The test documentation can then be used as evidence of compliance with the required level of performance.

The table entries cannot be used as the sole proof of performance of the door in question because there are too many unknown variables which could measurably affect fire performance. The wood may have dried over the years; coats of flammable varnish could have been added. Minor deviations in the internal construction of a door can result in significant differences in performance. Methods of securing inserts in panel doors can vary. The major non-destructive method of analysis, an x-ray, often cannot provide the necessary detail. It is for these, and similar reasons, that a fire test is still felt to be necessary.

It is often possible to upgrade the fire performance of an existing door. Sometimes, "as is" and modified doors are evaluated in a single series of tests when failure of the unmodified door is expected. Because doors upgraded after an initial failure must be tested again, there is a potential savings of time and money.

The most common problems encountered are plain glass, panel inserts of insufficient thickness, and improper fit of a door in its frame. The latter problem can be significant because a fire can develop a substantial positive pressure, and the fire will work its way through otherwise innocent-looking gaps between door and frame.

One approach to solving these problems is as follows. The plain glass is replaced with approved or listed wire glass in a steel frame. The panel inserts can be upgraded by adding an additional layer of material. Gypsum wallboard is often used for this purpose. Intumescent paint applied to the edges of the door and frame will expand when exposed to fire, forming an effective seal around the edges. This seal, coupled with the generally even thermal expansion of a wood door in a wood frame, can prevent the passage of flames and other fire gases. Figure 3 below illustrates these solutions.

Because the interior construction of a door cannot be determined by a visual inspection, there is no absolute guarantee that the remaining doors are identical to the one(s) removed from the building and tested. But the same is true for doors constructed today, and reason and judgment must be applied. Doors that appear identical upon visual inspection can be weighed. If the weights are reasonably close, the doors can be assumed to be identical and therefore provide the same level of fire performance. Another approach is to fire test more than one door or to dismantle doors selected at random to see if they had been constructed in the same manner. Original building plans showing door details or other records showing that doors were purchased at one time or obtained from a single supplier can also be evidence of similar construction.

More often though, it is what is visible to the eye that is most significant. The investigator should carefully check the condition and fit of the door and frame, and for frames out of plumb or separating from the wall. Door closers, latches, and hinges must be examined to see that they function properly and are tightly secured. If these are in order and the door and frame have passed a full-scale test, there can be a reasonable basis for allowing the existing doors to remain.

---

* Cover: the protective layer or membrane of material which slows the flow of heat to the structural elements.

FIGURE 3   **MODIFICATION DETAILS**

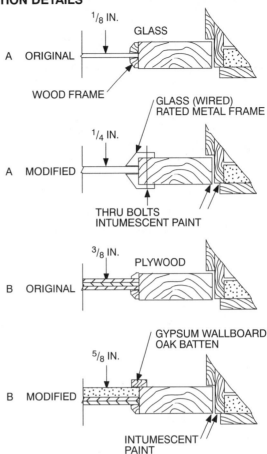

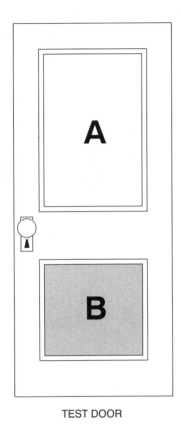

TEST DOOR

4
SUMMARY

This section summarizes the various approaches and design solutions discussed in the preceding sections of the guideline. The term "structural system" includes: frames, beams, columns, and other structural elements. "Cover" is a protective layer(s) of materials or membrane which slows the flow of heat to the structural elements. It cannot be stressed too strongly that the fire endurance of actual building elements can be greatly reduced or totally negated by removing part of the cover to allow pipes, ducts, or conduits to pass through the element. This must be repaired in the rehabilitation process.

The following approaches shall be considered equivalent.

4.1 The fire resistance of a building element can be established from the Appendix Tables. This is subject to the following limitations:

- The building element in the rehabilitated building shall be constructed of the same materials with the same nominal dimensions as stated in the tables.

- All penetrations in the building element or its cover for services such as electricity, plumbing, and HVAC shall be packed with noncombustible cementitious materials and so fixed that the packing material will not fall out when it loses its water of hydration.

The effects of age and wear and tear shall be repaired so that the building element is sound and the original thickness of all components, particularly covers and floor slabs, is maintained.

This approach essentially follows the approach taken by model building codes. The assembly must appear in a table either published in or accepted by the code for a given fire resistance rating to be recognized and accepted.

4.2 The fire resistance of a building element which does not explicitly appear in the Appendix Tables can be established if one or more elements of same design but different dimensions have been listed in the tables. For walls, the existing element must be thicker than the one listed. For floor/ceiling assemblies, the assembly listed in the table must have the same or less cover and the same or thinner slab constructed of the same material as the actual floor/ceiling assembly. For other structural elements, the element listed in the table must be of a similar design but with less cover thickness. The fire resistance in all instances shall be the fire resistance recommended in the table. This is subject to the following limitations:

- The actual element in the rehabilitated building shall be constructed of the same materials as listed in the table. Only the following dimensions may vary from those specified: for walls, the overall thickness must exceed that specified in the table; for floor/ceiling assemblies, the thickness of the cover and the slab must be greater than, or equal to, that specified in the table; for other structural elements, the thickness of the cover must be greater than that specified in the table.

- All penetrations in the building element or its cover for services such as electricity, plumbing, or HVAC shall be packed with noncombustible cementitious materials and so fixed that the packing material will not fall out when it loses its water of hydration.

- The effects of age and wear and tear shall be repaired so that the building element is sound and the original thickness of all components, particularly covers and floor slabs, is maintained.

This approach is an application of the "thickness design" concept presented in Part 3.3 of the guideline. There should be many instances when a thicker building element was utilized than the one listed in the Appendix Tables. This guideline recognizes the inherent superiority of a thicker design. Note: "thickness design" for floor/ceiling assemblies and structural elements refers to cover and slab thickness rather than total thickness.

The "thickness design" concept is essentially a special case of Harmathy's Rules (specifically Rules 1 and 2). It should be recognized that the only source of data is the Appendix Tables. If other data are used, it must be in connection with the approach below.

4.3 The fire resistance of building elements can be established by applying Harmathy's Ten Rules of Fire Resistance Ratings as set forth in Part 3.2 of the guideline. This is subject to the following limitations:

- The data from the tables can be utilized subject to the limitations in 4.2 above.
- Test reports from recognized journals or published papers can be used to support data utilized in applying Harmathy's Rules.
- Calculations utilizing recognized and well established computational techniques can be used in applying Harmathy's Rules. These include, but are not limited to, analysis of heat flow, mechanical properties, deflections, and load bearing capacity.

APPENDIX

TABLE OF CONTENTS

INTRODUCTION

The tables and histograms which follow are to be used only within the analytical framework detailed in the main body of this guideline.

Histograms precede any table with 10 or more entries. The use and interpretation of these histograms is explained in Part 2 of the guideline. The tables are in a format similar to that found in the model building codes. The following example, taken from an entry in Table 1.1.2, best explains the table format.

ITEM CODE	THICKNESS	CONSTRUCTION DETAILS	PERFORMANCE		REFERENCE NUMBER			NOTES	REC. HOURS
			LOAD	TIME	PRE-BMS-92	BMS-92	POST-BMS-92		
W-4-M-50	$4^5/_8''$	Core: structural clay tile, See notes 12, 16, 21; Facings on unexposed side only, see note 18	n/a	25 min.		1		3, 4, 24	$^1/_3$

1. Item Code: The item code consists of a four place series in the general form w-x-y-z in which each member of the series denotes the following:

   w = Type of building element (e.g., W=Walls; F=Floors, etc.)

   x = The building element thickness rounded down to the nearest one inch increment (e.g., $4^5/_8''$ is rounded off to 4″)

   y = The general type of material from which the building element is constructed (e.g., M=Masonry; W=Wood, etc.)

   z = The item number of the particular building element in a given table

   The item code shown in the example W-4-M-50 denotes the following:

   W = Wall, as the building element

   4 = Wall thickness in the range of 4″ to less than 5″

   M = Masonry construction

   50 = The 50th entry in Table 1.1.2

2. The specific name or heading of this column identifies the dimensions which, if varied, has the greatest impact on fire resistance. The critical dimension for walls, the example here, is thickness. It is different for other building elements (e.g., depth for beams; membrane thickness for some floor/ceiling assemblies). The table entry is the named dimension of the building element measured at the time of actual testing to within ± $^1/_8$ inch tolerance. The thickness tabulated includes facings where facings are a part of the wall construction.

3. Construction Details: The construction details provide a brief description of the manner in which the building element was constructed.

4. Performance: This heading is subdivided into two columns. The column labeled "Load" will either list the load that the building element was subjected to during the fire test or it will contain a note number which will list the load and any other significant details. If the building element was not subjected to a load during the test, this column will contain "n/a," which means "not applicable."

   The second column under performance is labeled "Time" and denotes the actual fire endurance time observed in the fire test.

5. Reference Number: This heading is subdivided into three columns: Pre-BMS-92; BMS-92; and Post-BMS-92. The table entry under this column is the number in the Bibliography of the original source reference for the test data.

6. Notes: Notes are provided at the end of each table to allow a more detailed explanation of certain aspects of the test. In certain tables the notes given to this column have also been listed under the "Construction Details" and/or "Load" columns.

7. Rec Hours: This column lists the recommended fire endurance rating, in hours, of a building element. In some cases, the recommended fire endurance will be less than that listed under the "Time" column. In no case is the "Rec Hours" greater than given in the "Time" column.

SECTION I – WALLS

FIGURE 1.1.1—WALLS—MASONRY
0″ TO LESS THAN 4″ THICK

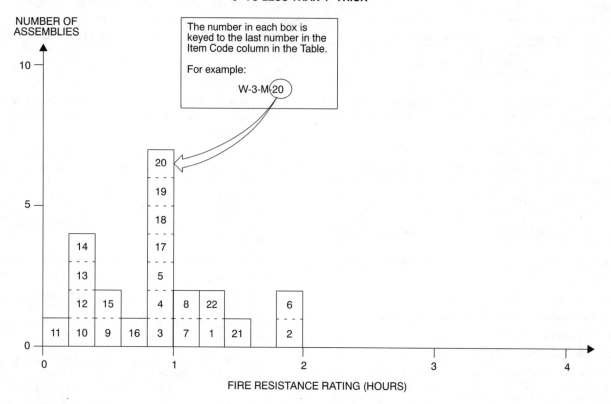

TABLE 1.1.1—MASONRY WALLS
0″ TO LESS THAN 4″ THICK

ITEM CODE	THICKNESS	CONSTRUCTION DETAILS	PERFORMANCE		REFERENCE NUMBER			NOTES	REC. HOURS
			LOAD	TIME	PRE-BMS-92	BMS-92	POST-BMS-92		
W-2-M-1	$2^1/_4''$	Solid partition; $^3/_4''$ gypsum plank - 10′ × 1′6″; $^3/_4''$ plus gypsum plaster each side.	N/A	1 hr. 22 min.			7	1	$1^1/_4$
W-3-M-2	3″	Concrete block (18″ × 9″ × 3″) of fuel ash, portland cement and plasticizer; cement/sand mortar.	N/A	2 hr.			7	2, 3	2
W-2-M-3	2″	Solid gypsum block wall; No facings.	N/A	1 hr.		1		4	1
W-3-M-4	3″	Solid gypsum blocks, laid in 1:3 sanded gypsum mortar.	N/A	1 hr.		1		4	1
W-3-M-5	3″	Magnesium oxysulfate wood fiber blocks; 2″ thick; laid in portland cement-lime mortar; Facings: $^1/_2''$ of 1:3 sanded gypsum plaster on both sides.	N/A	1 hr.		1		4	1
W-3-M-6	3″	Magnesium oxysulfate bound wood fiber blocks; 3″ thick; laid in portland cement-lime mortar; Facings: $^1/_2''$ of 1:3 sanded gypsum plaster on both sides.	N/A	2 hr.		1		4	2
W-3-M-7	3″	Clay tile; Ohio fire clay; single cell thick; Face plaster: $^5/_8''$ (both sides) 1:3 sanded gypsum; Design "E," Construction "A."	N/A	1 hr. 6 min.	0.		2	5, 6, 7, 11, 12, 39	1
W-3-M-8	3″	Clay tile; Illinois surface clay; single cell thick; Face plaster: $^5/_8''$ (both sides) 1:3 sanded gypsum; Design "A," Construction "E."	N/A	1 hr. 1 min.			2	5, 8, 9, 11, 12, 39	1

(Continued)

TABLE 1.1.1—MASONRY WALLS
0″ TO LESS THAN 4″ THICK—(Continued)

ITEM CODE	THICKNESS	CONSTRUCTION DETAILS	PERFORMANCE		REFERENCE NUMBER			NOTES	REC. HOURS
			LOAD	TIME	PRE-BMS-92	BMS-92	POST-BMS-92		
W-3-M-9	3″	Clay tile; Illinois surface clay; single cell thick; No face plaster; Design "A," Construction "C."	N/A	25 min.			2	5, 10, 11, 12, 39	$^1/_3$
W-3-M-10	$3^7/_8″$	8″ × $4^7/_8″$ glass blocks; weight 4 lbs. each; portland cement-lime mortar; horizontal mortar joints reinforced with metal lath.	N/A	15 min.		1		4	$^1/_4$
W-3-M-11	3″	Core: structural clay tile; see Notes 14, 18, 13; No facings.	N/A	10 min.		1		5, 11, 26	$^1/_6$
W-3-M-12	3″	Core: structural clay tile; see Notes 14, 19, 23; No facings.	N/A	20 min.		1		5, 11, 26	$^1/_3$
W-3-M-13	$3^5/_8″$	Core: structural clay tile; see Notes 14, 18, 23; Facings: unexposed side; see Note 20.	N/A	20 min.		1		5, 11, 26	$^1/_3$
W-3-M-14	$3^5/_8″$	Core: structural clay tile; see Notes 14, 19, 23; Facings: unexposed side only; see Note 20.	N/A	20 min.		1		5, 11, 26	$^1/_3$
W-3-M-15	$3^5/_8″$	Core: clay structural tile; see Notes 14, 18, 23; Facings: side exposed to fire; see Note 20.	N/A	30 min.		1		5, 11, 26	$^1/_2$
W-3-M-16	$3^5/_8″$	Core: clay structural tile; see Notes 14, 19, 23; Facings: side exposed to fire; see Note 20.	N/A	45 min.		1		5, 11, 26	$^3/_4$
W-2-M-17	2″	2″ thick solid gypsum blocks; see Note 27.	N/A	1 hr.		1		27	1
W-3-M-18	3″	Core: 3″ thick gypsum blocks 70% solid; see Note 2; No facings.	N/A	1 hr.		1		27	1
W-3-M-19	3″	Core: hollow concrete units; see Notes 29, 35, 36, 38; No facings.	N/A	1 hr.		1		27	1
W-3-M-20	3″	Core: hollow concrete units; see Notes 28, 35, 36, 37, 38; No facings.	N/A	1 hr.		1			1
W-3-M-21	$3^1/_2″$	Core: hollow concrete units; see Notes 28, 35, 36, 37, 38; Facings: one side; see Note 37.	N/A	$1^1/_2$ hr.		1			$1^1/_2$
W-3-M-22	$3^1/_2″$	Core: hollow concrete units; see Notes 29, 35, 36, 38; Facings: one side; see Note 37.	N/A	$1^1/_4$ hr.		1			$1^1/_4$

Notes:
1. Failure mode - flame thru.
2. Passed 2 hour fire test (Grade "C" fire res. - British).
3. Passed hose stream test.
4. Tested at NBS under ASA Spec. No. A2-1934. As nonload bearing partitions.
5. Tested at NBS under ASA Spec. No. 42-1934 (ASTM C 19-33) except that hose stream testing where carried was run on test specimens exposed for full test duration, not for a reduced period as is contemporarily done.
6. Failure by thermal criteria - maximum temperature rise 325°F.
7. Hose stream failure.
8. Hose stream - pass.
9. Specimen removed prior to any failure occurring.
10. Failure mode - collapse.
11. For clay tile walls, unless the source or density of the clay can be positively identified or determined, it is suggested that the lowest hourly rating for the fire endurance of a clay tile partition of that thickness be followed. Identified sources of clay showing longer fire endurance can lead to longer time recommendations.
12. See appendix for construction and design details for clay tile walls.
13. Load: 80 psi for gross wall area.
14. One cell in wall thickness.
15. Two cells in wall thickness.
16. Double shells plus one cell in wall thickness.
17. One cell in wall thickness, cells filled with broken tile, crushed stone, slag cinders or sand mixed with mortar.
18. Dense hard-burned clay or shale tile.
19. Medium-burned clay tile.
20. Not less than $^5/_8$ inch thickness of 1:3 sanded gypsum plaster.
21. Units of not less than 30 percent solid material.
22. Units of not less than 40 percent solid material.
23. Units of not less than 50 percent solid material.
24. Units of not less than 45 percent solid material.
25. Units of not less than 60 percent solid material.
26. All tiles laid in portland cement-lime mortar.
27. Blocks laid in 1:3 sanded gypsum mortar voids in blocks not to exceed 30 percent.
28. Units of expanded slag or pumice aggregate.
29. Units of crushed limestone, blast furnace, slag, cinders and expanded clay or shale.

TABLE 1.1.1—MASONRY WALLS
0″ TO LESS THAN 4″ THICK—(Continued)

30. Units of calcareous sand and gravel. Coarse aggregate, 60 percent or more calcite and dolomite.
31. Units of siliceous sand and gravel. Ninety percent or more quartz, chert or flint.
32. Unit at least 49 percent solid.
33. Unit at least 62 percent solid.
34. Unit at least 65 percent solid.
35. Unit at least 73 percent solid.
36. Ratings based on one unit and one cell in wall thickness.
37. Minimum of $^1/_2$ inch - 1:3 sanded gypsum plaster.
38. Nonload bearing.
39. See Clay Tile Partition Design Construction drawings, below.

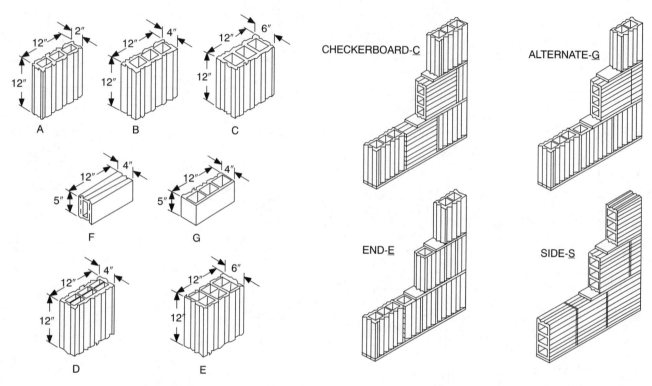

DESIGNS OF TILES USED IN FIRE-TEST PARTITIONS

THE FOUR TYPES OF CONSTRUCTION USED
IN FIRE-TEST PARTITIONS

FIGURE 1.1.2—WALLS—MASONRY
4″ TO LESS THAN 6″ THICK

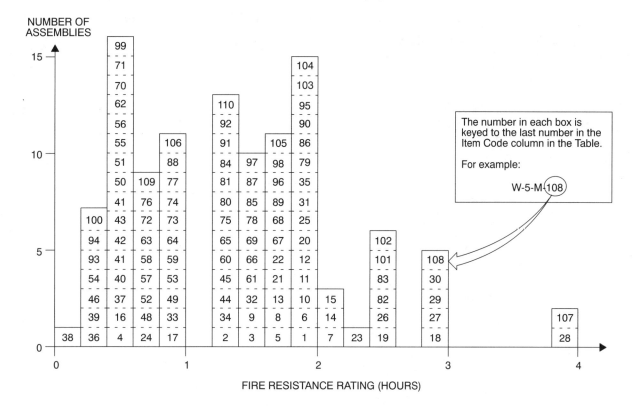

FIRE RESISTANCE RATING (HOURS)

TABLE 1.1.2—MASONRY WALLS
4″ TO LESS THAN 6″ THICK

ITEM CODE	THICKNESS	CONSTRUCTION DETAILS	PERFORMANCE		REFERENCE NUMBER			NOTES	REC. HOURS
			LOAD	TIME	PRE-BMS-92	BMS-92	POST-BMS-92		
W-4-M-1	4″	Solid 3″ thick, gypsum blocks laid in 1:3 sanded gypsum mortar; Facings: $1/2$″ of 1:3 sanded gypsum plaster (both sides).	N/A	2 hr.		1		1	2
W-4-M-2	4″	Solid clay or shale brick.	N/A	1 hr. 15 min.		1		1, 2	$1^1/4$
W-4-M-3	4″	Concrete; No facings.	N/A	1 hr. 30 min.		1		1	$1^1/2$
W-4-M-4	4″	Clay tile; Illinois surface clay; single cell thick; No face plaster; Design "B," Construction "C."	N/A	25 min.			2	3-7, 36	$1/3$
W-4-M-5	4″	Solid sand-lime brick.	N/A	1 hr. 45 min.		1		1	$1^3/4$
W-4-M-6	4″	Solid wall; 3″ thick block; $1/2$″ plaster each side; $17^3/4$″ × $8^3/4$″ × 3″ "Breeze Blocks"; portland cement/sand mortar.	N/A	1 hr. 52 min.			7	2	$1^3/4$
W-4-M-7	4″	Concrete (4020 psi); Reinforc×ment: vertical $3/8$″; horizontal $1/4$″; 6″ × 6″ grid.	3.4 tons/ft.	2 hr. 10 min.			7	2	2
W-4-M-8	4″	Concrete wall (4340 psi crush); reinforcement $1/4$″ diameter rebar on 8″ centers (vertical and horizontal).	N/A	1 hr. 40 min.			7	2	$1^2/3$
W-4-M-9	$4^3/16$″	$4^3/16$″ × $2^5/8$″ cellular fletton brick (1873 psi) with $1/2$″ sand mortar; bricks are U-shaped yielding hollow cover (approx. 2″ × 4″) in final cross-section configuration.	N/A	1 hr. 25 min.			7	2	$1^1/3$
W-4-M-10	$4^1/4$″	$4^1/4$″ × $2^1/2$″ fletton (1831 psi) brick in $1/2$″ sand mortar.	N/A	1 hr. 53 min.			7	2	$1^3/4$

(Continued)

97

TABLE 1.1.2—MASONRY WALLS
4″ TO LESS THAN 6″ THICK—(Continued)

ITEM CODE	THICKNESS	CONSTRUCTION DETAILS	PERFORMANCE		REFERENCE NUMBER			NOTES	REC. HOURS
			LOAD	TIME	PRE-BMS-92	BMS-92	POST-BMS-92		
W-4-M-11	$4^1/4''$	$4^1/4'' \times 2^1/2''$ London stock (683 psi) brick; $^1/2''$ grout.	N/A	1 hr. 52 min.			7	2	$1^3/4$
W-4-M-12	$4^1/2''$	$4^1/4'' \times 2^1/2''$ Leicester red, wire-cut brick (4465 psi) in $^1/2''$ sand mortar.	N/A	1 hr. 56 min.			7	6	$1^3/4$
W-4-M-13	$4^1/4''$	$4^1/4'' \times 2^1/2''$ stairfoot brick (7527 psi) $^1/2''$ sand mortar.	N/A	1 hr. 37 min.			7	2	$1^1/2$
W-4-M-14	$4^1/4''$	$4^1/4'' \times 2^1/2''$ sand-lime brick (2603 psi) $^1/2''$ sand mortar.	N/A	2 hrs. 6 min.			7	2	2
W-4-M-15	$4^1/4''$	$4^1/4'' \times 2^1/2''$ concrete brick (2527 psi) $^1/2''$ sand mortar.	N/A	2 hrs. 10 min.			7	2	2
W-4-M-16	$4^1/2''$	4″ thick clay tile; Ohio fire clay; single cell thick; No plaster exposed face; $^1/2''$ 1:2 gypsum back face; Design "F," Construction "S."	N/A	31 min.			2	3-6, 36	$^1/2$
W-4-M-17	$4^1/2''$	4″ thick clay tile; Ohio fire clay; single cell thick; Plaster exposed face; $^1/2''$ 1:2 sanded gypsum; Back Face: none; Construction "S," Design "F."	80 psi	50 min.			2	3-5, 8, 36	$^3/4$
W-4-M-18	$4^1/2''$	Core: solid sand-lime brick; $^1/2''$ sanded gypsum plaster facings on both sides.	80 psi	3 hrs.		1		1, 11	3
W-4-M-19	$4^1/2''$	Core: solid sand-lime brick; $^1/2''$ sanded gypsum plaster facings on both sides.	80 psi	2 hrs. 30 min.		1		1, 11	$2^1/2$
W-4-M-20	$4^1/2''$	Core: concrete brick $^1/2''$ of 1:3 sanded gypsum plaster facings on both sides.	80 psi	2 hrs.		1		1, 11	2
W-4-M-21	$4^1/2''$	Core: solid clay or shale brick; $^1/2''$ thick, 1:3 sanded gypsum plaster facings on fire sides.	80 psi	1 hr. 45 min.		1		1, 2, 11	$1^3/4$
W-4-M-22	$4^3/4''$	4″ thick clay tile; Ohio fire clay; single cell thick; cells filled with cement and broken tile concrete; Plaster on exposed face; none on unexposed face; $^3/4''$ 1:3 sanded gypsum; Design "G," Construction "E."	N/A	1 hr. 48 min.			2	2, 3-5, 9, 36	$1^3/4$
W-4-M-23	$4^3/4''$	4″ thick clay tile; Ohio fire clay; single cell thick; cells filled with cement and broken tile concrete; No plaster exposed faced; $^3/4''$ neat gypsum plaster on unexposed face; Design "G," Construction "E."	N/A	2 hrs. 14 min.			2	2, 3-5, 9, 36	2
W-5-M-24	5″	3″ × 13″ air space; 1″ thick metal reinforced concrete facings on both sides; faces connected with wood splines.	2,250 lbs./ft.	45 min.		1		1	$^3/4$
W-5-M-25	5″	Core: 3″ thick void filled with "nondulated" mineral wool weighing 10 lbs./ft.^{3}; 1″ thick metal reinforced concrete facings on both sides.	2,250 lbs./ft.	2 hrs.		1		1	2
W-5-M-26	5″	Core: solid clay or shale brick; $^1/2''$ thick, 1:3 sanded gypsum plaster facings on both sides.	40 psi	2 hrs. 30 min.		1		1, 2, 11	$2^1/2$
W-5-M-27	5″	Core: solid 4″ thick gypsum blocks, laid in 1:3 sanded gypsum mortar; $^1/2''$ of 1:3 sanded gypsum plaster facings on both sides.	N/A	3 hrs.		1		1	3
W-5-M-28	5″	Core: 4″ thick hollow gypsum blocks with 30% voids; blocks laid in 1:3 sanded gypsum mortar; No facings.	N/A	4 hrs.		1		1	4
W-5-M-29	5″	Core: concrete brick; $^1/2''$ of 1:3 sanded gypsum plaster facings on both sides.	160 psi	3 hrs.		1		1	3
W-5-M-30	$5^1/4''$	4″ thick clay tile; Illinois surface clay; double cell thick; Plaster: $^5/8''$ sanded gypsum 1:3 both faces; Design "D," Construction "S."	N/A	2 hrs. 53 min.			2	2-5, 9, 36	$2^3/4$

(Continued)

98

TABLE 1.1.2—MASONRY WALLS
4″ TO LESS THAN 6″ THICK—(Continued)

ITEM CODE	THICKNESS	CONSTRUCTION DETAILS	PERFORMANCE		REFERENCE NUMBER			NOTES	REC. HOURS
			LOAD	TIME	PRE-BMS-92	BMS-92	POST-BMS-92		
W-5-M-31	$5^1/_4''$	4″ thick clay tile; New Jersey fire clay; double cell thick; Plaster: $^5/_8''$ sanded gypsum 1:3 both faces; Design "D," Construction "S."	N/A	1 hr. 52 min.			2	2-5, 9, 36	$1^3/_4$
W-5-M-32	$5^1/_4''$	4″ thick clay tile; New Jersey fire clay; single cell thick; Plaster: $^5/_8''$ sanded gypsm 1:3 both faces; Design "D," Construction "S."	N/A	1 hr. 34 min.	2		2	2-5, 9, 36	$1^1/_2$
W-5-M-33	$5^1/_4''$	4″ thick clay tile; New Jersey fire clay; single cell thick; Face plaster: $^5/_8''$ both sides; 1:3 sanded gypsum; Design "B," Construction "S."	N/A	50 min.			2	3-5, 8, 36	$^3/_4$
W-5-M-34	$5^1/_4''$	4″ thick clay tile; Ohio fire clay; single cell thick; Face plaster: $^5/_8''$ both sides; 1:3 sanded gypsum; Design "B," Construction "A."	N/A	1 hr. 19 min.			2	2-5, 9, 36	$1^1/_4$
W-5-M-35	$5^1/_4''$	4″ thick clay tile; Illinois surface clay; single cell thick; Face plaster: $^5/_8''$ both sides; 1:3 sanded gypsum; Design "B," Construction "S."	N/A	1 hr. 59 min.			2	2-5, 10, 36	$1^3/_4$
W-4-M-36	4″	Core: structural clay tile; see Notes 12, 16, 21; No facings.	N/A	15 min.			1	3, 4, 24	$^1/_4$
W-4-M-37	4″	Core: structural clay tile; see Notes 12, 17, 21; No facings.	N/A	25 min.			1	3, 4, 24	$^1/_3$
W-4-M-38	4″	Core: structural clay tile; see Notes 12, 16, 20; No facings.	N/A	10 min.			1	3, 4, 24	$^1/_6$
W-4-M-39	4″	Core: structural clay tile; see Notes 12, 17, 20; No facings.	N/A	20 min.			1	3, 4, 24	$^1/_3$
W-4-M-40	4″	Core: structural clay tile; see Notes 13, 16, 23; No facings.	N/A	30 min.			1	3, 4, 24	$^1/_2$
W-4-M-41	4″	Core: structural clay tile; see Notes 13, 17, 23; No facings.	N/A	35 min.			1	3, 4, 24	$^1/_2$
W-4-M-42	4″	Core: structural clay tile; see Notes 13, 16, 21; No facings.	N/A	25 min.			1	3, 4, 24	$^1/_3$
W-4-M-43	4″	Core: structural clay tile; see Notes 13, 17, 21; No facings.	N/A	30 min.			1	3, 4, 24	$^1/_2$
W-4-M-44	4″	Core: structural clay tile; see Notes 15, 16, 20; No facings.	N/A	1 hr. 15 min.			1	3, 4, 24	$1^1/_4$
W-4-M-45	4″	Core: structural clay tile; see Notes 15, 17, 20; No facings.	N/A	1 hr. 15 min.			1	3, 4, 24	$1^1/_4$
W-4-M-46	4″	Core: structural clay tile; see Notes 14, 16, 22; No facings.	N/A	20 min.			1	3, 4, 24	$^1/_3$
W-4-M-47	4″	Core: structural clay tile; see Notes 14, 17, 22; No facings.	N/A	25 min.			1	3, 4, 24	$^1/_3$
W-4-M-48	$4^1/_4''$	Core: structural clay tile; see Notes 12, 16, 21; Facings: both sides; see Note 18.	N/A	45 min.			1	3, 4, 24	$^3/_4$
W-4-M-49	$4^1/_4''$	Core: structural clay tile; see Notes 12, 17, 21; Facings: both sides; see Note 18.	N/A	1 hr.			1	3, 4, 24	1
W-4-M-50	$4^5/_8''$	Core: structural clay tile; see Notes 12, 16, 21; Facings: unexposed side only; see Note 18.	N/A	25 min.			1	3, 4, 24	$^1/_3$
W-4-M-51	$4^5/_8''$	Core: structural clay tile; see Notes 12, 17, 21; Facings: unexposed side only; see Note 18.	N/A	30 min.			1	3, 4, 24	$^1/_2$
W-4-M-52	$4^5/_8''$	Core: structural clay tile; see Notes 12, 16, 21; Facings: unexposed side only; see Note 18.	N/A	45 min.			1	3, 4, 24	$^3/_4$
W-4-M-53	$4^5/_8''$	Core: structural clay tile; see Notes 12, 17, 21; Facings: fire side only; see Note 18.	N/A	1 hr.			1	3, 4, 24	1
W-4-M-54	$4^5/_8''$	Core: structural clay tile; see Notes 12, 16, 20; Facings: unexposed side; see Note 18.	N/A	20 min.			1	3, 4, 24	$^1/_3$

(Continued)

TABLE 1.1.2—MASONRY WALLS
4″ TO LESS THAN 6″ THICK—(Continued)

ITEM CODE	THICKNESS	CONSTRUCTION DETAILS	PERFORMANCE		REFERENCE NUMBER			NOTES	REC. HOURS
			LOAD	TIME	PRE-BMS-92	BMS-92	POST-BMS-92		
W-4-M-55	$4^5/_8''$	Core: structural clay tile; see Notes 12, 17, 20; Facings: exposed side; see Note 18.	N/A	25 min.		1		3, 4, 24	$^1/_3$
W-4-M-56	$4^5/_8''$	Core: structural clay tile; see Notes 12, 16, 20; Facings: fire side only; see Note 18.	N/A	30 min.		1		3, 4, 24	$^1/_2$
W-4-M-57	$4^5/_8''$	Core: structural clay tile; see Notes 12, 17, 20; Facings: fire side only; see Note 18.	N/A	45 min.		1		3, 4, 24	$^3/_4$
W-4-M-58	$4^5/_8''$	Core: structural clay tile; see Notes 13, 16, 23; Facings: unexposed side only; see Note 18.	N/A	40 min.		1		3, 4, 24	$^2/_3$
W-4-M-59	$4^5/_8''$	Core: structural clay tile; see Notes 13, 17, 23; Facings: unexposed side only; see Note 18.	N/A	1 hr.		1		3, 4, 24	1
W-4-M-60	$4^5/_8''$	Core: structural clay tile; see Notes 13, 16, 23; Facings: fire side only; see Note 18.	N/A	1 hr. 15 min.		1		3, 4, 24	$1^1/_4$
W-4-M-61	$4^5/_8''$	Core: structural clay tile; see Notes 13, 17, 23; Facings: fire side only; see Note 18.	N/A	1 hr. 30 min.		1		3, 4, 24	$1^1/_2$
W-4-M-62	$4^5/_8''$	Core: structural clay tile; see Notes 13, 16, 21; Facings: unexposed side only; see Note 18.	N/A	35 min.		1		3, 4, 24	$^1/_2$
W-4-M-63	$4^5/_8''$	Core: structural clay tile; see Notes 13, 17, 21; Facings: unexposed face only; see Note 18.	N/A	45 min.		1		3, 4, 24	$^3/_4$
W-4-M-64	$4^5/_8''$	Core: structural clay tile; see Notes 13, 16, 23; Facings: exposed face only; see Note 18.	N/A	1 hr.		1		3, 4, 24	1
W-4-M-65	$4^5/_8''$	Core: structural clay tile; see Notes 13, 17, 21; Facings: exposed side only; see Note 18.	N/A	1 hr. 15 min.		1		3, 4, 24	$1^1/_4$
W-4-M-66	$4^5/_8''$	Core: structural clay tile; see Notes 15, 17, 20; Facings: unexposed side only; see Note 18.	N/A	1 hr. 30 min.		1		3, 4, 24	$1^1/_2$
W-4-M-67	$4^5/_8''$	Core: structural clay tile; see Notes 15, 16, 20; Facings: exposed side only; see Note 18.	N/A	1 hr. 45 min.		1		3, 4, 24	$1^3/_4$
W-4-M-68	$4^5/_8''$	Core: structural clay tile; see Notes 15, 17, 20; Facings: exposed side only; see Note 18.	N/A	1 hr. 45 min.		1		3, 4, 24	$1^3/_4$
W-4-M-69	$4^5/_8''$	Core: structural clay tile; see Notes 15, 16, 20; Facings: unexposed side only; see Note 18.	N/A	1 hr. 30 min.		1		3, 4, 24	$1^3/_4$
W-4-M-70	$4^5/_8''$	Core: structural clay tile; see Notes 14, 16, 22; Facings: unexposed side only; see Note 18.	N/A	30 min.		1		3, 4, 24	$^1/_2$
W-4-M-71	$4^5/_8''$	Core: structural clay tile; see Notes 14, 17, 22; Facings: exposed side only; see Note 18.	N/A	35 min.		1		3, 4, 24	$^1/_2$
W-4-M-72	$4^5/_8''$	Core: structural clay tile; see Notes 14, 16, 22; Facings: fire side of wall only; see Note 18.	N/A	45 min.		1		3, 4, 24	$^3/_4$
W-4-M-73	$4^5/_8''$	Core: structural clay tile; see Notes 14, 17, 22; Facings: fire side of wall only; see Note 18.	N/A	1 hr.		1		3, 4, 24	1
W-5-M-74	$5^1/_4''$	Core: structural clay tile; see Notes 12, 16, 21; Facings: both sides; see Note 18.	N/A	1 hr.		1		3, 4, 24	1
W-5-M-75	$5^1/_4''$	Core: structural clay tile; see Notes 12, 17, 21; Facings: both sides; see Note 18.	N/A	1 hr. 15 min.		1		3, 4, 24	$1^1/_4$
W-5-M-76	$5^1/_4''$	Core: structural clay tile; see Notes 12, 16, 20; Facings: both sides; see Note 18.	N/A	45 min.		1		3, 4, 24	$^3/_4$

(Continued)

TABLE 1.1.2—MASONRY WALLS
4″ TO LESS THAN 6″ THICK—(Continued)

ITEM CODE	THICKNESS	CONSTRUCTION DETAILS	PERFORMANCE		REFERENCE NUMBER			NOTES	REC. HOURS
			LOAD	TIME	PRE-BMS-92	BMS-92	POST-BMS-92		
W-5-M-77	$5^1/_4″$	Core: structural clay tile; see Notes 12, 17, 20; Facings: both sides; see Note 18.	N/A	1 hr.		1		3, 4, 24	1
W-5-M-78	$5^1/_4″$	Core: structural clay tile; see Notes 13, 16, 23; Facings: both sides of wall; see Note 18.	N/A	1 hr. 30 min.		1		3, 4, 24	$1^1/_2$
W-5-M-79	$5^1/_4″$	Core: structural clay tile; see Notes 13, 17, 23; Facings: both sides of wall; see Note 18.	N/A	2 hrs.		1		3, 4, 24	2
W-5-M-80	$5^1/_4″$	Core: structural clay tile; see Notes 13, 16, 21; Facings: both sides of wall; see Note 18.	N/A	1 hr. 15 min.		1		3, 4, 24	$1^1/_4$
W-5-M-81	$5^1/_4″$	Core: structural clay tile; see Notes 13, 16, 21; Facings: both sides of wall; see Note 18.	N/A	1 hr. 30 min.		1		3, 4, 24	$1^1/_2$
W-5-M-82	$5^1/_4″$	Core: structural clay tile; see Notes 15, 16, 20; Facings: both sides; see Note 18.	N/A	2 hrs. 30 min.		1		3, 4, 24	$2^1/_2$
W-5-M-83	$5^1/_4″$	Core: structural clay tile; see Notes 15, 17, 20; Facings: both sides; see Note 18.	N/A	2 hrs. 30 min.		1		3, 4, 24	$2^1/_2$
W-5-M-84	$5^1/_4″$	Core: structural clay tile; see Notes 14, 16, 22; Facings: both sides of wall; see Note 18.	N/A	1 hr. 15 min.		1		3, 4, 24	$1^1/_4$
W-5-M-85	$5^1/_4″$	Core: structural clay tile; see Notes 14, 17, 22; Facings: both sides of wall; see Note 18.	N/A	1 hr. 30 min.		1		3, 4, 24	$1^1/_2$
W-4-M-86	4″	Core: 3″ thick gypsum blocks 70% solid; see Note 26; Facings: both sides; see Note 25.	N/A	2 hrs.		1			2
W-4-M-87	4″	Core: hollow concrete units; see Notes 27, 34, 35; No facings.	N/A	1 hr. 30 min.		1			$1^1/_2$
W-4-M-88	4″	Core: hollow concrete units; see Notes 28, 33, 35; No facings.	N/A	1 hr.		1			1
W-4-M-89	4″	Core: hollow concrete units; see Notes 28, 34, 35; Facings: both sides; see Note 25.	N/A	1 hr. 45 min.		1			$1^3/_4$
W-4-M-90	4″	Core: hollow concrete units; see Notes 27, 34, 35; Facings: both sides; see Note 25.	N/A	2 hrs.		1			2
W-4-M-91	4″	Core: hollow concrete units; see Notes 27, 32, 35; No facings.	N/A	1 hr. 15 min.		1			$1^1/_4$
W-4-M-92	4″	Core: hollow concrete units; see Notes 28, 34, 35; No facings.	N/A	1 hr. 15 min.		1			$1^1/_4$
W-4-M-93	4″	Core: hollow concrete units; see Notes 29, 32, 35; No facings.	N/A	20 min.		1			$^1/_3$
W-4-M-94	4″	Core: hollow concrete units; see Notes 30, 34, 35; No facings.	N/A	15 min.		1			$^1/_4$
W-4-M-95	$4^1/_2″$	Core: hollow concrete units; see Notes 27, 34, 35; Facings: one side only; see Note 25.	N/A	2 hrs.		1			2
W-4-M-96	$4^1/_2″$	Core: hollow concrete units; see Notes 27, 32, 35; Facings: one side only; see Note 25.	N/A	1 hr. 45 min.		1			$1^3/_4$
W-4-M-97	$4^1/_2″$	Core: hollow concrete units; see Notes 28, 33, 35; Facings: one side; see Note 25.	N/A	1 hr. 30 min.		1			$1^1/_2$
W-4-M-98	$4^1/_2″$	Core: hollow concrete units; see Notes 28, 34, 35; Facings: one side only; see Note 25.	N/A	1 hr. 45 min.		1			$1^3/_4$
W-4-M-99	$4^1/_2″$	Core: hollow concrete units; see Notes 29, 32, 35; Facings: one side; see Note 25.	N/A	30 min.		1			$^1/_2$

(Continued)

TABLE 1.1.2—MASONRY WALLS
4″ TO LESS THAN 6″ THICK—(Continued)

ITEM CODE	THICKNESS	CONSTRUCTION DETAILS	PERFORMANCE		REFERENCE NUMBER			NOTES	REC. HOURS
			LOAD	TIME	PRE-BMS-92	BMS-92	POST-BMS-92		
W-4-M-100	$4^1/_2″$	Core: hollow concrete units; see Notes 30, 34, 35; Facings: one side; see Note 25.	N/A	20 min.		1			$^1/_3$
W-5-M-101	5″	Core: hollow concrete units; see Notes 27, 34, 35; Facings: both sides; see Note 25.	N/A	2 hrs. 30 min.		1			$2^1/_2$
W5-M-102	5″	Core: hollow concrete units; see Notes 27, 32, 35; Facings: both sides; see Note 25.	N/A	2 hrs. 30 min.		1			$2^1/_2$
W-5-M-103	5″	Core: hollow concrete units; see Notes 28, 33, 35; Facings: both sides; see Note 25.	N/A	2 hrs.		1			2
W-5-M-104	5″	Core: hollow concrete units; see Notes 28, 31, 35; Facings: both sides; see Note 25.	N/A	2 hrs.		1			2
W-5-M-105	5″	Core: hollow concrete units; see Notes 29, 32, 35; Facings: both sides; see Note 25.	N/A	1 hr. 45 min.		1			$1^3/_4$
W-5-M-106	5″	Core: hollow concrete units; see Notes 30, 34, 35; Facings: both sides; see Note 25.	N/A	1 hr.		1			1
W-5-M-107	5″	Core: 5″ thick solid gypsum blocks; see Note 26; No facings.	N/A	4 hrs.		1			4
W-5-M-108	5″	Core: 4″ thick hollow gypsum blocks; see Note 26; Facings: both sides; see Note 25.	N/A	3 hrs.		1			3
W-5-M-108	4″	Concrete with 4″ × 4″ No. 6 welded wire mesh at wall center.	100 psi	45 min.			43	2	$^3/_4$
W-5-M-110	4″	Concrete with 4″ × 4″ No. 6 welded wire mesh at wall center.	N/A	1 hr. 15 min.			43	2	$1^1/_4$

Notes:
1. Tested as NBS under ASA Spec. No. A 2-1934.
2. Failure mode - maximum temperature rise.
3. Treated at NBS under ASA Spec. No. 42-1934 (ASTM C 19-53) except that hose stream testing where carried out was run on test specimens exposed for full test duration, not for or reduced period as is contemporarily done.
4. For clay tile walls, unless the source the clay can be positively identified, it is suggested that the most pessimistic hour rating for the fire endurance of a clay tile partition of that thickness to be followed. Identified sources of clay showing longer fire endurance can lead to longer time recommendations.
5. See appendix for construction and design details for clay tile walls.
6. Failure mode - flame thru or crack formation showing flames.
7. Hole formed at 25 minutes; partition collapsed at 42 minutes or removal from furnace.
8. Failure mode - collapse.
9. Hose stream pass.
10. Hose stream hole formed in specimen.
11. Load: 80 psi for gross wall cross sectional area.
12. One cell in wall thickness.
13. Two cells in wall thickness.
14. Double cells plus one cell in wall thickness.
15. One cell in wall thickness, cells filled with broken tile, crushed stone, slag, cinders or sand mixed with mortar.
16. Dense hard-burned clay or shale tile.
17. Medium-burned clay tile.
18. Not less than $^5/_8$ inch thickness of 1:3 sanded gypsum plaster.
19. Units of not less than 30 percent solid material.
20. Units of not less than 40 percent solid material.
21. Units of not less than 50 percent solid material.
22. Units of not less than 45 percent solid material.
23. Units of not less than 60 percent solid material.
24. All tiles laid in portland cement-lime mortar.
25. Minimum $^1/_2$ inch - 1:3 sanded gypsum plaster.
26. Laid in 1:3 sanded gypsum mortar. Voids in hollow units not to exceed 30 percent.
27. Units of expanded slag or pumice aggregate.
28. Units of crushed limestone, blast furnace slag, cinders and expanded clay or shale.
29. Units of calcareous sand and gravel. Coarse aggregate, 60 percent or more calcite and dolomite.
30. Units of siliceous sand and gravel. Ninety percent or more quartz, chert or flint.
31. Unit at least 49 percent solid.
32. Unit at least 62 percent solid.
33. Unit at least 65 percent solid.
34. Unit at least 73 percent solid.
35. Ratings based on one unit and one cell in wall thickness.
36. See Clay Tile Partition Design Construction drawings, below.

TABLE 1.1.2—MASONRY WALLS
4″ TO LESS THAN 6″ THICK—(Continued)

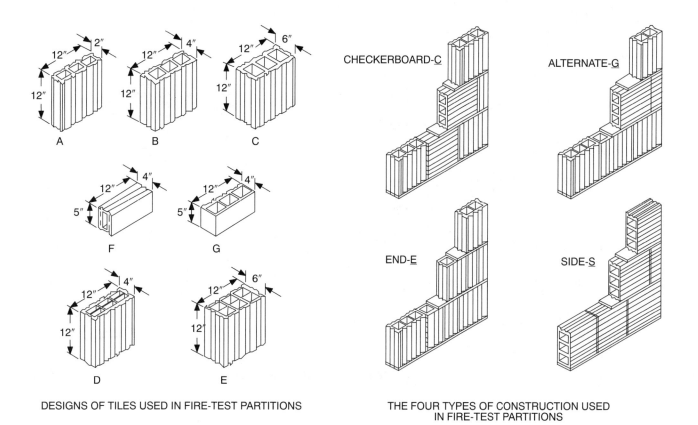

DESIGNS OF TILES USED IN FIRE-TEST PARTITIONS

THE FOUR TYPES OF CONSTRUCTION USED
IN FIRE-TEST PARTITIONS

FIGURE 1.1.3—WALLS—MASONRY
6″ TO LESS THAN 8″ THICK

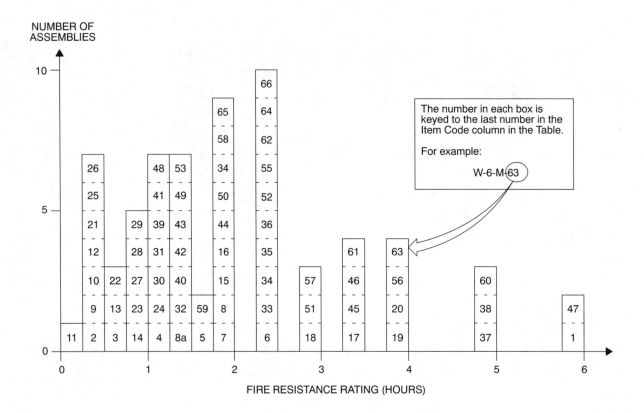

TABLE 1.1.3—MASONRY WALLS
6″ TO LESS THAN 8″ THICK

| ITEM CODE | THICKNESS | CONSTRUCTION DETAILS | PERFORMANCE | | REFERENCE NUMBER | | | NOTES | REC. HOURS |
			LOAD	TIME	PRE-BMS-92	BMS-92	POST-BMS-92		
W-6-M-1	6″	Core: 5″ thick, solid gypsum blocks laid in 1:3 sanded gypsum mortar; $1/2$″ of 1:3 sanded gypsum plaster facings on both sides.	N/A	6 hrs.		1			6
W-6-M-2	6″	6″ clay tile; Ohio fire clay; single cell thick; No plaster; Design "C," Construction "A."	N/A	17 min.			2	1, 3, 4, 6, 55	$1/4$
W-6-M-3	6″	6″ clay tile; Illinois surface clay; double cell thick; No plaster; Design "E," Construction "C."	N/A	45 min.			2	1-4, 7, 55	$3/4$
W-6-M-4	6″	6″ clay tile; New Jersey fire clay; double cell thick; No plaster; Design "E," Construction "S."	N/A	1 hr. 1 min.			2	1-4, 8, 55	1
W-7-M-5	$7^{1}/4$″	6″ clay tile; Illinois surface clay; double cell thick; Plaster: $5/8$″ - 1:3 sanded gypsum both faces; Design "E," Construction "A."	N/A	1 hr. 41 min.			2	1-4, 55	$1^{2}/3$
W-7-M-6	$7^{1}/4$″	6″ clay tile; New Jersey fire clay; double cell thick; Plaster: $5/8$″ - 1:3 sanded gypsum both faces; Design "E," Construction "S."	N/A	2 hrs. 23 min.			2	1-4, 9, 55	$2^{1}/3$
W-7-M-7	$7^{1}/4$″	6″ clay tile; Ohio fire clay; single cell thick; Plaster: $5/8$″ sanded gypsum; 1:3 both faces; Design "C," Construction "A."	N/A	1 hr. 54 min.			2	1-4, 9, 55	$2^{3}/4$
W-7-M-8	$7^{1}/4$″	6″ clay tile; Illinois surface clay; single cell thick; Plaster: $5/8$″ sanded gypsum 1:3 both faces; Design "C," Construction "S."	N/A	2 hrs.			2	1, 3, 4, 9, 10, 55	2

(Continued)

TABLE 1.1.3—MASONRY WALLS
6″ TO LESS THAN 8″ THICK—(Continued)

ITEM CODE	THICKNESS	CONSTRUCTION DETAILS	PERFORMANCE		REFERENCE NUMBER			NOTES	REC. HOURS
			LOAD	TIME	PRE-BMS-92	BMS-92	POST-BMS-92		
W-7-M-8a	7¼″	6″ clay tile; Illinois surface clay; single cell thick; Plaster: ⅝″ sanded gypsum 1:3 both faces; Design "C," Construction "E."	N/A	1 hr. 23 min.			2	1-4, 9, 10, 55	1¾
W-6-M-9	6″	Core: structural clay tile; see Notes 12, 16, 20; No facings.	N/A	20 min.		1		3, 5, 24	⅓
W-6-M-10	6″	Core: structural clay tile; see Notes 12, 17, 20; No facings.	N/A	25 min.		1		3, 5, 24	⅓
W-6-M-11	6″	Core: structural clay tile; see Notes 12, 16, 19; No facings.	N/A	15 min.		1		3, 5, 24	¼
W-6-M-12	6″	Core: structural clay tile; see Notes 12, 17, 19; No facings.	N/A	20 min.		1		3, 5, 24	⅓
W-6-M-13	6″	Core: structural clay tile; see Notes 13, 16, 22; No facings.	N/A	45 min.		1		3, 5, 24	¾
W-6-M-14	6″	Core: structural clay tile; see Notes 13, 17, 22; No facings.	N/A	1 hr.		1		3, 5, 24	1
W-6-M-15	6″	Core: structural clay tile; see Notes 15, 17, 19; No facings.	N/A	2 hrs.		1		3, 5, 24	2
W-6-M-16	6″	Core: structural clay tile; see Notes 15, 16, 19; No facings.	N/A	2 hrs.		1		3, 5, 24	2
W-6-M-17	6″	Cored concrete masonry; see Notes 12, 34, 36, 38, 41; No facings.	80 psi	3 hrs. 30 min.		1		5, 25	3½
W-6-M-18	6″	Cored concrete masonry; see Notes 12, 33, 36, 38, 41; No facings.	80 psi	3 hrs.		1		5, 25	3
W-6-M-19	6½″	Cored concrete masonry; see Notes 12, 34, 36, 38, 41; Facings: side 1; see Note 35.	80 psi	4 hrs.		1		5, 25	4
W-6-M-20	6½″	Cored concrete masonry; see Notes 12, 33, 36, 38, 41; Facings: side 1; see Note 35.	80 psi	4 hrs.		1		5, 25	4
W-6-M-21	6⅝″	Core: structural clay tile; see Notes 12, 16, 20; Facings: unexposed face only; see Note 18.	N/A	30 min.		1		3, 5, 24	½
W-6-M-22	6⅝″	Core: structural clay tile; see Notes 12, 17, 20; Facings: unexposed face only; see Note 18.	N/A	40 min.		1		3, 5, 24	⅔
W-6-M-23	6⅝″	Core: structural clay tile; see Notes 12, 16, 20; Facings: exposed face only; see Note 18.	N/A	1 hr.		1		3, 5, 24	1
W-6-M-24	6⅝″	Core: structural clay tile; see Notes 12, 17, 20; Facings: exposed face only; see Note 18.	N/A	1 hr. 5 min.		1		3, 5, 24	1
W-6-M-25	6⅝″	Core: structural clay tile; see Notes 12, 16, 19; Facings: unexposed side only; see Note 18.	N/A	25 min.		1		3, 5, 24	⅓
W-6-M-26	6⅝″	Core: structural clay tile; see Notes 12, 7, 19; Facings: unexposed face only; see Note 18.	N/A	30 min.		1		3, 5, 24	½
W-6-M-27	6⅝″	Core: structural clay tile; see Notes 12, 16, 19; Facings: exposed side only; see Note 18.	N/A	1 hr.		1		3, 5, 24	1
W-6-M-28	6⅝″	Core: structural clay tile; see Notes 12, 17, 19; Facings: fire side only; see Note 18.	N/A	1 hr.		1		3, 5, 24	1
W-6-M-29	6⅝″	Core: structural clay tile; see Notes 13, 16, 22; Facings: unexposed side only; see Note 18.	N/A	1 hr.		1		3, 5, 24	1
W-6-M-30	6⅝″	Core: structural clay tile; see Notes 13, 17, 22; Facings: unexposed side only; see Note 18.	N/A	1 hr. 15 min.		1		3, 5, 24	1¼
W-6-M-31	6⅝″	Core: structural clay tile; see Notes 13, 16, 22; Facings: fire side only; see Note 18.	N/A	1 hr. 15 min.		1		3, 5, 24	1¼

(Continued)

TABLE 1.1.3—MASONRY WALLS
6″ TO LESS THAN 8″ THICK—(Continued)

ITEM CODE	THICKNESS	CONSTRUCTION DETAILS	PERFORMANCE		REFERENCE NUMBER			NOTES	REC. HOURS
			LOAD	TIME	PRE-BMS-92	BMS-92	POST-BMS-92		
W-6-M-32	6⅝″	Core: structural clay tile; see Notes 13, 17, 22; Facings: fire side only; see Note 18.	N/A	1 hr. 30 min.		1		3, 5 , 24	1½
W-6-M-33	6⅝″	Core: structural clay tile; see Notes 15, 16, 19; Facings: unexposed side only; see Note 18.	N/A	2 hrs. 30 min.		1		3, 5 , 24	2½
W-6-M-34	6⅝″	Core: structural clay tile; see Notes 15, 17, 19; Facings: unexposed side only; see Note 18.	N/A	2 hrs. 30 min.		1		3, 5 , 24	2½
W-6-M-35	6⅝″	Core: structural clay tile; see Notes 15, 16, 19; Facings: fire side only; see Note 18.	N/A	2 hrs. 30 min.		1		3, 5 , 24	2½
W-6-M-36	6⅝″	Core: structural clay tile; see Notes 15, 17, 19; Facings: fire side only; see Note 18.	N/A	2 hrs. 30 min.		1		3, 5 , 24	2½
W-7-M-37	7″	Cored concrete masonry; see Notes 12, 34, 36, 38, 41; see Note 35 for facings on both sides.	80 psi	5 hrs.		1		5, 25	5
W-7-M-38	7″	Cored concrete masonry; see Notes 12, 33, 36, 38, 41; see Note 35 for facings.	80 psi	5 hrs.		1		5, 25	5
W-7-M-39	7¼″	Core: structural clay tile; see Notes 12, 16, 20; Facings: both sides; see Note 18.	N/A	1 hr. 15 min.		1		3, 5 , 24	1¼
W-7-M-40	7¼″	Core: structural clay tile; see Notes 12, 17, 20; Facings: both sides; see Note 18.	N/A	1 hr. 30 min.		1		3, 5 , 24	1½
W-7-M-41	7¼″	Core: structural clay tile; see Notes 12, 16, 19; Facings: both sides; see Note 18.	N/A	1 hr. 15 min.		1		3, 5 , 24	1¼
W-7-M-42	7¼″	Core: structural clay tile; see Notes 12, 17, 19; Facings: both sides; see Note 18.	N/A	1 hr. 30 min.		1		3, 5 , 24	1½
W-7-M-43	7¼″	Core: structural clay tile; see Notes 13, 16, 22; Facings: both sides of wall; see Note 18.	N/A	1 hr. 30 min.		1		3, 5 , 24	1½
W-7-M-44	7¼″	Core: structural clay tile; see Notes 13, 17, 22; Facings: both sides of wall; see Note 18.	N/A	2 hrs.		1		3, 5 , 24	1½
W-7-M-45	7¼″	Core: structural clay tile; see Notes 15, 16, 19; Facings: both sides; see Note 18.	N/A	3 hrs. 30 min.		1		3, 5 , 24	3½
W-7-M-46	7¼″	Core: structural clay tile; see Notes 15, 17, 19; Facings: both sides; see Note 18.	N/A	3 hrs. 30 min.		1		3, 5 , 24	3½
W-6-M-47	6″	Core: 5″ thick solid gypsum blocks; see Note 45; Facings: both sides; see Note 45.	N/A	6 hrs.		1			6
W-6-M-48	6″	Core: hollow concrete units; see Notes 47, 50, 54; No facings.	N/A	1 hr. 15 min.		1			1¼
W-6-M-49	6″	Core: hollow concrete units; see Notes 46, 50, 54; No facings.	N/A	1 hr. 30 min.		1			1½
W-6-M-50	6″	Core: hollow concrete units; see Notes 46, 41, 54; No facings.	N/A	2 hrs.		1			2
W-6-M-51	6″	Core: hollow concrete units; see Notes 46, 53, 54; No facings.	N/A	3 hrs.		1			3
W-6-M-52	6″	Core: hollow concrete units; see Notes 47, 53, 54; No facings.	N/A	2 hrs. 30 min.		1			2½
W-6-M-53	6″	Core: hollow concrete units; see Notes 47, 51, 54; No facings.	N/A	1 hr. 30 min.		1			1½
W-6-M-54	6½″	Core: hollow concrete units; see Notes 46, 50, 54; Facings: one side only; see Note 35.	N/A	2 hrs.		1			2

(Continued)

TABLE 1.1.3—MASONRY WALLS
6″ TO LESS THAN 8″ THICK—(Continued)

ITEM CODE	THICKNESS	CONSTRUCTION DETAILS	PERFORMANCE		REFERENCE NUMBER			NOTES	REC. HOURS
			LOAD	TIME	PRE-BMS-92	BMS-92	POST-BMS-92		
W-6-M-55	6½″	Core: hollow concrete units; see Notes 4, 51, 54; Facings: one side; see Note 35.	N/A	2 hrs. 30 min.		1			2½
W-6-M-56	6½″	Core: hollow concrete units; see Notes 46, 53, 54; Facings: one side; see Note 35.	N/A	4 hrs.		1			4
W-6-M-57	6½″	Core: hollow concrete units; see Notes 47, 53, 54; Facings: one side; see Note 35.	N/A	3 hrs.		1			3
W-6-M-58	6½″	Core: hollow concrete units; see Notes 47, 51, 54; Facings: one side; see Note 35.	N/A	2 hrs.		1			2
W-6-M-59	6½″	Core: hollow concrete units; see Notes 47, 50, 54; Facings: one side; see Note 35.	N/A	1 hr. 45 min.		1			1¾
W-7-M-60	7″	Core: hollow concrete units; see Notes 46, 53, 54; Facings: both sides; see Note 35.	N/A	5 hrs.		1			5
W-7-M-61	7″	Core: hollow concrete units; see Notes 46, 51, 54; Facings: both sides; see Note 35.	N/A	3 hrs. 30 min.		1			3½
W-7-M-62	7″	Core: hollow concrete units; see Notes 46, 50, 54; Facings: both sides; see Note 35.	N/A	2 hrs. 30 min.		1			2½
W-7-M-63	7″	Core: hollow concrete units; see Notes 47, 53, 54; Facings: both sides; see Note 35.	N/A	4 hrs.		1			4
W-7-M-64	7″	Core: hollow concrete units; see Notes 47, 51, 54; Facings: both sides; see Note 35.	N/A	2 hrs. 30 min.		1			2½
W-7-M-65	7″	Core: hollow concrete units; see Notes 47, 50, 54; Facings: both sides; see Note 35.	N/A	2 hrs.		1			2
W-6-M-66	6″	Concrete wall with 4″ × 4″ No. 6 wire fabric (welded) near wall center for reinforcement.	N/A	2 hrs. 30 min.			43	2	2½

Notes:

1. Tested at NBS under ASA Spec. No. 43-1934 (ASTM C 19-53) except that hose stream testing where carried out was run on test specimens exposed for full test duration, not for a reduced period as is contemporarily done.
2. Failure by thermal criteria - maximum temperature rise.
3. For clay tile walls, unless the source or density of the clay can be positively identified or determined, it is suggested that the lowest hourly rating for the fire endurance of a clay tile partition of that thickness be followed. Identified sources of clay showing longer fire endurance can lead to longer time recommendations.
4. See Note 55 for construction and design details for clay tile walls.
5. Tested at NBS under ASA Spec. No. A2-1934.
6. Failure mode - collapse.
7. Collapsed on removal from furnace at 1 hour 9 minutes.
8. Hose stream - failed.
9. Hose stream - passed.
10. No end point met in test.
11. Wall collapsed at 1 hour 28 minutes.
12. One cell in wall thickness.
13. Two cells in wall thickness.
14. Double shells plus one cell in wall thickness.
15. One cell in wall thickness, cells filled with broken tile, crushed stone, slag, cinders or sand mixed with mortar.
16. Dense hard-burned clay or shale tile.
17. Medium-burned clay tile.
18. Not less than ⅝ inch thickness of 1:3 sanded gypsum plaster.
19. Units of not less than 30 percent solid material.
20. Units of not less than 40 percent solid material.
21. Units of not less than 50 percent solid material.
22. Units of not less than 45 percent solid material.
23. Units of not less than 60 percent solid material.
24. All tiles laid in portland cement-lime mortar.
25. Load: 80 psi for gross cross sectional area of wall.
26. Three cells in wall thickness.
27. Minimum percent of solid material in concrete units = 52.
28. Minimum percent of solid material in concrete units = 54.
29. Minimum percent of solid material in concrete units = 55.
30. Minimum percent of solid material in concrete units = 57.
31. Minimum percent of solid material in concrete units = 62.

TABLE 1.1.3—MASONRY WALLS
6″ TO LESS THAN 8″ THICK—(Continued)

32. Minimum percent of solid material in concrete units = 65.
33. Minimum percent of solid material in concrete units = 70.
34. Minimum percent of solid material in concrete units = 76.
35. Not less than $^1/_2$ inch of 1:3 sanded gypsum plaster.
36. Noncombustible or no members framed into wall.
37. Combustible members framed into wall.
38. One unit in wall thickness.
39. Two units in wall thickness.
40. Three units in wall thickness.
41. Concrete units made with expanded slag or pumice aggregates.
42. Concrete units made with expanded burned clay or shale, crushed limestone, air cooled slag or cinders.
43. Concrete units made with calcareous sand and gravel. Coarse aggregate, 60 percent or more calcite and dolomite.
44. Concrete units made with siliceous sand and gravel. Ninety percent or more quartz, chert or flint.
45. Laid in 1:3 sanded gypsum mortar.
46. Units of expanded slag or pumice aggregate.
47. Units of crushed limestone, blast furnace, slag, cinder and expanded clay or shale.
48. Units of calcareous sand and gravel. Coarse aggregate, 60 percent or more calcite and dolomite.
49. Units of siliceous sand and gravel. Ninety percent or more quartz, chert or flint.
50. Unit minimum 49 percent solid.
51. Unit minimum 62 percent solid.
52. Unit minimum 65 percent solid.
53. Unit minimum 73 percent solid.
54. Ratings based on one unit and one cell in wall section.
55. See Clay Tile Partition Design Construction drawings, below.

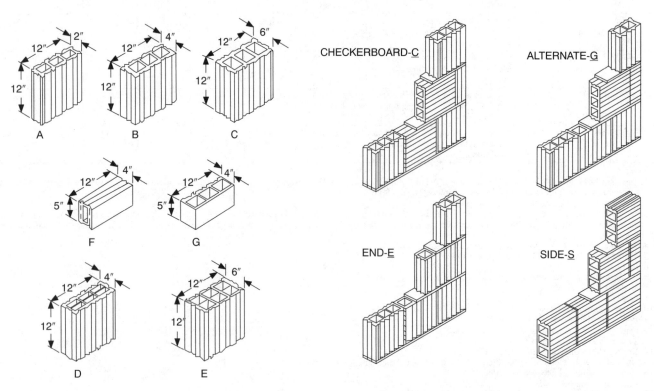

DESIGNS OF TILES USED IN FIRE-TEST PARTITIONS

THE FOUR TYPES OF CONSTRUCTION USED
IN FIRE-TEST PARTITIONS

FIGURE 1.1.4—WALLS—MASONRY
8″ TO LESS THAN 10″ THICK

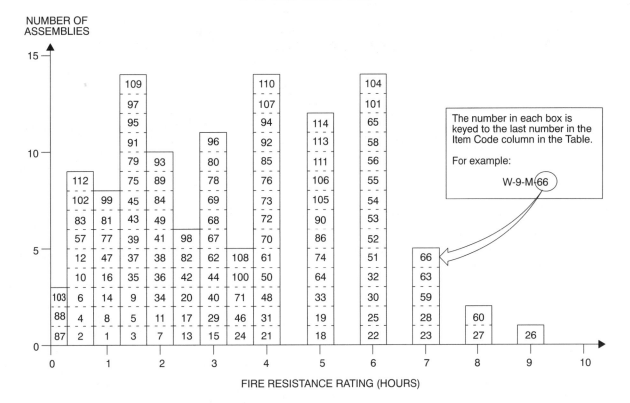

TABLE 1.1.4—MASONRY WALLS
8″ TO LESS THAN 10″ THICK

| ITEM CODE | THICKNESS | CONSTRUCTION DETAILS | PERFORMANCE | | REFERENCE NUMBER | | | NOTES | REC. HOURS |
			LOAD	TIME	PRE-BMS-92	BMS-92	POST-BMS-92		
W-8-M-1	8″	Core: clay or shale structural tile; Units in wall thickness: 1; Cells in wall thickness: 2; Minimum % solids in units: 40.	80 psi	1 hr. 15 min.		1		1, 20	$1^1/_4$
W-8-M-2	8″	Core: clay or shale structural tile; Units in wall thickness: 1; Cells in wall thickness: 2; Minimum % solids in units: 40; No facings; Result for wall with combustible members framed into interior.	80 psi	45 min.		1		1, 20	$3/_4$
W-8-M-3	8″	Core: clay or shale structural tile; Units in wall thickness: 1; Cells in wall thickness: 2; Minimum % solids in units: 43.	80 psi	1 hr. 30 min.		1		1, 20	$1^1/_2$
W-8-M-4	8″	Core: clay or shale structural tile; Units in wall thickness: 1; Cells in wall thickness: 2; Minimum % solids in units: 43; No facings; Combustible members framed into wall.	80 psi	45 min.		1		1, 20	$3/_4$
W-8-M-5	8″	Core: clay or shale structural tile; No facings.	See Notes	1 hr. 30 min.		1		1, 2, 5, 10, 18, 20, 21	$1^1/_2$
W-8-M-6	8″	Core: clay or shale structural tile; No facings.	See Notes	45 min.		1		1, 2, 5, 10, 19, 20, 21	$3/_4$
W-8-M-7	8″	Core: clay or shale structural tile; No facings.	See Notes	2 hrs.		1		1, 2, 5, 13, 18, 20, 21	2
W-8-M-8	8″	Core: clay or shale structural tile; No facings.	See Notes	1 hr. 45 min.		1		1, 2, 5, 13, 19, 20, 21	$1^1/_4$

(Continued)

TABLE 1.1.4—MASONRY WALLS
8″ TO LESS THAN 10″ THICK—(Continued)

ITEM CODE	THICKNESS	CONSTRUCTION DETAILS	PERFORMANCE		REFERENCE NUMBER			NOTES	REC. HOURS
			LOAD	TIME	PRE-BMS-92	BMS-92	POST-BMS-92		
W-8-M-9	8″	Core: clay or shale structural tile; No facings.	See Notes	1 hr. 15 min.		1		1, 2, 6, 9, 18, 20, 21	$1^3/_4$
W-8-M-10	8″	Core: clay or shale structural tile; No facings.	See Notes	45 min.		1		1, 2, 6, 9, 19, 20, 21	$^3/_4$
W-8-M-11	8″	Core: clay or shale structural tile; No facings.	See Notes	2 hrs.		1		1, 2, 6, 10, 18, 20, 21	2
W-8-M-12	8″	Core: clay or shale structural tile; No facings.	See Notes	45 min.		1		1, 2, 6, 10, 19, 20, 21	$^3/_4$
W-8-M-13	8″	Core: clay or shale structural tile; No facings.	See Notes	2 hrs. 30 min.		1		1, 3, 6, 12, 18, 20, 21	$2^1/_2$
W-8-M-14	8″	Core: clay or shale structural tile; No facings.	See Notes	1 hr.		1		1, 2, 6, 12, 19, 20, 21	1
W-8-M-15	8″	Core: clay or shale structural tile; No facings.	See Notes	3 hrs.		1		1, 2, 6, 16, 18, 20, 21	3
W-8-M-16	8″	Core: clay or shale structural tile; No facings.	See Notes	1 hr. 15 min.		1		1, 2, 6, 16, 19, 20, 21	$1^1/_4$
W-8-M-17	8″	Cored clay or shale brick; Units in wall thickness: 1; Cells in wall thickness: 1; Minimum % solids: 70; No facings.	See Notes	2 hrs. 30 min.		1		1, 44	$2^1/_2$
W-8-M-18	8″	Cored clay or shale brick; Units in wall thickness: 2; Cells in wall thickness: 2; Minimum % solids: 87; No facings.	See Notes	5 hrs.		1		1, 45	5
W-8-M-19	8″	Core: solid clay or shale brick; No facings.	See Notes	5 hrs.		1		1, 22, 45	5
W-8-M-20	8″	Core: hollow rolok of clay or shale.	See Notes	2 hrs. 30 min.		1		1, 22, 45	$2^1/_2$
W-8-M-21	8″	Core: hollow rolok bak of clay or shale; No facings.	See Notes	4 hrs.		1		1, 45	4
W-8-M-22	8″	Core: concrete brick; No facings.	See Notes	6 hrs.		1		1, 45	6
W-8-M-23	8″	Core: sand-lime brick; No facings.	See Notes	7 hrs.		1		1, 45	7
W-8-M-24	8″	Core: 4″, 40% solid clay or shale structural tile; 1 side 4″ brick facing.	See Notes	3 hrs. 30 min.		1		1, 20	$3^1/_2$
W-8-M-25	8″	Concrete wall (3220 psi); Reinforcing vertical rods 1″ from each face and 1″ diameter; horizontal rods $^5/_8$″ diameter.	22,200 lbs./ft.	6 hrs.			7		6
W-8-M-26	8″	Core: sand-line brick; $^1/_2$″ of 1:3 sanded gypsum plaster facings on one side.	See Notes	9 hrs.		1		1, 45	9
W-8-M-27	$8^1/_2$″	Core: sand-line brick; $^1/_2$″ of 1:3 sanded gypsum plaster facings on one side.	See Notes	8 hrs.		1		1, 45	8
W-8-M-28	$8^1/_2$″	Core: concrete; $^1/_2$″ of 1:3 sanded gypsum plaster facings on one side.	See Notes	7 hrs.		1		1, 45	7
W-8-M-29	$8^1/_2$″	Core: hollow rolok of clay or shale; $^1/_2$″ of 1:3 sanded gypsum plaster facings on one side.	See Notes	3 hrs.		1		1, 45	3
W-8-M-30	$8^1/_2$″	Core: solid clay or shale brick; $^1/_2$″ thick, 1:3 sanded gypsum plaster facings on one side.	See Notes	6 hrs.		1		1, 22, 45	6

(Continued)

TABLE 1.1.4—MASONRY WALLS
8″ TO LESS THAN 10″ THICK—(Continued)

ITEM CODE	THICKNESS	CONSTRUCTION DETAILS	PERFORMANCE		REFERENCE NUMBER			NOTES	REC. HOURS
			LOAD	TIME	PRE-BMS-92	BMS-92	POST-BMS-92		
W-8-M-31	$8^1/_2$″	Core: cored clay or shale brick; Units in wall thickness: 1; Cells in wall thickness: 1; Minimum % solids: 70; $^1/_2$″ of 1:3 sanded gypsum plaster facings on both sides.	See Notes	4 hrs.		1		1, 44	4
W-8-M-32	$8^1/_2$″	Core: cored clay or shale brick; Units in wall thickness: 2; Cells in wall thickness: 2; Minimum % solids: 87; $^1/_2$″ of 1:3 sanded gypsum plaster facings on one side.	See Notes	6 hrs.		1		1, 45	6
W-8-M-33	$8^1/_2$″	Core: hollow Rolok Bak of clay or shale; $^1/_2$″ of 1:3 sanded gypsum plaster facings on one side.	See Notes	5 hrs.		1		1, 45	5
W-8-M-34	$8^5/_8$″	Core: clay or shale structural tile; Units in wall thickness: 1; Cells in wall thickness: 2; Minimum % solids in units: 40; $^5/_8$″ of 1:3 sanded gypsum plaster facings on one side.	See Notes	2 hrs.		1		1, 20, 21	2
W-8-M-35	$8^5/_8$″	Core: clay or shale structural tile; Units in wall thickness: 1; Cells in wall thickness: 2; Minimum % solids in units: 40; Exposed face: $^5/_8$″ of 1:3 sanded gypsum plaster.	See Notes	1 hr. 30 min.		1		1, 20, 21	$1^1/_2$
W-8-M-36	$8^5/_8$″	Core: clay or shale structural tile; Units in wall thickness: 1; Cells in wall thickness: 2; Minimum % solids in units: 43; $^5/_8$″ of 1:3 sanded gypsum plaster facings on one side.	See Notes	2 hrs.		1		1, 20, 21	2
W-8-M-37	$8^5/_8$″	Core: clay or shale structural tile; Units in wall thickness: 1; Cells in wall thickness: 2; Minimum % solids in units: 43; $^5/_8$″ of 1:3 sanded gypsum plaster of the exposed face only.	See Notes	1 hr. 30 min.		1		1, 20, 21	$1^1/_2$
W-8-M-38	$8^5/_8$″	Core: clay or shale structural tile; Facings: side 1; see Note 17.	See Notes	2 hr.		1		1, 2, 5, 10, 18, 20, 21	2
W-8-M-39	$8^5/_8$″	Core: clay or shale structural tile; Facings: exposed side only; see Note 17.	See Notes	1 hr. 30 min.		1		1, 2, 5, 10, 19, 20, 21	$1^1/_2$
W-8-M-40	$8^5/_8$″	Core: clay or shale structural tile; Facings: exposed side only; see Note 17.	See Notes	3 hrs.		1		1, 2, 5, 13, 18, 20, 21	3
W-8-M-41	$8^5/_8$″	Core: clay or shale structural tile; Facings: exposed side only; see Note 17.	See Notes	2 hrs.		1		1, 2, 5, 13, 19, 20, 21	2
W-8-M-42	$8^5/_8$″	Core: clay or shale structural tile; Facings: side 1; see Note 17.	See Notes	2 hrs. 30 min.		1		1, 2, 9, 18, 20, 21	$2^1/_2$
W-8-M-43	$8^5/_8$″	Core: clay or shale structural tile; Facings: exposed side only; see Note 17.	See Notes	1 hr. 30 min.		1		1, 2, 6, 9, 19, 20, 21	$1^1/_2$
W-8-M-44	$8^5/_8$″	Core: clay or shale structural tile; Facings: side 1, see Note 17; side 2, none.	See Notes	3 hrs.		1		1, 2, 10, 18, 20, 21	3
W-8-M-45	$8^5/_8$″	Core: clay or shale structural tile; Facings: fire side only; see Note 17.	See Notes	1 hr. 30 min.		1		1, 2, 6, 10,19, 20, 21	$1^1/_2$
W-8-M-46	$8^5/_8$″	Core: clay or shale structural tile; Facings: side 1, see Note 17; side 2, none.	See Notes	3 hrs. 30 min.		1		1, 2, 6, 12, 18, 20, 21	$3^1/_2$
W-8-M-47	$8^5/_8$″	Core: clay or shale structural tile; Facings: exposed side only; see Note 17.	See Notes	1 hr. 45 min.		1		1, 2, 6, 12, 19 20, 21	$1^3/_4$
W-8-M-48	$8^5/_8$″	Core: clay or shale structural tile; Facings: side 1, see Note 17; side 2, none.	See Notes	4 hrs.		1		1, 2, 6, 16, 18, 20, 21	4

(Continued)

TABLE 1.1.4—MASONRY WALLS
8″ TO LESS THAN 10″ THICK—(Continued)

ITEM CODE	THICKNESS	CONSTRUCTION DETAILS	PERFORMANCE		REFERENCE NUMBER			NOTES	REC. HOURS
			LOAD	TIME	PRE-BMS-92	BMS-92	POST-BMS-92		
W-8-M-49	8⅝″	Core: clay or shale structural tile; Facings: fire side only; see Note 17.	See Notes	2 hrs.		1		1, 2, 6, 16, 19, 20, 21	2
W-8-M-50	8⅝″	Core: 4″, 40% solid clay or shale clay structural tile; 4″ brick plus ⅝″ of 1:3 sanded gypsum plaster facings on one side.	See Notes	4 hrs.		1		1, 20	4
W-8-M-51	8¾″	8¾″ × 2½″ and 4″ × 2½″ cellular fletton (1873 psi) single and triple cell hollow brick set in ½″ sand mortar in alternate courses.	3.6 tons/ft.	6 hrs.			7	23, 29	6
W-8-M-52	8¾″	8¾″ thick cement brick (2527 psi) with P.C. and sand mortar.	3.6 tons/ft.	6 hrs.			7	23, 24	6
W-8-M-53	8¾″	8¾″ × 2½″ fletton brick (1831 psi) in ½″ sand mortar.	3.6 tons/ft.	6 hrs.			7	23, 24	6
W-8-M-54	8¾″	8¾″ × 2½″ London stock brick (683 psi) in ½″ P.C. - sand mortar.	7.2 tons/ft.	6 hrs.			7	23, 24	6
W-9-M-55	9″	9″ × 2½″ Leicester red wire-cut brick (4465 psi) in ½″ P.C. - sand mortar.	6.0 tons/ft.	6 hrs.			7	23, 24	6
W-9-M-56	9″	9″ × 3″ sand-lime brick (2603 psi) in ½″ P.C. - sand mortar.	3.6 tons/ft.	6 hrs.			7	23, 24	6
W-9-M-57	9″	2 layers 2⅞″ fletton brick (1910 psi) with 3¼″ air space; Cement and sand mortar.	1.5 tons/ft.	32 min.			7	23, 25	⅓
W-9-M-58	9″	9″ × 3″ stairfoot brick (7527 psi) in ½″ sand-cement mortar.	7.2 tons/ft.	6 hrs.			7	23, 24	6
W-9-M-59	9″	Core: solid clay or shale brick; ½″ thick; 1:3 sanded gypsum plaster facings on both sides.	See Notes	7 hrs.		1		1, 22 45	7
W-9-M-60	9″	Core: concrete brick; ½″ of 1:3 sanded gypsum plaster facings on both sides.	See Notes	8 hrs.		1		1, 45	8
W-9-M-61	9″	Core: hollow Rolok of clay or shale; ½″ of 1:3 sanded gypsum plaster facings on both sides.	See Notes	4 hrs.		1		1, 45	4
W-9-M-62	9″	Cored clay or shale brick; Units in wall thickness: 1; Cells in wall thickness: 1; Minimum % solids: 70; ½″ of 1:3 sanded gypsum plaster facings on one side.	See Notes	3 hrs.		1		1, 44	3
W-9-M-63	9″	Cored clay or shale brick; Units in wall thickness: 2; Cells in wall thickness: 2; Minimum % solids: 87; ½″ of 1:3 sanded gypsum plaster facings on both sides.	See Notes	7 hrs.		1		1, 45	7
W-9-M-64	9-10″	Core: cavity wall of clay or shale brick; No facings.	See Notes	5 hrs.		1		1, 45	5
W-9-M-65	9-10″	Core: cavity construction of clay or shale brick; ½″ of 1:3 sanded gypsum plaster facings on one side.	See Notes	6 hrs.		1		1, 45	6
W-9-M-66	9-10″	Core: cavity construction of clay or shale brick; ½″ of 1:3 sanded gypsum plaster facings on both sides.	See Notes	7 hrs.		1		1, 45	7
W-9-M-67	9¼″	Core: clay or shale structural tile; Units in wall thickness: 1; Cells in wall thickness: 2; Minimum % solids in units: 40; ⅝″ of 1:3 sanded gypsum plaster facings on both sides.	See Notes	3 hrs.		1		1, 20, 21	3
W-9-M-68	9¼″	Core: clay or shale structural tile; Units in wall thickness: 1; Cells in wall thickness: 2; Minimum % solids in units: 43; ⅝″ of 1:3 sanded gypsum plaster facings on both sides.	See Notes	3 hrs.		1		1, 20, 21	3
W-9-M-69	9¼″	Core: clay or shale structural tile; Facings: sides 1 and 2; see Note 17.	See Notes	3 hrs.		1		1, 2, 5, 10, 18, 20, 21	3

(Continued)

TABLE 1.1.4—MASONRY WALLS
8″ TO LESS THAN 10″ THICK—(Continued)

| ITEM CODE | THICKNESS | CONSTRUCTION DETAILS | PERFORMANCE | | REFERENCE NUMBER | | | NOTES | REC. HOURS |
			LOAD	TIME	PRE-BMS-92	BMS-92	POST-BMS-92		
W-9-M-70	$9^1/_4″$	Core: clay or shale structural tile; Facings: sides 1 and 2; see Note 17.	See Notes	4 hrs.		1		1, 2, 5, 13, 18, 20, 21	4
W-9-M-71	$9^1/_4″$	Core: clay or shale structural tile; Facings: sides 1 and 2; see Note 17.	See Notes	3 hrs. 30 min.		1		1, 2, 6, 9, 18, 20, 21	$3^1/_2$
W-9-M-72	$9^1/_4″$	Core: clay or shale structural tile; Facings: sides 1 and 2; see Note 17.	See Notes	4 hrs.		1		1, 2, 6, 10, 18, 20, 21	4
W-9-M-73	$9^1/_4″$	Core: clay or shale structural tile; Facings: sides 1 and 2; see Note 17.	See Notes	4 hrs.		1		1, 2, 6, 12, 18, 20, 21	4
W-9-M-74	$9^1/_4″$	Core: clay or shale structural tile; Facings: sides 1 and 2; see Note 17.	See Notes	5 hrs.		1		1, 2, 6, 16, 18, 20, 21	5
W-9-M-75	8″	Cored concrete masonry; see Notes 2, 19, 26, 34, 40; No facings.	80 psi	1 hr. 30. min.		1		1, 20	$1^1/_2$
W-8-M-76	8″	Cored concrete masonry; see Notes 2, 18, 26, 34, 40; No facings.	80 psi	4 hrs.		1		1, 20	4
W-8-M-77	8″	Cored concrete masonry; see Notes 2, 19, 26, 31, 40; No facings.	80 psi	1 hr. 15 min.		1		1, 20	$1^1/_4$
W-8-M-78	8″	Cored concrete masonry; see Notes 2, 18, 26, 31, 40; No facings.	80 psi	3 hrs.		1		1, 20	3
W-8-M-79	8″	Cored concrete masonry; see Notes 2, 19, 26, 36, 42; No facings.	80 psi	1 hr. 30 min.		1		1, 20	$1^1/_2$
W-8-M-80	8″	Cored concrete masonry; see Notes 2, 18, 26, 36, 41; No facings.	80 psi	3 hrs.		1		1, 20	3
W-8-M-81	8″	Cored concrete masonry; see Notes 2, 19, 26, 34, 41; No facings.	80 psi	1 hr.		1		1, 20	1
W-8-M-82	8″	Cored concrete masonry; see Notes 2, 18, 26, 34, 41; No facings.	80 psi	2 hrs. 30 min.		1		1, 20	$2^1/_2$
W-8-M-83	8″	Cored concrete masonry; see Notes 2, 19, 26, 29, 41; No facings.	80 psi	45 min.		1		1, 20	$^3/_4$
W-8-M-84	8″	Cored concrete masonry; see Notes 2, 18, 26, 29, 41; No facings.	80 psi	2 hrs.		1		1, 20	2
W-8-M-85	$8^1/_2″$	Cored concrete masonry; see Notes 3, 18, 26, 34, 41; Facings: $2^1/_4″$ brick.	80 psi	4 hrs.		1		1, 20	4
W-8-M-86	8″	Cored concrete masonry; see Notes 3, 18, 26, 34, 41; Facings: $3^3/_4″$ brick face.	80 psi	5 hrs.		1		1, 20	5
W-8-M-87	8″	Cored concrete masonry; see Notes 2, 19, 26, 30, 43; No facings.	80 psi	12 min.		1		1, 20	$^1/_5$
W-8-M-88	8″	Cored concrete masonry; see Notes 2, 18, 26, 30, 43; No facings.	80 psi	12 min.		1		1, 20	$^1/_5$
W-8-M-89	$8^1/_2″$	Cored concrete masonry; see Notes 2, 19, 26, 34, 40; Facings: fire side only; see Note 38.	80 psi	2 hrs.		1		1, 20	2
W-8-M-90	$8^1/_2″$	Cored concrete masonry; see Notes 2, 18, 26, 34, 40; Facings: side 1; see Note 38.	80 psi	5 hrs.		1		1, 20	5
W-8-M-91	$8^1/_2″$	Cored concrete masonry; see Notes 2, 19, 26, 31, 40; Facings: fire side only; see Note 38.	80 psi	1 hr. 45 min.		1		1, 20	$1^3/_4$
W-8-M-92	$8^1/_2″$	Cored concrete masonry; see Notes 2, 18, 26, 31, 40; Facings: one side; see Note 38.	80 psi	4 hrs.		1		1, 20	4
W-8-M-93	$8^1/_2″$	Cored concrete masonry; see Notes 2, 19, 26, 36, 41; Facings: fire side only; see Note 38.	80 psi	2 hrs.		1		1, 20	2
W-8-M-94	$8^1/_2″$	Cored concrete masonry; see Notes 2, 18, 26, 36, 41; Facings: fire side only; see Note 38.	80 psi	4 hrs.		1		1, 20	4

(Continued)

TABLE 1.1.4—MASONRY WALLS
8″ TO LESS THAN 10″ THICK—(Continued)

ITEM CODE	THICKNESS	CONSTRUCTION DETAILS	PERFORMANCE		REFERENCE NUMBER			NOTES	REC. HOURS
			LOAD	TIME	PRE-BMS-92	BMS-92	POST-BMS-92		
W-8-M-95	$8^1/_2″$	Cored concrete masonry; see Notes 2, 19, 26, 34, 41; Facings: fire side only; see Note 38.	80 psi	1 hr. 30 min.		1		1, 20	$1^1/_2$
W-8-M-96	$8^1/_2″$	Cored concrete masonry; see Notes 2, 18, 26, 34, 41; Facings: one side; see Note 38.	80 psi	3 hrs.		1		1, 20	3
W-8-M-97	$8^1/_2″$	Cored concrete masonry; see Notes 2, 19, 26, 29, 41; Facings: fire side only; see Note 38.	80 psi	1 hr. 30 min.		1		1, 20	$1^1/_2$
W-8-M-98	$8^1/_2″$	Cored concrete masonry; see Notes 2, 18, 26, 29, 41; Facings: one side; see Note 38.	80 psi	2 hrs. 30 min.		1		1, 20	$2^1/_2$
W-8-M-99	$8^1/_2″$	Cored concrete masonry; see Notes 3, 19, 23, 27, 41; No facings.	80 psi	1 hr. 15 min.		1		1, 20	$1^1/_4$
W-8-M-100	$8^1/_2″$	Cored concrete masonry; see Notes 3, 18, 23, 27, 41; No facings.	80 psi	3 hrs. 30 min.		1		1, 20	$3^1/_2$
W-8-M-101	$8^1/_2″$	Cored concrete masonry; see Notes 3, 18, 26, 34, 41; Facings: $3^3/_4″$ brick face; one side only; see Note 38.	80 psi	6 hrs.		1		1, 20	6
W-8-M-102	$8^1/_2″$	Cored concrete masonry; see Notes 2, 19, 26, 30, 43; Facings: fire side only; see Note 38.	80 psi	30 min.		1		1, 20	$1/_2$
W-8-M-103	$8^1/_2″$	Cored concrete masonry; see Notes 2, 18, 26, 30, 43; Facings: one side only; see Note 38.	80 psi	12 min.		1		1, 20	$1/_5$
W-9-M-104	$9″$	Cored concrete masonry; see Notes 2, 18, 26, 34, 40; Facings: both sides; see Note 38.	80 psi	6 hrs.		1		1, 20	6
W-9-M-105	$9″$	Cored concrete masonry; see Notes 2, 18, 26, 31, 40; Facings: both sides; see Note 38.	80 psi	5 hrs.		1		1, 20	5
W-9-M-106	$9″$	Cored concrete masonry; see Notes 2, 18, 26, 36, 41; Facings: both sides of wall; see Note 38.	80 psi	5 hrs.		1		1, 20	5
W-9-M-107	$9″$	Cored concrete masonry; see Notes 2, 18, 26, 34, 41; Facings: both sides; see Note 38.	80 psi	4 hrs.		1		1, 20	4
W-9-M-108	$9″$	Cored concrete masonry; see Notes 2, 18, 26, 29, 41; Facings: both sides; see Note 38.	80 psi	3 hrs. 30 min.		1		1, 20	$3^1/_2$
W-9-M-109	$9″$	Cored concrete masonry; see Notes 3, 19, 23, 27, 40; Facings: fire side only; see Note 38.	80 psi	1 hr. 45 min.		1		1, 20	$1^3/_4$
W-9-M-110	$9″$	Cored concrete masonry; see Notes 3, 18, 23, 27, 41; Facings: one side only; see Note 38.	80 psi	4 hrs.		1		1, 20	4
W-9-M-111	$9″$	Cored concrete masonry; see Notes 3, 18, 26, 34, 41; $2^1/_4″$ brick face on one side only; see Note 38.	80 psi	5 hrs.		1		1, 20	5
W-9-M-112	$9″$	Cored concrete masonry; see Notes 2, 18, 26, 30, 43; Facings: both sides; see Note 38.	80 psi	30 min.		1		1, 20	$1/_2$
W-9-M-113	$9^1/_2″$	Cored concrete masonry; see Notes 3, 18, 23, 27, 41; Facings: both sides; see Note 38.	80 psi	5 hrs.		1		1, 20	5
W-8-M-114	$8″$		200 psi	5 hrs.			43	22	5

Notes:
1. Tested at NBS under ASA Spec. No. 43-1934 (ASTM C 19-53).
2. One unit in wall thickness.
3. Two units in wall thickness.
4. Two or three units in wall thickness.
5. Two cells in wall thickness.
6. Three or four cells in wall thickness.
7. Four or five cells in wall thickness.
8. Five or six cells in wall thickness.
9. Minimum percent of solid materials in units = 40%.
10. Minimum percent of solid materials in units = 43%.

TABLE 1.1.4—MASONRY WALLS
8″ TO LESS THAN 10″ THICK—(Continued)

11. Minimum percent of solid materials in units = 46%.
12. Minimum percent of solid materials in units = 48%.
13. Minimum percent of solid materials in units = 49%.
14. Minimum percent of solid materials in units = 45%.
15. Minimum percent of solid materials in units = 51%.
16. Minimum percent of solid materials in units = 53%.
17. Not less than $^5/_8$ inch thickness of 1:3 sanded gypsum plaster.
18. Noncombustible or no members framed into wall.
19. Combustible members framed into wall.
20. Load: 80 psi for gross cross-sectional area of wall.
21. Portland cement-lime mortar.
22. Failure mode thermal.
23. British test.
24. Passed all criteria.
25. Failed by sudden collapse with no preceding signs of impending failure.
26. One cell in wall thickness.
27. Two cells in wall thickness.
28. Three cells in wall thickness.
29. Minimum percent of solid material in concrete units = 52.
30. Minimum percent of solid material in concrete units = 54.
31. Minimum percent of solid material in concrete units = 55.
32. Minimum percent of solid material in concrete units = 57.
33. Minimum percent of solid material in concrete units = 60.
34. Minimum percent of solid material in concrete units = 62.
35. Minimum percent of solid material in concrete units = 65.
36. Minimum percent of solid material in concrete units = 70.
37. Minimum percent of solid material in concrete units = 76.
38. Not less than $^1/_2$ inch of 1:3 sanded gypsum plaster.
39. Three units in wall thickness.
40. Concrete units made with expanded slag or pumice aggregates.
41. Concrete units made with expanded burned clay or shale, crushed limestone, air cooled slag or cinders.
42. Concrete units made with calcareous sand and gravel. Coarse aggregate, 60 percent or more calcite and dolomite.
43. Concrete units made with siliceous sand and gravel. Ninety percent or more quartz, chert and dolomite.
44. Load: 120 psi for gross cross-sectional area of wall.
45. Load: 160 psi for gross cross-sectional area of wall.

FIGURE 1.1.5—WALLS—MASONRY
10″ TO LESS THAN 12″ THICK

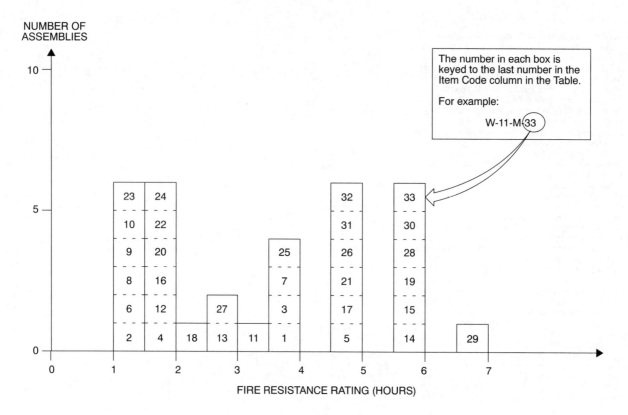

TABLE 1.1.5—WALLS—MASONRY
10″ TO LESS THAN 12″ THICK

ITEM CODE	THICKNESS	CONSTRUCTION DETAILS	PERFORMANCE		REFERENCE NUMBER			NOTES	REC. HOURS
			LOAD	TIME	PRE-BMS-92	BMS-92	POST-BMS-92		
W-10-M-1	10″	Core: two $3^3/_4$″, 40% solid clay or shale structural tiles with 2″ air space between; Facings: $3/_4$″ portland cement plaster on stucco on both sides.	80 psi	4 hrs.		1		1, 20	4
W-10-M-2	10″	Core: cored concrete masonry, 2″ air cavity; see Notes 3, 19, 27, 34, 40; No facings.	80 psi	1 hr. 30 min.		1		1, 20	$1^1/_2$
W-10-M-3	10″	Cored concrete masonry; see Notes 3, 18, 27, 34, 40; No facings.	80 psi	4 hrs.		1		1, 20	4
W-10-M-4	10″	Cored concrete masonry; see Notes 2, 19, 26, 34, 40; No facings.	80 psi	2 hrs.		1		1, 20	2
W-10-M-5	10″	Cored concrete masonry; see Notes 2, 18, 26, 33, 40; No facings.	80 psi	5 hrs.		1		1, 20	5
W-10-M-6	10″	Cored concrete masonry; see Notes 2, 19, 26, 33, 41; No facings.	80 psi	1 hr. 30 min.		1		1, 20	$1^1/_2$
W-10-M-7	10″	Cored concrete masonry; see Notes 2, 18, 26, 33, 41; No facings.	80 psi	4 hrs.		1		1, 20	4
W-10-M-8	10″	Cored concrete masonry (cavity type 2″ air space); see Notes 3, 19, 27, 34, 42; No facings.	80 psi	1 hr. 15 min.		1		1, 20	$1^1/_4$
W-10-M-9	10″	Cored concrete masonry (cavity type 2″ air space); see Notes 3, 18, 27, 34, 42; No facings.	80 psi	1 hr. 15 min.		1		1, 20	$1^1/_4$
W-10-M-10	10″	Cored concrete masonry (cavity type 2″ air space); see Notes 3, 19, 27, 34, 41; No facings.	80 psi	1 hr. 15 min.		1		1, 20	$1^1/_4$

(Continued)

TABLE 1.1.5—WALLS—MASONRY
10″ TO LESS THAN 12″ THICK—(Continued)

ITEM CODE	THICKNESS	CONSTRUCTION DETAILS	PERFORMANCE		REFERENCE NUMBER			NOTES	REC. HOURS
			LOAD	TIME	PRE-BMS-92	BMS-92	POST-BMS-92		
W-10-M-11	10″	Cored concrete masonry (cavity type 2″ air space); see Notes 3, 18, 27, 34, 41; No facings.	80 psi	3 hrs. 30 min.		1		1, 20	$3^1/_2$
W-10-M-12	10″	9″ thick concrete block ($11^3/_4″ \times 9″ \times 4^1/_4″$) with two 2″ thick voids included; $3/_8″$ P.C. plaster $1/_8″$ neat gypsum.	N/A	1 hr. 53 min.			7	23, 44	$1^3/_4$
W-10-M-13	10″	Holly clay tile block wall - $8^1/_2″$ block with two 3″ voids in each $8^1/_2″$ section; $3/_4″$ gypsum plaster - each face.	N/A	2 hrs. 42 min.			7	23, 25	$2^1/_2$
W-10-M-14	10″	Two layers $4^1/_4″$ brick with $1^1/_2″$ air space; No ties sand cement mortar. (Fletton brick - 1910 psi).	N/A	6 hrs.			7	23, 24	6
W-10-M-15	10″	Two layers $4^1/_4″$ thick Fletton brick (1910 psi); $1^1/_2″$ air space; Ties: 18″ o.c. vertical; 3′ o.c. horizontal.	N/A	6 hrs.			7	23, 24	6
W-10-M-16	$10^1/_2″$	Cored concrete masonry; 2″ air cavity; see Notes 3, 19, 27, 34, 40; Facings: fire side only; see Note 38.	80 psi	2 hrs.		1		1, 20	2
W-10-M-17	$10^1/_2″$	Cored concrete masonry; see Notes 3, 18, 27, 34, 40; Facings: side 1 only; see Note 38.	80 psi	5 hrs.		1		1, 20	5
W-10-M-18	$10^1/_2″$	Cored concrete masonry; see Notes 2, 19, 26, 33, 40; Facings: fire side only; see Note 38.	80 psi	2 hrs. 30 min.		1		1, 20	$2^1/_2$
W-10-M-19	$10^1/_2″$	Cored concrete masonry; see Notes 2, 18, 26, 33, 40; Facings: one side; see Note 38.	80 psi	6 hrs.		1		1, 20	6
W-10-M-20	$10^1/_2″$	Cored concrete masonry; see Notes 2, 19, 26, 33, 41; Facings: fire side of wall only; see Note 38.	80 psi	2 hrs.		1		1, 20	2
W-10-M-21	$10^1/_2″$	Cored concrete masonry; see Notes 2, 18, 26, 33, 41; Facings: one side only; see Note 38.	80 psi	5 hrs.		1		1, 20	5
W-10-M-22	$10^1/_2″$	Cored concrete masonry (cavity type 2″ air space); see Notes 3,19, 27, 34, 42; Facings: fire side only; see Note 38.	80 psi	1 hr. 45 min.		1		1, 20	$1^3/_4$
W-10-M-23	$10^1/_2″$	Cored concrete masonry (cavity type 2″ air space); see Notes 3, 18, 27, 34, 42; Facings: one side only; see Note 38.	80 psi	1 hr. 15 min.		1		1, 20	$1^1/_4$
W-10-M-24	$10^1/_2″$	Cored concrete masonry (cavity type 2″ air space); see Notes 3, 19, 27, 34, 41; Facings: fire side only; see Note 38.	80 psi	2 hrs.		1		1, 20	2
W-10-M-25	$10^1/_2″$	Cored concrete masonry (cavity type 2″ air space); see Notes 3, 18, 27, 34, 41; Facings: one side only; see Note 38.	80 psi	4 hrs.		1		1, 20	4
W-10-M-26	$10^5/_8″$	Core: 8″, 40% solid tile plus 2″ furring tile; $5/_8″$ sanded gypsum plaster between tile types; Facings: both sides $3/_4″$ portland cement plaster or stucco.	80 psi	5 hrs.		1		1, 20	5
W-10-M-27	$10^5/_8″$	Core: 8″, 40% solid tile plus 2″ furring tile; $5/_8″$ sanded gypsum plaster between tile types; Facings: one side $3/_4″$ portland cement plaster or stucco.	80 psi	3 hrs. 30 min.		1		1, 20	$3^1/_2$
W-11-M-28	11″	Cored concrete masonry; see Notes 3, 18, 27, 34, 40; Facings: both sides; see Note 38.	80 psi	6 hrs.		1		1, 20	6
W-11-M-29	11″	Cored concrete masonry; see Notes 2, 18, 26, 33, 40; Facings: both sides; see Note 38.	80 psi	7 hrs.		1		1, 20	7

(Continued)

TABLE 1.1.5—WALLS—MASONRY
10″ TO LESS THAN 12″ THICK—(Continued)

ITEM CODE	THICKNESS	CONSTRUCTION DETAILS	PERFORMANCE		REFERENCE NUMBER			NOTES	REC. HOURS
			LOAD	TIME	PRE-BMS-92	BMS-92	POST-BMS-92		
W-11-M-30	11″	Cored concrete masonry; see Notes 2, 18, 26, 33, 41; Facings: both sides of wall; see Note 38.	80 psi	6 hrs.		1		1, 20	6
W-11-M-31	11″	Cored concrete masonry (cavity type 2″ air space); see Notes 3, 18, 27, 34, 42; Facings: both sides; see Note 38.	80 psi	5 hrs.		1		1, 20	5
W-11-M-32	11″	Cored concrete masonry (cavity type 2″ air space); see Notes 3, 18, 27, 34, 41; Facings: both sides; see Note 38.	80 psi	5 hrs.		1		1, 20	5
W-11-M-33	11″	Two layers brick (4½″ Fletton, 2,428 psi) 2″ air space; galvanized ties; 18″ o.c. - horizontal; 3' o.c. - vertical.	3 tons/ft.	6 hrs.			7	23, 24	6

Notes:
1. Tested at NBS - ASA Spec. No. A2-1934.
2. One unit in wall thickness.
3. Two units in wall thickness.
4. Two or three units in wall thickness.
5. Two cells in wall thickness.
6. Three or four cells in wall thickness.
7. Four or five cells in wall thickness.
8. Five or six cells in wall thickness.
9. Minimum percent of solid materials in units = 40%.
10. Minimum percent of solid materials in units = 43%.
11. Minimum percent of solid materials in units = 46%.
12. Minimum percent of solid materials in units = 48%.
13. Minimum percent of solid materials in units = 49%.
14. Minimum percent of solid materials in units = 45%.
15. Minimum percent of solid materials in units = 51%.
16. Minimum percent of solid materials in units = 53%.
17. Not less than $^5/_8$ inch thickness of 1:3 sanded gypsum plaster.
18. Noncombustible or no members framed into wall.
19. Combustible members framed into wall.
20. Load: 80 psi for gross cross sectional area of wall.
21. Portland cement-lime mortar.
22. Failure mode - thermal.
23. British test.
24. Passed all criteria.
25. Failed by sudden collapse with no preceding signs of impending failure.
26. One cell in wall thickness.
27. Two cells in wall thickness.
28. Three cells in wall thickness.
29. Minimum percent of solid material in concrete units = 52%.
30. Minimum percent of solid material in concrete units = 54%.
31. Minimum percent of solid material in concrete units = 55%.
32. Minimum percent of solid material in concrete units = 57%.
33. Minimum percent of solid material in concrete units = 60%.
34. Minimum percent of solid material in concrete units = 62%.
35. Minimum percent of solid material in concrete units = 65%.
36. Minimum percent of solid material in concrete units = 70%.
37. Minimum percent of solid material in concrete units = 76%.
38. Not less than $^1/_2$″ of 1:3 sanded gypsum plaster.
39. Three units in wall thickness.
40. Concrete units made with expanded slag or pumice aggregates.
41. Concrete units made with expanded burned clay or shale, crushed limestone, air cooled slag or cinders.
42. Concrete units made with calcareous sand and gravel. Coarse aggregate, 60 percent or more calcite and dolomite.

FIGURE 1.1.6—WALLS—MASONRY
12″ TO LESS THAN 14″ THICK

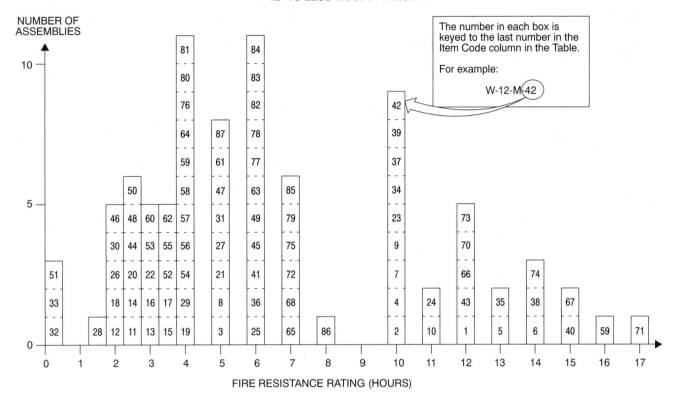

TABLE 1.1.6—WALLS—MASONRY
12″ TO LESS THAN 14″ THICK

ITEM CODE	THICKNESS	CONSTRUCTION DETAILS	PERFORMANCE		REFERENCE NUMBER			NOTES	REC. HOURS
			LOAD	TIME	PRE-BMS-92	BMS-92	POST-BMS-92		
W-12-M-1	12″	Core: solid clay or shale brick; No facings.	N/A	12 hrs.		1		1	12
W-12-M-2	12″	Core: solid clay or shale brick; No facings.	160 psi	10 hrs.		1		1, 44	10
W-12-M-3	12″	Core: hollow Rolok of clay or shale; No facings.	160 psi	5 hrs.		1		1, 44	5
W-12-M-4	12″	Core: hollow Rolok Bak of clay or shale; No facings.	160 psi	10 hrs.		1		1, 44	10
W-12-M-5	12″	Core: concrete brick; No facings.	160 psi	13 hrs.		1		1, 44	13
W-12-M-6	12″	Core: sand-lime brick; No facings.	N/A	14 hrs.		1		1	14
W-12-M-7	12″	Core: sand-lime brick; No facings.	160 psi	10 hrs.		1		1, 44	10
W-12-M-8	12″	Cored clay or shale brick; Units in wall thickness: 1; Cells in wall thickness: 2; Minimum % solids: 70; No facings.	120 psi	5 hrs.		1		1, 45	5
W-12-M-9	12″	Cored clay or shale brick; Units in wall thickness: 3; Cells in wall thickness: 3; Minimum % solids: 87; No facings.	160 psi	10 hrs.		1		1, 44	10
W-12-M-10	12″	Cored clay or shale brick; Units in wall thickness: 3; Cells in wall thickness: 3; Minimum % solids: 87; No facings.	N/A	11 hrs.		1		1	11
W-12-M-11	12″	Core: clay or shale structural tile; see Notes 2, 6, 9, 18; No facings.	80 psi	2 hrs.		1		1, 20	$2^1/_2$
W-12-M-12	12″	Core: clay or shale structural tile; see Notes 2, 4, 9, 19; No facings.	80 psi	2 hrs.		1		1, 20	2
W-12-M-13	12″	Core: clay or shale structural tile; see Notes 2, 6, 14, 19; No facings.	80 psi	3 hrs.		1		1, 20	3

(Continued)

TABLE 1.1.6—WALLS—MASONRY
12″ TO LESS THAN 14″ THICK—(Continued)

ITEM CODE	THICKNESS	CONSTRUCTION DETAILS	PERFORMANCE		REFERENCE NUMBER			NOTES	REC. HOURS
			LOAD	TIME	PRE-BMS-92	BMS-92	POST-BMS-92		
W-12-M-14	12″	Core: clay or shale structural tile; see Notes 2, 6,14, 18; No facings.	80 psi	2 hrs. 30 min.		1		1, 20	$2^1/_2$
W-12-M-15	12″	Core: clay or shale structural tile; see Notes 2, 4, 13, 18; No facings.	80 psi	3 hrs. 30 min		1		1, 20	$3^1/_2$
W-12-M-16	12″	Core: clay or shale structural tile; see Notes 2, 4, 13, 19; No facings.	80 psi	3 hrs.		1		1, 20	3
W-12-M-17	12″	Core: clay or shale structural tile; see Notes 3, 6, 9, 18; No facings.	80 psi	3 hrs. 30 min.		1		1, 20	$3^1/_2$
W-12-M-18	12″	Core: clay or shale structural tile; see Notes 3, 6, 9, 19; No facings.	80 psi	2 hrs.		1		1, 20	2
W-12-M-19	12″	Core: clay or shale structural tile; see Notes 3, 6, 14, 18; No facings.	80 psi	4 hrs.		1		1, 20	4
W-12-M-20	12″	Core: clay or shale structural tile; see Notes 3, 6, 14, 19; No facings.	80 psi	2 hrs. 30 min.		1		1, 20	$2^1/_2$
W-12-M-21	12″	Core: clay or shale structural tile; see Notes 3, 6, 16, 18; No facings.	80 psi	5 hrs.		1		1, 20	5
W-12-M-22	12″	Core: clay or shale structural tile; see Notes 3, 6, 16, 19; No facings.	80 psi	3 hrs.		1		1, 20	3
W-12-M-23	12″	Core: 8″, 70% solid clay or shale structural tile; 4″ brick facings on one side.	80 psi	10 hrs.		1		1, 20	10
W-12-M-24	12″	Core: 8″, 70% solid clay or shale structural tile; 4″ brick facings on one side.	N/A	11 hrs.		1		1	11
W-12-M-25	12″	Core: 8″, 40% solid clay or shale structural tile; 4″ brick facings on one side.	80 psi	6 hrs.		1		1, 20	6
W-12-M-26	12″	Cored concrete masonry; see Notes 1, 9, 15, 16, 20; No facings.	80 psi	2 hrs.		1		1, 20	2
W-12-M-27	12″	Cored concrete masonry; see Notes 2, 18, 26, 34, 41; No facings.	80 psi	5 hrs.		1		1, 20	5
W-12-M-28	12″	Cored concrete masonry; see Notes 2, 19, 26, 31, 41; No facings.	80 psi	1 hr. 30 min.		1		1, 20	$1^1/_2$
W-12-M-29	12″	Cored concrete masonry; see Notes 2, 18, 26, 31, 41; No facings.	80 psi	4 hrs.		1		1, 20	4
W-12-M-30	12″	Cored concrete masonry; see Notes 3, 19, 27, 31, 43; No facings.	80 psi	2 hrs.		1		1, 20	2
W-12-M-31	12″	Cored concrete masonry; see Notes 3, 18, 27, 31, 43; No facings.	80 psi	5 hrs.		1		1, 20	5
W-12-M-32	12″	Cored concrete masonry; see Notes 2, 19, 26, 32, 43; No facings.	80 psi	25 min.		1		1, 20	$1/_3$
W-12-M-33	12″	Cored concrete masonry; see Notes 2, 18, 26, 32, 43; No facings.	80 psi	25 min.		1		1, 20	$1/_3$
W-12-M-34	$12^1/_2$″	Core: solid clay or shale brick; $1/_2$″ of 1:3 sanded gypsum plaster facings on one side.	160 psi	10 hrs.		1		1, 44	10
W-12-M-35	$12^1/_2$″	Core: solid clay or shale brick; $1/_2$″ of 1:3 sanded gypsum plaster facings on one side.	N/A	13 hrs.		1		1	13
W-12-M-36	$12^1/_2$″	Core: hollow Rolok of clay or shale; $1/_2$″ of 1:3 sanded gypsum plaster facings on one side.	160 psi	6 hrs.		1		1, 44	6
W-12-M-37	$12^1/_2$″	Core: hollow Rolok Bak of clay or shale; $1/_2$″ of 1:3 sanded gypsum plaster facings on one side.	160 psi	10 hrs.		1		1, 44	10
W-12-M-38	$12^1/_2$″	Core: concrete; $1/_2$″ of 1:3 sanded gypsum plaster facings on one side.	160 psi	14 hrs.		1		1, 44	14
W-12-M-39	$12^1/_2$″	Core: sand-lime brick; $1/_2$″ of 1:3 sanded gypsum plaster facings on one side.	160 psi	10 hrs.		1		1, 44	10
W-12-M-40	$12^1/_2$″	Core: sand-lime brick; $1/_2$″ of 1:3 sanded gypsum plaster facings on one side.	N/A	15 hrs.		1		1	15

(Continued)

TABLE 1.1.6—WALLS—MASONRY
12″ TO LESS THAN 14″ THICK—(Continued)

ITEM CODE	THICKNESS	CONSTRUCTION DETAILS	PERFORMANCE		REFERENCE NUMBER			NOTES	REC. HOURS
			LOAD	TIME	PRE-BMS-92	BMS-92	POST-BMS-92		
W-12-M-41	$12^1/_2''$	Cored clay or shale brick; Units in wall thickness: 1; Cells in wall thickness: 2; Minimum % solids: 70; $^1/_2''$ of 1:3 sanded gypsum plaster facings on one side.	120 psi	6 hrs.		1		1, 45	6
W-12-M-42	$12^1/_2''$	Cored clay or shale brick; Units in wall thickness: 3; Cells in wall thickness: 3; Minimum % solids: 87; $^1/_2''$ of 1:3 sanded gypsum plaster facings on one side.	160 psi	10 hrs.		1		1, 44	10
W-12-M-43	$12^1/_2''$	Cored clay or shale brick; Units in wall thickness: 3; Cells in wall thickness: 3; Minimum % solids: 87; $^1/_2''$ of 1:3 sanded gypsum plaster facings on one side.	N/A	12 hrs.		1		1	12
W-12-M-44	$12^1/_2''$	Cored concrete masonry; see Notes 2, 19, 26, 34, 41; Facings: fire side only; see Note 38.	80 psi	2 hrs. 30 min.		1		1, 20	$2^1/_2$
W-12-M-45	$12^1/_2''$	Cored concrete masonry; see Notes 2, 18, 26, 34, 39, 41; Facings: one side only; see Note 38.	80 psi	6 hrs.		1		1, 20	6
W-12-M-46	$12^1/_2''$	Cored concrete masonry; see Notes 2, 19, 26, 31, 41; Facings: fire side only; see Note 38.	80 psi	2 hrs.		1		1, 20	2
W-12-M-47	$12^1/_2''$	Cored concrete masonry; see Notes 2, 18, 26, 31, 41; Facings: one side of wall only; see Note 38.	80 psi	5 hrs.		1		1, 20	5
W-12-M-48	$12^1/_2''$	Cored concrete masonry; see Notes 3, 19, 27, 31, 43; Facings: fire side only; see Note 38.	80 psi	2 hrs. 30 min.		1		1, 20	$2^1/_2$
W-12-M-49	$12^1/_2''$	Cored concrete masonry; see Notes 3, 18, 27, 31, 43; Facings: one side only; see Note 38.	80 psi	6 hrs.		1		1, 20	6
W-12-M-50	$12^1/_2''$	Cored concrete masonry; see Notes 2, 19, 26, 32, 43; Facings: fire side only; see Note 38.	80 psi	2 hrs. 30 min.		1		1, 20	$2^1/_2$
W-12-M-51	$12^1/_2''$	Cored concrete masonry; see Notes 2, 18, 26, 32, 43; Facings: one side only; see Note 38.	80 psi	25 min.		1		1, 20	$^1/_3$
W-12-M-52	$12^5/_8''$	Clay or shale structural tile; see Notes 2, 6, 9, 18; Facings: side 1, see Note 17; side 2, none.	80 psi	3 hrs. 30 min.		1		1, 20	$3^1/_2$
W-12-M-53	$12^5/_8''$	Clay or shale structural tile; see Notes 2, 6, 9, 19; Facings: fire side only; see Note 17.	80 psi	3 hrs.		1		1, 20	3
W-12-M-54	$12^5/_8''$	Clay or shale structural tile; see Notes 2, 6, 14, 19; Facings: side 1, see Note 17; side 2, none.	80 psi	4 hrs.		1		1, 20	4
W-12-M-55	$12^5/_8''$	Clay or shale structural tile; see Notes 2, 6, 14, 18; Facings: exposed side only; see note 17.	80 psi	3 hrs. 30 min.		1		1, 20	$3^1/_2$
W-12-M-56	$12^5/_8''$	Clay or shale structural tile; see Notes 2, 4, 13, 18; Facings: side 1, see Note 17; side 2, none.	80 psi	4 hrs.		1		1, 20	4
W-12-M-57	$12^5/_8''$	Clay or shale structural tile; see Notes 1, 4, 13, 19; Facings: fire side only; see Note 17.	80 psi	4 hrs.		1		1, 20	4
W-12-M-58	$12^5/_8''$	Clay or shale structural tile; see Notes 3, 6, 9, 18; Facings: side 1, see Note 17; side 2, none.	80 psi	4 hrs.		1		1, 20	4
W-12-M-59	$12^5/_8''$	Clay or shale structural tile; see Notes 3, 6, 9, 19; Facings: fire side only; see Note 17.	80 psi	3 hrs.		1		1, 20	3
W-12-M-60	$12^5/_8''$	Clay or shale structural tile; see Notes 3, 6, 14, 18; Facings: side 1, see Note 17; side 2, none.	80 psi	5 hrs.		1		1, 20	5

(Continued)

TABLE 1.1.6—WALLS—MASONRY
12″ TO LESS THAN 14″ THICK—(Continued)

ITEM CODE	THICKNESS	CONSTRUCTION DETAILS	PERFORMANCE		REFERENCE NUMBER			NOTES	REC. HOURS
			LOAD	TIME	PRE-BMS-92	BMS-92	POST-BMS-92		
W-12-M-61	12⅝″	Clay or shale structural tile; see Notes 3, 6, 14, 19; Facings: fire side only; see Note 17.	80 psi	3 hrs. 30 min.		1		1, 20	3½
W-12-M-62	12⅝″	Clay or shale structural tile; see Notes 3, 6, 16, 18; Facings: side 1, see Note 17; side 2, none.	80 psi	6 hrs.		1		1, 20	6
W-12-M-63	12⅝″	Clay or shale structural tile; see Notes 3, 6, 16, 19; Facings: fire side only; see Note 17.	80 psi	4 hrs.		1		1, 20	4
W-12-M-64	12⅝″	Core: 8″, 40% solid clay or shale structural tile; Facings: 4″ brick plus ⅝″ of 1:3 sanded gypsum plaster on one side.	80 psi	7 hrs.		1		1, 20	7
W-13-M-65	13″	Core: solid clay or shale brick; ½″ of 1:3 sanded gypsum plaster facings on both sides.	160 psi	12 hrs.		1		1, 44	12
W-13-M-66	13″	Core: solid clay or shale brick; ½″ of 1:3 sanded gypsum plaster facings on both sides.	N/A	15 hrs.		1		1, 20	15
W-13-M-67	13″	Core: solid clay or shale brick; ½″ of 1:3 sanded gypsum plaster facings on both sides.	N/A	15 hrs.		1		1	15
W-13-M-68	13″	Core: hollow Rolok of clay or shale; ½″ of 1:3 sanded gypsum plaster facings on both sides.	80 psi	7 hrs.		1		1, 20	7
W-13-M-69	13″	Core: concrete brick; ½″ of 1:3 sanded gypsum plaster facings on both sides.	160 psi	16 hrs.		1		1, 44	16
W-13-M-70	13″	Core: sand-lime brick; ½″ of 1:3 sanded gypsum plaster facings on both sides.	160 psi	12 hrs.		1		1, 44	12
W-13-M-71	13″	Core: sand-lime brick; ½″ of 1:3 sanded gypsum plaster facings on both sides.	N/A	17 hrs.		1		1	17
W-13-M-72	13″	Cored clay or shale brick; Units in wall thickness: 1; Cells in wall thickness: 2; Minimum % solids: 70; ½″ of 1:3 sanded gypsum plaster facings on both sides.	120 psi	7 hrs.		1		1, 45	7
W-13-M-73	13″	Cored clay or shale brick; Units in wall thickness: 3; Cells in wall thickness: 3; Minimum % solids: 87; ½″ of 1:3 sanded gypsum plaster facings on both sides.	160 psi	12 hrs.		1		1, 44	12
W-13-M-74	13″	Cored clay or shale brick; Units in wall thickness: 3; Cells in wall thickness: 2; Minimum % solids: 87; ½″ of 1:3 sanded gypsum plaster facings on both sides.	N/A	14 hrs.		1		1	14
W-13-M-75	13″	Cored concrete masonry; see Notes 18, 23, 28, 39, 41; No facings.	80 psi	7 hrs.		1		1, 20	7
W-13-M-76	13″	Cored concrete masonry; see Notes 19, 23, 28, 39, 41; No facings.	80 psi	4 hrs.		1		1, 20	4
W-13-M-77	13″	Cored concrete masonry; see Notes 3, 18, 27, 31, 43; Facings: both sides; see Note 38.	80 psi	6 hrs.		1		1, 20	6
W-13-M-78	13″	Cored concrete masonry; see Notes 2, 18, 26, 31, 41; Facings: both sides; see Note 38.	80 psi	6 hrs.		1		1, 20	6
W-13-M-79	13″	Cored concrete masonry; see Notes 2, 18, 26, 34, 41; Facings: both sides of wall; see Note 38.	80 psi	7 hrs.		1		1, 20	7
W-13-M-80	13¼″	Core: clay or shale structural tile; see Notes 2, 6, 9, 18; Facings: both sides; see Note 17.	80 psi	4 hrs.		1		1, 20	4

(Continued)

TABLE 1.1.6—WALLS—MASONRY
12″ TO LESS THAN 14″ THICK—(Continued)

ITEM CODE	THICKNESS	CONSTRUCTION DETAILS	PERFORMANCE		REFERENCE NUMBER			NOTES	REC. HOURS
			LOAD	TIME	PRE-BMS-92	BMS-92	POST-BMS-92		
W-13-M-81	13¼″	Core: clay or shale structural tile; see Notes 2, 6, 14, 19; Facings: both sides; see Note 17.	80 psi	4 hrs.		1		1, 20	4
W-13-M-82	13¼″	Core: clay or shale structural tile; see Notes 2, 4, 13, 18; Facings: both sides; see Note 17.	80 psi	6 hrs.		1		1, 20	6
W-13-M-83	13¼″	Core: clay or shale structural tile; see Notes 3, 6, 9, 18; Facings: both sides; see Note 17.	80 psi	6 hrs.		1		1, 20	6
W-13-M-84	13¼″	Core: clay or shale structural tile; see Notes 3, 6, 14, 18; Facings: both sides; see Note 17.	80 psi	6 hrs.		1		1, 20	6
W-13-M-85	13¼″	Core: clay or shale structural tile; see Notes 3, 6, 16, 18; Facings: both sides; see Note 17.	80 psi	7 hrs.		1		1, 20	7
W-13-M-86	13½″	Cored concrete masonry; see Notes 18, 23, 28, 39, 41; Facings: one side only; see Note 38.	80 psi	8 hrs.		1		1, 20	8
W-13-M-87	13½″	Cored concrete masonry; see Notes 19, 23, 28, 39, 41; Facings: fire side only; see Note 38.	80 psi	5 hrs.		1		1, 20	5

Notes:
1. Tested at NBS - ASA Spec. No. A2-1934.
2. One unit in wall thickness.
3. Two units in wall thickness.
4. Two or three units in wall thickness.
5. Two cells in wall thickness.
6. Three or four cells in wall thickness.
7. Four or five cells in wall thickness.
8. Five or six cells in wall thickness.
9. Minimum percent of solid materials in units = 40%.
10. Minimum percent of solid materials in units = 43%.
11. Minimum percent of solid materials in units = 46%.
12. Minimum percent of solid materials in units = 48%.
13. Minimum percent of solid materials in units = 49%.
14. Minimum percent of solid materials in units = 45%.
15. Minimum percent of solid materials in units = 51%.
16. Minimum percent of solid materials in units = 53%.
17. Not less than ⅝ inch thickness of 1:3 sanded gypsum plaster.
18. Noncombustible or no members framed into wall.
19. Combustible members framed into wall.
20. Load: 80 psi for gross area.
21. Portland cement-lime mortar.
22. Failure mode - thermal.
23. British test.
24. Passed all criteria.
25. Failed by sudden collapse with no preceding signs of impending failure.
26. One cell in wall thickness.
27. Two cells in wall thickness.
28. Three cells in wall thickness.
29. Minimum percent of solid material in concrete units = 52%.
30. Minimum percent of solid material in concrete units = 54%.
31. Minimum percent of solid material in concrete units = 55%.
32. Minimum percent of solid material in concrete units = 57%.
33. Minimum percent of solid material in concrete units = 60%.
34. Minimum percent of solid material in concrete units = 62%.
35. Minimum percent of solid material in concrete units = 65%.
36. Minimum percent of solid material in concrete units = 70%.
37. Minimum percent of solid material in concrete units = 76%.
38. Not less than ½″ of 1:3 sanded gypsum plaster.
39. Three units in wall thickness.
40. Concrete units made with expanded slag or pumice aggregates.
41. Concrete units made with expanded burned clay or shale, crushed limestone, air cooled slag or cinders.
42. Concrete units made with calcareous sand and gravel. Coarse aggregate, 60 percent or more calcite and dolomite.
43. Concrete units made with siliceous sand and gravel. Ninety percent or more quartz, chert or flint.
44. Load: 160 psi of gross wall cross sectional area.
45. Load: 120 psi of gross wall cross sectional area.

FIGURE 1.1.7—WALL—SMASONRY
14″ OR MORE THICK

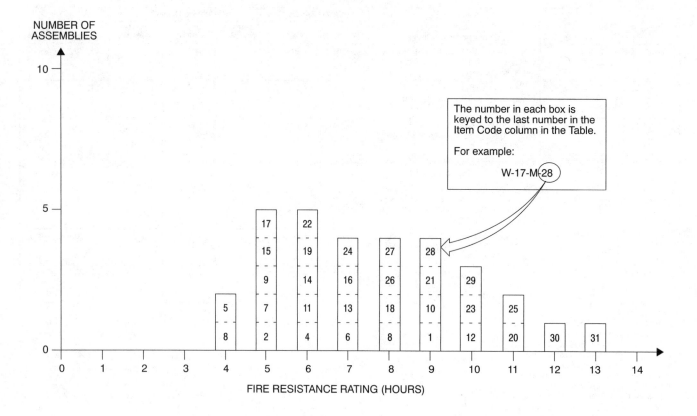

TABLE 1.1.7—WALLS—MASONRY
14″ OR MORE THICK

ITEM CODE	THICKNESS	CONSTRUCTION DETAILS	PERFORMANCE		REFERENCE NUMBER			NOTES	REC. HOURS
			LOAD	TIME	PRE-BMS-92	BMS-92	POST-BMS-92		
W-14-M-1	14″	Core: cored masonry; see Notes 18, 28, 33, 39, 41; Facings: both sides; see Note 38.	80 psi	9 hrs.		1		1, 20	9
W-16-M-2	16″	Core: clay or shale structural tile; see Notes 4, 7, 9, 19; No facings.	80 psi	5 hrs.		1		1, 20	5
W-16-M-3	16″	Core: clay or shale structural tile; see Notes 4, 7, 9, 19; No facings.	80 psi	4 hrs.		1		1, 20	4
W-16-M-4	16″	Core: clay or shale structural tile; see Notes 4, 7, 10, 18; No facings.	80 psi	6 hrs.		1		1, 20	6
W-16-M-5	16″	Core: clay or shale structural tile; see Notes 4, 7, 10, 19; No facings.	80 psi	4 hrs.		1		1, 20	4
W-16-M-6	16″	Core: clay or shale structural tile; see Notes 4, 7, 11, 18; No facings.	80 psi	7 hrs.		1		1, 20	7
W-16-M-7	16″	Core: clay or shale structural tile; see Notes 4, 7, 11, 19; No facings.	80 psi	5 hrs.		1		1, 20	5
W-16-M-8	16″	Core: clay or shale structural tile; see Notes 4, 8, 13, 18; No facings.	80 psi	8 hrs.		1		1, 20	8
W-16-M-9	16″	Core: clay or shale structural tile; see Notes 4, 8, 13, 19; No facings.	80 psi	5 hrs.		1		1, 20	5
W-16-M-10	16″	Core: clay or shale structural tile; see Notes 4, 8, 15, 18; No facings.	80 psi	9 hrs.		1		1, 20	9
W-16-M-11	16″	Core: clay or shale structural tile; see Notes 3, 7, 14, 18; No facings.	80 psi	6 hrs.		1		1, 20	6
W-16-M-12	16″	Core: clay or shale structural tile; see Notes 4, 8, 16, 18; No facings.	80 psi	10 hrs.		1		1, 20	10
W-16-M-13	16″	Core: clay or shale structural tile; see Notes 4, 6, 16, 19; No facings.	80 psi	7 hrs.		1		1, 20	7

(Continued)

TABLE 1.1.7—WALLS—MASONRY
14″ OR MORE THICK—(Continued)

ITEM CODE	THICKNESS	CONSTRUCTION DETAILS	PERFORMANCE		REFERENCE NUMBER			NOTES	REC. HOURS
			LOAD	TIME	PRE-BMS-92	BMS-92	POST-BMS-92		
W-16-M-14	16⅝″	Core: clay or shale structural tile; see Notes 4, 7, 9, 18; Facings: side 1, see Note 17; side 2, none.	80 psi	6 hrs.		1		1, 20	6
W-16-M-15	16⅝″	Core: clay or shale structural tile; see Notes 4, 7, 9, 19; Facings: fire side only; see Note 17.	80 psi	5 hrs.		1		1, 20	5
W-16-M-16	16⅝″	Core: clay or shale structural tile; see Notes 4, 7, 10, 18; Facings: side 1, see Note 17; side 2, none.	80 psi	7 hrs.		1		1, 20	7
W-16-M-17	16⅝″	Core: clay or shale structural tile; see Notes 4, 7, 10, 19; Facings: fire side only; see Note 17.	80 psi	5 hrs.		1		1, 20	5
W-16-M-18	16⅝″	Core: clay or shale structural tile; see Notes 4, 7, 11, 18; Facings: side 1, see Note 17; side 2, none.	80 psi	5 hrs.		1		1, 20	8
W-16-M-19	16⅝″	Core: clay or shale structural tile; see Notes 4, 7, 11, 19; Facings: fire side only; see Note 17.	80 psi	6 hrs.		1		1, 20	6
W-16-M-20	16⅝″	Core: clay or shale structural tile; see Notes 4, 8, 13, 18; Facings: sides 1 and 2; see Note 17.	80 psi	11 hrs.		1		1, 20	11
W-16-M-21	16⅝″	Core: clay or shale structural tile; see Notes 4, 8, 13 18; Facings: side 1, see Note 17; side 2, none.	80 psi	9 hrs.		1		1, 20	9
W-16-M-22	16⅝″	Core: clay or shale structural tile; see Notes 4, 8, 13, 19; Facings: fire side only; see Note 17.	80 psi	6 hrs.		1		1, 20	6
W-16-M-23	16⅝″	Core: clay or shale structural tile; see Notes 4, 8, 15, 18; Facings: side 1, see Note 17; side 2, none.	80 psi	10 hrs.		1		1, 20	10
W-16-M-24	16⅝″	Core: clay or shale structural tile; see Notes 4, 8, 15, 19; Facings: fire side only; see Note 17.	80 psi	7 hrs.		1		1, 20	7
W-16-M-25	16⅝″	Core: clay or shale structural tile; see Notes 4, 6, 16, 18; Facings: side 1, see Note 17; side 2, none.	80 psi	11 hrs.		1		1, 20	11
W-16-M-26	16⅝″	Core: clay or shale structural tile; see Notes 4, 6, 16, 19; Facings: fire side only; see Note 17.	80 psi	8 hrs.		1		1, 20	8
W-17-M-27	17¼″	Core: clay or shale structural tile; see Notes 4, 7, 9, 18; Facings: sides 1 and 2; see Note 17.	80 psi	8 hrs.		1		1, 20	8
W-17-M-28	17¼″	Core: clay or shale structural tile; see Notes 4, 7, 10, 18; Facings: sides 1 and 2; see Note 17.	80 psi	9 hrs.		1		1, 20	9
W-17-M-29	17¼″	Core: clay or shale structural tile; see Notes 4, 7, 11, 18; Facings: sides 1 and 2; see Note 17.	80 psi	10 hrs.		1		1, 20	10
W-17-M-30	17¼″	Core: clay or shale structural tile; see Notes 4, 8, 15, 18; Facings: sides 1 and 2; see Note 17.	80 psi	12 hrs.		1		1, 20	12
W-17-M-31	17¼″	Core: clay or shale structural tile; see Notes 4, 6, 16, 18; Facings: sides 1 and 2; see Note 17.	80 psi	13 hrs.		1		1, 20	13

Notes:
1. Tested at NBS - ASA Spec. No. A2-1934.
2. One unit in wall thickness.
3. Two units in wall thickness.
4. Two or three units in wall thickness.
5. Two cells in wall thickness.
6. Three or four cells in wall thickness.
7. Four or five cells in wall thickness.
8. Five or six cells in wall thickness.
9. Minimum percent of solid materials in units = 40%.
10. Minimum percent of solid materials in units = 43%.
11. Minimum percent of solid materials in units = 46%.
12. Minimum percent of solid materials in units = 48%.
13. Minimum percent of solid materials in units = 49%.

TABLE 1.1.7—WALLS—MASONRY
14″ OR MORE THICK—(Continued)

14. Minimum percent of solid materials in units = 45%.
15. Minimum percent of solid materials in units = 51%.
16. Minimum percent of solid materials in units = 53%.
17. Not less than $5/8$ inch thickness of 1:3 sanded gypsum plaster.
18. Noncombustible or no members framed into wall.
19. Combustible members framed into wall.
20. Load: 80 psi for gross area.
21. Portland cement-lime mortar.
22. Failure mode - thermal.
23. British test.
24. Passed all criteria.
25. Failed by sudden collapse with no preceding signs of impending failure.
26. One cell in wall thickness.
27. Two cells in wall thickness.
28. Three cells in wall thickness.
29. Minimum percent of solid material in concrete units = 52%.
30. Minimum percent of solid material in concrete units = 54%.
31. Minimum percent of solid material in concrete units = 55%.
32. Minimum percent of solid material in concrete units = 57%.
33. Minimum percent of solid material in concrete units = 60%.
34. Minimum percent of solid material in concrete units = 62%.
35. Minimum percent of solid material in concrete units = 65%.
36. Minimum percent of solid material in concrete units = 70%.
37. Minimum percent of solid material in concrete units = 76%.
38. Not less than $1/2''$ of 1:3 sanded gypsum plaster.
39. Three units in wall thickness.
40. Concrete units made with expanded slag or pumice aggregates.
41. Concrete units made with expanded burned clay or shale, crushed limestone, air cooled slag or cinders.
42. Concrete units made with calcareous sand and gravel. Coarse aggregate, 60 percent or more calcite and dolomite.
43. Concrete units made with siliceous sand and gravel. Ninety percent or more quartz, chert or flint.

FIGURE 1.2.1—WALLS—METAL FRAME
0″ TO LESS THAN 4″ THICK

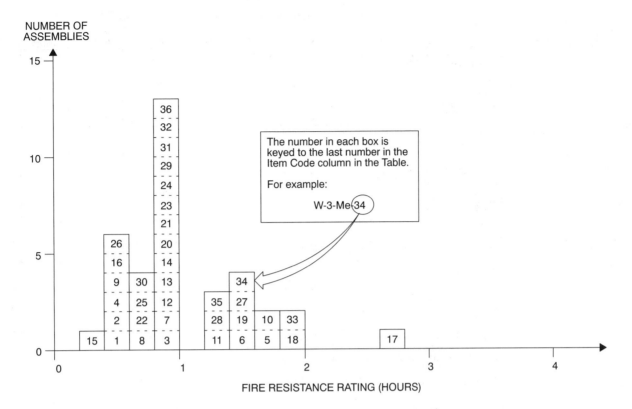

TABLE 1.2.1—WALLS—METAL FRAME
0″ TO LESS THAN 4″ THICK

ITEM CODE	THICKNESS	CONSTRUCTION DETAILS	PERFORMANCE		REFERENCE NUMBER			NOTES	REC. HOURS
			LOAD	TIME	PRE-BMS-92	BMS-92	POST-BMS-92		
W-3-Me-1	3″	Core: steel channels having three rows of 4″ × 1/8″ staggered slots in web; core filled with heat expanded vermiculite weighing 1.5 lbs./ft.^{2} of wall area; Facings: sides 1 and 2, 18 gage steel, spot welded to core.	N/A	25 min.		1			1/3
W-3-Me-2	3″	Core: steel channels having three rows of 4″ × 1/8″ staggered slots in web; core filled with heat expanded vermiculite weighing 2 lbs./ft.^{2} of wall area; Facings: sides 1 and 2, 18 gage steel, spot welded to core.	N/A	30 min.		1			1/2
W-3-Me-3	2 1/2″	Solid partition: 3/8″ tension rods (vertical) 3′ o.c. with metal lath; Scratch coat: cement/sand/lime plaster; Float coats: cement/sand/lime plaster; Finish coats: neat gypsum plaster.	N/A	1 hr.			7	1	1
W-2-Me-4	2″	Solid wall: steel channel per Note 1; 2″ thickness of 1:2; 1:3 portland cement on metal lath.	N/A	30 min.		1			1/2
W-2-Me-5	2″	Solid wall: steel channel per Note 1; 2″ thickness of neat gypsum plaster on metal lath.	N/A	1 hr. 45 min.		1			1 3/4
W-2-Me-6	2″	Solid wall: steel channel per Note 1; 2″ thickness of 1:1 1/2; 1:1 1/2 gypsum plaster on metal lath.	N/A	1 hr. 30 min.		1			1 1/2
W-2-Me-7	2″	Solid wall: steel channel per Note 2; 2″ thickness of 1:1; 1:1 gypsum plaster on metal lath.	N/A	1 hr.		1			1

(Continued)

TABLE 1.2.1—WALLS—METAL FRAME
0″ TO LESS THAN 4″ THICK—(Continued)

ITEM CODE	THICKNESS	CONSTRUCTION DETAILS	PERFORMANCE		REFERENCE NUMBER			NOTES	REC. HOURS
			LOAD	TIME	PRE-BMS-92	BMS-92	POST-BMS-92		
W-2-Me-8	2″	Solid wall: steel channel per Note 1; 2″ thickness of 1:2; 1:2 gypsum plaster on metal lath.	N/A	45 min.		1			$^3/_4$
W-2-Me-9	$2^1/_4$″	Solid wall: steel channel per Note 2; $2^1/_4$″ thickness of 1:2; 1:3 portland cement on metal lath.	N/A	30 min.		1			$1/_2$
W-2-Me-10	$2^1/_4$″	Solid wall: steel channel per Note 2; $2^1/_4$″ thickness of neat gypsum plaster on metal lath.	N/A	2 hrs.		1			2
W-2-Me-11	$2^1/_4$″	Solid wall: steel channel per Note 2; $2^1/_4$″ thickness of 1:$1/_2$; 1:$1/_2$ gypsum plaster on metal lath.	N/A	1 hr. 45 min.		1			$1^3/_4$
W-2-Me-12	$2^1/_4$″	Solid wall: steel channel per Note 2; $2^1/_4$″ thickness of 1:1; 1:1 gypsum plaster on metal lath.	N/A	1 hr. 15 min.		1			$1^1/_4$
W-2-Me-13	$2^1/_4$″	Solid wall: steel channel per Note 2; $2^1/_4$″ thickness of 1:2; 1:2 gypsum plaster on metal lath.	N/A	1 hr.		1			1
W-2-Me-14	$2^1/_2$″	Solid wall: steel channel per Note 1; $2^1/_2$″ thickness of 4.5:1:7; 4.5:1:7 portland cement, sawdust and sand sprayed on wire mesh; see Note 3.	N/A	1 hr.		1			1
W-2-Me-15	$2^1/_2$″	Solid wall: steel channel per Note 2; $2^1/_2$″ thickness of 1:4; 1:4 portland cement sprayed on wire mesh; see Note 3.	N/A	20 min.		1			$1/_3$
W-2-Me-16	$2^1/_2$″	Solid wall: steel channel per Note 2; $2^1/_2$″ thickness of 1:2; 1:3 portland cement on metal lath.	N/A	30 min.		1			$1/_2$
W-2-Me-17	$2^1/_2$″	Solid wall: steel channel per Note 2; $2^1/_2$″ thickness of neat gypsum plaster on metal lath.	N/A	2 hrs. 30 min.		1			$2^1/_2$
W-2-Me-18	$2^1/_2$″	Solid wall: steel channel per Note 2; $2^1/_2$″ thickness of 1:$1/_2$; 1:$1/_2$ gypsum plaster on metal lath.	N/A	2 hrs.		1			2
W-2-Me-19	$2^1/_2$″	Solid wall: steel channel per Note 2; $2^1/_2$″ thickness of 1:1; 1:1 gypsum plaster on metal lath.	N/A	1 hr. 30 min.		1			$1^1/_2$
W-2-Me-20	$2^1/_2$″	Solid wall: steel channel per Note 2; $2^1/_2$″ thickness of 1:2; 1:2 gypsum plaster on metal lath.	N/A	1 hr.		1			1
W-2-Me-21	$2^1/_2$″	Solid wall: steel channel per Note 2; $2^1/_2$″ thickness of 1:2; 1:3 gypsum plaster on metal lath.	N/A	1 hr.		1			1
W-3-Me-22	3″	Core: steel channel per Note 2; 1:2; 1:2 gypsum plaster on $3/_4$″ soft asbestos lath; plaster thickness 2″.	N/A	45 min.		1			$^3/_4$
W-3-Me-23	$3^1/_2$″	Solid wall: steel channel per Note 2; $2^1/_2$″ thickness of 1:2; 1:2 gypsum plaster on $3/_4$″ asbestos lath.	N/A	1 hr.		1			1
W-3-Me-24	$3^1/_2$″	Solid wall: steel channel per Note 2; lath over and 1:$2^1/_2$; 1:$2^1/_2$ gypsum plaster on 1″ magnesium oxysulfate wood fiberboard; plaster thickness $2^1/_2$″.	N/A	1 hr.		1			1
W-3-Me-25	$3^1/_2$″	Core: steel studs; see Note 4; Facings: $3/_4$″ thickness of 1:$1/_{30}$:2; 1:$1/_{30}$:3 portland cement and asbestos fiber plaster.	N/A	45 min.		1			$^3/_4$
W-3-Me-26	$3^1/_2$″	Core: steel studs; see Note 4; Facings: both sides $3/_4$″ thickness of 1:2; 1:3 portland cement.	N/A	30 min.		1			$1/_2$
W-3-Me-27	$3^1/_2$″	Core: steel studs; see Note 4; Facings: both sides $3/_4$″ thickness of neat gypsum plaster.	N/A	1 hr. 30 min.		1			$1^1/_2$

(Continued)

TABLE 1.2.1—WALLS—METAL FRAME
0″ TO LESS THAN 4″ THICK—(Continued)

ITEM CODE	THICKNESS	CONSTRUCTION DETAILS	PERFORMANCE		REFERENCE NUMBER			NOTES	REC. HOURS
			LOAD	TIME	PRE-BMS-92	BMS-92	POST-BMS-92		
W-3-Me-28	$3^1/_2''$	Core: steel studs; see Note 4; Facings: both sides $^3/_4''$ thickness of 1:$^1/_2$; 1:$^1/_2$ gypsum plaster.	N/A	1 hr. 15 min.		1			$1^1/_4$
W-3-Me-29	$3^1/_2''$	Core: steel studs; see Note 4; Facings: both sides $^3/_4''$ thickness of 1:2; 1:2 gypsum plaster.	N/A	1 hr.		1			1
W-3-Me-30	$3^1/_2''$	Core: steel studs; see Note 4; Facings: both sides $^3/_4''$ thickness of 1:2; 1:3 gypsum plaster.	N/A	45 min.		1			$^3/_4$
W-3-Me-31	$3^3/_4''$	Core: steel studs; see Note 4; Facings: both sides $^7/_8''$ thickness of 1:$^1/_{30}$:2; 1:$^1/_{30}$:3 portland cement and asbestos fiber plaster.	N/A	1 hr.		1			1
W-3-Me-32	$3^3/_4''$	Core: steel studs; see Note 4; Facings: both sides $^7/_8''$ thickness of 1:2; 1:3 portland cement.	N/A	45 min.		1			$^3/_4$
W-3-Me-33	$3^3/_4''$	Core: steel studs; see Note 4; Facings: both sides $^7/_8''$ thickness of neat gypsum plaster.	N/A	2 hrs.		1			2
W-3-Me-34	$3^3/_4''$	Core: steel studs; see Note 4; Facings: both sides $^7/_8''$ thickness of 1:$^1/_2$; 1:$^1/_2$ gypsum plaster.	N/A	1 hr. 30 min.		1			$1^1/_2$
W-3-Me-35	$3^3/_4''$	Core: steel studs; see Note 4; Facings: both sides $^7/_8''$ thickness of 1:2; 1:2 gypsum plaster.	N/A	1 hr. 15 min.		1			$1^1/_4$
W-3-Me-36	$3^3/_4''$	Core: steel; see Note 4; Facings: $^7/_8''$ thickness of 1:2; 1:3 gypsum plaster on both sides.	N/A	1 hr.		1			1

Notes:
1. Failure mode - local temperature rise - back face.
2. Three-fourths inch or 1 inch channel framing - hot-rolled or strip-steel channels.
3. Reinforcement is 4-inch square mesh of No. 6 wire welded at intersections (no channels).
4. Ratings are for any usual type of nonload-bearing metal framing providing 2 inches (or more) air space.

General Note:
The construction details of the wall assemblies are as complete as the source documentation will permit. Data on the method of attachment of facings and the gauge of steel studs was provided when known. The cross-sectional area of the steel stud can be computed, thereby permitting a reasoned estimate of actual loading conditions. For load-bearing assemblies, the maximum allowable stress for the steel studs has been provided in the table "Notes." More often, it is the thermal properties of the facing materials, rather than the specific gauge of the steel, that will determine the degree of fire resistance. This is particularly true for non-bearing wall assemblies.

FIGURE 1.2.2—WALLS—METAL FRAME
4″ TO LESS THAN 6″ THICK

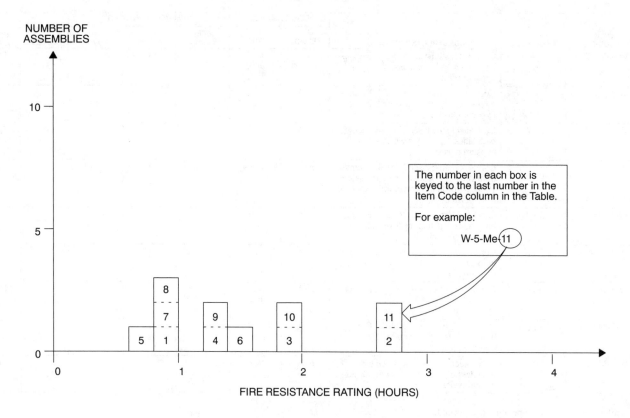

TABLE 1.2.2—WALLS—METAL FRAME
4″ TO LESS THAN 6″ THICK

ITEM CODE	THICKNESS	CONSTRUCTION DETAILS	PERFORMANCE		REFERENCE NUMBER			NOTES	REC. HOURS
			LOAD	TIME	PRE-BMS-92	BMS-92	POST-BMS-92		
W-5-Me-1	5 1/2″	3″ cavity with 16 ga. channel studs (3 1/2″ o.c.) of 1/2″ × 1/2″ channel and 3″ spacer; Metal lath on ribs with plaster (three coats) 3/4″ over face of lath; Plaster (each side): scratch coat, cement/lime/sand with hair; float coat, cement/lime/sand; finish coat, neat gypsum.	N/A	1 hr. 11 min.			7	1	1
W-4-Me-2	4″	Core: steel studs; see Note 2; Facings: both sides 1″ thickness of neat gypsum plaster.	N/A	2 hrs. 30 min.		1			2 1/2
W-4-Me-3	4″	Core: steel studs; see Note 2; Facings: both sides 1″ thickness of 1:1 1/2; 1:1 1/2 gypsum plaster.	N/A	2 hrs.		1			2
W-4-Me-4	4″	Core: steel; see Note 2; Facings: both sides 1″ thickness of 1:2; 1:3 gypsum plaster.	N/A	1 hr. 15 min.		1			1 1/4
W-4-Me-5	4 1/2″	Core: lightweight steel studs 3″ in depth; Facings: both sides 3/4″ thick sanded gypsum plaster, 1:2 scratch coat, 1:3 brown coat applied on metal lath.	See Note 4	45 min.		1		5	3/4
W-4-Me-6	4 1/2″	Core: lightweight steel studs 3″ in depth; Facings: both sides 3/4″ thick neat gypsum plaster on metal lath.	See Note 4	1 hr. 30 min.		1		5	1 1/2
W-4-Me-7	4 1/2″	Core: lightweight steel studs 3″ in depth; Facings: both sides 3/4″ thick sanded gypsum plaster, 1:2 scratch and brown coats applied on metal lath.	See Note 4	1 hr.		1		5	1

(Continued)

130

TABLE 1.2.2—WALLS—METAL FRAME
4″ TO LESS THAN 6″ THICK—(Continued)

ITEM CODE	THICKNESS	CONSTRUCTION DETAILS	PERFORMANCE		REFERENCE NUMBER			NOTES	REC. HOURS
			LOAD	TIME	PRE-BMS-92	BMS-92	POST-BMS-92		
W-4-Me-8	$4^3/_4''$	Core: lightweight steel studs 3″ in depth; Facings: both sides $^7/_8''$ thick sanded gypsum plaster, 1:2 scratch coat, 1:3 brown coat, applied on metal lath.	See Note 4	1 hr.		1		5	1
W-4-Me-9	$4^3/_4''$	Core: lightweight steel studs 3″ in depth; Facings: both sides $^7/_8''$ thick sanded gypsum plaster, 1:2 scratch and 1:3 brown coats applied on metal lath.	See Note 4	1 hr. 15 min.		1		5	$1^1/_4$
W-5-Me-10	5″	Core: lightweight steel studs 3″ in depth; Facings: both sides 1″ thick neat gypsum plaster on metal lath.	See Note 4	2 hrs.		1		5	2
W-5-Me-11	5″	Core: lightweight steel studs 3″ in depth; Facings: both sides 1″ thick neat gypsum plaster on metal lath.	See Note 4	2 hrs. 30 min.		1		5, 6	$2^1/_2$

Notes:
1. Failure mode - local back face temperature rise.
2. Ratings are for any usual type of non-bearing metal framing providing a minimum 2 inches air space.
3. Facing materials secured to lightweight steel studs not less than 3 inches deep.
4. Rating based on loading to develop a maximum stress of 7270 psi for net area of each stud.
5. Spacing of steel studs must be sufficient to develop adequate rigidity in the metal-lath or gypsum-plaster base.
6. As per Note 4 but load/stud not to exceed 5120 psi.

General Note:
The construction details of the wall assemblies are as complete as the source documentation will permit. Data on the method of attachment of facings and the gauge of steel studs was provided when known. The cross sectional area of the steel stud can be computed, thereby permitting a reasoned estimate of actual loading conditions. For load-bearing assemblies, the maximum allowable stress for the steel studs has been provided in the table "Notes." More often, it is the thermal properties of the facing materials, rather than the specific gauge of the steel, that will determine the degree of fire resistance. This is particularly true for non-bearing wall assemblies.

TABLE 1.2.3—WALLS—METAL FRAME
6″ TO LESS THAN 8″ THICK

ITEM CODE	THICKNESS	CONSTRUCTION DETAILS	PERFORMANCE		REFERENCE NUMBER			NOTES	REC. HOURS
			LOAD	TIME	PRE-BMS-92	BMS-92	POST-BMS-92		
W-6-Me-1	$6^5/_8''$	On one side of 1″ magnesium oxysulfate wood fiberboard sheathing attached to steel studs (see Notes 1 and 2), 1″ air space, $3^3/_4''$ brick secured with metal ties to steel frame every fifth course; Inside facing of $^7/_8''$ 1:2 sanded gypsum plaster on metal lath secured directly to studs; Plaster side exposed to fire.	See Note 2	1 hr. 45 min.		1		1	$1^3/_4$
W-6-Me-2	$6^5/_8''$	On one side of 1″ magnesium oxysulfate wood fiberboard sheathing attached to steel studs (see Notes 1 and 2), 1″ air space, $3^3/_4''$ brick secured with metal ties to steel frame every fifth course; Inside facing of $^7/_8''$ 1:2 sanded gypsum plaster on metal lath secured directly to studs; Brick face exposed to fire.	See Note 2	4 hrs.		1		1	4
W-6-Me-3	$6^5/_8''$	On one side of 1″ magnesium oxysulfate wood fiberboard sheathing attached to steel studs (see Notes 1 and 2), 1″ air space, $3^3/_4''$ brick secured with metal ties to steel frame every fifth course; Inside facing of $^7/_8''$ vermiculite plaster on metal lath secured directly to studs; Plaster side exposed to fire.	See Note 2	2 hrs.		1		1	2

Notes:
1. Lightweight steel studs (minimum 3 inches deep) used. Stud spacing dependent on loading, but in each case, spacing is to be such that adequate rigidity is provided to the metal lath plaster base.
2. Load is such that stress developed in studs is not greater than 5120 psi calculated from net stud area.

General Note:
The construction details of the wall assemblies are as complete as the source documentation will permit. Data on the method of attachment of facings and the gauge of steel studs was provided when known. The cross sectional area of the steel stud can be computed, thereby permitting a reasoned estimate of actual loading conditions. For load-bearing assemblies, the maximum allowable stress for the steel studs has been provided in the table "Notes." More often, it is the thermal properties of the facing materials, rather than the specific gauge of the steel, that will determine the degree of fire resistance. This is particularly true for non-bearing wall assemblies.

TABLE 1.2.4—WALLS—METAL FRAME
8″ TO LESS THAN 10″ THICK

ITEM CODE	THICKNESS	CONSTRUCTION DETAILS	PERFORMANCE		REFERENCE NUMBER			NOTES	REC. HOURS
			LOAD	TIME	PRE-BMS-92	BMS-92	POST-BMS-92		
W-9-Me-1	$9^1/_{16}''$	On one side of $1/_2''$ wood fiberboard sheathing next to studs, $3/_4''$ air space formed with $3/_4''$ x $1^5/_8''$ wood strips placed over the fiberboard and secured to the studs, paper backed wire lath nailed to strips $3^3/_4''$ brick veneer held in place by filling a $3/_4''$ space between the brick and paper backed lath with mortar; Inside facing of $3/_4''$ neat gypsum plaster on metal lath attached to $5/_{16}''$ plywood strips secured to edges of steel studs; Rated as combustible because of the sheathing; See Notes 1 and 2; Plaster exposed.	See Note 2	1 hr. 45 min.		1		1	$1^3/_4$
W-9-Me-2	$9^1/_{16}''$	Same as above with brick exposed.	See Note 2	4 hrs.		1		1	4
W-8-Me-3	$8^1/_2''$	On one side of paper backed wire lath attached to studs and $3^3/_4''$ brick veneer held in place by filling a 1″ space between the brick and lath with mortar; Inside facing of 1″ paper-enclosed mineral wool blanket weighing .6 lb./ft.^{2} attached to studs, metal lath or paper backed wire lath laid over the blanket and attached to the studs, $3/_4''$ sanded gypsum plaster 1:2 for the scratch coat and 1:3 for the brown coat; See Notes 1 and 2; Plaster face exposed.	See Note 2	4 hrs.		1		1	4
W-8-Me-4	$8^1/_2''$	Same as above with brick exposed.	See Note 2	5 hrs.		1		1	5

Notes:
1. Lightweight steel studs ≥ 3 inches in depth. Stud spacing dependent on loading, but in any case, the spacing is to be such that adequate rigidity is provided to the metal-lath plaster base.
2. Load is such that stress developed in studs is ≤ 5120 psi calculated from the net area of the stud.

General Note:
The construction details of the wall assemblies are as complete as the source documentation will permit. Data on the method of attachment of facings and the gauge of steel studs was provided when known. The cross sectional area of the steel stud can be computed, thereby permitting a reasoned estimate of actual loading conditions. For load-bearing assemblies, the maximum allowable stress for the steel studs has been provided in the table "Notes." More often, it is the thermal properties of the facing materials, rather than the specific gauge of the steel, that will determine the degree of fire resistance. This is particularly true for non-bearing wall assemblies.

TABLE 1.3.1—WOOD FRAME WALLS
0″ TO LESS THAN 4″ THICK

ITEM CODE	THICKNESS	CONSTRUCTION DETAILS	PERFORMANCE		REFERENCE NUMBER			NOTES	REC. HOURS
			LOAD	TIME	PRE-BMS-92	BMS-92	POST-BMS-92		
W-3-W-1	$3^3/_4''$	Solid wall: $2^1/_4''$ wood-wool slab core; $3/_4''$ gypsum plaster each side.	N/A	2 hrs.			7	1, 6	2
W-3-W-2	$3^7/_8''$	2 × 4 stud wall; $3/_{16}''$ thick cement asbestos board on both sides of wall.	360 psi net area	10 min.		1		2-5	$1/_6$
W-3-W-3	$3^7/_8''$	Same as W-3-W-2 but stud cavities filled with 1 lb./ft.^{2} mineral wool batts.	360 psi net area	40 min.		1		2-5	$2/_3$

Notes:
1. Achieved "Grade C" fire resistance (British).
2. Nominal 2 × 4 wood studs of No. 1 common or better lumber set edgewise, 2 × 4 plates at top and bottom and blocking at mid height of wall.
3. All horizontal joints in facing material backed by 2 × 4 blocking in wall.
4. Load: 360 psi of net stud cross sectional area.
5. Facings secured with 6d casing nails. Nail holes predrilled and 0.02 inch to 0.03 inch smaller than nail diameter.
6. The wood-wool core is a pressed excelsior slab which possesses insulating properties similar to cellulosic insulation.

FIGURE 1.3.2—WOOD FRAME WALLS
4″ TO LESS THAN 6″ THICK

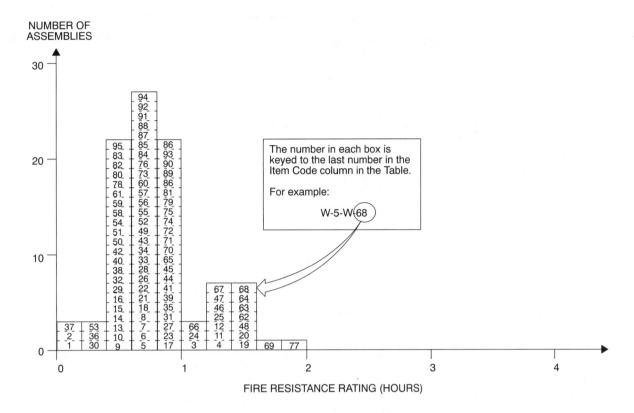

TABLE 1.3.2—WOOD FRAME WALLS
4″ TO LESS THAN 6″ THICK

ITEM CODE	THICKNESS	CONSTRUCTION DETAILS	PERFORMANCE		REFERENCE NUMBER			NOTES	REC. HOURS
			LOAD	TIME	PRE-BMS-92	BMS-92	POST-BMS-92		
W-4-W-1	4″	2″ × 4″ stud wall; $^3/_{16}$″ CAB; no insulation; Design A.	35 min.	10 min.			4	1-10	$^1/_6$
W-4-W-2	$4^1/_8$″	2″ × 4″ stud wall; $^3/_{16}$″ CAB; no insulation; Design A.	38 min.	9 min.			4	1-10	$^1/_6$
W-4-W-3	$4^3/_4$″	2″ × 4″ stud wall; $^3/_{16}$″ CAB and $^3/_8$″ gypsum board face (both sides); Design B.	62 min.	64 min.			4	1-10	1
W-5-W-4	5″	2″ × 4″ stud wall; $^3/_{16}$″ CAB and $^1/_2$″ gypsum board (both sides); Design B.	79 min.	Greater than 90 min.			4	1-10	1
W-4-W-5	$4^3/_4$″	2″ × 4″ stud wall; $^3/_{16}$″ CAB and $^3/_8$″ gypsum board (both sides); Design B.	45 min.	45 min.			4	1-12	—
W-5-W-6	5″	2″ × 4″ stud wall; $^3/_{16}$″ CAB and $^1/_2$″ gypsum board face (both sides); Design B.	45 min.	45 min.			4	1-10, 12, 13	—
W-4-W-7	4″	2″ × 4″ stud wall; $^3/_{16}$″ CAB face; $3^1/_2$″ mineral wool insulation; Design C.	40 min.	42 min.			4	1-10	$^2/_3$
W-4-W-8	4″	2″ × 4″ stud wall; $^3/_{16}$″ CAB face; $3^1/_2$″ mineral wool insulation; Design C.	46 min.	46 min.			4	1-10, 43	$^2/_3$
W-4-W-9	4″	2″ × 4″ stud wall; $^3/_{16}$″ CAB face; $3^1/_2$″ mineral wool insulation; Design C.	30 min.	30 min.			4	1-10, 12, 14	—
W-4-W-10	$4^1/_8$″	2″ × 4″ stud wall; $^3/_{16}$″ CAB face; $3^1/_2$″ mineral wool insulation; Design C.	—	30 min.			4	1-8, 12, 14	—
W-4-W-11	$4^3/_4$″	2″ × 4″ stud wall; $^3/_{16}$″ CAB face; $^3/_8$″ gypsum strips over studs; $5^1/_2$″ mineral wool insulation; Design D.	79 min.	79 min.			4	1-10	1

(Continued)

TABLE 1.3.2—WOOD FRAME WALLS
4″ TO LESS THAN 6″ THICK—(Continued)

ITEM CODE	THICKNESS	CONSTRUCTION DETAILS	PERFORMANCE		REFERENCE NUMBER			NOTES	REC. HOURS
			LOAD	TIME	PRE-BMS-92	BMS-92	POST-BMS-92		
W-4-W-12	$4^3/_4''$	2″ × 4″ stud wall; $^3/_{16}''$ CAB face; $^3/_8''$ gypsum strips at stud edges; $7^1/_2''$ mineral wool insulation; Design D.	82 min.	82 min.			4	1-10	1
W-4-W-13	$4^3/_4''$	2″ × 4″ stud wall; $^3/_{16}''$ CAB face; $^3/_8''$ gypsum board strips over studs; $5^1/_2''$ mineral wool insulation; Design D.	30 min.	30 min.			4	1-12	—
W-4-W-14	$4^3/_4''$	2″ × 4″ stud wall; $^3/_{16}''$ CAB face; $^3/_8''$ gypsum board strips over studs; 7″ mineral wool insulation; Design D.	30 min.	30 min.			4	1-12	—
W-5-W-15	$5^1/_2''$	2″ × 4″ stud wall; Exposed face: CAB shingles over 1″ × 6″; Unexposed face: $^1/_8''$ CAB sheet; $^7/_{16}''$ fiberboard (wood); Design E.	34 min.	—			4	1-10	$^1/_2$
W-5-W-16	$5^1/_2''$	2″ × 4″ stud wall; Exposed face: $^1/_8''$ CAB sheet; $^7/_{16}''$ fiberboard; Unexposed face: CAB shingles over 1″ × 6″; Design E.	32 min.	33 min.			4	1-10	$^1/_2$
W-5-W-17	$5^1/_2''$	2″ × 4″ stud wall; Exposed face: CAB shingles over 1″ × 6″; Unexposed face: $^1/_8''$ CAB sheet; gypsum at stud edges; $3^1/_2''$ mineral wood insulation; Design F.	51 min.	—			4	1-10	$^3/_4$
W-5-W-18	$5^1/_2''$	2″ × 4″ stud wall; Exposed face: $^1/_8''$ CAB sheet; gypsum board at stud edges; Unexposed face: CAB shingles over 1″ × 6″; $3^1/_2''$ mineral wool insulation; Design F.	42 min.	—			4	1-10	$^2/_3$
W-5-W-19	$5^5/_8''$	2″ × 4″ stud wall; Exposed face: CAB shingles over 1″ × 6″; Unexposed face: $^1/_8''$ CAB sheet; gypsum board at stud edges; $5^1/_2''$ mineral wool insulation; Design G.	74 min.	85 min.			4	1-10	1
W-5-W-20	$5^5/_8''$	2″ × 4″ stud wall; Exposed face: $^1/_8''$ CAB sheet; gypsum board at $^3/_{16}''$ stud edges; $^7/_{16}''$ fiberboard; Unexposed face: CAB shingles over 1″ × 6″; $5^1/_2''$ mineral wool insulation; Design G.	79 min.	85 min.			4	1-10	$1^1/_4$
W-5-W-21	$5^5/_8''$	2″ × 4″ stud wall; Exposed face: CAB shingles 1″ × 6″ sheathing; Unexposed face: CAB sheet; gypsum board at stud edges; $5^1/_2''$ mineral wool insulation; Design G.	38 min.	38 min.			4	1-10, 12, 14	—
W-5-W-22	$5^5/_8''$	2″ × 4″ stud wall; Exposed face: CAB sheet; gypsum board at stud edges; Unexposed face: CAB shingles 1″ × 6″ sheathing; $5^1/_2''$ mineral wool insulation; Design G.	38 min.	38 min.			4	1-12	—
W-6-W-23	6″	2″ × 4″ stud wall; 16″ o.c.; $^1/_2''$ gypsum board each side; $^1/_2''$ gypsum plaster each side.	N/A	60 min.			7	15	1
W-6-W-24	6″	2″ × 4″ stud wall; 16″ o.c.; $^1/_2''$ gypsum board each side; $^1/_2''$ gypsum plaster each side.	N/A	68 min.			7	16	1
W-6-W-25	$6^7/_8''$	2″ × 4″ stud wall; 18″ o.c.; $^3/_4''$ gypsum plank each side; $^3/_{16}''$ gypsum plaster each side.	N/A	80 min.			7	15	$1^1/_3$
W-5-W-26	$5^1/_8''$	2″ × 4″ stud wall; 16″ o.c.; $^3/_8''$ gypsum board each side; $^3/_{16}''$ gypsum plaster each side.	N/A	37 min.			7	15	$^1/_2$
W-5-W-27	$5^3/_4''$	2″ × 4″ stud wall; 16″ o.c.; $^3/_8''$ gypsum lath each side; $^1/_2''$ gypsum plaster each side.	N/A	52 min.			7	15	$^3/_4$
W-5-W-28	5″	2″ × 4″ stud wall; 16″ o.c.; $^1/_2''$ gypsum board each side.	N/A	37 min.			7	16	$^1/_2$
W-5-W-29	5″	2″ × 4″ stud wall; $^1/_2''$ fiberboard both sides 14% M.C. with F.R. paint at 35 gm./ft.^{2}.	N/A	28 min.			7	15	$^1/_3$

(Continued)

TABLE 1.3.2—WOOD FRAME WALLS
4″ TO LESS THAN 6″ THICK—(Continued)

ITEM CODE	THICKNESS	CONSTRUCTION DETAILS	PERFORMANCE		REFERENCE NUMBER			NOTES	REC. HOURS
			LOAD	TIME	PRE-BMS-92	BMS-92	POST-BMS-92		
W-4-W-30	$4^3/_4″$	2″ × 4″ stud wall; Fire side: $^1/_2″$ (wood) fiberboard; Back side: $^1/_4″$ CAB; 16″ o.c.	N/A	17 min.			7	15,1 6	$^1/_4$
W-5-W-31	$5^1/_8″$	2″ × 4″ stud wall; 16″ o.c.; $^1/_2″$ fiberboard insulation with $^1/_{32}″$ asbestos (both sides of each board).	N/A	50 min.			7	16	$^3/_4$
W-4-W-32	$4^1/_4″$	2″ × 4″ stud wall; $^3/_8″$ thick gypsum wallboard on both faces; insulated cavities.	See Note 23	25 min.		1		17, 18, 23	$^1/_3$
W-4-W-33	$4^1/_2″$	2″ × 4″ stud wall; $^1/_2″$ thick gypsum wallboard on both faces.	See Note 17	40 min.		1		17, 23	$^1/_3$
W-4-W-34	$4^1/_2″$	2″ × 4″ stud wall; $^1/_2″$ thick gypsum wallboard on both faces; insulated cavities.	See Note 17	45 min.		1		17, 18, 23	$^3/_4$
W-4-W-35	$4^1/_2″$	2″ × 4″ stud wall; $^1/_2″$ thick gypsum wallboard on both faces; insulated cavities.	N/A	1 hr.		1		17, 18, 24	1
W-4-W-36	$4^1/_2″$	2″ × 4″ stud wall; $^1/_2″$ thick, 1.1 lbs./ft.^{2} wood fiberboard sheathing on both faces.	See Note 23	15 min.		1		17, 23	$^1/_4$
W-4-W-37	$4^1/_2″$	2″ × 4″ stud wall; $^1/_2″$ thick, 0.7 lb./ft.^{2} wood fiberboard sheathing on both faces.	See Note 23	10 min.		1		17, 23	$^1/_6$
W-4-W-38	$4^1/_2″$	2″ × 4″ stud wall; $^1/_2″$ thick, flameproofed 1.6 lbs./ft.^{2} wood fiberboard sheathing on both faces.	See Note 23	30 min.		1		17, 23	$^1/_2$
W-4-W-39	$4^1/_2″$	2″ × 4″ stud wall; $^1/_2″$ thick gypsum wallboard on both faces; insulated cavities.	See Note 23	1 hr.		1		17, 18, 23	1
W-4-W-40	$4^1/_2″$	2″ × 4″ stud wall; $^1/_2″$ thick, 1:2; 1:3 gypsum plaster on wood lath on both faces.	See Note 23	30 min.		1		17, 21, 23	$^1/_2$
W-4-W-41	$4^1/_2″$	2″ × 4″ stud wall; $^1/_2″$, 1:2; 1:3 gypsum plaster on wood lath on both faces; insulated cavities.	See Note 23	1 hr.		1		17, 18, 21, 24	1
W-4-W-42	$4^1/_2″$	2″ × 4″ stud wall; $^1/_2″$, 1:5; 1:7.5 lime plaster on wood lath on both wall faces.	See Note 23	30 min.		1		17, 21, 23	$^1/_2$
W-4-W-43	$4^1/_2″$	2″ × 4″ stud wall; $^1/_2″$ thick 1:5; 1:7.5 lime plaster on wood lath on both faces; insulated cavities.	See Note 23	45 min.		1		17, 18, 21, 23	$^3/_4$
W-4-W-44	$4^5/_8″$	2″ × 4″ stud wall; $^3/_{16}″$ thick cement-asbestos over $^3/_8″$ thick gypsum board on both faces.	See Note 23	1 hr.		1		23, 25, 26, 27	1
W-4-W-45	$4^5/_8″$	2″ × 4″ stud wall; studs faced with 4″ wide strips of $^3/_8″$ thick gypsum board; $^3/_{16}″$ thick gypsum cement-asbestos board on both faces; insulated cavities.	See Note 23	1 hr.		1		23, 25, 27, 28	1
W-4-W-46	$4^5/_8″$	Same as W-4-W-45 but nonload bearing.	N/A	1 hr. 15 min.		1		24, 28	$1^1/_4$
W-4-W-47	$4^7/_8″$	2″ × 4″ stud wall; $^3/_{16}″$ thick cement-asbestos board over $^1/_2″$ thick gypsum sheathing on both faces.	See Note 23	1 hr. 15 min.		1		23, 25, 26, 27	$1^1/_4$
W-4-W-48	$4^7/_8″$	Same as W-4-W-47 but nonload bearing.	N/A	1 hr. 30 min.		1		24, 27	$1^1/_2$
W-5-W-49	5″	2″ × 4″ stud wall; Exterior face: $^3/_4″$ wood sheathing; asbestos felt 14 lbs./100 ft.^{2} and $^5/_{32}″$ cement-asbestos shingles; Interior face: 4″ wide strips of $^3/_8″$ gypsum board over studs; wall faced with $^3/_{16}″$ thick cement-asbestos board.	See Note 23	40 min.		1		18, 23, 25, 26, 29	$^2/_3$

(Continued)

TABLE 1.3.2—WOOD FRAME WALLS
4″ TO LESS THAN 6″ THICK—(Continued)

ITEM CODE	THICKNESS	CONSTRUCTION DETAILS	PERFORMANCE		REFERENCE NUMBER			NOTES	REC. HOURS
			LOAD	TIME	PRE-BMS-92	BMS-92	POST-BMS-92		
W-5-W-50	5″	2″ × 4″ stud wall; Exterior face: as per W-5-W-49; Interior face: $9/16$″ composite board consisting of $7/16$″ thick wood fiberboard faced with $1/8$″ thick cement-asbestos board; Exterior side exposed to fire.	See Note 23	30 min.		1		23, 25, 26, 30	$1/2$
W-5-W-51	5″	Same as W-5-W-50 but interior side exposed to fire.	See Note 23	30 min.		1		23, 25, 26	$1/2$
W-5-W-52	5″	Same as W-5-W-49 but exterior side exposed to fire.	See Note 23	45 min.		1		18, 23, 25, 26	$3/4$
W-5-W-53	5″	2″ × 4″ stud wall; $3/4$″ thick T&G wood boards on both sides.	See Note 23	20 min.		1		17, 23	$1/3$
W-5-W-54	5″	Same as W-5-W-53 but with insulated cavities.	See Note 23	35 min.		1		17, 18, 23	$1/2$
W-5-W-55	5″	2″ × 4″ stud wall; $3/4$″ thick T&G wood boards on both sides with 30 lbs./100 ft.^{2} asbestos; paper, between studs and boards.	See Note 23	45 min.		1		17, 23	$3/4$
W-5-W-56	5″	2″ × 4″ stud wall; $1/2$″ thick, 1:2; 1:3 gypsum plaster on metal lath on both sides of wall.	See Note 23	45 min.		1		17, 21, 34	$3/4$
W-5-W-57	5″	2″ × 4″ stud wall; $3/4$″ thick 2:1:8; 2:1:12 lime and Keene's cement plaster over metal lath on both sides of wall.	See Note 23	45 min.		1		17, 21, 23	$1/2$
W-5-W-58	5″	2″ × 4″ stud wall; $3/4$″ thick 2:1:8; 2:1:10 lime portland cement plaster over metal lath on both sides of wall.	See Note 23	30 min.		1		17, 21, 23	$1/2$
W-5-W-59	5″	2″ × 4″ stud wall; $3/4$″ thick 1:5; 1:7.5 lime plaster on metal lath on both sides of wall.	See Note 23	30 min.		1		17, 21, 23	$1/2$
W-5-W-60	5″	2″ × 4″ stud wall; $3/4$″ thick 1:$1/30$:2; 1:$1/30$:3 portland cement, asbestos fiber plaster on metal lath on both sides of wall.	See Note 23	45 min.		1		17, 21, 23	$3/4$
W-5-W-61	5″	2″ × 4″ stud wall; $3/4$″ thick 1:2; 1:3 portland cement plaster on metal lath on both sides of wall.	See Note 23	30 min.		1		17, 21, 23	$1/2$
W-5-W-62	5″	2″ × 4″ stud wall; $3/4$″ thick neat gypsum plaster on metal lath on both sides of wall.	N/A	1 hr. 30 min.		1		17, 22, 24	$1^1/2$
W-5-W-63	5″	2″ × 4″ stud wall; $3/4$″ thick neat gypsum plaster on metal lath on both sides of wall.	See Note 23	1 hr. 30 min.		1		17, 21, 23	$1^1/2$
W-5-W-64	5″	2″ × 4″ stud wall; $3/4$″ thick 1:2; 1:2 gypsum plaster on metal lath on both sides of wall; insulated cavities.	See Note 23	1 hr. 30 min.		1		17, 18, 21, 23	$1^1/2$
W-5-W-65	5″	2″ × 4″ stud wall; same as W-5-W-64 but cavities not insulated.	See Note 23	1 hr.		1		17, 21, 23	1
W-5-W-66	5″	2″ × 4″ stud wall; $3/4$″ thick 1:2; 1:3 gypsum plaster on metal lath on both sides of wall; insulated cavities.	See Note 23	1 hr. 15 min.		1		17, 18, 21, 23	$1^1/4$
W-5-W-67	$5^1/16$″	Same as W-5-W-49 except cavity insulation of 1.75 lbs./ft.^{2} mineral wool bats; rating applies when either wall side exposed to fire.	See Note 23	1 hr. 15 min.		1		23, 26, 25	$1^1/4$
W-5-W-68	$5^1/4$″	2″ × 4″ stud wall, $7/8$″ thick 1:2; 1:3 gypsum plaster on metal lath on both sides of wall; insulated cavities.	See Note 23	1 hr. 30 min.		1		17, 18, 21, 23	$1^1/2$
W-5-W-69	$5^1/4$″	2″ × 4″ stud wall; $7/8$″ thick neat gypsum plaster applied on metal lath on both sides of wall.	N/A	1 hr. 45 min.		1		17, 22, 24	$1^3/4$
W-5-W-70	$5^1/4$″	2″ × 4″ stud wall; $1/2$″ thick neat gypsum plaster on $3/8$″ plain gypsum lath on both sides of wall.	See Note 23	1 hr.		1		17, 22, 23	1

(Continued)

TABLE 1.3.2—WOOD FRAME WALLS
4″ TO LESS THAN 6″ THICK—(Continued)

ITEM CODE	THICKNESS	CONSTRUCTION DETAILS	PERFORMANCE		REFERENCE NUMBER			NOTES	REC. HOURS
			LOAD	TIME	PRE-BMS-92	BMS-92	POST-BMS-92		
W-5-W-71	$5^1/_4''$	2″ × 4″ stud wall; $^1/_2''$ thick of 1:2; 1:2 gypsum plaster on $^3/_8''$ thick plain gypsum lath with $1^3/_4''$ x $1^3/_4''$ metal lath pads nailed 8″ o.c. vertically and 16″ o.c. horizontally on both sides of wall.	See Note 23	1 hr.		1		17, 21, 23	1
W-5-W-72	$5^1/_4''$	2″ × 4″ stud wall; $^1/_2''$ thick of 1:2; 1:2 gypsum plaster on $^3/_8''$ perforated gypsum lath, one $^3/_4''$ diameter hole or larger per 16″ square of lath surface, on both sides of wall.	See Note 23	1 hr.		1		17, 21, 23	1
W-5-W-73	$5^1/_4''$	2″ × 4″ stud wall; $^1/_2''$ thick of 1:2; 1:2 gypsum plaster on $^3/_8''$ gypsum lath (plain, indented or perforated) on both sides of wall.	See Note 23	45 min.		1		17, 21, 23	$^3/_4$
W-5-W-74	$5^1/_4''$	2″ × 4″ stud wall; $^7/_8''$ thick of 1:2; 1:3 gypsum plaster over metal lath on both sides of wall.	See Note 23	1 hr.		1		17, 21, 23	1
W-5-W-75	$5^1/_4''$	2″ × 4″ stud wall; $^7/_8''$ thick of $1{:}^1/_{30}{:}2$; $1{:}^1/_{30}{:}3$ portland cement, asbestos plaster applied over metal lath on both sides of wall.	See Note 23	1 hr.		1		17, 21, 23	1
W-5-W-76	$5^1/_4''$	2″ × 4″ stud wall; $^7/_8''$ thick of 1:2; 1:3 portland cement plaster over metal lath on both sides of wall.	See Note 23	45 min.		1		17, 21, 23	$^3/_4$
W-5-W-77	$5^1/_2''$	2″ × 4″ stud wall; 1″ thick neat gypsum plaster over metal lath on both sides of wall; nonload bearing.	N/A	2 hrs.		1		17, 22, 24	2
W-5-W-78	$5^1/_2''$	2″ × 4″ stud wall; $^1/_2''$ thick of 1:2; 1:2 gypsum plaster on $^1/_2''$ thick, 0.7 lb./ft.^{2} wood fiberboard on both sides of wall.	See Note 23	35 min.		1		17, 21, 23	$^1/_2$
W-4-W-79	$4^3/_4''$	2″ × 4″ wood stud wall; $^1/_2''$ thick of 1:2; 1:2 gypsum plaster over wood lath on both sides of wall; mineral wool insulation.	N/A	1 hr.			43	21, 31, 35, 38	1
W-4-W-80	$4^3/_4''$	Same as W-4-W-79 but uninsulated.	N/A	35 min.			43	21, 31, 35	$^1/_2$
W-4-W-81	$4^3/_4''$	2″ × 4″ wood stud wall; $^1/_2''$ thick of 3:1:8; 3:1:12 lime, Keene's cement, sand plaster over wood lath on both sides of wall; mineral wool insulation.	N/A	1 hr.			43	21, 31, 35, 40	1
W-4-W-82	$4^3/_4''$	2″ × 4″ wood stud wall; $^1/_2''$ thick of $1{:}6^1/_4$; $1{:}6^1/_4$ lime Keene's cement plaster over wood lath on both sides of wall; mineral wool insulation.	N/A	30 min.			43	21, 31, 35, 40	$^1/_2$
W-4-W-83	$4^3/_4''$	2″ × 4″ wood stud wall; $^1/_2''$ thick of 1:5; 1:7.5 lime plaster over wood lath on both sides of wall.	N/A	30 min.			43	21, 31, 35	$^1/_2$
W-5-W-84	$5^1/_8''$	2″ × 4″ wood stud wall; $^{11}/_{16}''$ thick of 1:5; 1:7.5 lime plaster over wood lath on both sides of wall; mineral wool insulation.	N/A	45 min.			43	21, 31, 35, 39	$^1/_2$
W-5-W-85	$5^1/_4''$	2″ × 4″ wood stud wall; $^3/_4''$ thick of 1:5; 1:7 lime plaster over wood lath on both sides of wall; mineral wool insulation.	N/A	40 min.			43	21, 31, 35, 40	$^2/_3$
W-5-W-86	$5^1/_4''$	2″ × 4″ wood stud wall; $^1/_2''$ thick of 2:1:12 lime, Keene's cement and sand scratch coat; $^1/_2''$ thick 2:1:18 lime, Keene's cement and sand brown coat over wood lath on both sides of wall; mineral wool insulation.	N/A	1 hr.			43	21, 31, 35, 40	1
W-5-W-87	$5^1/_4''$	2″ × 4″ wood stud wall; $^1/_2''$ thick of 1:2; 1:2 gypsum plaster over $^3/_8''$ plaster board on both sides of wall.	N/A	45 min.			43	21, 31	$^3/_4$
W-5-W-88	$5^1/_4''$	2″ × 4″ wood stud wall; $^1/_2''$ thick of 1:2; 1:2 gypsum plaster over $^3/_8''$ gypsum lath on both sides of wall.	N/A	45 min.			43	21, 31	$^3/_4$

(Continued)

TABLE 1.3.2—WOOD FRAME WALLS
4″ TO LESS THAN 6″ THICK—(Continued)

| ITEM CODE | THICKNESS | CONSTRUCTION DETAILS | PERFORMANCE | | REFERENCE NUMBER | | | NOTES | REC. HOURS |
			LOAD	TIME	PRE-BMS-92	BMS-92	POST-BMS-92		
W-5-W-89	$5^1/_4''$	2″ × 4″ wood stud wall; $^1/_2''$ thick of 1:2; 1:2 gypsum plaster over $^3/_8''$ gypsum lath on both sides of wall.	N/A	1 hr.			43	21, 31, 33	1
W-5-W-90	$5^1/_4''$	2″ × 4″ wood stud wall; $^1/_2''$ thick neat plaster over $^3/_8''$ thick gypsum lath on both sides of wall.	N/A	1 hr.			43	21, 22, 31	1
W-5-W-91	$5^1/_4''$	2″ × 4″ wood stud wall; $^1/_2''$ thick of 1:2; 1:2 gypsum plaster over $^3/_8''$ thick indented gypsum lath on both sides of wall.	N/A	45 min.			43	21, 31	$^3/_4$
W-5-W-92	$5^1/_4''$	2″ × 4″ wood stud wall; $^1/_2''$ thick of 1:2; 1:2 gypsum plaster over $^3/_8''$ thick perforated gypsum lath on both sides of wall.	N/A	45 min.			43	21, 31, 34	$^3/_4$
W-5-W-93	$5^1/_4''$	2″ × 4″ wood stud wall; $^1/_2''$ thick of 1:2; 1:2 gypsum plaster over $^3/_8''$ perforated gypsum lath on both sides of wall.	N/A	1 hr.			43	21, 31	1
W-5-W-94	$5^1/_4''$	2″ × 4″ wood stud wall; $^1/_2''$ thick of 1:2; 1:2 gypsum plaster over $^3/_8''$ thick perforated gypsum lath on both sides of wall.	N/A	45 min.			43	21, 31, 34	$^3/_4$
W-5-W-95	$5^1/_2''$	2″ × 4″ wood stud wall; $^1/_2''$ thick of 1:2; 1:2 gypsum plaster over $^1/_2''$ thick wood fiberboard plaster base on both sides of wall.	N/A	35 min.			43	21, 31, 36	$^1/_2$
W-5-W-96	$5^3/_4''$	2″ × 4″ wood stud wall; $^1/_2''$ thick of 1:2; 1:2 gypsum plaster over $^7/_8''$ thick flameproofed wood fiberboard on both sides of wall.	N/A	1 hr.			43	21, 31, 37	1

Notes:
1. All specimens 8 feet or 8 feet 8 inches by 10 feet, 4 inches, i.e. one-half of furnace size. See Note 42 for design cross section.
2. Specimens tested in tandem (two per exposure).
3. Test per ASA No. A2-1934 except where unloaded. Also, panels were of "half" size of furnace opening. Time value signifies a thermal failure time.
4. Two-inch by 4-inch studs: 16 inches on center.; where 10 feet 4 inches, blocking at 2-foot 4-inch height.
5. Facing 4 feet by 8 feet, cement-asbestos board sheets, $^3/_{16}$ inch thick.
6. Sheathing (diagonal): $^{25}/_{22}$ inch by $5^1/_2$ inch, 1 inch by 6 inches pine.
7. Facing shingles: 24 inches by 12 inches by $^5/_{32}$ inch where used.
8. Asbestos felt: asphalt sat between sheathing and shingles.
9. Load: 30,500 pounds or 360 psi/stud where load was tested.
10. Walls were tested beyond achievement of first test end point. A load-bearing time in excess of performance time indicates that although thermal criteria were exceeded, load-bearing ability continued.
11. Wall was rated for one hour combustible use in original source.
12. Hose steam test specimen. See table entry of similar design above for recommended rating.
13. Rated one and one-fourth hour load bearing. Rated one and one-half hour nonload bearing.
14. Failed hose stream.
15. Test terminated due to flame penetration.
16. Test terminated - local back face temperature rise.
17. Nominal 2-inch by 4-inch wood studs of No. 1 common or better lumber set edgewise. Two-inch by four-inch plates at top and bottom and blocking ad mid height of wall.
18. Cavity insulation consists of rock wool bats 1.0 lb./ft.^{2} of filled cavity area.
19. Cavity insulation consists of glass wool bats 0.6 lb./ft.^{2} of filled cavity area.
20. Cavity insulation consists of blown-in forck wool 2.0 lbs./ft.^{2} of filled cavity area
21. Mix proportions for plastered walls as follows: first ratio indicates scratch coat mix, weight of dry plaster: dry sand; second ratio indicates brown coat mix.
22. "Neat" plaster is taken to mean unsanded wood-fiber gypsum plaster.
23. Load: 360 psi of net stud cross sectional area.
24. Rated as nonload bearing.
25. Nominal 2-inch by 4-inch studs per Note 17, spaced at 16 inches on center.
26. Horizontal joints in facing material supported by 2-inch by 4-inch blocking within wall.
27. Facings secured with 6d casing nails. Nail holes predrilled and were 0.02 to 0.03 inch smaller than nail diameter.
28. Cavity insulation consists of mineral wool bats weighing 2 lbs./ft.^{2} of filled cavity area.
29. Interior wall face exposed to fire.
30. Exterior wall faced exposed to fire.
31. Nominal 2-inch by 4-inch studs of yellow pine or Douglas-fir spaced 16 inches on center in a single row.
32. Studs as in Note 31 except double row, with studs in rows staggered.
33. Six roofing nails with metal-lath pads around heats to each 16-inch by 48-inch lath.
34. Areas of holes less than $2^3/_4$ percent of area of lath.
35. Wood laths were nailed with either 3d or 4d nails, one nail to each bearing, and the end joining broken every seventh course.
36. One-half-inch thick fiberboard plaster base nailed with 3d or 4d common wire nails spaced 4 to 6 inches on center.
37. Seven-eighths-inch thick fiberboard plaster base nailed with 5d common wire nails spaced 4 to 6 inches on center.
38. Mineral wood bats 1.05 to 1.25 lbs./ft.^{2} with waterproofed-paper backing.
39. Blown-in mineral wool insulation, 2.2 lbs./ft.^{2}.
40. Mineral wool bats, 1.4 lbs./ft.^{2} with waterproofed-paper backing.

TABLE 1.3.2—WOOD FRAME WALLS
4″ TO LESS THAN 6″ THICK—(Continued)

41. Mineral wood bats, 0.9 lb./ft.^{2}.
42. See wall design diagram, below.

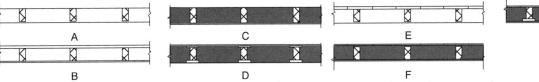

43. Duplicate specimen of W-4-W-7, tested simultaneously with W-4-W-7 in 18-foot test furnace.

TABLE 1.3.3—WOOD FRAME WALLS
6″ TO LESS THAN 8″ THICK

ITEM CODE	THICKNESS	CONSTRUCTION DETAILS	PERFORMANCE		REFERENCE NUMBER			NOTES	REC. HOURS
			LOAD	TIME	PRE-BMS-92	BMS-92	POST-BMS-92		
W-6-W-1	$6^1/_4$″	2 × 4 stud wall; $^1/_2$″ thick, 1:2; 1:2 gypsum plaster on $^7/_8$″ flameproofed wood fiberboard weighing 2.8 lbs./ft.^{2} on both sides of wall.	See Note 3	1 hr.		1		1-3	1
W-6-W-2	$6^1/_2$″	2 × 4 stud wall; $^1/_2$″ thick, 1:3; 1:3 gypsum plaster on 1″ thick magnesium oxysulfate wood fiberboard on both sides of wall.	See Note 3	45 min.		1		1-3	$^3/_4$
W-7-W-3	$7^1/_4$″	Double row of 2 × 4 studs, $^1/_2$″ thick of 1:2; 1:2 gypsum plaster applied over $^3/_8$″ thick perforated gypsum lath on both sides of wall; mineral wool insulation.	N/A	1 hr.			43	2, 4, 5	1
W-7-W-4	$7^1/_2$″	Double row of 2 × 4 studs, $^5/_8$″ thick of 1:2; 1:2 gypsum plaster applied over $^3/_8$″ thick perforated gypsum lath over laid with 2″ × 2″, 16 gage wire fabric, on both sides of wall.	N/A	1 hr. 15 min.			43	2, 4	$1^1/_4$

Notes:
1. Nominal 2-inch by 4-inch wood studs of No. 1 common or better lumber set edgewise. Two-inch by 4-inch plates at top and bottom and blocking at mid height of wall.
2. Mix proportions for plastered walls as follows: first ratio indicates scratch coat mix, weight of dry plaster:dry sand; second ratio indicates brown coat mix.
3. Load: 360 psi of net stud cross sectional area.
4. Nominal 2-inch by 4-inch studs of yellow pine of Douglas-fir spaced 16 inches in a double row, with studs in rows staggered.
5. Mineral wool bats, 0.19 lb./ft.^{2}.

TABLE 1.4.1—WALLS—MISCELLANEOUS MATERIALS
0″ TO LESS THAN 4″ THICK

ITEM CODE	THICKNESS	CONSTRUCTION DETAILS	PERFORMANCE		REFERENCE NUMBER			NOTES	REC. HOURS
			LOAD	TIME	PRE-BMS-92	BMS-92	POST-BMS-92		
W-3-Mi-1	$3^7/_8$″	Glass brick wall: (bricks $5^3/_4$″ x $5^3/_4$″ × $3^7/_8$″) $^1/_4$″ mortar bed, cement/lime/sand; mounted in brick (9″) wall with mastic and $^1/_2$″ asbestos rope.	N/A	1 hr.			7	1, 2	1
W-3-Mi-2	3″	Core: 2″ magnesium oxysulfate wood-fiber blocks; laid in portland cement-lime mortar; Facings: on both sides; see Note 3.	N/A	1 hr.		1		3	1
W-3-Mi-3	$3^7/_8$″	Core: 8″ × $4^7/_8$″ glass blocks $3^7/_8$″ thick weighing 4 lbs. each; laid in portland cement-lime mortar; horizontal mortar joints reinforced with metal lath.	N/A	15 min.		1			$^1/_4$

Notes:
1. No failure reached at 1 hour.
2. These glass blocks are assumed to be solid based on other test data available for similar but hollow units which show significantly reduced fire endurance.
3. Minimum of $^1/_2$ inch of 1:3 sanded gypsum plaster required to develop this rating.

TABLE 1.4.2—WALLS—MISCELLANEOUS MATERIALS
4″ TO LESS THAN 6″ THICK

ITEM CODE	THICKNESS	CONSTRUCTION DETAILS	PERFORMANCE		REFERENCE NUMBER			NOTES	REC. HOURS
			LOAD	TIME	PRE-BMS-92	BMS-92	POST-BMS-92		
W-4-Mi-1	4″	Core: 3″ magnesium oxysulfate wood-fiber blocks; laid in portland cement mortar; Facings: both sides; see Note 1.	N/A	2 hrs.		1			2

Notes:
1. One-half inch sanded gypsum plaster. Voids in hollow blocks to be not more than 30 percent.

FIGURE 1.5.1—FINISH RATINGS—INORGANIC MATERIALS

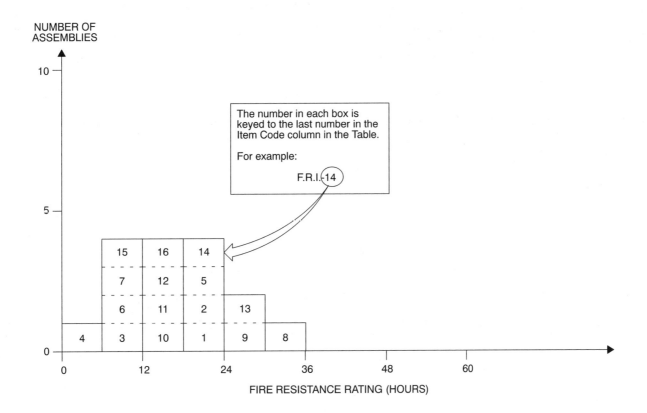

TABLE 1.5.1—FINISH RATINGS—INORGANIC MATERIALS

ITEM CODE	THICKNESS	CONSTRUCTION DETAILS	PERFORMANCE	REFERENCE NUMBER			NOTES	REC. F.R. (MIN.)
			FINISH RATING	PRE-BMS-92	BMS-92	POST-BMS-92		
F.R.-I-1	$^9/_{16}"$	$^3/_8"$ gypsum wallboard faced with $^3/_{16}"$ cement-asbestos board.	20 minutes		1		1, 2	15
F.R.-I-2	$^{11}/_{16}"$	$^1/_2"$ gypsum sheathing faced with $^3/_{16}"$ cement-asbestos board.	20 minutes		1		1, 2	20
F.R.-I-3	$^3/_{16}"$	$^3/_{16}"$ cement-asbestos board over uninsulated cavity.	10 minutes		1		1, 2	5
F.R.-I-4	$^3/_{16}"$	$^3/_{16}"$ cement-asbestos board over insulated cavities.	5 minutes		1		1, 2	5
F.R.-I-5	$^3/_4"$	$^3/_4"$ thick 1:2; 1:3 gypsum plaster over paper backed metal lath.	20 minutes		1		1, 2, 3	20
F.R.-I-6	$^3/_4"$	$^3/_4"$ thick portland cement plaster on metal lath.	10 minutes		1		1, 2	10
F.R.-I-7	$^3/_4"$	$^3/_4"$ thick 1:5; 1:7.5 lime plaster on metal lath.	10 minutes		1		1, 2	10
F.R.-I-8	$1"$	$1"$ thick neat gypsum plaster on metal lath.	35 minutes		1		1, 2, 4	35
F.R.-I-9	$^3/_4"$	$^3/_4"$ thick neat gypsum plaster on metal lath.	30 minutes		1		1, 2, 4	30
F.R.-I-10	$^3/_4"$	$^3/_4"$ thick 1:2; 1:2 gypsum plaster on metal lath.	15 minutes		1		1, 2, 3	15
F.R.-I-11	$^1/_2"$	Same as F.R.-1-7, except $^1/_2"$ thick on wood lath.	15 minutes		1		1, 2, 3	15
F.R.-I-12	$^1/_2"$	$^1/_2"$ thick 1:2; 1:3 gypsum plaster on wood lath.	15 minutes		1		1, 2, 3	15
F.R.-I-13	$^7/_8"$	$^1/_2"$ thick 1:2; 1:2 gypsum plaster on $^3/_8"$ perforated gypsum lath.	30 minutes		1		1, 2, 3	30

(Continued)

TABLE 1.5.1—FINISH RATINGS—INORGANIC MATERIALS—(Continued)

ITEM CODE	THICKNESS	CONSTRUCTION DETAILS	PERFORMANCE FINISH RATING	REFERENCE NUMBER PRE-BMS-92	BMS-92	POST-BMS-92	NOTES	REC. F.R. (MIN.)
F.R.-I-14	$7/8''$	$1/2''$ thick 1:2; 1:2 gypsum plaster on $3/8''$ thick plain or indented gypsum plaster.	20 minutes		1		1, 2, 3	20
F.R.-I-15	$3/8''$	$3/8''$ gypsum wallboard.	10 minutes		1		1, 2	10
F.R.-I-16	$1/2''$	$1/2''$ gypsum wallboard.	15 minutes		1		1, 2	15

Notes:
1. The finish rating is the time required to obtain an average temperature rise of 250°F., or a single point rise of 325°F., at the interface between the material being rated and the substrate being protected.
2. Tested in accordance with the Standard Specifications for Fire Tests of Building Construction and Materials, ASA No. A2-1932.
3. Mix proportions for plasters as follows: first ratio, dry weight of plaster: dry weight of sand for scratch coat; second ratio, plaster: sand for brown coat.
4. Neat plaster means unsanded wood-fiber gypsum plaster.

General Note:
The finish rating of modern building materials can be found in the current literature.

TABLE 1.5.2—FINISH RATINGS—ORGANIC MATERIALS

ITEM CODE	THICKNESS	CONSTRUCTION DETAILS	PERFORMANCE FINISH RATING	REFERENCE NUMBER PRE-BMS-92	BMS-92	POST-BMS-92	NOTES	REC. F.R. (MIN.)
F.R.-O-1	$9/16''$	$7/16''$ wood fiberboard faced with $1/8''$ cement-asbestos board.	15 minutes		1		1, 2	15
F.R.-O-2	$29/32''$	$3/4''$ wood sheathing, asbestos felt weighing 14 lbs./100 ft.^{2} and $5/32''$ cement-asbestos shingles.	20 minutes		1		1, 2	20
F.R.-O-3	$1 1/2''$	1″ thick magnesium oxysulfate wood fiberboard faced with 1:3; 1:3 gypsum plaster, $1/2''$ thick.	20 minutes		1		1, 2, 3	20
F.R.-O-4	$1/2''$	$1/2''$ thick wood fiberboard	5 minutes		1		1, 2	5
F.R.-O-5	$1/2''$	$1/2''$ thick flameproofed wood fiberboard.	10 minutes		1		1, 2	10
F.R.-O-6	1″	$1/2''$ thick wood fiberboard faced with $1/2''$ thick 1:2; 1:2 gypsum plaster.	15 minutes		1		1, 2, 3	30
F.R.-O-7	$1 3/8''$	$7/8''$ thick flameproofed wood fiberboard faced with $1/2''$ thick 1:2; 1:2 gypsum plaster.	30 minutes		1		1, 2, 3	30
F.R.-O-8	$1 1/4''$	$1 1/4''$ thick plywood.	30 minutes			35		30

Notes:
1. The finish rating is the time required to obtain an average temperature rise of 250°F., or a single point rise of 325°F., at the interface between the material being rated and he substrate being protected.
2. Tested in accordance with the Standard Specifications for Fire Tests of Building Construction and Materials, ASA No. A2-1932.
3. Plaster ratios as follows: first ratio is for scratch coat, weight of dry plaster: weight of dry sand; second ratio is for the brown coat.

General Note:
The finish rating of thinner materials, particularly thinner woods, have not bee listed because the possible effects of shrinkage, warpage and aging cannot be predicted.

SECTION II—COLUMNS

TABLE 2.1.1—REINFORCED CONCRETE COLUMNS
MINIMUM DIMENSION 0″ TO LESS THAN 6″

ITEM CODE	MINIMUM DIMENSION	CONSTRUCTION DETAILS	PERFORMANCE		REFERENCE NUMBER			NOTES	REC-HOURS
			LOAD	TIME	PRE-BMS-92	BMS-92	POST-BMS-92		
C-6-RC-1	6″	6″ × 6″ square columns; gravel aggregate concrete (4030 psi); Reinforcement: vertical, four $^7/_8$″ rebars; horizontal, $^5/_{16}$″ ties at 6″ pitch; Cover: 1″.	34.7 tons	62 min.			7	1, 2	1
C-6-RC-2	6″	6″ × 6″ square columns; gravel aggregate concrete (4200 psi); Reinforcement: vertical, four $^1/_2$″ rebars; horizontal, $^5/_{16}$″ ties at 6″ pitch; Cover: 1″.	21 tons	69 min.			7	1, 2	1

Notes:
1. Collapse.
2. British Test.

FIGURE 2.1.2—REINFORCED CONCRETE COLUMNS
MINIMUM DIMENSION 10″ TO LESS THAN 12″

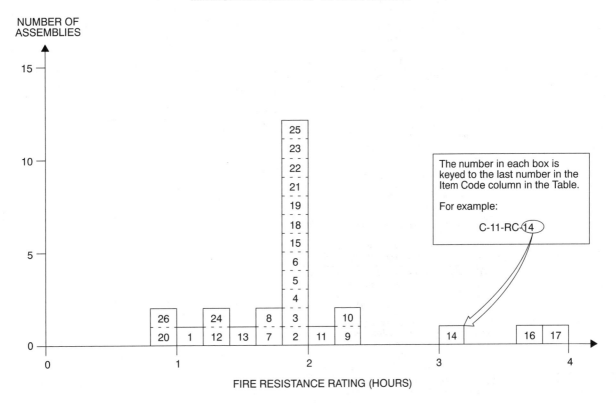

TABLE 2.1.2—REINFORCED CONCRETE COLUMN
MINIMUM DIMENSION 10″ TO LESS THAN 12″

ITEM CODE	MINIMUM DIMENSION	CONSTRUCTION DETAILS	PERFORMANCE		REFERENCE NUMBER			NOTES	REC-HOURS
			LOAD	TIME	PRE-BMS-92	BMS-92	POST-BMS-92		
C-10-RC-1	10″	10″ square columns; aggregate concrete (4260 psi); Reinforcement: vertical, four $1^1/_4$″ rebars; horizontal, $^3/_8$″ ties at 6 pitch; Cover: $1^1/_4$″.	92.2 tons	1 hr. 2 min.			7	1	1
C-10-RC-2	10″	10″ square columns; aggregate concrete (2325 psi); Reinforcement: vertical, four $^1/_2$″ rebars; horizontal, $^5/_{16}$″ ties at 6″ pitch; Cover: 1″.	46.7 tons	1 hr. 52 min.			7	1	$1^3/_4$

(Continued)

143

ITEM CODE	MINIMUM DIMENSION	CONSTRUCTION DETAILS	PERFORMANCE		REFERENCE NUMBER			NOTES	REC-HOURS
			LOAD	TIME	PRE-BMS-92	BMS-92	POST-BMS-92		
C-10-RC-3	10″	10″ square columns; aggregate concrete (5370 psi); Reinforcement: vertical, four $^1/_2$″ rebars; horizontal, $^5/_{16}$″ ties at 6″ pitch; Cover: 1″.	46.5 tons	2 hrs.			7	2, 3, 11	2
C-10-RC-4	10″	10″ square columns; aggregate concrete (5206 psi); Reinforcement: vertical, four $^1/_2$″ rebars; horizontal, $^5/_{16}$″ ties at 6″ pitch; Cover: 1″.	46.5 tons	2 hrs.			7	2, 7	2
C-10-RC-5	10″	10″ square columns; aggregate concrete (5674 psi); Reinforcement: vertical, four $^1/_2$″ rebars; horizontal, $^5/_{16}$″ ties at 6″ pitch; Cover: 1″.	46.7 tons	2 hrs.			7	1	2
C-10-RC-6	10″	10″ square columns; aggregate concrete (5150 psi); Reinforcement: vertical, four $1^1/_2$″ rebars; horizontal, $^5/_{16}$″ ties at 6 pitch; Cover: 1″.	66 tons	1 hr. 43 min.			7	1	$1^3/_4$
C-10-RC-7	10″	10″ square columns; aggregate concrete (5580 psi); Reinforcement: vertical, four $^1/_2$″ rebars; horizontal, $^5/_{16}$″ ties at 6″ pitch; Cover: $1^1/_8$″.	62.5 tons	1 hr. 38 min.			7	1	$1^1/_2$
C-10-RC-8	10″	10″ square columns; aggregate concrete (4080 psi); Reinforcement: vertical, four $1^1/_8$″ rebars; horizontal, $^5/_{16}$″ ties at 6″ pitch; Cover: $1^1/_8$″.	72.8 tons	1 hr. 48 min.			7	1	$1^3/_4$
C-10-RC-9	10″	10″ square columns; aggregate concrete (2510 psi); Reinforcement: vertical, four $^1/_2$″ rebars; horizontal, $^5/_{16}$″ ties at 6″ pitch; Cover: 1″.	51 tons	2 hrs 16 min.			7	1	$2^1/_4$
C-10-RC-10	10″	10″ square columns; aggregate concrete (2170 psi); Reinforcement: vertical, four $^1/_2$″ rebars; horizontal, $^5/_{16}$″ ties at 6″ pitch; Cover: 1″.	45 tons	2 hrs. 14 min.			7	12	$2^1/_4$
C-10-RC-11	10″	10″ square columns; gravel aggregate concrete (4015 psi); Reinforcement: vertical, four $^1/_2$″ rebars; horizontal, $^5/_{16}$″ ties at 6″ pitch; Cover: $1^1/_8$″.	46.5 tons	2 hrs. 6 min.			7	1	2
C-11-RC-12	11″	11″ square columns; gravel aggregate concrete (4150 psi); Reinforcement: vertical, four $1^1/_4$″ rebars; horizontal, $^3/_8$″ ties at $7^1/_2$″ pitch; Cover: $1^1/_2$″.	61 tons	1 hr. 23 min.			7	1	$1^1/_4$
C-11-RC-13	11″	11″ square columns; gravel aggregate concrete (4380 psi); Reinforcement: vertical, four $1^1/_4$″ rebars; horizontal, $^3/_8$″ ties at $7^1/_2$″ pitch; Cover: $1^1/_2$″.	61 tons	1 hr. 26 min.			7	1	$1^1/_4$
C-11-RC-14	11″	11″ square columns; gravel aggregate concrete (4140 psi); Reinforcement: vertical, four $1^1/_4$″ rebars; horizontal, $^3/_8$″ ties at $7^1/_2$″ pitch; steel mesh around reinforcement; Cover: $1^1/_2$″.	61 tons	3 hrs. 9 min.			7	1	3
C-11-RC-15	11″	11″ square columns; slag aggregate concrete (3690 psi); Reinforcement: vertical, four $1^1/_4$″ rebars; horizontal, $^3/_8$″ ties at $7^1/_2$″ pitch; Cover: $1^1/_2$″.	91 tons	2 hrs.			7	2, 3, 4, 5	2
C-11-RC-16	11″	11″ square columns; limestone aggregate concrete (5230 psi); Reinforcement: vertical, four $1^1/_4$″ rebars; horizontal, $^3/_8$″ ties at $7^1/_2$″ pitch; Cover: $1^1/_2$″.	91.5 tons	3 hrs. 41 min.			7	1	$3^1/_2$
C-11-RC-17	11″	11″ square columns; limestone aggregate concrete (5530 psi); Reinforcement: vertical, four $1^1/_4$″ rebars; horizontal, $^3/_8$″ ties at $7^1/_2$″ pitch; Cover: $1^1/_2$″.	91.5 tons	3 hrs. 47 min.			7	1	$3^1/_2$
C-11-RC-18	11″	11″ square columns; limestone aggregate concrete (5280 psi); Reinforcement: vertical, four $1^1/_4$″ rebars; horizontal, $^3/_8$″ ties at $7^1/_2$″ pitch; Cover: $1^1/_2$″.	91.5 tons	2 hrs.			7	2, 3, 4, 6	2

(Continued)

TABLE 2.1.2—REINFORCED CONCRETE COLUMN
MINIMUM DIMENSION 10″ TO LESS THAN 12″—(Continued)

ITEM CODE	MINIMUM DIMENSION	CONSTRUCTION DETAILS	PERFORMANCE		REFERENCE NUMBER			NOTES	REC-HOURS
			LOAD	TIME	PRE-BMS-92	BMS-92	POST-BMS-92		
C-11-RC-19	11″	11″ square columns; limestone aggregate concrete (4180 psi); Reinforcement: vertical, four $^5/_8$″ rebars; horizontal, $^3/_8$″ ties at 7″ pitch; Cover: $1^1/_2$″.	71.4 tons	2 hrs.			7	2, 7	2
C-11-RC-20	11″	11″ square columns; gravel concrete (4530 psi); Reinforcement: vertical, four $^5/_8$″ rebars; horizontal, $^3/_8$″ ties at 7″ pitch; Cover: $1^1/_2$″ with $^1/_2$″ plaster.	58.8 tons	2 hrs.			7	2, 3, 9	$1^1/_4$
C-11-RC-21	11″	11″ square columns; gravel concrete (3520 psi); Reinforcement: vertical, four $^5/_8$″ rebars; horizontal, $^3/_8$″ ties at 7″ pitch; Cover: $1^1/_2$″.	Variable	1 hr. 24 min.			7	1, 8	2
C-11-RC-22	11″	11″ square columns; aggregate concrete (3710 psi); Reinforcement: vertical, four $^5/_8$″ rebars; horizontal, $^3/_8$″ ties at 7″ pitch; Cover: $1^1/_2$″.	58.8 tons	2 hrs.			7	2, 3, 10	2
C-11-RC-23	11″	11″ square columns; aggregate concrete (3190 psi); Reinforcement: vertical, four $^5/_8$″ rebars; horizontal, $^3/_8$″ ties at 7″ pitch; Cover: $1^1/_2$″.	58.8 tons	2 hrs.			7	2, 3, 10	2
C-11-RC-24	11″	11″ square columns; aggregate concrete (4860 psi); Reinforcement: vertical, four $^5/_8$″ rebars; horizontal, $^3/_8$″ ties at 7″ pitch; Cover: $1^1/_2$″.	86.1 tons	1 hr. 20 min.			7	1	$1^1/_3$
C-11-RC-25	11″	11″ square columns; aggregate concrete (4850 psi); Reinforcement: vertical, four $^5/_8$″ rebars; horizontal, $^3/_8$″ ties at 7″ pitch; Cover: $1^1/_2$″.	58.8 tons	1 hr. 59 min.			7	1	$1^3/_4$
C-11-RC-26	11″	11″ square columns; aggregate concrete (3834 psi); Reinforcement: vertical, four $^5/_8$″ rebars; horizontal, $^5/_{16}$″ ties at $4^1/_2$″ pitch; Cover: $1^1/_2$″.	71.4 tons	53 min.			7	1	$^3/_4$

Notes:
1. Failure mode - collapse.
2. Passed 2 hour fire exposure.
3. Passed hose stream test.
4. Reloaded effectively after 48 hours but collapsed at load in excess of original test load.
5. Failing load was 150 tons.
6. Failing load was 112 tons.
7. Failed during hose stream test.
8. Range of load 58.8 tons (initial) to 92 tons (92 minutes) to 60 tons (80 minutes).
9. Collapsed at 44 tons in reload after 96 hours.
10. Withstood reload after 72 hours.
11. Collapsed on reload after 48 hours.

TABLE 2.1.3—REINFORCED CONCRETE COLUMNS
MINIMUM DIMENSION 12″ TO LESS THAN 14″

ITEM CODE	MINIMUM DIMENSION	CONSTRUCTION DETAILS	PERFORMANCE		REFERENCE NUMBER			NOTES	REC-HOURS
			LOAD	TIME	PRE-BMS-92	BMS-92	POST-BMS-92		
C-12-RC-1	12″	12″ square columns; gravel aggregate concrete (2647 psi); Reinforcement: vertical, four $^5/_8$″ rebars; horizontal, $^5/_{16}$″ ties at $4^1/_2$″ pitch; Cover: 2″.	78.2 tons	38 min.		1	7	1	$^1/_2$
C-12-RC-2	12″	Reinforced columns with $1^1/_2$″ concrete outside of reinforced steel; Gross diameter or side of column: 12″; Group I, Column A.	—	6 hrs.		1		2, 3	6
C-12-RC-3	12″	Description as per C-12-RC-2; Group I, Column B.	—	4 hrs.		1		2, 3	4
C-12-RC-4	12″	Description as per C-12-RC-2; Group II, Column A.	—	4 hrs.		1		2, 3	4
C-12-RC-5	12″	Description as per C-12-RC-2; Group II, Column B.	—	2 hrs. 30 min.		1		2, 3	$2^1/_2$
C-12-RC-6	12″	Description as per C-12-RC-2; Group III, Column A.	—	3 hrs.		1		2, 3	3
C-12-RC-7	12″	Description as per C-12-RC-2; Group III, Column B.	—	2 hrs.		1		2, 3	2
C-12-RC-8	12″	Description as per C-12-RC-2; Group IV, Column A.	—	2 hrs.		1		2, 3	2
C-12-RC-9	12″	Description as per C-12-RC-2; Group IV, Column B.	—	1 hr. 30 min.		1		2, 3	$1^1/_2$

Notes:

1. Failure mode - unspecified structural.
2. Group I: includes concrete having calcareous aggregate containing a combined total of not more than 10 percent of quartz, chert and flint for the coarse aggregate.

   Group II: includes concrete having trap-rock aggregate applied without metal ties and also concrete having cinder, sandstone or granite aggregate, if held in place with wire mesh or expanded metal having not larger than 4-inch mesh, weighing not less than 1.7 lbs./yd.^{2}, placed not more than 1 inch from the surface of the concrete.

   Group III: includes concrete having cinder, sandstone or granite aggregate tied with No. 5 gage steel wire, wound spirally over the column section on a pitch of 8 inches, or equivalent ties, and concrete having siliceous aggregates containing a combined total of 60 percent or more of quartz, chert and flint, if held in place with wire mesh or expanded metal having not larger than 4-inch mesh, weighing not less than 1.7 lbs./yd.^{2}, placed not more than 1 inch from the surface of the concrete.

   Group IV: includes concrete having siliceous aggregates containing a combined total of 60 percent or more of quartz, chert and flint, and tied with No. 5 gage steel wire wound spirally over the column section on a pitch of 8 inches, or equivalent ties.
3. Groupings of aggregates and ties are the same as for structural steel columns protected solidly with concrete, the ties to be placed over the vertical reinforcing bars and the mesh where required, to be placed within 1 inch from the surface of the column.

   Column A: working loads are assumed as carried by the area of the column inside of the lines circumscribing the reinforcing steel.

   Column B: working loads are assumed as carried by the gross area of the column.

TABLE 2.1.4—REINFORCED CONCRETE COLUMNS
MINIMUM DIMENSION 14″ TO LESS THAN 16″

| ITEM CODE | MINIMUM DIMENSION | CONSTRUCTION DETAILS | PERFORMANCE | | REFERENCE NUMBER | | | NOTES | REC-HOURS |
			LOAD	TIME	PRE-BMS-92	BMS-92	POST-BMS-92		
C-14-RC-1	14″	14″ square columns; gravel aggregate concrete (4295 psi); Reinforcement: vertical four $3/4$″ rebars; horizontal: $1/4$″ ties at 9″ pitch; Cover: $1^1/_2$″.	86 tons	1 hr. 22 min.			7	1	$1^1/_4$
C-14-RC-2	14″	Reinforced concrete columns with $1^1/_2$″ concrete outside reinforcing steel; Gross diameter or side of column: 12″; Group I, Column A.	—	7 hrs.		1		2, 3	7
C-14-RC-3	14″	Description as per C-14-RC-2; Group II, Column B.	—	5 hrs.		1		2, 3	5
C-14-RC-4	14″	Description as per C-14-RC-2; Group III, Column A.	—	5 hrs.		1		2, 3	5
C-14-RC-5	14″	Description as per C-14-RC-2; Group IV, Column B.	—	3 hrs. 30 min.		1		2, 3	$3^1/_2$
C-14-RC-6	14″	Description as per C-14-RC-2; Group III, Column A.	—	4 hrs.		1		2, 3	4
C-14-RC-7	14″	Description as per C-14-RC-2; Group III, Column B.	—	2 hrs. 30 min.		1		2, 3	$2^1/_2$
C-14-RC-8	14″	Description as per C-14-RC-2; Group IV, Column A.	—	2 hrs. 30 min.		1		2, 3	$2^1/_2$
C-14-RC-9	14″	Description as per C-14-RC-2; Group IV, Column B.	—	1 hr. 30 min.		1		2, 3	$1^1/_2$

Notes:
1. Failure mode - main rebars buckled between links at various points.
2. Group I: includes concrete having calcareous aggregate containing a combined total of not more than 10 percent of quartz, chert and flint for the coarse aggregate.

   Group II: includes concrete having trap-rock aggregate applied without metal ties and also concrete having cinder, sandstone or granite aggregate, if held in place with wire mesh or expanded metal having not larger than 4-inch mesh, weighing not less than 1.7 lbs./yd.^{2}, placed not more than 1 inch from the surface of the concrete.

   Group III: includes concrete having cinder, sandstone or granite aggregate tied with No. 5 gage steel wire, wound spirally over the column section on a pitch of 8 inches, or equivalent ties, and concrete having siliceous aggregates containing a combined total of 60 percent or more of quartz, chert and flint, if held in place with wire mesh or expanded metal having not larger than 4-inch mesh, weighing not less than 1.7 lbs./yd.^{2}, placed not more than 1 inch from the surface of the concrete.

   Group IV: includes concrete having siliceous aggregates containing a combined total of 60 percent or more of quartz, chert and flint, and tied with No. 5 gage steel wire wound spirally over the column section on a pitch of 8 inches, or equivalent ties.
3. Groupings of aggregates and ties are the same as for structural steel columns protected solidly with concrete, the ties to be placed over the vertical reinforcing bars and the mesh where required, to be placed within 1 inch from the surface of the column.

   Column A: working loads are assumed as carried by the area of the column inside of the lines circumscribing the reinforcing steel.

   Column B: working loads are assumed as carried by the gross area of the column.

FIGURE 2.1.5—REINFORCED CONCRETE COLUMNS
MINIMUM DIMENSION 16″ TO LESS THAN 18″

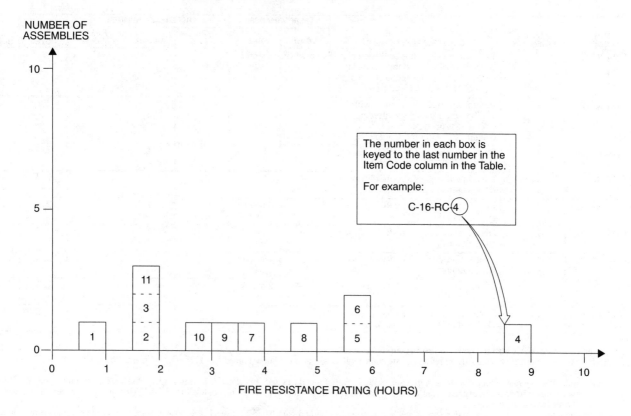

TABLE 2.1.5—REINFORCED CONCRETE COLUMN
MINIMUM DIMENSION 16″ TO LESS THAN 18″

ITEM CODE	MINIMUM DIMENSION	CONSTRUCTION DETAILS	PERFORMANCE		REFERENCE NUMBER			NOTES	REC-HOURS
			LOAD	TIME	PRE-BMS-92	BMS-92	POST-BMS-92		
C-16-RC-1	16″	16″ square columns; gravel aggregate concrete (4550 psi); Reinforcement: vertical, eight $1^3/_8$″ rebars; horizontal, $^5/_{16}$″ ties at 6″ pitch $1^3/_8$″ below column surface and $^5/_{16}$″ ties at 6″ pitch linking center rebars of each face forming a smaller square in column cross section.	237 tons	1 hr.			7	1, 2, 3	1
C-16-RC-2	16″	16″ square columns; gravel aggregate concrete (3360 psi); Reinforcement: vertical, eight $1^3/_8$″ rebars; horizontal, $^5/_{16}$″ ties at 6″ pitch; Cover: $1^3/_8$″.	210 tons	2 hrs.			7	2, 4, 5, 6	2
C-16-RC-3	16″	16″ square columns; gravel aggregate concrete (3980 psi); Reinforcement: vertical, four $^7/_8$″ rebars; horizontal, $^3/_8$″ ties at 6″ pitch; Cover: 1″.	123.5 tons	2 hrs.			7	2, 4, 7	2
C-16-RC-4	16″	Reinforced concrete columns with $1^1/_2$″ concrete outside reinforcing steel; Gross diameter or side of column: 16″; Group I, Column A.	—	9 hrs.	1			8, 9	9
C-16-RC-5	16″	Description as per C-16-RC-4; Group I, Column B.	—	6 hrs.	1			8, 9	6
C-16-RC-6	16″	Description as per C-16-RC-4; Group II, Column A.	—	6 hrs.	1			8, 9	6
C-16-RC-7	16″	Description as per C-16-RC-4; Group II, Column B.	—	4 hrs.	1			8, 9	4
C-16-RC-8	16″	Description as per C-16-RC-4; Group III, Column A.	—	5 hrs.	1			8, 9	5
C-16-RC-9	16″	Description as per C-16-RC-4; Group III, Column B.	—	3 hrs. 30 min.	1			8, 9	$3^1/_2$

(Continued)

ITEM CODE	MINIMUM DIMENSION	CONSTRUCTION DETAILS	PERFORMANCE		REFERENCE NUMBER			NOTES	REC-HOURS
			LOAD	TIME	PRE-BMS-92	BMS-92	POST-BMS-92		
C-16-RC-10	16″	Description as per C-16-RC-4; Group IV, Column A.	—	3 hrs.		1		8, 9	3
C-16-RC-11	16″	Description as per C-16-RC-4; Group IV, Column B.	—	2 hrs.		1		8, 9	2

Notes:
1. Column passed 1 hour fire test.
2. Column passed hose stream test.
3. No reload specified.
4. Column passed 2 hour fire test.
5. Column reloaded successfully after 24 hours.
6. Reinforcing details same as C-16-RC-1.
7. Column passed reload after 72 hours.
8. Group I: includes concrete having calcareous aggregate containing a combined total of not more than 10 percent of quartz, chert and flint for the coarse aggregate.

   Group II: includes concrete having trap-rock aggregate applied without metal ties and also concrete having cinder, sandstone or granite aggregate, if held in place with wire mesh or expanded metal having not larger than 4-inch mesh, weighing not less than 1.7 lbs./yd.^{2}, placed not more than 1 inch from the surface of the concrete.

   Group III: includes concrete having cinder, sandstone or granite aggregate tied with No. 5 gage steel wire, wound spirally over the column section on a pitch of 8 inches, or equivalent ties, and concrete having siliceous aggregates containing a combined total of 60 percent or more of quartz, chert and flint, if held in place with wire mesh or expanded metal having not larger than 4-inch mesh, weighing not less than 1.7 lbs./yd.^{2}, placed not more than 1 inch from the surface of the concrete.

   Group IV: includes concrete having siliceous aggregates containing a combined total of 60 percent or more of quartz, chert and flint, and tied with No. 5 gage steel wire wound spirally over the column section on a pitch of 8 inches, or equivalent ties.
9. Groupings of aggregates and ties are the same as for structural steel columns protected solidly with concrete, the ties to be placed over the vertical reinforcing bars and the mesh where required, to be placed within 1 inch from the surface of the column.

   Column A: working loads are assumed as carried by the area of the column inside of the lines circumscribing the reinforcing steel.

   Column B: working loads are assumed as carried by the gross area of the column.

ITEM CODE	MINIMUM DIMENSION	CONSTRUCTION DETAILS	PERFORMANCE		REFERENCE NUMBER			NOTES	REC-HOURS
			LOAD	TIME	PRE-BMS-92	BMS-92	POST-BMS-92		
C-18-RC-1	18″	Reinforced concrete columns with 1$\frac{1}{2}$″ concrete outside reinforced steel; Gross diameter or side of column: 18″; Group I, Column A.	—	11 hrs.		1		1, 2	11
C-18-RC-2	18″	Description as per C-18-RC-1; Group I, Column B.	—	8 hrs.		1		1, 2	8
C-18-RC-3	18″	Description as per C-18-RC-1; Group II, Column A.	—	7 hrs.		1		1, 2	7
C-18-RC-4	18″	Description as per C-18-RC-1; Group II, Column B.	—	5 hrs.		1		1, 2	5
C-18-RC-5	18″	Description as per C-18-RC-1; Group III, Column A.	—	6 hrs.		1		1, 2	6
C-18-RC-6	18″	Description as per C-18-RC-1; Group III, Column B.	—	4 hrs.		1		1, 2	4
C-18-RC-7	18″	Description as per C-18-RC-1; Group IV, Column A.	—	3 hrs. 30 min.		1		1, 2	3$\frac{1}{2}$
C-18-RC-8	18″	Description as per C-18-RC-1; Group IV, Column B.	—	2 hrs. 30 min.		1		1, 2	2$\frac{1}{2}$

Notes:
1. Group I: includes concrete having calcareous aggregate containing a combined total of not more than 10 percent of quartz, chert and flint for the coarse aggregate.

   Group II: includes concrete having trap-rock aggregate applied without metal ties and also concrete having cinder, sandstone or granite aggregate, if held in place with wire mesh or expanded metal having not larger than 4-inch mesh, weighing not less than 1.7 lbs./yd.^{2}, placed not more than 1 inch from the surface of the concrete.

   Group III: includes concrete having cinder, sandstone or granite aggregate tied with No. 5 gage steel wire, wound spirally over the column section on a pitch of 8 inches, or equivalent ties, and concrete having siliceous aggregates containing a combined total of 60 percent or more of quartz, chert and flint, if held in place with wire mesh or expanded metal having not larger than 4-inch mesh, weighing not less than 1.7 lbs./yd.^{2}, placed not more than 1 inch from the surface of the concrete.

   Group IV: includes concrete having siliceous aggregates containing a combined total of 60 percent or more of quartz, chert and flint and, tied with No. 5 gage steel wire wound spirally over the column section on a pitch of 8 inches, or equivalent ties.
2. Groupings of aggregates and ties are the same as for structural steel columns protected solidly with concrete, the ties to be placed over the vertical reinforcing bars and the mesh where required, to be placed within 1 inch from the surface of the column.

   Column A: working loads are assumed as carried by the area of the column inside of the lines circumscribing the reinforcing steel.

   Column B: working loads are assumed as carried by the gross area of the column.

FIGURE 2.1.7—REINFORCED CONCRETE COLUMNS
MINIMUM DIMENSION 20″ TO LESS THAN 22″

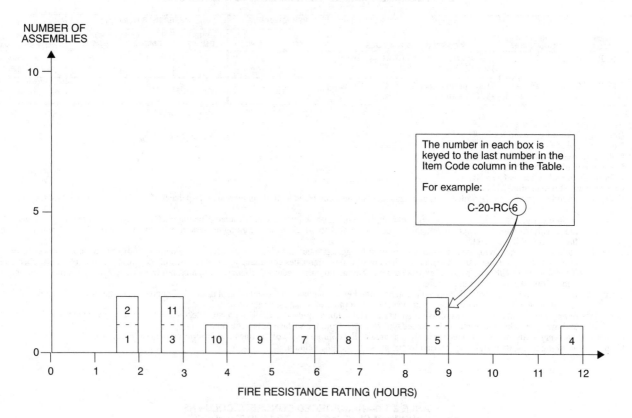

TABLE 2.1.7—REINFORCED CONCRETE COLUMNS
MINIMUM DIMENSION 20″ TO LESS THAN 22″

| ITEM CODE | MINIMUM DIMENSION | CONSTRUCTION DETAILS | PERFORMANCE | | REFERENCE NUMBER | | | NOTES | REC-HOURS |
			LOAD	TIME	PRE-BMS-92	BMS-92	POST-BMS-92		
C-20-RC-1	20″	20″ square columns; gravel aggregate concrete (6690 psi); Reinforcement: vertical, four $1^3/_4$″ rebars; horizontal, $^3/_8$″ wire at 6″ pitch; Cover $1^3/_4$″.	367 tons	2 hrs.			7	1, 2, 3	2
C-20-RC-2	20″	20″ square columns; gravel aggregate concrete (4330 psi); Reinforcement: vertical, four $1^3/_4$″ rebars; horizontal, $^3/_8$″ ties at 6″ pitch; Cover $1^3/_4$″.	327 tons	2 hrs.			7	1, 2, 4	2
C-20-RC-3	$20^1/_4$″	20″ squarecolumns; gravel aggregate concrete (4230 psi); Reinforcement: vertical, four $1^1/_8$″ rebars; horizontal, $^3/_8$″ wire at 5″ pitch; Cover $1^1/_8$″.	199 tons	2 hrs. 56 min.			7	5	$2^3/_4$
C-20-RC-4	20″	Reinforced concrete columns with $1^1/_2$″ concrete outside of reinforcing steel; Gross diameter or side of column: 20″; Group I, Column A.	—	12 hrs.		1		6, 7	12
C-20-RC-5	20″	Description as per C-20-RC-4; Group I, Column B.	—	9 hrs.		1		6, 7	9
C-20-RC-6	20″	Description as per C-20-RC-4; Group II, Column A.	—	9 hrs.		1		6, 7	9
C-20-RC-7	20″	Description as per C-20-RC-4; Group II, Column B.	—	6 hrs.		1		6, 7	6
C-20-RC-8	20″	Description as per C-20-RC-4; Group III, Column A.	—	7 hrs.		1		6, 7	7
C-20-RC-9	20″	Description as per C-20-RC-4; Group III, Column B.	—	5 hrs.		1		6, 7	5
C-20-RC-10	20″	Description as per C-20-RC-4; Group IV, Column A.	—	4 hrs.		1		6, 7	4
C-20-RC-11	20″	Description as per C-20-RC-4; Group IV, Column B.	—	3 hrs.		1		6, 7	3

Notes:
1. Passed 2 hour fire test.
2. Passed hose stream test.
3. Failed during reload at 300 tons.
4. Passed reload after 72 hours.
5. Failure mode - collapse.
6. Group I: includes concrete having calcareous aggregate containing a combined total of not more than 10 percent of quartz, chert and flint for the coarse aggregate.

   Group II: includes concrete having trap-rock aggregate applied without metal ties and also concrete having cinder, sandstone or granite aggregate, if held in place with wire mesh or expanded metal having not larger than 4-inch mesh, weighing not less than 1.7 lbs./yd.^{2}, placed not more than 1 inch from the surface of the concrete.

   Group III: includes concrete having cinder, sandstone or granite aggregate tied with No. 5 gage steel wire, wound spirally over the column section on a pitch of 8 inches, or equivalent ties, and concrete having siliceous aggregates containing a combined total of 60 percent or more of quartz, chert and flint, if held in place with wire mesh or expanded metal having not larger than 4-inch mesh, weighing not less than 1.7 lbs./yd.^{2}, placed not more than 1 inch from the surface of the concrete.

   Group IV: includes concrete having siliceous aggregates containing a combined total of 60 percent or more of quartz, chert and flint, and tied with No. 5 gage steel wire wound spirally over the column section on a pitch of 8 inches, or equivalent ties.
7. Groupings of aggregates and ties are the same as for structural steel columns protected solidly with concrete, the ties to be placed over the vertical reinforcing bars and the mesh where required, to be placed within 1 inch from the surface of the column.

   Column A: working loads are assumed as carried by the area of the column inside of the lines circumscribing the reinforcing steel.

   Column B: working loads are assumed as carried by the gross area of the column.

TABLE 2.1.8—HEXAGONAL REINFORCED CONCRETE COLUMNS
MINIMUM DIMENSION 12″ TO LESS THAN 14″

| ITEM CODE | MINIMUM DIMENSION | CONSTRUCTION DETAILS | PERFORMANCE | | REFERENCE NUMBER | | | NOTES | REC-HOURS |
			LOAD	TIME	PRE-BMS-92	BMS-92	POST-BMS-92		
C-12-HRC-1	12″	12″ hexagonal columns; gravel aggregate concrete (4420 psi); Reinforcement: vertical, eight $^1/_2$″ rebars; horizontal, $^5/_{16}$″ helical winding at $1^1/_2$″ pitch; Cover: $^1/_2$″.	88 tons	58 min.			7	1	$^3/_4$
C-12-HRC-2	12″	12″ hexagonal columns; gravel aggregate concrete (3460 psi); Reinforcement: vertical, eight $^1/_2$″ rebars; horizontal, $^5/_{16}$″ helical winding at $1^1/_2$″ pitch; Cover: $^1/_2$″.	78.7 tons	1 hr.			7	2	1

Notes:
1. Failure mode - collapse.
2. Test stopped at 1 hour.

TABLE 2.1.9—HEXAGONAL REINFORCED CONCRETE COLUMNS
MINIMUM DIMENSION 14″ TO LESS THAN 16″

| ITEM CODE | MINIMUM DIMENSION | CONSTRUCTION DETAILS | PERFORMANCE | | REFERENCE NUMBER | | | NOTES | REC-HOURS |
			LOAD	TIME	PRE-BMS-92	BMS-92	POST-BMS-92		
C-14-HRC-1	14″	14″ hexagonal columns; gravel aggregate concrete (4970 psi); Reinforcement: vertical, eight $^1/_2$″ rebars; horizontal, $^5/_{16}$″ helical winding on 2″ pitch; Cover: $^1/_2$″.	90 tons	2 hrs.			7	1, 2, 3	2

Notes:
1. Withstood 2 hour fire test.
2. Withstood hose stream test.
3. Withstood reload after 48 hours.

TABLE 2.1.10—HEXAGONAL REINFORCED CONCRETE COLUMNS
DIAMETER — 16″ TO LESS THAN 18″

| ITEM CODE | MINIMUM DIMENSION | CONSTRUCTION DETAILS | PERFORMANCE | | REFERENCE NUMBER | | | NOTES | REC-HOURS |
			LOAD	TIME	PRE-BMS-92	BMS-92	POST-BMS-92		
C-16-HRC-1	16″	16″ hexagonal columns; gravel concrete (6320 psi); Reinforcement: vertical, eight $^5/_8$″ rebars; horizontal, $^5/_{16}$″ helical winding on $^3/_4$″ pitch; Cover: $^1/_2$″.	140 tons	1 hr. 55 min.			7	1	$1^3/_4$
C-16-HRC-2	16″	16″ hexagonal columns; gravel aggregate concrete (5580 psi); Reinforcement: vertical, eight $^5/_8$″ rebars; horizontal, $^5/_{16}$″ helical winding on $1^3/_4$″ pitch; Cover: $^1/_2$″.	124 tons	2 hrs.			7	2	2

Notes:
1. Failure mode - collapse.
2. Failed on furnace removal.

TABLE 2.1.11—HEXAGONAL REINFORCED CONCRETE COLUMNS
DIAMETER — 20″ TO LESS THAN 22″

| ITEM CODE | MINIMUM DIMENSION | CONSTRUCTION DETAILS | PERFORMANCE | | REFERENCE NUMBER | | | NOTES | REC. HOURS |
			LOAD	TIME	PRE-BMS-92	BMS-92	POST-BMS-92		
C-20-HRC-1	20″	20″ hexagonal columns; gravel concrete (6080 psi); Reinforcement: vertical, $^3/_4$″ rebars; horizontal, $^5/_6$″ helical winding on $1^3/_4$″ pitch; Cover: $^1/_2$″.	211 tons	2 hrs.			7	1	2
C-20-HRC-2	20″	20″ hexagonal columns; gravel concrete (5080 psi); Reinforcement: vertical, $^3/_4$″ rebars; horizontal, $^5/_{16}$″ wire on $1^3/_4$″ pitch; Cover: $^1/_2$″.	184 tons	2 hrs. 15 min.			7	2, 3, 4	$2^1/_4$

Notes:
1. Column collapsed on furnace removal.
2. Passed $2^1/_4$ hour fire test.
3. Passed hose stream test.
4. Withstood reload after 48 hours.

TABLE 2.2—ROUND CAST IRON COLUMNS

| ITEM CODE | MINIMUM DIMENSION | CONSTRUCTION DETAILS | PERFORMANCE | | REFERENCE NUMBER | | | NOTES | REC-HOURS |
			LOAD	TIME	PRE-BMS-92	BMS-92	POST-BMS-92		
C-7-CI-1	7″ O.D.	Column: .6″ minimum metal thickness; unprotected.	—	30 min.		1			$^1/_2$
C-7-CI-2	7″ O.D.	Column: .6″ minimum metal thickness concrete filled, outside unprotected.	—	45 min.		1			$^3/_4$
C-11-CI-3	11″ O.D.	Column: .6″ minimum metal thickness; Protection: $1^1/_2$″ portland cement plaster on high ribbed metal lath, $^1/_2$″ broken air space.	—	3 hrs.		1			3
C-11-CI-4	11″ O.D.	Column: .6″ minimum metal thickness; Protection: 2″ concrete other than siliceous aggregate.	—	2 hrs. 30 min.		1			$2^1/_2$
C-12-CI-5	12.5″ O.D.	Column: 7″ O.D. .6″ minimum metal thickness; Protection: 2″ porous hollow tile, $^3/_4$″ mortar between tile and column, outside wire ties.	—	3 hrs.		1			3
C-7-CI-6	7.6″ O.D.	Column: 7″ I.D., $^3/_{10}$″ minimum metal thickness, concrete filled unprotected.	—	30 min.		1			$^1/_2$
C-8-CI-7	8.6″ O.D.	Column: 8″ I.D., $^3/_{10}$″ minimum metal thickness; concrete filled reinforced with four $3^1/_2$″ × $^3/_8$″ angles, in fill; unprotected outside.	—	1 hr.		1			1

TABLE 2.3—STEEL COLUMNS—GYPSUM ENCASEMENTS

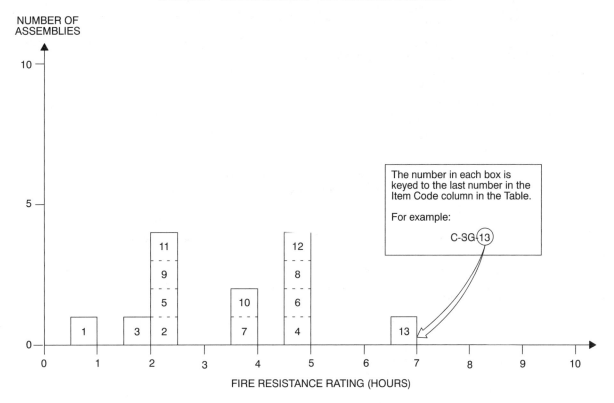

FIRE RESISTANCE RATING (HOURS)

The number in each box is keyed to the last number in the Item Code column in the Table.

For example:

C-SG-(13)

TABLE 2.3—STEEL COLUMNS—GYPSUM ENCASEMENTS

ITEM CODE	MINIMUM AREA OF SOLID MATERIAL	CONSTRUCTION DETAILS	PERFORMANCE		REFERENCE NUMBER			NOTES	REC-HOURS
			LOAD	TIME	PRE-BMS-92	BMS-92	POST-BMS-92		
C-SG-1	—	Steel protected with $^3/_4''$ 1:3 sanded gypsum or 1″ 1:2$^1/_2$ portland cement plaster on wire or lath; one layer.	—	1 hr.		1			1
C-SG-2	—	Same as C-SG-1; two layers.	—	2 hrs. 30 min.		1			2$^1/_2$
C-SG-3	130 in.^{2}	2″ solid blocks with wire mesh in horizontal joints; 1″ mortar on flange; reentrant space filled with block and mortar.	—	2 hrs.		1			2
C-SG-4	150 in.^{2}	Same as C-130-SG-3 with $^1/_2''$ sanded gypsum plaster.	—	5 hrs.		1			5
C-SG-5	130 in.^{2}	2″ solid blocks with wire mesh in horizontal joints; 1″ mortar on flange; reentrant space filled with gypsum concrete.	—	2 hrs. 30 min.		1			2$^1/_2$
C-SG-6	150 in.^{2}	Same as C-130-SG-5 with $^1/_2''$ sanded gypsum plaster.	—	5 hrs.		1			5
C-SG-7	300 in.^{2}	4″ solid blocks with wire mesh in horizontal joints; 1″ mortar on flange; reentrant space filled with block and mortar.	—	4 hrs.		1			4
C-SG-8	300 in.^{2}	Same as C-300-SG-7 with reentrant space filled with gypsum concrete.	—	5 hrs.		1			5
C-SG-9	85 in.^{2}	2″ solid blocks with cramps at horizontal joints; mortar on flange only at horizontal joints; reentrant space not filled.	—	2 hrs. 30 min.		1			2$^1/_2$
C-SG-10	105 in.^{2}	Same as C-85-SG-9 with $^1/_2''$ sanded gypsum plaster.	—	4 hrs.		1			4
C-SG-11	95 in.^{2}	3″ hollow blocks with cramps at horizontal joints; mortar on flange only at horizontal joints; reentrant space not filled.	—	2 hrs. 30 min.		1			2$^1/_2$

(Continued)

TABLE 2.3—STEEL COLUMNS—GYPSUM ENCASEMENTS—(Continued)

ITEM CODE	MINIMUM AREA OF SOLID MATERIAL	CONSTRUCTION DETAILS	PERFORMANCE		REFERENCE NUMBER			NOTES	REC-HOURS
			LOAD	TIME	PRE-BMS-92	BMS-92	POST-BMS-92		
C-SG-12	120 in.^{2}	Same as C-95-SG-11 with $^1/_2$" sanded gypsum plaster.	—	5 hrs.		1			5
C-SG-13	130 in.^{2}	2" neat fibered gypsum reentrant space filled poured solid and reinforced with 4" × 4" wire mesh $^1/_2$" sanded gypsum plaster.	—	7 hrs.		1			7

TABLE 2.4—TIMBER COLUMNS
MINIMUM DIMENSION

ITEM CODE	MINIMUM DIMENSION	CONSTRUCTION DETAILS	PERFORMANCE		REFERENCE NUMBER			NOTES	REC-HOURS
			LOAD	TIME	PRE-BMS-92	BMS-92	POST-BMS-92		
C-11-TC-1	11"	With unprotected steel plate cap.	—	30 min.		1		1, 2	$^1/_2$
C-11-TC-2	11"	With unprotected cast iron cap and pintle.	—	45 min.		1		1, 2	$^3/_4$
C-11-TC-3	11"	With concrete or protected steel or cast iron cap.	—	1 hr. 15 min.		1		1, 2	$1^1/_4$
C-11-TC-4	11"	With $^3/_8$" gypsum wallboard over column and over cast iron or steel cap.	—	1 hr. 15 min.		1		1, 2	$1^1/_4$
C-11-TC-5	11"	With 1" portland cement plaster on wire lath over column and over cast iron or steel cap; $^3/_4$" air space.	—	2 hrs.		1		1, 2	2

Notes:
1. Minimum area: 120 square inches.
2. Type of wood: long leaf pine or Douglas fir.

TABLE 2.5.1.1—STEEL COLUMNS—CONCRETE ENCASEMENTS
MINIMUM DIMENSION LESS THAN 6"

ITEM CODE	MINIMUM DIMENSION	CONSTRUCTION DETAILS	PERFORMANCE		REFERENCE NUMBER			NOTES	REC-HOURS
			LOAD	TIME	PRE-BMS-92	BMS-92	POST-BMS-92		
C-5-SC-1	5"	5" × 6" outer dimensions; 4" × 3" × 10 lbs. "H" beam; Protection: gravel concrete (4900 psi) 6" × 4" - 13 SWG mesh.	12 tons	1 hr. 29 min.			7	1	$1^1/_4$

Notes:
1. Failure mode - collapse.

TABLE 2.5.1.2—STEEL COLUMNS—CONCRETE ENCASEMENTS
6" TO LESS THAN 8" THICK

ITEM CODE	MINIMUM DIMENSION	CONSTRUCTION DETAILS	PERFORMANCE		REFERENCE NUMBER			NOTES	REC-HOURS
			LOAD	TIME	PRE-BMS-92	BMS-92	POST-BMS-92		
C-7-SC-1	7"	7" × 8" column; 4" × 3" × 10 lbs. "H" beam; Protection: brick filled concrete (6220 psi); 6" × 4" mesh - 13 SWG; 1" below column surface.	12 tons	2 hrs. 46 min.			7	1	3
C-7-SC-2	7"	7" × 8" column; 4" × 3" × 10 lbs. "H" beam; Protection: gravel concrete (5140 psi); 6" × 4" 13 SWG mesh 1" below surface.	12 tons	3 hrs. 1 min.			7	1	$2^3/_4$
C-7-SC-3	7"	7" × 8" column; 4" × 3" × 10 lbs. "H" beam; Protection: concrete (4540 psi); 6" × 4" - 13 SWG mesh; 1" below column surface.	12 tons	3 hrs. 9 min.			7	1	3
C-7-SC-4	7"	7" × 8" column; 4" × 3" × 10 lbs. "H" beam; Protection: gravel concrete (5520 psi); 4" × 4" mesh; 16 SWG	12 tons	2 hrs. 50 min.			7	1	$2^3/_4$

Notes:
1. Failure mode - collapse.

FIGURE 2.5.1.3—STEEL COLUMNS—CONCRETE ENCASEMENTS
MINIMUM DIMENSION 8″ TO LESS THAN 10″

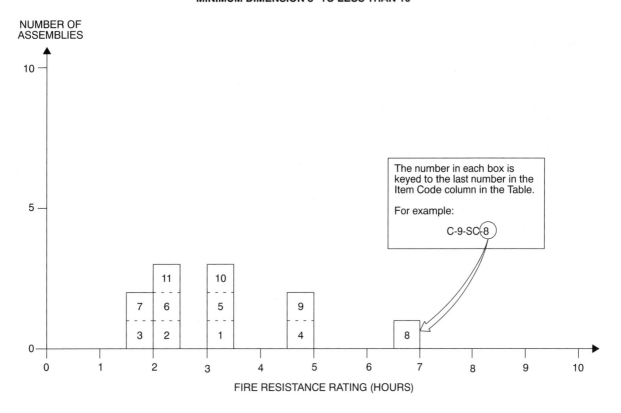

TABLE 2.5.1.3—STEEL COLUMNS—CONCRETE ENCASEMENTS
MINIMUM DIMENSION 8″ TO LESS THAN 10″

| ITEM CODE | MINIMUM DIMENSION | CONSTRUCTION DETAILS | PERFORMANCE | | REFERENCE NUMBER | | | NOTES | REC-HOURS |
			LOAD	TIME	PRE-BMS-92	BMS-92	POST-BMS-92		
C-8-SC-1	$8^1/_2$″	$8^1/_2$″ × 10″ column; 6″ × $4^1/_2$″ × 20 lbs. "H" beam; Protection: gravel concrete (5140 psi); 6″ × 4″ - 13 SWG mesh.	39 tons	3 hrs. 8 min.			7	1	3
C-8-SC-2	8″	8″ × 10″ column; 8″ × 6″ × 35 lbs. "I" beam; Protection: gravel concrete (4240 psi); 4″ × 6″ - 13 SWG mesh; $^1/_2$″ cover.	90 tons	2 hrs. 1 min.			7	1	2
C-8-SC-3	8″	8″ × 10″ concrete encased column; 8″ × 6″ × 35 lbs. "H" beam; protection: aggregate concrete (3750 psi); 4″ mesh - 16 SWG reinforcing $^1/_2$″ below column surface.	90 tons	1 hr. 58 min.			7	1	$1^3/_4$
C-8-SC-4	8″	6″ × 6″ steel column; 2″ outside protection; Group I.	—	5 hrs.		1		2	5
C-8-SC-5	8″	6″ × 6″ steel column; 2″ outside protection; Group II.	—	3 hrs. 30 min.		1		2	$3^1/_2$
C-8-SC-6	8″	6″ × 6″ steel column; 2″ outside protection; Group III.	—	2 hrs. 30 min.		1		2	$2^1/_2$
C-8-SC-7	8″	6″ × 6″ steel column; 2″ outside protection; Group IV.	—	1 hr. 45 min.		1		2	$1^3/_4$
C-9-SC-8	9″	6″ × 6″ steel column; 3″ outside protection; Group I.	—	7 hrs.		1		2	7
C-9-SC-9	9″	6″ × 6″ steel column; 3″ outside protection; Group II.	—	5 hrs.		1		2	5
C-9-SC-10	9″	6″ × 6″ steel column; 3″ outside protection; Group III.	—	3 hrs. 30 min.		1		2	$3^1/_2$
C-9-SC-11	9″	6″ × 6″ steel column; 3″ outside protection; Group IV.	—	2 hrs. 30 min.		1		2	$2^1/_2$

Notes:
1. Failure mode - collapse.
2. Group I: includes concrete having calcareous aggregate containing a combined total of not more than 10 percent of quartz, chert and flint for the coarse aggregate.

   Group II: includes concrete having trap-rock aggregate applied without metal ties and also concrete having cinder, sandstone or granite aggregate, if held in place with wire mesh or expanded metal having not larger than 4-inch mesh, weighing not less than 1.7 lbs./yd.[2], placed not more than 1 inch from the surface of the concrete.

   Group III: includes concrete having cinder, sandstone or granite aggregate tied with No. 5 gage steel wire, wound spirally over the column section on a pitch of 8 inches, or equivalent ties, and concrete having siliceous aggregates containing a combined total of 60 percent or more of quartz, chert and flint, if held in place with wire mesh or expanded metal having not larger than 4-inch mesh, weighing not less than 1.7 lbs./yd.[2], placed not more than 1 inch from the surface of the concrete.

   Group IV: includes concrete having siliceous aggregates containing a combined total of 60 percent or more of quartz, chert and flint, and tied with No. 5 gage steel wire wound spirally over the column section on a pitch of 8 inches, or equivalent ties.

**FIGURE 2.5.1.4—STEEL COLUMNS—CONCRETE ENCASEMENTS
MINIMUM DIMENSION 10″ TO LESS THAN 12″**

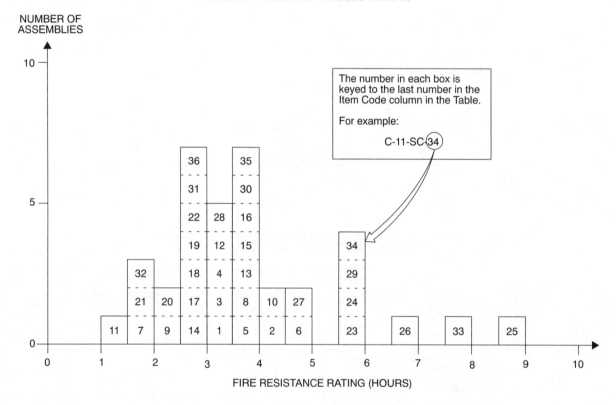

**TABLE 2.5.1.4—STEEL COLUMNS—CONCRETE ENCASEMENTS
MINIMUM DIMENSION 10″ TO LESS THAN 12″**

| ITEM CODE | MINIMUM DIMENSION | CONSTRUCTION DETAILS | PERFORMANCE | | REFERENCE NUMBER | | | NOTES | REC-HOURS |
			LOAD	TIME	PRE-BMS-92	BMS-92	POST-BMS-92		
C-10-SC-1	10″	10″ × 12″ concrete encased steel column; 8″ × 6″ 35 lbs. "H" beam; Protection: gravel aggregate concrete (3640 psi); Mesh 6″ × 4″ 13 SWG, 1″ below column surface.	90 tons	3 hrs. 7 min.			7	1, 2	3
C-10-SC-2	10″	10″ × 16″ column; 8″ × 6″ × 35 lbs. "H" beam; Protection: clay brick concrete (3630 psi); 6″ × 4″ mesh; 13 SWG, 1″ below column surface.	90 tons	4 hrs. 6 min.			7	2	4
C-10-SC-3	10″	10″ × 12″ column; 8″ × 6″ × 35 lbs. "H" beam; Protection: crushed stone and sand concrete (3930 psi); 6″ × 4″ - 13 SWG mesh; 1″ below column surface.	90 tons	3 hrs. 17 min.			7	2	3$\frac{1}{4}$

(Continued)

ITEM CODE	MINIMUM DIMENSION	CONSTRUCTION DETAILS	PERFORMANCE		REFERENCE NUMBER			NOTES	REC-HOURS
			LOAD	TIME	PRE-BMS-92	BMS-92	POST-BMS-92		
C-10-SC-4	10″	10″ × 12″ column; 8″ × 6″ × 35 lbs. "H" beam; Protection: crushed basalt and sand concrete (4350 psi); 6″ × 4″ - 13 SWG mesh; 1″ below column surface.	90 tons	3 hrs. 22 min.			7	2	$3^1/_3$
C-10-SC-5	10″	10″ × 12″ column; 8″ × 6″ × 35 lbs. "H" beam; Protection: gravel aggregate concrete (5570 psi); 6″ × 4″ mesh; 13 SWG.	90 tons	3 hrs. 39 min.			7	2	$3^1/_2$
C-10-SC-6	10″	10″ × 16″ column; 8″ × 6″ × 35 lbs. "I" beam; Protection: gravel concrete (4950 psi); mesh; 6″ × 4″ 13 SWG 1″ below column surface.	90 tons	4 hrs. 32 min.			7	2	$4^1/_2$
C-10-SC-7	10″	10″ × 12″ concrete encased steel column; 8″ × 6″ × 35 lbs. "H" beam; Protection: aggregate concrete (1370 psi); 6″ × 4″ mesh; 13 SWG reinforcing 1″ below column surface.	90 tons	2 hrs.			7	3, 4	2
C-10-SC-8	10″	10″ × 12″ concrete encased steel column; 8″ × 6″ × 35 lbs. "H" column; Protection: aggregate concrete (4000 psi); 13 SWG iron wire loosely around column at 6″ pitch about 2″ beneath column surface.	86 tons	3 hrs. 36 min.			7	2	$3^1/_2$
C-10-SC-9	10″	10″ × 12″ concrete encased steel column; 8″ × 6″ × 35 lbs. "H" beam; Protection: aggregate concrete (3290 psi); 2″ cover minimum.	86 tons	2 hrs. 8 min.			7	2	2
C-10-SC-10	10″	10″ × 14″ concrete encased steel column; 8″ x 6″ × 35 lbs. "H" column; Protection: crushed brick filled concrete (5310 psi); 6″ × 4″ mesh; 13 SWG reinforcement 1″ below column surface.	90 tons	4 hrs. 28 min.			7	2	$4^1/_3$
C-10-SC-11	10″	10″ × 12″ concrete encased column; 8″ × 6″ 35 lbs. "H" beam; Protection: aggregate concrete (342 psi); 6″ × 4″ mesh; 13 SWG reinforcement 1″ below surface.	90 tons	1 hr. 2 min.			7	2	1
C-10-SC-12	10″	10″ × 12″ concrete encased steel column; 8″ × 6″ × 35 lbs. "H" beam; Protection: aggregate concrete (4480 psi); four $^3/_8$″ vertical bars at "H" beam edges with $^3/_{16}$″ spacers at beam surface at 3′ pitch and $^3/_{16}$″ binders at 10″ pitch; 2″ concrete cover.	90 tons	3 hrs. 2 min.			7	2	3
C-10-SC-13	10″	10″ × 12″ concrete encased steel column; 8″ × 6″ × 35 lbs. "H" beam; Protection: aggregate concrete (5070 psi); 6″ × 4″ mesh; 13 SWG reinforcing at 6″ beam sides wrapped and held by wire ties across (open) 8″ beam face; reinforcements wrapped in 6″ × 4″ mesh; 13 SWG throughout; $^1/_2$″ cover to column surface.	90 tons	3 hrs. 59 min.			7	2	$3^3/_4$
C-10-SC-14	10″	10″ × 12″ concrete encased steel column; 8″ × 6″ × 35 lbs. "H" beam; Protection: aggregate concrete (4410 psi); 6″ × 4″ mesh; 13 SWG reinforcement $1^1/_4$″ below column surface; $^1/_2$″ limestone cement plaster with $^3/_8$″ gypsum plaster finish.	90 tons	2 hrs. 50 min.			7	2	$2^3/_4$
C-10-SC-15	10″	10″ × 12″ concrete encased steel column; 8″ × 6″ × 35 lbs. "H" beam; Protection: crushed clay brick filled concrete (4,260 psi); 6″ × 4″ mesh; 13 SWG reinforcing 1″ below column surface.	90 tons	3 hrs. 54 min.			7	2	$3^3/_4$

(Continued)

ITEM CODE	MINIMUM DIMENSION	CONSTRUCTION DETAILS	PERFORMANCE		REFERENCE NUMBER			NOTES	REC-HOURS
			LOAD	TIME	PRE-BMS-92	BMS-92	POST-BMS-92		
C-10-SC-16	10″	10″ × 12″ concrete encased steel column; 8″ × 6″ × 35 lbs. "H" beam; Protection: limestone aggregate concrete (4350 psi); 6″ × 4″ mesh; 13 SWG reinforcing 1″ below column surface.	90 tons	3 hrs. 54 min.			7	2	$3^3/_4$
C-10-SC-17	10″	10″ × 12″ concrete encased steel column; 8″ × 6″ × 35 lbs. "H" beam; Protection: limestone aggregate concrete (5300 psi); 6″ × 4″; 13 SWG wire mesh 1″ below column surface.	90 tons	3 hrs.			7	4, 5	3
C-10-SC-18	10″	10″ × 12″ concrete encased steel column; 8″ × 6″ × 35 lbs. "H" beam; Protection: limestone aggregate concrete (4800 psi) with 6″ × 4″; 13 SWG mesh reinforcement 1″ below surface.	90 tons	3 hrs.			7	4, 5	3
C-10-SC-19	10″	10″ × 14″ concrete encased steel column; 12″ × 8″ × 65 lbs. "H" beam; Protection: aggregate concrete (3900 psi); 4″ mesh; 16 SWG reinforcing $^1/_2$″ below column surface.	118 tons	2 hrs. 42 min.			7	2	2
C-10-SC-20	10″	10″ × 14″ concrete encased steel column; 12″ × 8″ × 65 lbs. "H" beam; Protection: aggregate concrete (4930 psi); 4″ mesh; 16 SWG reinforcing $^1/_2$″ below column surface.	177 tons	2 hrs. 8 min.			7	2	2
C-10-SC-21	$10^3/_8$″	$10^3/_8$″ × $12^3/_8$″ concrete encased steel column; 8″ × 6″ × 35 lbs. "H" beam; Protection: aggregate concrete (835 psi) with 6″ × 4″ mesh; 13 SWG reinforcing $1^3/_{16}$″ below column surface; $^3/_{16}$″ gypsum plaster finish.	90 tons	2 hrs.			7	3, 4	2
C-11-SC-22	11″	11″ × 13″ concrete encased steel column; 8″ × 6″ × 35 lbs. "H" beam; Protection: "open texture" brick filled concrete (890 psi) with 6″ × 4″ mesh; 13 SWG reinforcing $1^1/_2$″ below column surface; $^3/_8$″ lime cement plaster; $^1/_8$″ gypsum plaster finish.	90 tons	3 hrs.			7	6, 7	3
C-11-SC-23	11″	11″ × 12″ column; 4″ × 3″ × 10 lbs. "H" beam; gravel concrete (4550 psi); 6″ × 4″ - 13 SWG mesh reinforcing; 1″ below column surface.	12 tons	6 hrs.			7	7, 8	6
C-11-SC-24	11″	11″ × 12″ column; 4″ × 3″ × 10 lbs. "H" beam; Protection: gravel aggregate concrete (3830 psi); with 4″ × 4″ mesh; 16 SWG, 1″ below column surface.	16 tons	5 hrs. 32 min.			7	2	$5^1/_2$
C-10-SC-25	10″	6″ × 6″ steel column with 4″ outside protection; Group I.	—	9 hrs.		1		9	9
C-10-SC-26	10″	Description as per C-SC-25; Group II.	—	7 hrs.		1		9	7
C-10-SC-27	10″	Description as per C-10-SC-25; Group III.	—	5 hrs.		1		9	5
C-10-SC-28	10″	Description as per C-10-SC-25; Group IV.	—	3 hrs. 30 min.		1		9	$3^1/_2$
C-10-SC-29	10″	8″ × 8″ steel column with 2″ outside protection; Group I.	—	6 hrs.		1		9	6
C-10-SC-30	10″	Description as per C-10-SC-29; Group II.	—	4 hrs.		1		9	4
C-10-SC-31	10″	Description as per C-10-SC-29; Group III.	—	3 hrs.		1		9	3
C-10-SC-32	10″	Description as per C-10-SC-29; Group IV.	—	2 hrs.		1		9	2
C-11-SC-33	11″	8″ × 8″ steel column with 3″ outside protection; Group I.	—	8 hrs.		1		9	8

(Continued)

TABLE 2.5.1.4—STEEL COLUMNS—CONCRETE ENCASEMENTS
MINIMUM DIMENSION 10″ TO LESS THAN 12″—(Continued)

ITEM CODE	MINIMUM DIMENSION	CONSTRUCTION DETAILS	PERFORMANCE		REFERENCE NUMBER			NOTES	REC-HOURS
			LOAD	TIME	PRE-BMS-92	BMS-92	POST-BMS-92		
C-11-SC-34	11″	Description as per C-10-SC-33; Group II.	—	6 hrs.		1		9	6
C-11-SC-35	11″	Description as per C-10-SC-33; Group III.	—	4 hrs.		1		9	4
C-11-SC-36	11″	Description as per C-10-SC-33; Group IV.	—	3 hrs.		1		9	3

Notes:
1. Tested under total restraint load to prevent expansion - minimum load 90 tons.
2. Failure mode - collapse.
3. Passed 2 hour fire test (Grade "C," British).
4. Passed hose stream test.
5. Column tested and passed 3 hour grade fire resistance (British).
6. Column passed 3 hour fire test.
7. Column collapsed during hose stream testing.
8. Column passed 6 hour fire test.
9. Group I: includes concrete having calcareous aggregate containing a combined total of not more than 10 percent of quartz, chert and flint for the coarse aggregate.
   Group II: includes concrete having trap-rock aggregate applied without metal ties and also concrete having cinder, sandstone or granite aggregate, if held in place with wire mesh or expanded metal having not larger than 4-inch mesh, weighing not less than 1.7 lbs./yd.^{2}, placed not more than 1 inch from the surface of the concrete.
   Group III: includes concrete having cinder, sandstone or granite aggregate tied with No. 5 gage steel wire, wound spirally over the column section on a pitch of 8 inches, or equivalent ties, and concrete having siliceous aggregates containing a combined total of 60 percent or more of quartz, chert and flint, if held in place with wire mesh or expanded metal having not larger than 4-inch mesh, weighing not less than 1.7 lbs./yd.^{2}, placed not more than 1 inch from the surface of the concrete.
   Group IV: includes concrete having siliceous aggregates containing a combined total of 60 percent or more of quartz, chert and flint, and tied with No. 5 gage steel wire wound spirally over the column section on a pitch of 8 inches, or equivalent ties.

FIGURE 2.5.1.5—STEEL COLUMNS—CONCRETE ENCASEMENTS
MINIMUM DIMENSION 12″ TO LESS THAN 14″

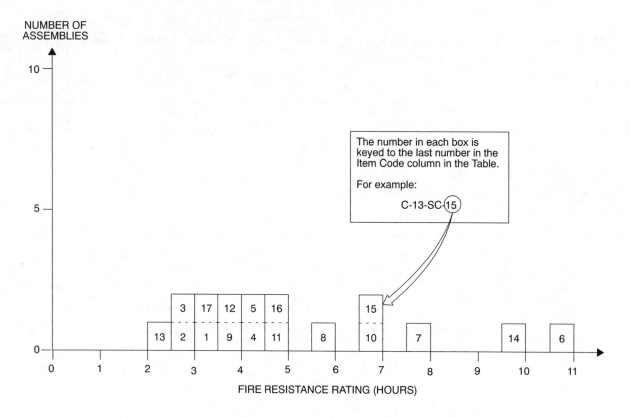

TABLE 2.5.1.5—STEEL COLUMNS—CONCRETE ENCASEMENTS
MINIMUM DIMENSION 12″ TO LESS THAN 14″

ITEM CODE	MINIMUM DIMENSION	CONSTRUCTION DETAILS	PERFORMANCE		REFERENCE NUMBER			NOTES	REC-HOURS
			LOAD	TIME	PRE-BMS-92	BMS-92	POST-BMS-92		
C-12-SC-1	12″	12″ × 14″ concrete encased steel column; 8″ × 6″ × 35 lbs. "H" beam; Protection: aggregate concrete (4150 psi) with 4″ mesh; 16 SWG reinforcing 1″ below column surface.	120 tons	3 hrs. 24 min.			7	1	$3^1/_3$
C-12-SC-2	12″	12″ × 16″ concrete encased column; 8″ × 6″ × 35 lbs. "H" beam; Protection: aggregate concrete (4300 psi) with 4″ mesh; 16 SWG reinforcing 1″ below column surface.	90 tons	2 hrs. 52 min.			7	1	$2^3/_4$
C-12-SC-3	12″	12″ × 16″ concrete encased steel column; 12″ × 8″ × 65 lbs. "H" column; Protection: gravel aggregate concrete (3550 psi) with 4″ mesh; 16 SWG reinforcement 1″ below column surface.	177 tons	2 hrs. 31 min.			7	1	$2^1/_2$
C-12-SC-4	12″	12″ × 16″ concrete encased column; 12″ × 8″ × 65 lbs. "H" beam; Protection: aggregate concrete (3450 psi) with 4″ mesh; 16 SWG reinforcement 1″ below column surface.	118 tons	4 hrs. 4 min.			7	1	4
C-12-SC-5	$12^1/_2$″	$12^1/_2$″ × 14″ column; 6″ × $4^1/_2$″ × 20 lbs. "H" beam; Protection: gravel aggregate concrete (3750 psi) with 4″ × 4″ mesh; 16 SWG reinforcing 1″ below column surface.	52 tons	4 hrs. 29 min.			7	1	$4^1/_3$
C-12-SC-6	12″	8″ × 8″ steel column; 2″ outside protection; Group I.	—	11 hrs.			1	2	11
C-12-SC-7	12″	Description as per C-12-SC-6; Group II.	—	8 hrs.		1		2	8

(Continued)

TABLE 2.5.1.5—STEEL COLUMNS—CONCRETE ENCASEMENTS
MINIMUM DIMENSION 12″ TO LESS THAN 14″—(Continued)

| ITEM CODE | MINIMUM DIMENSION | CONSTRUCTION DETAILS | PERFORMANCE | | REFERENCE NUMBER | | | NOTES | REC-HOURS |
			LOAD	TIME	PRE-BMS-92	BMS-92	POST-BMS-92		
C-12-SC-8	12″	Description as per C-12-SC-6; Group III.	—	6 hrs.		1		2	6
C-12-SC-9	12″	Description as per C-12-SC-6; Group IV.	—	4 hrs.		1		2	4
C-12-SC-10	12″	10″ × 10″ steel column; 2″ outside protection; Group I.	—	7 hrs.		1		2	7
C-12-SC-11	12″	Description as per C-12-SC-10; Group II.	—	5 hrs.		1		2	5
C-12-SC-12	12″	Description as per C-12-SC-10; Group III.	—	4 hrs.		1		2	4
C-12-SC-13	12″	Description as per C-12-SC-10; Group IV.	—	2 hrs. 30 min.		1		2	$2^1/_2$
C-13-SC-14	13″	10″ × 10″ steel column; 3″ outside protection; Group I.	—	10 hrs.		1		2	10
C-13-SC-15	13″	Description as per C-12-SC-14; Group II.	—	7 hrs.		1		2	7
C-13-SC-16	13″	Description as per C-12-SC-14; Group III.	—	5 hrs.		1		2	5
C-13-SC-17	13″	Description as per C-12-SC-14; Group IV.	—	3 hrs. 30 hrs.		1		2	$3^1/_2$

Notes:

1. Failure mode - collapse.
2. Group I: includes concrete having calcareous aggregate containing a combined total of not more than 10 percent of quartz, chert and flint for the coarse aggregate.

   Group II: includes concrete having trap-rock aggregate applied without metal ties and also concrete having cinder, sandstone or granite aggregate, if held in place with wire mesh or expanded metal having not larger than 4-inch mesh, weighing not less than 1.7 lbs./yd.^{2}, placed not more than 1 inch from the surface of the concrete.

   Group III: includes concrete having cinder, sandstone or granite aggregate tied with No. 5 gage steel wire, wound spirally over the column section on a pitch of 8 inches, or equivalent ties, and concrete having siliceous aggregates containing a combined total of 60 percent or more of quartz, chert and flint, if held in place with wire mesh or expanded metal having not larger than 4-inch mesh, weighing not less than 1.7 lbs./yd.^{2}, placed not more than 1 inch from the surface of the concrete.

   Group IV: includes concrete having siliceous aggregates containing a combined total of 60 percent or more of quartz, chert and flint, and tied with No. 5 gage steel wire wound spirally over the column section on a pitch of 8 inches, or equivalent ties.

FIGURE 2.5.1.6—STEEL COLUMNS—CONCRETE ENCASEMENTS
MINIMUM DIMENSION 14″ TO LESS THAN 16″

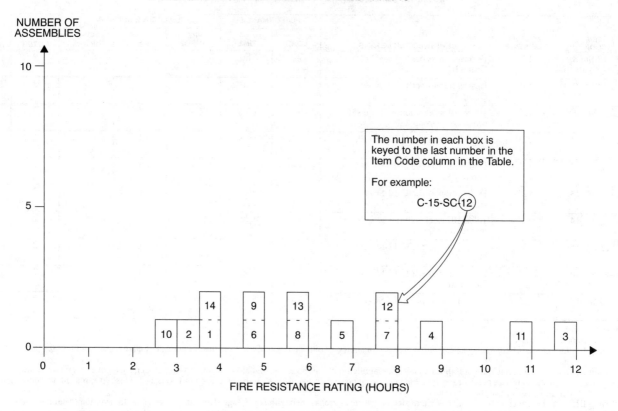

TABLE 2.5.1.6—STEEL COLUMNS—CONCRETE ENCASEMENTS
MINIMUM DIMENSION 14″ TO LESS THAN 16″

ITEM CODE	MINIMUM DIMENSION	CONSTRUCTION DETAILS	PERFORMANCE		REFERENCE NUMBER			NOTES	REC-HOURS
			LOAD	TIME	PRE-BMS-92	BMS-92	POST-BMS-92		
C-14-SC-1	14″	14″ × 16″ concrete encased steel column; 8″ × 6″ × 35 lbs. "H" column; Protection: aggregate concrete (4240 psi); 4″ mesh - 16 SWG reinforcing 1″ below column surface.	90 tons	3 hrs. 40 min.			7	1	3
C-14-SC-2	14″	14″ × 18″ concrete encased steel column; 12″ × 8″ × 65 lbs. "H" beam; Protection: gravel aggregate concrete (4,000 psi) with 4″ - 16 SWG wire mesh reinforcement 1″ below column surface.	177 tons	3 hrs. 20 min.			7	1	3
C-14-SC-3	14″	10″ × 10″ steel column; 4″ outside protection; Group I.	—	12 hrs		1		2	12
C-14-SC-4	14″	Description as per C-14-SC-3; Group II.	—	9 hrs		1		2	9
C-14-SC-5	14″	Description as per C-14-SC-3; Group III.	—	7 hrs		1		2	7
C-14-SC-6	14″	Description as per C-14-SC-3; Group IV.	—	5 hrs		1		2	5
C-14-SC-7	14″	12″ × 12″ steel column; 2″ outside protection; Group I.	—	8 hrs		1		2	8
C-14-SC-8	14″	Description as per C-14-SC-7; Group II.	—	6 hrs		1		2	6
C-14-SC-9	14″	Description as per C-14-SC-7; Group III.	—	5 hrs		1		2	5
C-14-SC-10	14″	Description as per C-14-SC-7; Group IV.	—	3 hrs		1		2	3
C-15-SC-11	15″	12″ × 12″ steel column; 3″ outside protection; Group I.	—	11 hrs		1		2	11

(Continued)

TABLE 2.5.1.6—STEEL COLUMNS—CONCRETE ENCASEMENTS
MINIMUM DIMENSION 14″ TO LESS THAN 16″—(Continued)

ITEM CODE	MINIMUM DIMENSION	CONSTRUCTION DETAILS	PERFORMANCE		REFERENCE NUMBER			NOTES	REC-HOURS
			LOAD	TIME	PRE-BMS-92	BMS-92	POST-BMS-92		
C-15-SC-12	15″	Description as per C-15-SC-11; Group II.	—	8 hrs		1		2	8
C-15-SC-13	15″	Description as per C-15-SC-11; Group III.	—	6 hrs		1		2	6
C-15-SC-14	15″	Description as per C-15-SC-11; Group IV.	—	4 hrs		1		2	4

Notes:
1. Collapse.
2. Group I: includes concrete having calcareous aggregate containing a combined total of not more than 10 percent of quartz, chert and flint for the coarse aggregate.

   Group II: includes concrete having trap-rock aggregate applied without metal ties and also concrete having cinder, sandstone or granite aggregate, if held in place with wire mesh or expanded metal having not larger than 4-inch mesh, weighing not less than 1.7 lbs./yd.^{2}, placed not more than 1 inch from the surface of the concrete.

   Group III: includes concrete having cinder, sandstone or granite aggregate tied with No. 5 gage steel wire, wound spirally over the column section on a pitch of 8 inches, or equivalent ties, and concrete having siliceous aggregates containing a combined total of 60 percent or more of quartz, chert and flint, if held in place with wire mesh or expanded metal having not larger than 4-inch mesh, weighing not less than 1.7 lbs./yd.^{2}, placed not more than 1 inch from the surface of the concrete.

   Group IV: includes concrete having siliceous aggregates containing a combined total of 60 percent or more of quartz, chert and flint, and tied with No. 5 gage steel wire wound spirally over the column section on a pitch of 8 inches, or equivalent ties.

TABLE 2.5.1.7—STEEL COLUMNS—CONCRETE ENCASEMENTS
MINIMUM DIMENSION 16″ TO LESS THAN 18″

ITEM CODE	MINIMUM DIMENSION	CONSTRUCTION DETAILS	PERFORMANCE		REFERENCE NUMBER			NOTES	REC-HOURS
			LOAD	TIME	PRE-BMS-92	BMS-92	POST-BMS-92		
C-16-SC-1	16″	12″ × 12″ steel column; 4″ outside protection; Group I.	—	14 hrs.		1		1	14
C-16-SC-2	16″	Description as per C-16-SC-1; Group II.	—	10 hrs.		1		1	10
C-16-SC-3	16″	Description as per C-16-SC-1; Group III.	—	8 hrs.		1		1	8
C-16-SC-4	16″	Description as per C-16-SC-1; Group IV.	—	5 hrs.		1		1	5

Notes:
1. Group I: includes concrete having calcareous aggregate containing a combined total of not more than 10 percent of quartz, chert and flint for the coarse aggregate.

   Group II: includes concrete having trap-rock aggregate applied without metal ties and also concrete having cinder, sandstone or granite aggregate, if held in place with wire mesh or expanded metal having not larger than 4-inch mesh, weighing not less than 1.7 lbs./yd.^{2}, placed not more than 1 inch from the surface of the concrete.

   Group III: includes concrete having cinder, sandstone or granite aggregate tied with No. 5 gage steel wire, wound spirally over the column section on a pitch of 8 inches, or equivalent ties, and concrete having siliceous aggregates containing a combined total of 60 percent or more of quartz, chert and flint, if held in place with wire mesh or expanded metal having not larger than 4-inch mesh, weighing not less than 1.7 lbs./yd.^{2}, placed not more than 1 inch from the surface of the concrete.

   Group IV: includes concrete having siliceous aggregates containing a combined total of 60 percent or more of quartz, chert and flint, and tied with No. 5 gage steel wire wound spirally over the column section on a pitch of 8 inches, or equivalent ties.

TABLE 2.5.2.1—STEEL COLUMNS—BRICK AND BLOCK ENCASEMENTS
MINIMUM DIMENSION 10″ TO LESS THAN 12″

ITEM CODE	MINIMUM DIMENSION	CONSTRUCTION DETAILS	PERFORMANCE		REFERENCE NUMBER			NOTES	REC-HOURS
			LOAD	TIME	PRE-BMS-92	BMS-92	POST-BMS-92		
C-10-SB-1	$10^1/_2$″	$10^1/_2$″ × 13″ brick encased steel columns; 8″ × 6″ × 35 lbs. "H" beam; Protection. Fill of broken brick and mortar; 2″ brick on edge; joints broken in alternate courses; cement-sand grout; 13 SWG wire reinforcement in every third horizontal joint.	90 tons	3 hrs. 6 min.			7	1	3
C-10-SB-2	$10^1/_2$″	$10^1/_2$″ × 13″ brick encased steel columns; 8″ × 6″ × 35 lbs. "H" beam; Protection: 2″ brick; joints broken in alternate courses; cement-sand grout; 13 SWG iron wire reinforcement in alternate horizontal joints.	90 tons	2 hrs.			7	2, 3, 4	2
C-10-SB-3	10″	10″ × 12″ block encased columns; 8″ × 6″ × 35 lbs. "H" beam; Protection: 2″ foamed slag concrete blocks; 13 SWG wire at each horizontal joint; mortar at each joint.	90 tons	2 hrs.			7	5	2
C-10-SB-4	$10^1/_2$″	$10^1/_2$″ × 12″ block encased steel columns; 8″ × 6″ × 35 lbs. "H" beam; Protection: gravel aggregate concrete fill (unconsolidated) 2″ thick hollow clay tiles with mortar at edges.	86 tons	56 min.			7	1	$^3/_4$
C-10-SB-5	$10^1/_2$″	$10^1/_2$″ × 12″ block encased steel columns; 8″ × 6″ × 35 lbs. "H" beam; Protection: 2″ hollow clay tiles with mortar at edges.	86 tons	22 min.			7	1	$^1/_4$

Notes:
1. Failure mode - collapse.
2. Passed 2 hour fire test (Grade "C" - British).
3. Passed hose stream test.
4. Passed reload test.
5. Passed 2 hour fire exposure but collapsed immediately following hose stream test.

TABLE 2.5.2.2—STEEL COLUMNS—BRICK AND BLOCK ENCASEMENTS
MINIMUM DIMENSION 12″ TO LESS THAN 14″

ITEM CODE	MINIMUM DIMENSION	CONSTRUCTION DETAILS	PERFORMANCE		REFERENCE NUMBER			NOTES	REC-HOURS
			LOAD	TIME	PRE-BMS-92	BMS-92	POST-BMS-92		
C-12-SB-1	12″	12″ × 15″ brick encased steel columns; 8″ × 6″ × 35 lbs. "H" beam; Protection: $2^5/_8$″ thick brick; joints broken in alternate courses; cement-sand grout; fill of broken brick and mortar.	90 tons	1 hr. 49 min.			7	1	$1^3/_4$

Notes:
1. Failure mode - collapse.

TABLE 2.5.2.3—STEEL COLUMNS—BRICK AND BLOCK ENCASEMENTS
MINIMUM DIMENSION 14″ TO LESS THAN 16″

ITEM CODE	MINIMUM DIMENSION	CONSTRUCTION DETAILS	PERFORMANCE		REFERENCE NUMBER			NOTES	REC-HOURS
			LOAD	TIME	PRE-BMS-92	BMS-92	POST-BMS-92		
C-15-SB-1	15″	15″ × 17″ brick encased steel columns; 8″ × 6″ × 35 lbs. "H" beam; Protection: 4$^1/_2$″ thick brick; joints broken in alternate courses; cement-sand grout; fill of broken brick and mortar.	45 tons	6 hrs.			7	1	6
C-15-SB-2	15″	15″ × 17″ brick encased steel columns; 8″ × 6″ × 35 lbs. "H" beam; Protection. Fill of broken brick and mortar; 4$^1/_2$″ brick; joints broken in alternate courses; cement-sand grout.	86 tons	6 hrs.			7	2, 3, 4	6
C-15-SB-3	15″	15″ × 18″ brick encased steel columns; 8″ × 6″ × 35 lbs. "H" beam; Protection: 4$^1/_2$″ brick work; joints alternating; cement-sand grout.	90 tons	4 hrs.			7	5, 6	4
C-14-SB-4	14″	14″ × 16″ block encased steel columns; 8″ × 6″ × 35 lbs. "H" beam; Protection: 4″ thick foam slag concrete blocks; 13 SWG wire reinforcement in each horizontal joint; mortar in joints.	90 tons	5 hrs. 52 min.			7	7	4$^3/_4$

Notes:
1. Only a nominal load was applied to specimen.
2. Passed 6 hour fire test (Grade "A" - British).
3. Passed (6 minute) hose stream test.
4. Reload not specified.
5. Passed 4 hour fire exposure.
6. Failed by collapse between first and second minute of hose stream exposure.
7. Mode of failure - collapse.

TABLE 2.5.3.1—STEEL COLUMNS—PLASTER ENCASEMENTS
MINIMUM DIMENSION 6″ TO LESS THAN 8″

ITEM CODE	MINIMUM DIMENSION	CONSTRUCTION DETAILS	PERFORMANCE		REFERENCE NUMBER			NOTES	REC-HOURS
			LOAD	TIME	PRE-BMS-92	BMS-92	POST-BMS-92		
C-7-SP-1	7$^1/_2$″	7$^1/_2$″ × 9$^1/_2$″ plaster protected steel columns; 8″ × 6″ × 35 lbs. "H" beam; Protection: 24 SWG wire metal lath; 1$^1/_4$″ lime plaster.	90 tons	57 min.			7	1	$^3/_4$
C-7-SP-2	7$^7/_8$″	7$^7/_8$″ × 10″ plaster protected steel columns; 8″ × 6″ × 35 lbs. "H" beam; Protection: $^3/_8$″ gypsum bal wire wound with 16 SWG wire helically wound at 4″ pitch; $^1/_2$″ gypsum plaster.	90 tons	1 hr. 13 min.			7	1	1
C-7-SP-3	7$^1/_4$″	7$^1/_4$″ × 9$^3/_8$″ plaster protected steel columns; 8″ × 6″ × 35 lbs. "H" beam; Protection: $^3/_8$″ gypsum board; wire helically wound 16 SWG at 4″ pitch; $^1/_4$″ gypsum plaster finish.	90 tons	1 hr. 14 min.			7	1	1

Notes:
1. Failure mode - collapse.

TABLE 2.5.3.2—STEEL COLUMNS—PLASTER ENCASEMENTS
MINIMUM DIMENSION 8" TO LESS THAN 10"

ITEM CODE	MINIMUM DIMENSION	CONSTRUCTION DETAILS	PERFORMANCE		REFERENCE NUMBER			NOTES	REC-HOURS
			LOAD	TIME	PRE-BMS-92	BMS-92	POST-BMS-92		
C-8-SP-1	8″	8″ × 10″ plaster protected steel columns; 8″ × 6″ × 35 lbs. "H" beam; Protection: 24 SWG wire lath; 1″ gypsum plaster.	86 tons	1 hr. 23 min.			7	1	$1^1/_4$
C-8-SP-2	$8^1/_2$″	$8^1/_2$″ × $10^1/_2$″ plaster protected steel columns; 8″ × 6″ × 35 lbs. "H" beam; Protection: 24 SWG metal lath wrap; $1^1/_4$″ gypsum plaster.	90 tons	1 hr. 36 min.			7	1	$1^1/_2$
C-9-SP-3	9″	9″ × 11″ plaster protected steel columns; 8″ × 6″ × 35 lbs. "H" beam; Protection: 24 SWG metal lath wrap; $1/_8$″ M.S. ties at 12″ pitch wire netting $1^1/_2$″ × 22 SWG between first and second plaster coats; $1^1/_2$″ gypsum plaster.	90 tons	1 hr. 33 min.			7	1	$1^1/_2$
C-8-SP-4	$8^3/_4$″	$8^3/_4$″ × $10^3/_4$″ plaster protected steel columns; 8″ × 6″ × 35 lbs. "H" beam; Protection: $3/_4$″ gypsum board; wire wound spirally (#16 SWG) at $1^1/_2$″ pitch; $1/_2$″ gypsum plaster.	90 tons	2 hrs.			7	2, 3, 4	2

Notes:
1. Failure mode - collapse.
2. Passed 2 hour fire exposure test (Grade "C" - British).
3. Passed hose stream test.
4. Passed reload test.

TABLE 2.5.4.1—STEEL COLUMNS—MISCELLANEOUS ENCASEMENTS
MINIMUM DIMENSION 6″ TO LESS THAN 8″

ITEM CODE	MINIMUM DIMENSION	CONSTRUCTION DETAILS	PERFORMANCE		REFERENCE NUMBER			NOTES	REC-HOURS
			LOAD	TIME	PRE-BMS-92	BMS-92	POST-BMS-92		
C-7-SM-1	$7^5/_8$″	$7^5/_8$″ × $9^1/_2$″ (asbestos plaster) protected steel columns; 8″ × 6″ × 35 lbs. "H" beam; Protection: 20 gage $1/_2$″ metal lath; $9/_{16}$″ asbestos plaster (minimum).	90 tons	1 hr. 52 min.			7	1	$1^3/_4$

Notes:
1. Failure mode - collapse.

TABLE 2.5.4.2—STEEL COLUMNS—MISCELLANEOUS ENCASEMENTS
MINIMUM DIMENSION 8″ TO LESS THAN 10″

ITEM CODE	MINIMUM DIMENSION	CONSTRUCTION DETAILS	PERFORMANCE		REFERENCE NUMBER			NOTES	REC-HOURS
			LOAD	TIME	PRE-BMS-92	BMS-92	POST-BMS-92		
C-9-SM-1	$9^5/_8$″	$9^5/_8$″ × $11^3/_8$″ asbestos slab and cement plaster protected columns; 8″ × 6″ × 35 lbs. "H" beam; Protection: 1″ asbestos slab; wire wound; $5/_8$″ plaster.	90 tons	2 hrs.			7	1, 2	2

Notes:
1. Passed 2 hour fire exposure test.
2. Collapsed during hose stream test.

TABLE 2.5.4.3—STEEL COLUMNS—MISCELLANEOUS ENCASEMENTS
MINIMUM DIMENSION 10″ TO LESS THAN 12″

| ITEM CODE | MINIMUM DIMENSION | CONSTRUCTION DETAILS | PERFORMANCE | | REFERENCE NUMBER | | | NOTES | REC-HOURS |
			LOAD	TIME	PRE-BMS-92	BMS-92	POST-BMS-92		
C-11-SM-1	11$^1/_2$″	11$^1/_2$″ × 13$^1/_2$″ wood wool and plaster protected steel columns; 8″ × 6″ × 35 lbs. "H" beam; Protection: wood-wool-cement paste as fill and to 2″ cover over beam; $^3/_4$″ gypsum plaster finish.	90 tons	2 hrs.			7	1, 2, 3	2
C-10-SM-1	10″	10″ × 12″ asbestos protected steel columns; 8″ × 6″ × 35 lbs. "H" beam; Protection: sprayed on asbestos paste to 2″ cover over column.	90 tons	4 hrs.			7	2, 3, 4	4

Notes:
1. Passed 2 hour fire exposure (Grade "C" - British).
2. Passed hose stream test.
3. Passed reload test.
4. Passed 4 hour fire exposure test.

TABLE 2.5.4.4—STEEL COLUMNS—MISCELLANEOUS ENCASEMENTS
MINIMUM DIMENSION 12″ TO LESS THAN 14″

| ITEM CODE | MINIMUM DIMENSION | CONSTRUCTION DETAILS | PERFORMANCE | | REFERENCE NUMBER | | | NOTES | REC-HOURS |
			LOAD	TIME	PRE-BMS-92	BMS-92	POST-BMS-92		
C-12-SM-1	12″	12″ × 14$^1/_4$″ cement and asbestos protected columns; 8″ × 6″ × 35 lbs. "H" beam; Protection: fill of asbestos packing pieces 1″ thick 1′ 3″ o.c.; cover of 2″ molded asbestos inner layer; 1″ molded asbestos outer layer; held in position by 16 SWG nichrome wire ties; wash of refractory cement on outer surface.	86 tons	4 hrs. 43 min.			7	1, 2, 3	4$^2/_3$

Notes:
1. Passed 4 hour fire exposure (Grade "B" - British).
2. Passed hose stream test.
3. Passed reload test.

SECTION III—FLOOR/CEILING ASSEMBLIES

FIGURE 3.1—FLOOR/CEILING ASSEMBLIES—REINFORCED CONCRETE

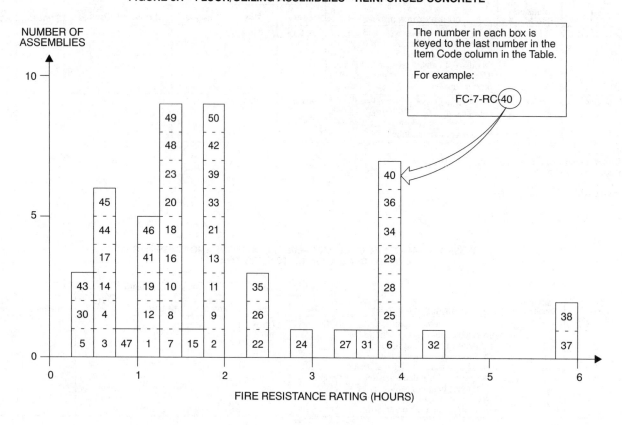

TABLE 3.1—FLOOR/CEILING ASSEMBLIES—REINFORCED CONCRETE

ITEM CODE	ASSEMBLY THICKNESS	CONSTRUCTION DETAILS	PERFORMANCE		REFERENCE NUMBER			NOTES	REC. HOURS
			LOAD	TIME	PRE-BMS-92	BMS-92	POST-BMS-92		
F/C-3-RC-1	$3^3/_4''$	$3^3/_4''$ thick floor; $3^1/_4''$ (5475 psi) concrete deck; $^1/_2''$ plaster under deck; $^3/_8''$ main reinforcement bars at $5^1/_2''$ pitch with $^7/_8''$ concrete cover; $^3/_8''$ main reinforcement bars at $4^1/_2''$ pitch perpendicular with $^1/_2''$ concrete cover; 13'1" span restrained.	195 psf	24 min.			7	1, 2	1
F/C-3-RC-2	$3^1/_4''$	$3^1/_4''$ deep (3540 psi) concrete deck; $^3/_8''$ main reinforcement bars at $5^1/_2''$ pitch with $^7/_8''$ cover; $^3/_8''$ main reinforcement bars at $4^1/_2''$ pitch perpendicular with $^1/_2''$ cover; 13'1" span restrained.	195 psf	2 hrs.			7	1, 3, 4	$1^3/_4$
F/C-3-RC-3	$3^1/_4''$	$3^1/_4''$ deep (4175 psi) concrete deck; $^3/_8''$ main reinforcement bars at $5^1/_2''$ pitch with $^7/_8''$ cover; $^3/_8''$ main reinforcement bars at $4^1/_2''$ pitch perpendicular with $^1/_2''$ cover; 13'1" span restrained.	195 psf	31 min.			7	1, 5	$^1/_2$
F/C-3-RC-4	$3^1/_4''$	$3^1/_4''$ deep (4355 psi) concrete deck; $^3/_8''$ main reinforcement bars at $5^1/_2''$ pitch with $^7/_8''$ cover; $^3/_8''$ main reinforcement bars at $4^1/_2''$ pitch perpendicular with $^1/_2''$ cover; 13'1" span restrained.	195 psf	41 min.			7	1, 5, 6	$^1/_2$
F/C-3-RC-5	$3^1/_4''$	$3^1/_4''$ thick (3800 psi) concrete deck; $^3/_8''$ main reinforcement bars at $5^1/_2''$ pitch with $^7/_8''$ cover; $^3/_8''$ main reinforcement bars at $4^1/_2''$ pitch perpendicular with $^1/_2''$ cover; 13'1" span restrained.	195 psf	1 hr. 5 min.			7	1, 5	$^1/_4$

(Continued)

TABLE 3.1—FLOOR/CEILING ASSEMBLIES—REINFORCED CONCRETE—(Continued)

ITEM CODE	ASSEMBLY THICKNESS	CONSTRUCTION DETAILS	PERFORMANCE		REFERENCE NUMBER			NOTES	REC. HOURS
			LOAD	TIME	PRE-BMS-92	BMS-92	POST-BMS-92		
F/C-4-RC-6	$4^1/_4''$	$4^1/_4''$ thick; $3^1/_4''$ (4000 psi) concrete deck; 1" sprayed asbestos lower surface; $^3/_8''$ main reinforcement bars at $5^7/_8''$ pitch with $^7/_8''$ concrete cover; $^3/_8''$ main reinforcement bars at $4^1/_2''$ pitch perpendicular with $^1/_2''$ concrete cover; 13'1" span restrained.	195 psf	4 hrs.			7	1, 7	4
F/C-4-RC-7	4"	4" (5025 psi) concrete deck; $^1/_4''$ reinforcement bars at $7^1/_2''$ pitch with $^3/_4''$ cover; $^3/_8''$ main reinforcement bars at $3^3/_4''$ pitch perpendicular with $^1/_2''$ cover; 13'1" span restrained.	140 psf	1 hr. 16 min.			7	1, 2	$1^1/_4$
F/C-4-RC-8	4"	4" thick (4905 psi) deck; $^1/_4''$ reinforcement bars at $7^1/_2''$ pitch with $^7/_8''$ cover; $^3/_8''$ main reinforcement bars at $3^3/_4''$ pitch perpendicular with $^1/_2''$ cover; 13'1" span restrained.	100 psf	1 hr. 23 min.			7	1, 2	$1^1/_3$
F/C-4-RC-9	4"	4" deep (4370 psi); $^1/_4''$ reinforcement bars at 6" pitch with $^3/_4''$ cover; $^1/_4''$ main reinforcement bars at 4" pitch perpendicular with $^1/_2''$ cover; 13'1" span restrained.	150 psf	2 hrs.			7	1, 3	2
F/C-4-RC-10	4"	4" thick (5140 psi) deck; $^1/_4''$ reinforcement bars at $7^1/_2''$ pitch with $^7/_8''$ cover; $^3/_8''$ main reinforcement bars at $3^3/_4''$ pitch perpendicular with $^1/_2''$ cover; 13'1" span restrained.	140 psf	1 hr. 16 min.			7	1, 5	$1^1/_4$
F/C-4-RC-11	4"	4" thick (4000 psi) concrete deck; 3" × $1^1/_2''$ × 4 lbs. R.S.J.; 2'6" C.R.S.; flush with top surface; 4" × 6" x 13 SWG mesh reinforcement 1" from bottom of slab; 6'6" span restrained.	150 psf	2 hrs.			7	1, 3	2
F/C-4-RC-12	4"	4" deep (2380 psi) concrete deck; 3" × $1^1/_2''$ × 4 lbs. R.S.J.; 2'6" C.R.S.; flush with top surface; 4" × 6" x 13 SWG mesh reinforcement 1" from bottom surface; 6'6" span restrained.	150 psf	1 hr. 3 min.			7	1, 2	1
F/C-4-RC-13	$4^1/_2''$	$4^1/_2''$ thick (5200 psi) deck; $^1/_4''$ reinforcement bars at $7^1/_4''$ pitch with $^7/_8''$ cover; $^3/_8''$ main reinforcement bars at $3^3/_4''$ pitch perpendicular with $^1/_2''$ cover; 13'1" span restrained.	140 psf	2 hrs.			7	1, 3	2
F/C-4-RC-14	$4^1/_2''$	$4^1/_2''$ deep (2525 psi) concrete deck; $^1/_4''$ reinforcement bars at $7^1/_2''$ pitch with $^7/_8''$ cover; $^3/_8''$ main reinforcement bars at $3^3/_8''$ pitch perpendicular with $^1/_2''$ cover; 13'1" span restrained.	150 psf	42 min.			7	1, 5	$^2/_3$
F/C-4-RC-15	$4^1/_2''$	$4^1/_2''$ deep (4830 psi) concrete deck; $1^1/_2''$ × No. 15 gauge wire mesh; $^3/_8''$ reinforcement bars at 15" pitch with 1" cover; $^1/_2''$ main reinforcement bars at 6" pitch perpendicular with $^1/_2''$ cover; 12' span simply supported.	75 psf	1 hr. 32 min.			7	1, 8	$1^1/_2$
F/C-4-RC-16	$4^1/_2''$	$4^1/_2''$ deep (4595 psi) concrete deck; $^1/_4''$ reinforcement bars at $7^1/_2''$ pitch with $^7/_8''$ cover; $^3/_8''$ main reinforcement bars at $3^1/_2''$ pitch perpendicular with $^1/_2''$ cover; 12' span simply supported.	75 psf	1 hr. 20 min.			7	1, 8	$1^1/_3$
F/C-4-RC-17	$4^1/_2''$	$4^1/_2''$ deep (3625 psi) concrete deck; $^1/_4''$ reinforcement bars at $7^1/_2''$ pitch with $^7/_8''$ cover; $^3/_8''$ main reinforcement bars at $3^1/_2''$ pitch perpendicular with $^1/_2''$ cover; 12' span simply supported.	75 psf	35 min.			7	1, 8	$^1/_2$
F/C-4-RC-18	$4^1/_2''$	$4^1/_2''$ deep (4410 psi) concrete deck; $^1/_4''$ reinforcement bars at $7^1/_2''$ pitch with $^7/_8''$ cover; $^3/_8''$ main reinforcement bars at $3^1/_2''$ pitch perpendicular with $^1/_2''$ cover; 12' span simply supported.	85 psf	1 hr. 27 min.			7	1, 8	$1^1/_3$

(Continued)

TABLE 3.1—FLOOR/CEILING ASSEMBLIES—REINFORCED CONCRETE—(Continued)

ITEM CODE	ASSEMBLY THICKNESS	CONSTRUCTION DETAILS	PERFORMANCE		REFERENCE NUMBER			NOTES	REC. HOURS
			LOAD	TIME	PRE-BMS-92	BMS-92	POST-BMS-92		
F/C-4-RC-19	$4^1/_2''$	$4^1/_2''$ deep (4850 psi) deck; $^3/_8''$ reinforcement bars at 15" pitch with 1" cover; $^1/_2''$ main reinforcement bars at 6" pitch perpendicular with $^1/_2''$ cover; 12' span simply supported.	75 psf	2 hrs. 15 min.			7	1, 9	$1^1/_4$
F/C-4-RC-20	$4^1/_2''$	$4^1/_2''$ deep (3610 psi) deck; $^1/_4''$ reinforcement bars at $7^1/_2''$ pitch with $^7/_8''$ cover; $^3/_8''$ main reinforcement bars at $3^1/_2''$ pitch perpendicular with $^1/_2''$ cover; 12' span simply supported.	75 psf	1 hr. 22 min.			7	1, 8	$1^1/_3$
F/C-5-RC-21	5"	5" deep; $4^1/_2''$ (5830 psi) concrete deck; $^1/_2''$ plaster finish bottom of slab; $^1/_4''$ reinforcement bars at $7^1/_2''$ pitch with $^7/_8''$ cover; $^3/_8''$ main reinforcement bars at $3^1/_2''$ pitch perpendicular with $^1/_2''$ cover; 12' span simply supported.	69 psf	2 hrs.			7	1, 3	2
F/C-5-RC-22	5"	$4^1/_2''$ (5290 psi) concrete deck; $^1/_2''$ plaster finish bottom of slab; $^1/_4''$ reinforcement bars at $7^1/_2''$ pitch with $^7/_8''$ cover; $^3/_8''$ main reinforcement bars at $3^1/_2''$ pitch perpendicular with $^1/_2''$ cover; 12' span simply supported.	No load	2 hrs. 28 min.			7	1, 10, 11	$2^1/_4$
F/C-5-RC-23	5"	5" (3020 psi) concrete deck; 3" × $1^1/_2''$ × 4 lbs. R.S.J.; 2' C.R.S. with 1" cover on bottom and top flanges; 8' span restrained.	172 psf	1 hr. 24 min.			7	1, 2, 12	$1^1/_2$
F/C-5-RC-24	$5^1/_2''$	5" (5180 psi) concrete deck; $^1/_2''$ retarded plaster underneath slab; $^1/_4''$ reinforcement bars at $7^1/_2''$ pitch with $1^3/_8''$ cover; $^3/_8''$ main reinforcement bars at $3^1/_2''$ pitch perpendicular with 1" cover; 12' span simply supported.	60 psf	2 hrs. 48 min.			7	1, 10	$2^3/_4$
F/C-6-RC-25	6"	6" deep (4800 psi) concrete deck; $^1/_4''$ reinforcement bars at $7^1/_2''$ pitch with $^7/_8''$ cover; $^3/_8''$ main reinforcement bars at $3^1/_2''$ pitch perpendicular with $^7/_8''$ cover; 13'1" span restrained.	195 psf	4 hrs.			7	1, 7	4
F/C-6-RC-26	6"	6" (4650 psi) concrete deck; $^1/_4''$ reinforcement bars at $7^1/_2''$ pitch with $^7/_8''$ cover; $^3/_8''$ main reinforcement bars at $3^1/_2''$ pitch perpendicular with $^1/_2''$ cover; 13'1" span restrained.	195 psf	2 hrs. 23 min.			7	1, 2	$2^1/_4$
F/C-6-RC-27	6"	6" deep (6050 psi) concrete deck; $^1/_4''$ reinforcement bars at $7^1/_2''$ pitch $^7/_8''$ cover; $^3/_8''$ reinforcement bars at $3^1/_2''$ pitch perpendicular with $^1/_2''$ cover; 13'1" span restrained.	195 psf	3 hrs. 30 min.			7	1, 10	$3^1/_2$
F/C-6-RC-28	6"	6" deep (5180 psi) concrete deck; $^1/_4''$ reinforcement bars at 8" pitch $^3/_4''$ cover; $^1/_4''$ reinforcement bars at $5^1/_2''$ pitch perpendicular with $^1/_2''$ cover; 13'1" span restrained.	150 psf	4 hrs.			7	1, 7	4
F/C-6-RC-29	6"	6" thick (4180 psi) concrete deck; 4" × 3" × 10 lbs. R.S.J.; 2'6" C.R.S. with 1" cover on both top and bottom flanges; 13'1" span restrained.	160 psf	3 hrs. 48 min.			7	1, 10	$3^3/_4$
F/C-6-RC-30	6"	6" thick (3720 psi) concrete deck; 4" × 3" × 10 lbs. R.S.J.; 2'6" C.R.S. with 1" cover on both top and bottom flanges; 12' span simply supported.	115 psf	29 min.			7	1, 5, 13	$^1/_4$
F/C-6-RC-31	6"	6" deep (3450 psi) concrete deck; 4" × $1^3/_4''$ × 5 lbs. R.S.J.; 2'6" C.R.S. with 1" cover on both top and bottom flanges; 12' span simply supported.	25 psf	3 hrs. 35 min.			7	1, 2	$3^1/_2$
F/C-6-RC-32	6"	6" deep (4460 psi) concrete deck; 4" × $1^3/_4''$ × 5 lbs. R.S.J.; 2' C.R.S.; with 1" cover on both top and bottom flanges; 12' span simply supported.	60 psf	4 hrs. 30 min.			7	1, 10	$4^1/_2$

(Continued)

TABLE 3.1—FLOOR/CEILING ASSEMBLIES—REINFORCED CONCRETE—(Continued)

ITEM CODE	ASSEMBLY THICKNESS	CONSTRUCTION DETAILS	PERFORMANCE		REFERENCE NUMBER			NOTES	REC. HOURS
			LOAD	TIME	PRE-BMS-92	BMS-92	POST-BMS-92		
F/C-6-RC-33	6″	6″ deep (4360 psi) concrete deck; 4″ × 1³/₄″ × 5 lbs. R.S.J.; 2′ C.R.S.; with 1″ cover on both top and bottom flanges; 13′1″ span restrained.	60 psf	2 hrs.			7	1, 3	2
F/C-6-RC-34	6¹/₄″	6¹/₄″ thick; 4³/₄″ (5120 psi) concrete core; 1″ T&G board flooring; ¹/₂″ plaster undercoat; 4″ × 3″ × 10 lbs. R.S.J.; 3′ C.R.S. flush with top surface concrete; 12′ span simply supported; 2″ × 1′3″ clinker concrete insert.	100 psf	4 hrs.			7	1, 7	4
F/C-6-RC-35	6¹/₄″	4³/₄″ (3600 psi) concrete core; 1″ T&G board flooring; ¹/₂″ plaster undercoat; 4″ × 3″ × 10 lbs. R.S.J.; 3′ C.R.S.; flush with top surface concrete; 12′ span simply supported; 2″ × 1′3″ clinker concrete insert.	100 psf	2 hrs. 30 min.			7	1, 5	2¹/₂
F/C-6-RC-36	6¹/₄″	4³/₄″ (2800 psi) concrete core; 1″ T&G board flooring; ¹/₂″ plaster undercoat; 4″ × 3″ × 10 lbs. R.S.J.; 3′ C.R.S.; flush with top surface concrete; 12″ span simply supported; 2″ × 1′3″ clinker concrete insert.	80 psf	4 hrs.			7	1, 7	4
F/C-7-RC-37	7″	(3640 psi) concrete deck; ¹/₄″ reinforcement bars at 6″ pitch with 1¹/₂″ cover; ¹/₄″ reinforcement bars at 5″ pitch perpendicular with 1¹/₂″ cover; 13′1″ span restrained.	169 psf	6 hrs.			7	1, 14	6
F/C-7-RC-38	7″	(4060 psi) concrete deck; 4″ × 3″ × 10 lbs. R.S.J.; 2′6″ C.R.S. with 1¹/₂″ cover on both top and bottom flanges; 4″ × 6″ × 13 SWG mesh reinforcement 1¹/₂″ from bottom of slab; 13′1″ span restrained.	175 psf	6 hrs.			7	1, 14	6
F/C-7-RC-39	7¹/₄″	5³/₄″ (4010 psi) concrete core; 1″ T&G board flooring; ¹/₂″ plaster undercoat; 4″ × 3″ × 10 lbs. R.S.J.; 2′6″ C.R.S.; 1″ down from top surface of concrete; 12′ simply supported span; 2″ × 1′3″ clinker concrete insert.	95 psf	2 hrs.			7	1, 3	2
F/C-7-RC-40	7¹/₄″	5³/₄″ (3220 psi) concrete core; 1″ T&G flooring; ¹/₂″ plaster undercoat; 4″ × 3″ × 10 lbs. R.S.J.; 2′6″ C.R.S.; 1″ down from top surface of concrete; 12′ simply supported span; 2″ × 1′3″ clinker concrete insert.	95 psf	4 hrs.			7	1, 7	4
F/C-7-RC-41	10″ (2¹/₄″ Slab)	Ribbed floor, see Note 15 for details; slab 2¹/₂″ deep (3020 psi); ¹/₄″ reinforcement bars at 6″ pitch with ³/₄″ cover; beams 7¹/₂″ deep × 5″ wide; 24″ C.R.S.; ⁵/₈″ reinforcement bars two rows ¹/₂″ vertically apart with 1″ cover; 13′1″ span restricted.	195 psf	1 hr. 4. min.			7	1, 2, 15	1
F/C-5-RC-42	5¹/₂″	Composite ribbed concrete slab assembly; see Note 17 for details.	See Note 16	2 hrs.			43	16, 17	2
F/C-3-RC-43	3″	2500 psi concrete; ⁵/₈″ cover; fully restrained at test.	See Note 16	30 min.			43	16	¹/₂
F/C-3-RC-44	3″	2000 psi concrete; ⁵/₈″ cover; free or partial restraint at test.	See Note 16	45 min.			43	16	³/₄
F/C-4-RC-45	4″	2500 psi concrete; ⁵/₈″ cover; fully restrained at test.	See Note 16	40 min.			43	16	²/₃
F/C-4-RC-46	4″	2000 psi concrete; ³/₄″ cover; free or partial restraint at test.	See Note 16	1 hr. 15 min.			43	16	1¹/₄
F/C-5-RC-47	5″	2500 psi concrete; ³/₄″ cover; fully restrained at test.	See Note 16	1 hr.			43	16	1
F/C-5-RC-48	5″	2000 psi concrete; ³/₄″ cover; free or partial restraint at test.	See Note 16	1 hr. 30 min.			43	16	1¹/₂

(Continued)

TABLE 3.1—FLOOR/CEILING ASSEMBLIES—REINFORCED CONCRETE—(Continued)

ITEM CODE	ASSEMBLY THICKNESS	CONSTRUCTION DETAILS	PERFORMANCE		REFERENCE NUMBER			NOTES	REC. HOURS
			LOAD	TIME	PRE-BMS-92	BMS-92	POST-BMS-92		
F/C-6-RC-49	6″	2500 psi concrete; 1″ cover; fully restrained at test.	See Note 16	1 hr. 30 min.			43	16	1¹/₂
F/C-6-RC-50	6″	2000 psi concrete; 1″ cover; free or partial restraint at test.	See Note 16	2 hrs.			43	16	2

Notes:
1. British test.
2. Failure mode - local back face temperature rise.
3. Tested for Grade "C" (2 hour) fire resistance.
4. Collapse imminent following hose stream.
5. Failure mode - flame thru.
6. Void formed with explosive force and report.
7. Achieved Grade "B" (4 hour) fire resistance (British).
8. Failure mode - collapse.
9. Test was run to 2 hours, but specimen was partially supported by the furnace at $1^1/_4$ hours.
10. Failure mode - average back face temperature.
11. Recommended endurance for nonload bearing performance only.
12. Floor maintained load bearing ability to 2 hours at which point test was terminated.
13. Test was run to 3 hours at which time failure mode 2 (above) was reached in spite of crack formation at 29 minutes.
14. Tested for Grade "A" (6 hour) fire resistance.
15.

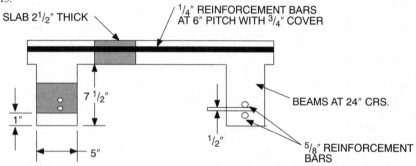

16. Load unspecified.
17. Total assembly thickness $5^1/_2$ inches. Three-inch thick blocks of molded excelsior bonded with portland cement used as inserts with $2^1/_2$-inch cover (concrete) above blocks and $^3/_4$-inch gypsum plaster below. Nine-inch wide ribs containing reinforcing steel of unspecified size interrupted 20-inch wide segments of slab composite (i.e., plaster, excelsior blocks, concrete cover).

FIGURE 3.2—FLOOR/CEILING ASSEMBLIES—STEEL STRUCTURAL ELEMENTS

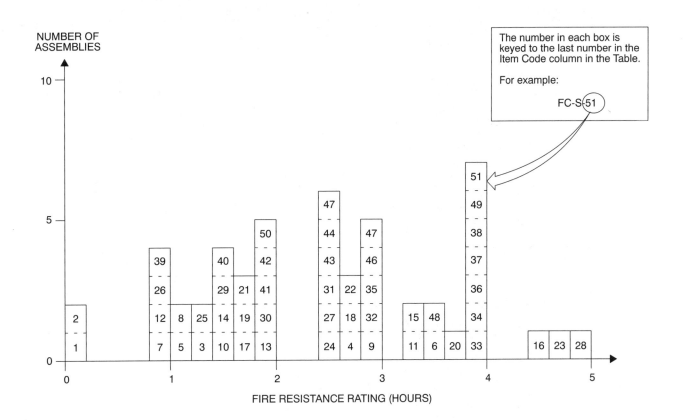

TABLE 3.2—FLOOR/CEILING ASSEMBLIES—STEEL STRUCTURAL ELEMENTS

ITEM CODE	MEMBRANCE THICKNESS	CONSTRUCTION DETAILS	PERFORMANCE		REFERENCE NUMBER			NOTES	REC. HOURS
			LOAD	TIME	PRE-BMS-92	BMS-92	POST-BMS-92		
F/C-S-1	0″	- 10′ × 13′6″; S.J. 103 - 24″ o.c.; Deck: 2″ concrete; Membrane: none.	145 psf	7 min.			3	1, 2, 3, 8	0
F/C-S-2	0″	- 10′ × 13′6″; S.J. 103 - 24″ o.c.; Deck: 2″ concrete; Membrane: none	145 psf	7 min.			3	1, 2, 3, 8	0
F/C-S-3	$^1/_2$″	- 10′ × 13′6″; S.J. 103 - 24″ o.c.; Deck: 2″ concrete 1:2:4; Membrane: furring 12″ o.c.; Clips A, B, G; No extra reinforcement; $^1/_2$″ plaster - 1.5:2.5.	145 psf	1 hr. 15 min.			3	2, 3, 8	$1^1/_4$
F/C-S-4	$^1/_2$″	- 10′ × 13′6″; S.J. 103 - 24″ o.c.; Deck: 2″ concrete 1:2:4; Membrane: furring 16″ o.c.; Clips D, E, F, G; Diagonal wire reinforcement; $^1/_2$″ plaster - 1.5:2.5.	145 psf	2 hrs. 46 min.			3	3, 8	$2^3/_4$
F/C-S-5	$^1/_2$″	- 10′ × 13′6″; S.J. 103 - 24″ o.c.; Deck: 2″ concrete 1:2:4; Membrane: furring 16″ o.c.; Clips A, B, G; No extra reinforcement; $^1/_2$″ plaster - 1.5:2.5.	145 psf	1 hr. 4 min.			3	2, 3, 8	1
F/C-S-6	$^1/_2$″	10′ × 13′6″; S.J. 103 - 24″ o.c.; Deck: 2″ concrete 1:2:4; Membrane: furring 16″ o.c.; Clips D, E, F, G; Hexagonal mesh reinforcement; $^1/_2$″ plaster.	145 psf	3 hrs. 28 min.			3	2, 3, 8	$2^1/_3$
F/C-S-7	$^1/_2$″	10′ × 13′6″; S.J. 103 - 24″ o.c.; Deck: 4 lbs. rib lath; 6″ × 6″ - 10 × 10 ga. reinforcement; 2″ deck gravel concrete; Membrane: furring 16″ o.c.; Clips C, E; Reinforcement: none; $^1/_2$″ plaster - 1.5:2.5 mill mix.	N/A	55 min.			3	5, 8	$^3/_4$

(Continued)

TABLE 3.2—FLOOR/CEILING ASSEMBLIES—STEEL STRUCTURAL ELEMENTS—(Continued)

ITEM CODE	MEMBRANCE THICKNESS	CONSTRUCTION DETAILS	PERFORMANCE		REFERENCE NUMBER			NOTES	REC. HOURS
			LOAD	TIME	PRE-BMS-92	BMS-92	POST-BMS-92		
F/C-S-8	$1/2''$	Spec. 9' × 4'4"; S.J. 103 bar joists - 18" o.c.; Deck: 4 lbs. rib lath base; 6" × 6" - 10 × 10 ga. reinforcement; 2" deck 1:2:4 gravel concrete; Membrane: furring, $3/4''$ C.R.S., 16" o.c.; Clips C, E; Reinforcement: none; $1/2''$ plaster - 1.5:2.5 mill mix.	300 psf	1 hr. 10 min.			3	2, 3, 8	1
F/C-S-9	$5/8''$	10' × 13'6"; S.J. 103 - 24" o.c.; Deck: 2" concrete 1:2:4; Membrane: furring 12" o.c.; Clips A, B, G; Extra "A" clips reinforcement; $5/8''$ plaster - 1.5:2; 1.5:3.	145 psf	3 hrs.			3	6, 8	3
F/C-S-10	$5/8''$	18' × 13'6"; Joists, S.J. 103 - 24" o.c.; Deck: 4 lbs. rib lath; 6" × 6" - 10 x 10 ga. reinforcement; 2" deck 1:2:3.5 gravel concrete; Membrane: furring, spacing 16" o.c.; Clips C, E; Reinforcement: none; $5/8''$ plaster - 1.5:2.5 mill mix.	145 psf	1 hr. 25 min.			3	2, 3, 8	$1^1/3$
F/C-S-11	$5/8''$	10' × 13'6"; S.J. 103 - 24" o.c.; Deck: 2" concrete 1:2:4; Membrane: furring 12" o.c.; Clips D, E, F, G; Diagonal wire reinforcement; $5/8''$ plaster - 1.5:2; 0.5:3.	145 psf	3 hrs. 15 min.			3	2, 4, 8	$3^1/4$
F/C-S-12	$5/8''$	10' × 13'6"; Joists, S.J. 103 - 24" o.c.; Deck: 3.4 lbs. rib lath; 6" × 6" - 10 × 10 ga. reinforcement; 2" deck 1:2:4 gravel concrete; Membrane: furring 16" o.c.; Clips D, E, F, G; Reinforcement: none; $5/8''$ plaster - 1.5:2.5.	145 psf	1 hr.			3	7, 8	1
F/C-S-13	$3/4''$	Spec. 9' × 4'4"; S.J. 103 - 18" o.c.; Deck: 4 lbs. rib lath; 6" × 6" - 10 x 10 ga. reinforcement; 2" deck 1:2:4 gravel concrete; Membrane: furring, $3/4''$ C.R.S., 16" o.c.; Clips C, E; Reinforcement: none; $3/4''$ plaster - 1.5:2.5 mill mix.	300 psf	1 hr. 56 min.			3	3, 8	$1^3/4$
F/C-S-14	$7/8''$	Floor finish: 1" concrete; plate cont. weld; 4" - 7.7 lbs. "I" beams; Ceiling: $1/4''$ rods 12" o.c.; $7/8''$ gypsum sand plaster.	105 psf	1 hr. 35 min.			6	2, 4, 9, 10	$1^1/2$
F/C-S-15	1"	Floor finish: $1^1/2''$ L.W. concrete; $1/2''$ limestone cement; plate cont. weld; 5" - 10 lbs. "I" beams; Ceiling: $1/4''$ rods 12" o.c. tack welded to beams metal lath; 1" P. C. plaster.	165 psf	3 hrs. 20 min.			6	4, 9, 11	
F/C-S-16	1"	10' × 13'6"; S.J. 103 - 24" o.c.; Deck: 2" concrete 1:2:4; Membrane: furring 12" o.c.; Clips D, E, F, G; Hexagonal mesh reinforcement; 1" thick plaster - 1.5:2; 1.5:3.	145 psf	4 hr. 26 min.			3	2, 4, 8	$4^1/3$
F/C-S-17	1"	10' × 13'6"; Joists - S.J. 103 - 24" o.c.; Deck: 3.4 lbs. rib lath; 6" × 6" - 10 × 10 ga. reinforcement; 2" deck 1:2:4 gravel concrete; Membrane: furring 16" o.c.; Clips D, E, F, G; 1" plaster.	145 psf	1 hr. 42 min.			3	2, 4, 8	$1^2/3$
F/C-S-18	$1^1/8''$	10' × 13'6"; S. J. 103 - 24" o.c.; Deck: 2" concrete 1:2:4; Membrane: furring 12" o.c.; Clips C, E, F, G; Diagonal wire reinforcement; $1^1/8''$ plaster.	145 psf	2 hrs. 44 min.			3	2, 4, 8	$2^2/3$
F/C-S-19	$1^1/8''$	10' × 13'6"; Joists - S.J. 103 - 24" o.c.; Deck: $1^1/2''$ gypsum concrete over; $1/2''$ gypsum board; Membrane: furring 12" o.c.; Clips D, E, F, G; $1^1/8''$ plaster - 1.5:2; 1.5:3.	145 psf	1 hr. 40 min.			3	2, 3, 8	$1^2/3$
F/C-S-20	$1^1/8''$	$2^1/2''$ cinder concrete; $1/2''$ topping; plate 6" welds 12" o.c.; 5" - 18.9 lbs. "H" center; 5" - 10 lbs. "I" ends; 1" channels 18" o.c.; $1^1/8''$ gypsum sand plaster.	150 psf	3 hr. 43 min.			6	2, 4, 9, 11	$3^2/3$

(Continued)

TABLE 3.2—FLOOR/CEILING ASSEMBLIES—STEEL STRUCTURAL ELEMENTS—(Continued)

ITEM CODE	MEMBRANCE THICKNESS	CONSTRUCTION DETAILS	PERFORMANCE		REFERENCE NUMBER			NOTES	REC. HOURS
			LOAD	TIME	PRE-BMS-92	BMS-92	POST-BMS-92		
F/C-S-21	$1^1/_4''$	$10' \times 13'6''$; Joists - S.J. 103 - 24'' o.c.; Deck: $1^1/_2''$ gypsum concrete over; $^1/_2''$ gypsum board base; Membrane: furring 12'' o.c.; Clips D, E, F, G; $1^1/_4''$ plaster - 1.5:2; 1.5:3.	145 psf	1 hr. 48 min.			3	2, 3, 8	$1^2/_3$
F/C-S-22	$1^1/_4''$	Floor finish: $1^1/_2''$ limestone concrete; $^1/_2''$ sand cement topping; plate to beams $3^1/_2''$; 12'' o.c. welded; 5'' - 10 lbs. "I" beams; 1'' channels 18'' o.c.; $1^1/_4''$ wood fiber gypsum sand plaster on metal lath.	292 psf	2 hrs. 45 min.			6	2, 4, 9, 10	$2^3/_4$
F/C-S-23	$1^1/_2''$	$2^1/_2''$ L.W. (gas exp.) concrete; Deck: $^1/_2''$ topping; plate $6^1/_4''$ welds 12'' o.c.; Beams: 5'' - 18.9 lbs. "H" center; 5'' - 10 lbs. "I" ends; Membrane: 1'' channels 18'' o.c.; $1^1/_2''$ gypsum sand plaster.	150 psf	4 hrs. 42 min.			6	2, 4, 9	$4^2/_3$
F/C-S-24	$1^1/_2''$	Floor finish: $1^1/_2''$ limestone concrete; $^1/_2''$ cement topping; plate $3^1/_2''$ - 12'' o.c. welded; 5'' - 10 lbs. "I" beams; Ceiling: 1'' channels 18'' o.c.; $1^1/_2''$ gypsum plaster.	292 psf	2 hrs. 34 min.			6	2, 4, 9, 10	$2^1/_2$
F/C-S-25	$1^1/_2''$	Floor finish: $1^1/_2''$ gravel concrete on exp. metal; plate cont. weld; 4'' - 7.7 lbs. "I" beams; Ceiling: $^1/_4''$ rods 12'' o.c. welded to beams; $1^1/_2''$ fiber gypsum sand plaster.	70 psf	1 hr. 24 min.			6	2, 4, 9, 10	$1^1/_3$
F/C-S-26	$2^1/_2''$	Floor finish: bare plate; $6^1/_4''$ welding - 12'' o.c.; 5'' - 18.9 lbs. "H" girders (inner); 5'' - 10 lbs "I" girders (two outer); 1'' channels 18'' o.c.; 2'' reinforced gypsum tile; $^1/_2''$ gypsum sand plaster.	122 psf	1 hr.			6	7, 9, 11	1
F/C-S-27	$2^1/_2''$	Floor finish: 2'' gravel concrete; plate to beams $3^1/_2''$ - 12'' o.c. welded; 4'' - 7.7 lbs. "I" beams; 2'' gypsum ceiling tiles; $^1/_2''$ 1:3 gypsum sand plaster.	105 psf	2 hrs. 31 min.			6	2, 4, 9, 10	$2^1/_2$
F/C-S-28	$2^1/_2''$	Floor finish: $1^1/_2''$ gravel concrete; $^1/_2''$ gypsum asphalt; plate continuous weld; 4'' - 7.7 lbs. "I" beams; 12'' - 31.8 lbs. "I" beams - girder at 5' from one end; 1'' channels 18'' o.c.; 2'' reinforcement gypsum tile; $^1/_2''$ 1:3 gypsum sand plaster.	200 psf	4 hrs. 55 min.			6	2, 4, 9, 11	$4^2/_3$
F/C-S-29	$^3/_4''$	Floor: 2'' reinforced concrete or 2'' precast reinforced gypsum tile; Ceiling: $^3/_4''$ portland cement-sand plaster 1:2 for scratch coat and 1:3 for brown coat with 15 lbs. hydrated lime and 3 lbs. of short asbestos fiber bag per cement or $^3/_4''$ sanded gypsum plaster 1:2 for scratch coat and 1:3 for brown coat.	See Note 12	1 hr. 30 min.		1		12, 13, 14	$1^1/_2$
F/C-S-30	$^3/_4''$	Floor: $2^1/_4''$ reinforced concrete or 2'' reinforced gypsum tile; the latter with $^1/_4''$ mortar finish; Ceiling: $^3/_4''$ sanded gypsum plaster; 1:2 for scratch coat and 1:3 for brown coat.	See Note 12	2 hrs.		1		12, 13, 14	2
F/C-S-31	$^3/_4''$	Floor: $2^1/_2''$ reinforced concrete or 2'' reinforced gypsum tile; the latter with $^1/_4''$ mortar finish; Ceiling: 1'' neat gypsum plaster or $^3/_4''$ gypsum-vermiculite plaster, ratio of gypsum to fine vermiculite 2:1 to 3:1.	See Note 12	2 hrs. 30 min.		1		12, 13, 14	$2^1/_2$
F/C-S-32	$^3/_4''$	Floor: $2^1/_2''$ reinforced concrete or 2'' reinforced gypsum tile; the latter with $^1/_2''$ mortar finish; Ceiling: 1'' neat gypsum plaster or $^3/_4''$ gypsum-vermiculite plaster, ratio of gypsum to fine vermiculite 2:1 to 3:1.	See Note 12	3 hrs.		1		12, 13, 14	3

(Continued)

TABLE 3.2—FLOOR/CEILING ASSEMBLIES—STEEL STRUCTURAL ELEMENTS—(Continued)

ITEM CODE	MEMBRANE THICKNESS	CONSTRUCTION DETAILS	PERFORMANCE		REFERENCE NUMBER			NOTES	REC. HOURS
			LOAD	TIME	PRE-BMS-92	BMS-92	POST-BMS-92		
F/C-S-33	1″	Floor: 2$\frac{1}{2}$″ reinforced concrete or 2″ reinforced gypsum slabs; the latter with $\frac{1}{2}$″ mortar finish; Ceiling: 1″ gypsum-vermiculite plaster applied on metal lath and ratio 2:1 to 3:1 gypsum to vermiculite by weight.	See Note 12	4 hrs.		1		12, 13, 14	4
F/C-S-34	2$\frac{1}{2}$″	Floor: 2″ reinforced concrete or 2″ precast reinforced portland cement concrete or gypsum slabs; precast slabs to be finished with $\frac{1}{4}$″ mortar top coat; Ceiling: 2″ precast reinforced gypsum tile, anchored into beams with metal ties or clips and covered with $\frac{1}{2}$″ 1:3 sanded gypsum plaster.	See Note 12	4 hrs.		1		12, 13, 14	4
F/C-S-35	1″	Floor: 1:3:6 portland cement, sand and gravel concrete applied directly to the top of steel units and 1$\frac{1}{2}$″ thick at top of cells, plus $\frac{1}{2}$″ 1:2$\frac{1}{2}$″ cement-sand finish, total thickness at top of cells, 2″; Ceiling: 1″ neat gypsum plaster, back of lath 2″ or more from underside of cellular steel.	See Note 15	3 hrs.		1		15, 16, 17, 18	3
F/C-S-36	1″	Floor: same as F/C-S-35; Ceiling: 1″ gypsum-vermiculite plaster (ratio of gypsum to vermiculite 2:1 to 3:1), the back of lath 2″ or more from under-side of cellular steel.	See Note 15	4 hrs.		1		15, 16, 17, 18	4
F/C-S-37	1″	Floor: same as F/C-S-35; Ceiling: 1″ neat gypsum plaster; back of lath 9″ or more from underside of cellular steel.	See Note 15	4 hrs.		1		15, 16, 17, 18	4
F/C-S-38	1″	Floor: same as F/C-S-35; Ceiling: 1″ gypsum-vermiculite plaster (ratio of gypsum to vermiculite 2:1 to 3:1), the back of lath being 9″ or more from underside of cellular steel.	See Note 15	5 hrs.		1		15, 16, 17, 18	5
F/C-S-39	$\frac{3}{4}$″	Floor: asbestos paper 14 lbs./100 ft.² cemented to steel deck with waterproof linoleum cement, wood screeds and $\frac{7}{8}$″ wood floor; Ceiling: $\frac{3}{4}$″ sanded gypsum plaster 1:2 for scratch coat and 1:3 for brown coat.	Note 19	1 hr.		1		19, 20, 21, 22	1
F/C-S-40	$\frac{3}{4}$″	Floor: 1$\frac{1}{2}$″, 1:2:4 portland cement concrete; Ceiling: $\frac{3}{4}$″ sanded gypsum plaster 1:2 for scratch coat and 1:3 for brown coat.	Note 19	1 hr. 30 min.		1		19, 20, 21, 22	1$\frac{1}{2}$
F/C-S-41	$\frac{3}{4}$″	Floor: 2″, 1:2:4 portland cement concrete; Ceiling: $\frac{3}{4}$″ sanded gypsum plaster, 1:2 for scratch coat and 1:3 for brown coat.	Note 19	2 hrs.		1		19, 20, 21, 22	2
F/C-S-42	1″	Floor: 2″, 1:2:4 portland cement concrete; Ceiling: 1″ portland cement-sand plaster with 10 lbs. of hydrated lime for @ bag of cement 1:2 for scratch coat and 1:2$\frac{1}{2}$″ for brown coat.	Note 19	2 hrs.		1		19, 20, 21, 22	2
F/C-S-43	1$\frac{1}{2}$″	Floor: 2″, 1:2:4 portland cement concrete; Ceiling: 1$\frac{1}{2}$″, 1:2 sanded gypsum plaster on ribbed metal lath.	Note 19	2 hrs. 30 min.		1		19, 20, 21, 22	2$\frac{1}{2}$
F/C-S-44	1$\frac{1}{8}$″	Floor: 2″, 1:2:4 portland cement concrete; Ceiling: 1$\frac{1}{8}$″, 1:1 sanded gypsum plaster.	Note 19	2 hrs. 30 min.		1		19, 20, 21, 22	2$\frac{1}{2}$
F/C-S-45	1″	Floor: 2$\frac{1}{2}$″, 1:2:4 portland cement concrete; Ceiling: 1″, 1:2 sanded gypsum plaster.	Note 19	2 hrs. 30 min.		1		19, 20, 21, 22	2$\frac{1}{2}$
F/C-S-46	$\frac{3}{4}$″	Floor: 2$\frac{1}{2}$″, 1:2:4 portland cement concrete; Ceiling: 1″ neat gypsum plaster or $\frac{3}{4}$″ gypsum-vermiculite plaster, ratio of gypsum to vermiculite 2:1 to 3:1.	Note 19	3 hrs.		1		19, 20, 21, 22	3

(Continued)

TABLE 3.2—FLOOR/CEILING ASSEMBLIES—STEEL STRUCTURAL ELEMENTS—(Continued)

ITEM CODE	MEMBRANCE THICKNESS	CONSTRUCTION DETAILS	PERFORMANCE		REFERENCE NUMBER			NOTES	REC. HOURS
			LOAD	TIME	PRE-BMS-92	BMS-92	POST-BMS-92		
F/C-S-47	$1^1/_8''$	Floor: $2^1/_2''$, 1:2:4 portland cement, sand and cinder concrete plus $^1/_2''$, 1:2$^1/_2''$ cement-sand finish; total thickness 3″; Ceiling: $1^1/_8''$, 1:1 sanded gypsum plaster.	Note 19	3 hrs.		1		19, 20, 21, 22	3
F/C-S-48	$1^1/_8''$	Floor: $2^1/_2''$, gas expanded portland cement- sand concrete plus $^1/_2''$, 1:2.5 cement-sand finish; total thickness 3″; Ceiling: $1^1/_8''$, 1:1 sanded gypsum plaster.	Note 19	3 hrs. 30 min.		1		19, 20, 21, 22	$3^1/_2$
F/C-S-49	1″	Floor: $2^1/_2''$, 1:2:4 portland cement concrete; Ceiling: 1″ gypsum-vermiculite plaster; ratio of gypsum to vermiculite 2:1 to 3:1.	Note 19	4 hrs.		1		19, 20, 21, 22	4
F/C-S-50	$2^1/_2''$	Floor: 2″, 1:2:4 portland cement concrete; Ceiling: 2″ interlocking gypsum tile supported on upper face of lower flanges of beams, $^1/_2''$ 1:3 sanded gypsum plaster.	Note 19	2 hrs.		1		19, 20, 21, 22	2
F/C-S-51	$2^1/_2''$	Floor: 2″, 1:2:4 portland cement concrete; Ceiling: 2″ precast metal reinforced gypsum tile, $^1/_2''$ 1:3 sanded gypsum plaster (tile clipped to channels which are clipped to lower flanges of beams).	Note 19	4 hrs.		1		19, 20, 21, 22	4

Notes:
1. No protective membrane over structural steel.
2. Performance time indicates first endpoint reached only several tests were continued to points where other failures occurred.
3. Load failure.
4. Thermal failure.
5. This is an estimated time to load bearing failure. The same joist and deck specimen ws used for a later test with different membrane protection.
6. Test stopped at 3 hours to reuse specimen; no endpoint reached.
7. Test stopped at 1 hour to reuse specimen; no endpoint reached.
8. All plaster used = gypsum.
9. Specimen size - 18 feet by 13$^1/_2$ inches. Floor deck - base material - $^1/_4$-inch by 18-foot steel plate welded to "I" beams.
10. "I" beams - 24 inches o.c.
11. "I" beams - 48 inches o.c.
12. Apply to open web joists, pressed steel joists or rolled steel beams, which are not stressed beyond 18,000 lbs./in.^{2} in flexure for open-web pressed or light rolled joists, and 20,000 lbs./in.^{2} for American standard or heavier rolled beams.
13. Ratio of weight of portland cement to fine and coarse aggregates combined for floor slabs shall be not less than 1:6$^1/_2$.
14. Plaster for ceiling shall be applied on metal lath which shall be tied to supports to give the equivalent of single No. 18 gage steel wires 5 inches o.c.
15. Load: maximum fiber stress in steel not to exceed 16,000 psi.
16. Prefabricated units 2 feet wide with length equal to the span, composed of two pieces of No. 18 gage formed steel welded together to give four longitudinal cells.
17. Depth not less than 3 inches and distance between cells no less than 2 inches.
18. Ceiling: metal lath tied to furring channels secured to runner channels hung from cellular steel.
19. Load: rolled steel supporting beams and steel plate base shall not be stressed beyond 20,000 psi in flexure.
Formed steel (with wide upper flange) construction shall not be stressed beyond 16,000 psi.
20. Some type of expanded metal or woven wire shall be embedded to prevent cracking in concrete flooring.
21. Ceiling plaster shall be metal lath wired to rods or channels with are clipped or welded to steel construction. Lath shall be no smaller than 18 gage steel wire and not more than 7 inches o.c.
22. The securing rods or channels shall be at least as effective as single $^3/_{16}$-inch rods with 1-inch of their length bent over the lower flanges of beams with the rods or channels tied to this clip with 14 gage iron wire.

FIGURE 3.3—FLOOR/CEILING ASSEMBLIES—WOOD JOIST

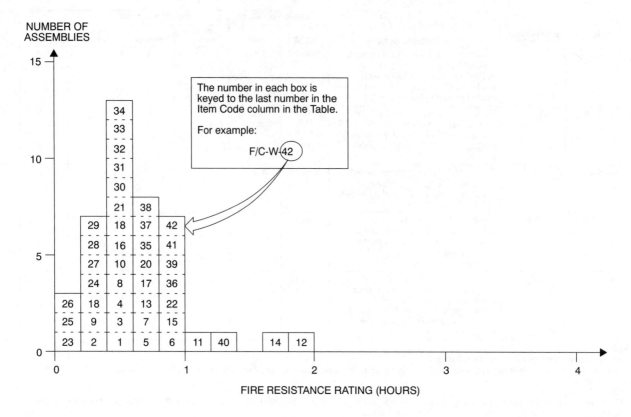

TABLE 3.3—FLOOR/CEILING ASSEMBLIES—WOOD JOIST

ITEM CODE	MEMBRANCE THICKNESS	CONSTRUCTION DETAILS	PERFORMANCE		REFERENCE NUMBER			NOTES	REC. HOURS
			LOAD	TIME	PRE-BMS-92	BMS-92	POST-BMS-92		
F/C-W-1	$3/8''$	12' clear span - 2" × 9" wood joists; 18" o.c.; Deck: 1" T&G; Filler: 3" of ashes on $1/2''$ boards nailed to joist sides 2" from bottom; 2" air space; Membrane: $3/8''$ gypsum board.	60 psf	36 min.			7	1, 2	$1/2$
F/C-W-2	$1/2''$	12' clear span - 2" × 7" joists; 15" o.c.; Deck: 1" nominal lumber; Membrane: $1/2''$ fiber board.	60 psf	22 min.			7	1, 2, 3	$1/4$
F/C-W-3	$1/2''$	12' clear span - 2" × 7" wood joists; 16" o.c.; 2" × $1^1/2''$ bridging at center; Deck: 1" T&G; Membrane: $1/2''$ fiber board; 2 coats "distemper" paint.	30 psf	28 min.			7	1, 3, 15	$1/3$
F/C-W-4	$3/16''$	12' clear span - 2" × 7" wood joists; 16" o.c.; 2" × $1^1/2''$ bridging at center span; Deck: 1" nominal lumber; Membrane: $1/2''$ fiber board under $3/16''$ gypsum plaster.	30 psf	32 min.			7	1, 2	$1/2$
F/C-W-5	$5/8''$	As per previous F/C-W-4 except membrane is $5/8''$ lime plaster.	70 psf	48 min.			7	1, 2	$3/4$
F/C-W-6	$5/8''$	As per previous F/C-W-5 except membrane is $5/8''$ gypsum plaster on 22 gage $3/8''$ metal lath.	70 psf	49 min.			7	1, 2	$3/4$
F/C-W-7	$1/2''$	As per previous F/C-W-6 except membrane is $1/2''$ fiber board under $1/2''$ gypsum plaster.	60 psf	43 min.			7	1, 2, 3	$2/3$
F/C-W-8	$1/2''$	As per previous F/C-W-7 except membrane is $1/2''$ gypsum board.	60 psf	33 min.			7	1, 2, 3	$1/2$
F/C-W-9	$9/16''$	12' clear span - 2" × 7" wood joists; 15" o.c.; 2" × $1^1/2''$ bridging at center; Deck: 1" nominal lumber; Membrane: $3/8''$ gypsum board; $3/16''$ gypsum plaster.	60 psf	24 min.			7	1, 2, 3	$1/3$

(Continued)

TABLE 3.3—FLOOR/CEILING ASSEMBLIES—WOOD JOIST—(Continued)

ITEM CODE	MEMBRANCE THICKNESS	CONSTRUCTION DETAILS	PERFORMANCE		REFERENCE NUMBER			NOTES	REC. HOURS
			LOAD	TIME	PRE-BMS-92	BMS-92	POST-BMS-92		
F/C-W-10	$5/8''$	As per F/C-W-9 except membrane is $5/8''$ gypsum plaster on wood lath.	60 psf	27 min.			7	1, 2, 3	$1/3$
F/C-W-11	$7/8''$	12' clear span - 2" × 9" wood joists; 15" o.c.; 2" × 1$1/2$" bridging at center span; Deck: 1" T&G; Membrane: original ceiling joists have $3/8''$ plaster on wood lath; 4" metal hangers attached below joists creating 15" chases filled with mineral wool and closed with $7/8''$ plaster (gypsum) on $3/8''$ S.W.M. metal lath to form new ceiling surface.	75 psf	1 hr. 10 min.			7	1, 2	1
F/C-W-12	$7/8''$	12' clear span - 2" × 9" wood joists; 15" o.c.; 2" × 1$1/2$" bridging at center; Deck: 1" T&G; Membrane: 3" mineral wood below joists; 3" hangers to channel below joists; $7/8''$ gypsum plaster on metal lath attached to channels.	75 psf	2 hrs.			7	1, 4	2
F/C-W-13	$7/8''$	12' clear span - 2" × 9" wood joists; 16" o.c.; 2" × 1$1/2$" bridging at center span; Deck: 1" T&G on 1" bottoms on $3/4''$ glass wool strips on $3/4''$ gypsum board nailed to joists; Membrane: $3/4''$ glass wool strips on joists; $3/8''$ perforated gyspum lath; $1/2''$ gypsum plaster.	60 psf	41 min.			7	1, 3	$2/3$
F/C-W-14	$7/8''$	12' clear span - 2" × 9" wood joists; 15" o.c.; Deck: 1" T&G; Membrane: 3" foam concrete in cavity on $1/2''$ boards nailed to joists; wood lath nailed to 1" × 1$1/4$" straps 14 o.c. across joists; $7/8''$ gypsum plaster.	60 psf	1 hr. 40 min.			7	1, 5	1$2/3$
F/C-W-15	$7/8''$	12' clear span - 2" × 9" wood joists; 18" o.c.; Deck: 1" T&G; Membrane: 2" foam concrete on $1/2''$ boards nailed to joist sides 2" from joist bottom; 2" air space; 1" × 1$1/4$" wood straps 14" o.c. across joists; $7/8''$ lime plaster on wood lath.	60 psf	53 min.			7	1, 2	$3/4$
F/C-W-16	$7/8''$	12' clear span - 2" × 9" wood joists; Deck: 1" T&G; Membrane: 3" ashes on $1/2''$ boards nailed to joist sides 2" from joist bottom; 2" air space; 1" × 1$1/4$" wood straps 14" o.c.; $7/8''$ gypsum plaster on wood lath.	60 psf	28 min.			7	1, 2	$1/3$
F/C-W-17	$7/8''$	As per previous F/C-W-16 but with lime plaster mix.	60 psf	41 min.			7	1, 2	$2/3$
F/C-W-18	$7/8''$	12' clear span - 2" × 9" wood joists; 18" o.c.; 2" × 1$1/2$" bridging at center; Deck: 1" T&G; Membrane: $7/8''$ gypsum plster on wood lath.	60 psf	36 min.			7	1, 2	$1/2$
F/C-W-19	$7/8''$	As per previous F/C-W-18 except with lime plaster membrane and deck is 1" nominal boards (plain edge).	60 psf	19 min.			7	1, 2	$1/4$
F/C-W-20	$7/8''$	As per F/C-W-19, except deck is 1" T&G boards.	60 psf	43 min.			7	1, 2	$2/3$
F/C-W-21	1"	12' clear span - 2" × 9" wood joists; 16" o.c.; 2" × 1$1/2$" bridging at center; Deck: 1" T&G; Membrane: $3/8''$ gypsum base board; $5/8''$ gypsum plaster.	70 psf	29 min.			7	1, 2	$1/3$
F/C-W-22	1$1/8$"	12' clear span - 2" × 9" wood joists; 16" o.c.; 2" × 2" wood bridging at center; Deck: 1" T&G; Membrane: hangers, channel with $3/8''$ gypsum baseboard affixed under $3/4''$ gypsum plaster.	60 psf	1 hr.			7	1, 2, 3	1
F/C-W-23	$3/8''$	Deck: 1" nominal lumber; Joists: 2" × 7"; 15" o.c.; Membrane: $3/8''$ plasterboard with plaster skim coat.	60 psf	11$1/2$ min.			12	2, 6	$1/6$

(Continued)

TABLE 3.3—FLOOR/CEILING ASSEMBLIES—WOOD JOIST—(Continued)

ITEM CODE	MEMBRANE THICKNESS	CONSTRUCTION DETAILS	PERFORMANCE		REFERENCE NUMBER			NOTES	REC. HOURS
			LOAD	TIME	PRE-BMS-92	BMS-92	POST-BMS-92		
F/C-W-24	$1/2''$	Deck: 1" T&G lumber; Joists: 2" × 9"; 16" o.c.; Membrane: $1/2''$ plasterboard.	60 psf	18 min.			12	2, 7	$1/4$
F/C-W-25	$1/2''$	Deck: 1" T&G lumber; Joists: 2" × 7"; 16" o.c.; Membrane: $1/2''$ fiber insulation board.	30 psf	8 min.			12	2, 8	$2/15$
F/C-W-26	$1/2''$	Deck: 1" nominal lumber; Joists: 2" × 7"; 15" o.c.; Membrane: $1/2''$ fiber insulation board.	60 psf	8 min.			12	2, 9	$2/15$
F/C-W-27	$5/8''$	Deck: 1" nominal lumber; Joists: 2" × 7"; 15" o.c.; Membrane: $5/8''$ gypsum plaster on wood lath.	60 psf	17 min.			12	2, 10	$1/4$
F/C-W-28	$5/8''$	Deck: 1" T&G lumber; Joists: 2" × 9"; 16" o.c.; Membrane: $1/2''$ fiber insulation board; $1/2''$ plaster	60 psf	20 min.			12	2, 11	$1/3$
F/C-W-29	No Membrane	Exposed wood joists.	See Note 13	15 min.		1		1, 12, 13, 14	$1/4$
F/C-W-30	$3/8''$	Gypsum wallboard: $3/8''$ or $1/2''$ with $1\ 1/2''$ No. 15 gage nails with $3/16''$ heads spaced 6" centers with asbestos paper applied with paperhangers paste and finished with casein paint.	See Note 13	25 min.		1		1, 12, 13, 14	$1/2$
F/C-W-31	$1/2''$	Gypsum wallboard: $1/2''$ with $1\ 3/4''$ No. 12 gage nails with $1/2''$ heads, 6" o.c., and finished with casein paint.	See Note 13	25 min.		1		1, 12, 13, 14	$1/2$
F/C-W-32	$1/2''$	Gypsum wallboard: $1/2''$ with $1\ 1/2''$ No. 12 gage nails with $1/2''$ heads, 18" o.c., with asbestos paper applied with paperhangers paste and secured with $1\ 1/2''$ No. 15 gage nails with $3/16''$ heads and finished with casein paint; combined nail spacing 6" o.c.	See Note 13	30 min.		1		1, 12, 13, 14	$1/2$
F/C-W-33	$3/8''$	Gypsum wallboard: two layers $3/8''$ secured with $1\ 1/2''$ No. 15 gage nails with $3/8''$ heads, 6" o.c.	See Note 13	30 min.		1		1, 12, 13, 14	$1/2$
F/C-W-34	$1/2''$	Perforated gypsum lath: $3/8''$, plastered with $1\ 1/8''$ No. 13 gage nails with $5/16''$ heads, 4" o.c.; $1/2''$ sanded gypsum plaster.	See Note 13	30 min.		1		1, 12, 13, 14	$1/2$
F/C-W-35	$1/2''$	Same as F/C-W-34, except with $1\ 1/8''$ No. 13 gage nails with $3/8''$ heads, 4" o.c.	See Note 13	45 min.		1		1, 12, 13, 14	$3/4$
F/C-W-36	$1/2''$	Perforated gypsum lath: $3/8''$, nailed with $1\ 1/8''$ No. 13 gage nails with $3/8''$ heads, 4" o.c.; joints covered with 3" strips of metal lath with $1\ 3/4''$ No. 12 nails with $1/2''$ heads, 5" o.c.; $1/2''$ sanded gypsum plaster.	See Note 13	1 hr.		1		1, 12, 13, 14	1
F/C-W-37	$1/2''$	Gypsum lath: $3/8''$ and lower layer of $3/8''$ perforated gypsum lath nailed with $1\ 3/4''$ No. 13 nails with $5/16''$ heads, 4" o.c.; $1/2''$ sanded gypsum plaster or $1/2''$ portland cement plaster.	See Note 13	45 min.		1		1, 12, 13, 14	$3/4$
F/C-W-38	$3/4''$	Metal lath: nailed with $1\ 1/4''$ No. 11 nails with $3/8''$ heads or 6d common driven 1" and bent over, 6" o.c.; $3/4''$ sanded gypsum plaster.	See Note 13	45 min.		1		1, 12, 13, 14	$3/4$
F/C-W-39	$3/4''$	Same as F/C-W-38, except nailed with $1\ 1/2''$ No. 11 barbed roof nails with $7/16''$ heads, 6" o.c.	See Note 13	1 hr.		1		1, 12, 13, 14	1
F/C-W-40	$3/4''$	Same as F/C-W-38, except with lath nailed to joists with additional supports for lath 27" o.c.; attached to alternate joists and consisting of two nails driven $1\ 1/4''$, 2" above bottom on opposite sides of the joists, one loop of No. 18 wire slipped over each nail; the ends twisted together below lath.‘	See Note 13	1 hr. 15 min.		1		1, 12, 13, 14	$1\ 1/4$

(Continued)

TABLE 3.3—FLOOR/CEILING ASSEMBLIES—WOOD JOIST—(Continued)

ITEM CODE	MEMBRANCE THICKNESS	CONSTRUCTION DETAILS	PERFORMANCE		REFERENCE NUMBER			NOTES	REC. HOURS
			LOAD	TIME	PRE-BMS-92	BMS-92	POST-BMS-92		
F/C-W-41	$3/4''$	Metal lath: nailed with $1^1/2''$ No. 11 barbed roof nails with $7/16''$ heads, 6 o.c., with $3/4''$ portland cement plaster for scratch coat and 1:3 for brown coat, 3 lbs. of asbestos fiber and 15 lbs. of hydrated lime/94 lbs. bag of cement.	See Note 13	1 hr.		1		1, 12, 13, 14	1
F/C-W-42	$3/4''$	Metal lath: nailed with 8d, No. $11^1/2$ gage barbed box nails, $2^1/2''$ driven, $1^1/4''$ on slant and bent over, 6'' o.c.; $3/4''$ sanded gypsum plaster, 1:2 for scratch coat and 1:3 for below coat.	See Note 13	1 hr.		1		1, 12, 13, 14	1

Notes:
1. Thickness indicates thickness of first membrane protection on ceiling surface.
2. Failure mode - flame thru.
3. Failure mode - collapse.
4. No endpoint reached at termination of test.
5. Failure imminent - test terminated.
6. Joist failure - 11.5 minutes; flame thru - 13.0 minutes.; collapse - 24 minutes.
7. Joist failure - 17 minutes; flame thru - 18 minutes.; collapse - 33 minutes.
8. Joist failure - 18 minutes; flame thru - 8 minutes.; collapse - 30 minutes.
9. Joist failure - 12 minutes; flame thru - 8 minutes.; collapse - 22 minutes.
10. Joist failure - 11 minutes; flame thru - 17 minutes.; collapse - 27 minutes.
11. Joist failure - 17 minutes; flame thru - 20 minutes.; collapse - 43 minutes.
12. Joists: 2-inch by 10-inch southern pine or Douglas fir; No. 1 common or better. Subfloor: $3/4$-inch wood sheating diaphragm of asbestos paper, and finish of tongue-and-groove wood flooring.
13. Loadings: not more than 1,000 psi maximum fiber stress in joists.
14. Perforations in gypsum lath are to be not less than $3/4$-inch diameter with one perforation for not more than 16/in.^{2} diameter.
15. "Distemper" is a British term for a water based paint such as white was or calcimine.

FIGURE 3.4—FLOOR/CEILING ASSEMBLIES—HOLLOW CLAY TILE WITH REINFORCED CONCRETE

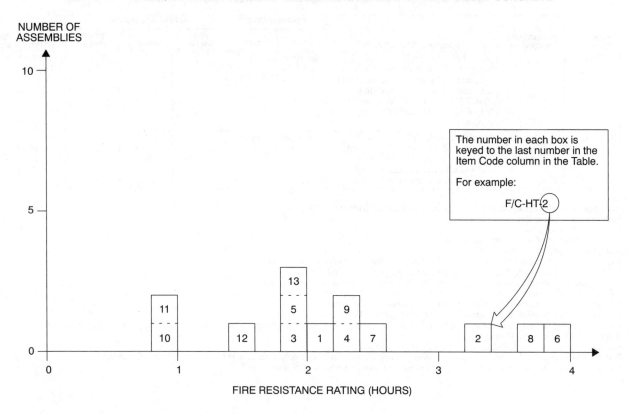

TABLE 3.4—FLOOR/CEILING ASSEMBLIES—HOLLOW CLAY TILE WITH REINFORCED CONCRETE

ITEM CODE	ASSEMBLY THICKNESS	CONSTRUCTION DETAILS	PERFORMANCE		REFERENCE NUMBER			NOTES	REC. HOURS
			LOAD	TIME	PRE-BMS-92	BMS-92	POST-BMS-92		
F/C-HT-1	6″	Cover: $1^1/_2$″ concrete (6080 psi); three cell hollow clay tiles, 12″ × 12″ × 4″; $3^1/_4$″ concrete between tiles including two $^1/_2$″ rebars with $^3/_4$″ concrete cover; $^1/_2$″ plaster cover, lower.	75 psf	2 hrs. 7 min.			7	1, 2, 3	2
F/C-HT-2	6″	Cover: $1^1/_2$″ concrete (5840 psi); three cell hollow clay tiles, 12″ × 12″ × 4″; $3^1/_4$″ concrete between tiles including two $^1/_2$″ rebars each with $^1/_2$″ concrete cover and $^5/_8$″ filler tiles between hollow tiles; $^1/_2$″ plaster cover, lower.	61 psf	3 hrs. 23 min.			7	3, 4, 6	$3^1/_3$
F/C-HT-3	6″	Cover: $1^1/_2$″ concrete (6280 psi); three cell hollow clay tiles, 12″ × 12″ × 4″; $3^1/_4$″ concrete between tiles including two $^1/_2$″ rebars with $^1/_2$″ cover; $^1/_2$″ plaster cover, lower.	122 psf	2 hrs.			7	1, 3, 5, 8	2
F/C-HT-4	6″	Cover: $1^1/_2$″ concrete (6280 psi); three cell hollow clay tiles, 12″ × 12″ × 4″; $3^1/_4$″ concrete between tiles including two $^1/_2$″ rebars with $^3/_4$″ cover; $^1/_2$″ plaster cover, lower.	115 psf	2 hrs. 23 min.			7	1, 3, 7	$2^1/_3$
F/C-HT-5	6″	Cover: $1^1/_2$″ concrete (6470 psi); three cell hollow clay tiles, 12″ × 12″ × 4″; $3^1/_4$″ concrete between tiles including two $^1/_2$″ rebars with $^1/_2$″ cover; $^1/_2$″ plaster cover, lower.	122 psf	2 hrs.			7	1, 3, 5, 8	2
F/C-HT-6	8″	Floor cover: $1^1/_2$″ gravel cement (4300 psi); three cell, 12″ × 12″ × 6″; $3^1/_2$″ space between tiles including two $^1/_2$″ rebars with 1″ cover from concrete bottom; $^1/_2$″ plaster cover, lower.	165 psf	4 hrs.			7	1, 3, 9, 10	4

(Continued)

TABLE 3.4—FLOOR/CEILING ASSEMBLIES—HOLLOW CLAY TILE WITH REINFORCED CONCRETE—(Continued)

ITEM CODE	ASSEMBLY THICKNESS	CONSTRUCTION DETAILS	PERFORMANCE		REFERENCE NUMBER			NOTES	REC. HOURS
			LOAD	TIME	PRE-BMS-92	BMS-92	POST-BMS-92		
F/C-HT-7	9″ (nom.)	Deck: $^7/_8$″ T&G on 2″ × $1^1/_2$″ bottoms (18″ o.c.) $1^1/_2$″ concrete cover (4600 psi); three cell hollow clay tiles, 12″ × 12″ × 4″; 3″ concrete between tiles including one $^3/_4$″ rebar $^3/_4$″ from tile bottom; $^1/_2$″ plaster cover.	95 psf	2 hrs. 26 min.			7	4, 11, 12, 13	$2^1/_3$
F/C-HT-8	9″ (nom.)	Deck: $^7/_8$″ T&G on 2″ × $1^1/_2$″ bottoms (18″ o.c.) $1^1/_2$″ concrete cover (3850 psi); three cell hollow clay tiles, 12″ × 12″ × 4″; 3″ concrete between tiles including one $^3/_4$″ rebar $^3/_4$″ from tile bottoms; $^1/_2$″ plaster cover.	95 psf	3 hrs. 28 min.			7	4, 11, 12, 13	
F/C-HT-9	9″ (nom.)	Deck: $^7/_8$″ T&G on 2″ × $1^1/_2$″ bottoms (18″ o.c.) $1^1/_2$″ concrete cover (4200 psi); three cell hollow clay tiles, 12″ × 12″ × 4″; 3″ concrete between tiles including one $^3/_4$″ rebar $^3/_4$″ from tile bottoms; $^1/_2$″ plaster cover.	95 psf	2 hrs. 14 min.			7	3, 5, 8, 11	
F/C-HT-10	$5^1/_2$″	Fire clay tile (4″ thick); $1^1/_2$″ concrete cover; for general details, see Note 15.	See Note 14	1 hr.			43	15	1
F/C-HT-11	8″	Fire clay tile (6″ thick); 2″ cover.	See Note 14	1 hr.			43	15	1
F/C-HT-12	$5^1/_2$″	Fire clay tile (4″ thick); $1^1/_2$″ cover; $^5/_8$″ gypsum plaster, lower.	See Note 14	1 hr. 30 min.			43	15	$1^1/_2$
F/C-HT-13	8″	Fire clay tile (6″ thick); 2″ cover; $^5/_8$″ gypsum plaster, lower.	See Note 14	2 hrs.			43	15	$1^1/_2$

Notes:

1. A generalized cross section of this floor type follows:

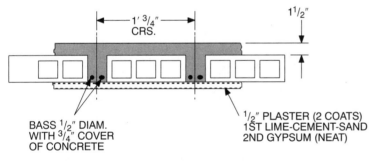

2. Failure mode - structural.
3. Plaster: base coat - lime-cement-sand; top coat - gypsum (neat).
4. Failure mode - collapse.
5. Test stopped before any endpoints were reached.
6. A generalized cross section of this floor type follows:

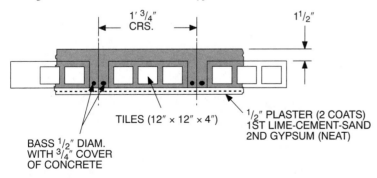

7. Failure mode - thermal - back face temperature rise.
8. Passed hose stream test.
9. Failed hose stream test.
10. Test stopped at 4 hours before any endpoints were reached.
11. A generalized cross section of this floor type follows:

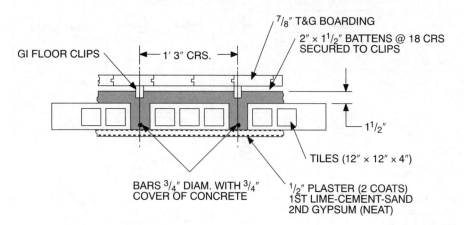

12. Plaster: base coat - retarded hemihydrate gypsum-sand; second coat - neat gypsum.
13. Concrete in Item 7 is P.C. based but with crushed brick aggregates while in Item 8 river sand and river gravels are used with the P.C.
14. Load - unspecified.
15. The 12-inch by 12-inch fire-clay tiles were laid end to end in rows spaced $2^1/_2$ inches or 4 inches apart. The reinforcing steel was placed between these rows and the concrete cast around them and over the tile to form the structural floor.

SECTION IV—BEAMS

TABLE 4.1.1—REINFORCED CONCRETE BEAMS
DEPTH 10″ TO LESS THAN 12″

| ITEM CODE | DEPTH | CONSTRUCTION DETAILS | PERFORMANCE | | REFERENCE NUMBER | | | NOTES | REC. HOURS |
			LOAD	TIME	PRE-BMS-92	BMS-92	POST-BMS-92		
B-11-RC-1	11″	24″ wide × 11″ deep reinforced concrete "T" beam (3290 psi); Details: see Note 5 figure.	8.8 tons	4 hrs. 2 min.			7	1, 2, 14	4
B-10-RC-2	10″	24″ wide × 10″ deep reinforced concrete "T" beam (4370 psi); Details: see Note 6 figure.	8.8 tons	1 hr. 53 min.			7	1, 3	$1^3/_4$
B-10-RC-3	$10^1/_2$″	24″ wide × $10^1/_2$″ deep reinforced concrete "T" beam (4450 psi); Details: see Note 7 figure.	8.8 tons	2 hrs. 40 min.			7	1, 3	$2^2/_3$
B-11-RC-4	11″	24″ wide × 11″ deep reinforced concrete "T" beam (2400 psi); Details: see Note 8 figure.	8.8 tons	3 hrs. 32 min.			7	1, 3, 14	$3^1/_2$
B-11-RC-5	11″	24″ wide × 11″ deep reinforced concrete "T" beam (4250 psi); Details: see Note 9 figure.	8.8 tons	3 hrs. 3 min.			7	1, 3, 14	3
B-11-RC-6	11″	Concrete flange: 4″ deep × 2′ wide (4895 psi) concrete; Concrete beam: 7″ deep × $6^1/_2$″ wide beam; "I" beam reinforcement; 10″ × $4^1/_2$″ × 25 lbs. R.S.J.; 1″ cover on flanges; Flange reinforcement: $3/_8$″ diameter bars at 6″ pitch parallel to "T"; $1/_4$″ diameter bars perpendicular to "T"; Beam reinforcement: 4″ × 6″ wire mesh No. 13 SWG; Span: 11′ restrained; Details: see Note 10 figure.	10 tons	6 hrs.			7	1, 4	6
B-11-RC-7	11″	Concrete flange: 6″ deep × 1′$6^1/_2$″ wide (3525 psi) concrete; Concrete beam: 5″ deep × 8″ wide precast concrete blocks $8^3/_4$″ long; "I" beam reinforcement; 7″ × 4″ x 16 lbs. R.S.J.; 2″ cover on bottom; $1^1/_2$″ cover on top; Flange reinforcement: two rows $1/_2$″ diameter rods parallel to "T"; Beam reinforcement: $1/_8$″ wire mesh perpendicular to 1″; Span: 1′3″ simply supported; Details: see Note 11 figure.	3.9 tons	4 hrs.			7	1, 2	4
B-11-RC-8	11″	Concrete flange: 4″ deep × 2′ wide (3525 psi) concrete; Concrete beam 7″ deep × $4^1/_2$″ wide; (scaled from drawing); "I" beam reinforcement; 10″ × $4^1/_2$″ × 25 lbs. R.S.J.; no concrete cover on bottom; Flange reinforcement: $3/_8$″ diameter bars at 6 pitch parallel to "T"; $1/_4$″ diameter bars perpendicular to "T"; Span: 11′ restricted.	10 tons	4 hrs.			7	1, 2, 12	4
B-11-RC-9	$11^1/_2$″	24″ wide × $11^1/_2$″ deep reinforced concrete "T" beam (4390 psi); Details: see Note 12 figure.	8.8 tons	3 hrs. 24 min.			7	1, 3	$3^1/_3$

Notes:
1. Load concentrated at mid span.
2. Achieved 4 hour performance (Class "B," British).
3. Failure mode - collapse.
4. Achieved 6 hour performance (Class "A," British).
5.

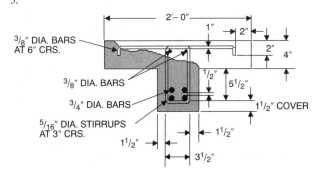

6.

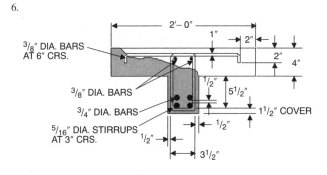

7.

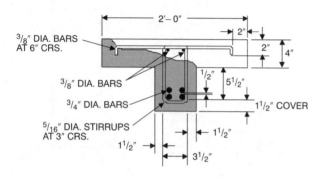

8.

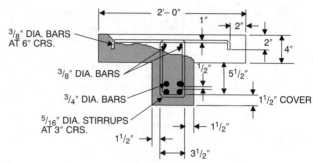

9.

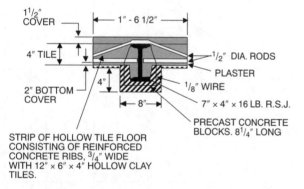

10.

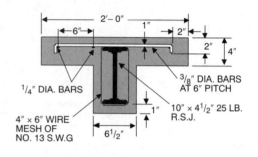

11.

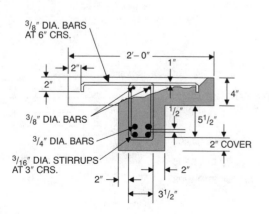

STRIP OF HOLLOW TILE FLOOR
CONSISTING OF REINFORCED
CONCRETE RIBS, 3/4″ WIDE
WITH 12″ × 6″ × 4″ HOLLOW CLAY
TILES.

SPAN AND END CONDITIONS:–10′–3″ (CLEAR). SIMPLY
SUPPORTED.

12.

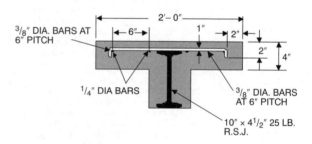

13.

14.

The different performances achieved by B-11-RC-1, B-11-RC-4 and
B-11-RC-5 are attributable to differences in concrete aggregate
compositions reported in the source document but unreported in this
table. This demonstrates the significance of material composition in
addition to other details.

TABLE 4.1.2—REINFORCED CONCRETE BEAMS
DEPTH 12″ TO LESS THAN 14″

ITEM CODE	DEPTH	CONSTRUCTION DETAILS	PERFORMANCE		REFERENCE NUMBER			NOTES	REC. HOURS
			LOAD	TIME	PRE-BMS-92	BMS-92	POST-BMS-92		
B-12-RC-1	12″	12″ × 8″ section; 4160 psi aggregate concrete; Reinforcement: 4-⅞″ rebars at corners; 1″ below each surface; ¼″ stirrups 10″ o.c.	5.5 tons	2 hrs.			7	1	2
B-12-RC-2	12″	Concrete flange: 4″ deep × 2′ wide (3045 psi) concrete at 35 days; Concrete beam: 8″ deep; "I" beam reinforcement: 10″ × 4½″ × 25 lbs. R.S.J.; 1″ cover on flanges; Flange reinforcement: ⅜″ diameter bars at 6″ pitch parallel to "T"; ¼″ diameter bars perpendicular to "T"; Beam reinforcement: 4″ × 6″ wire mesh No. 13 SWG; Span: 10′ 3″ simply supported.	10 tons	4 hrs.			7	2, 3, 5	4
B-13-RC-3	13″	Concrete flange: 4″ deep × 2′ wide (3825 psi) concrete at 46 days; Concrete beam: 9″ deep × 8½″ wide; (scaled from drawing); "I" beam reinforcement: 10″ × 4½″ × 25 lbs. R.S.J.; 3″ cover on bottom flange; 1″ cover on top flange; Flange reinforcement: ⅜″ diameter bars at 6″ pitch parallel to "T"; ¼″ diameter bars perpendicular to "T"; Beam reinforcement: 4″ × 6″ wire mesh No. 13 SWG; Span: 11′ restrained.	10 tons	6 hrs.			7	2, 3, 6, 8, 9	4
B-12-RC-4	12″	Concrete flange: 4″ deep × 2′ wide (3720 psi) concrete at 42 days; Concrete beam: 8″ deep × 8½″ wide; (scaled from drawing); "I" beam reinforcement: 10″ × 4½″ × 25 lbs. R.S.J.; 2″ cover bottom flange; 1″ cover top flange; Flange reinforcement: ⅜″ diameter bars at 6″ pitch parallel to "T"; ¼″ diameter bars perpendicular to "T"; Beam reinforcement: 4″ × 6″ wire mesh No. 13 SWG; Span: 11′ restrained.	10 tons	6 hrs.			7	2, 3, 4, 7, 8, 9 1	4

Notes:
1. Qualified for 2 hour use. (Grade "C," British) Test included hose stream and reload at 48 hours.
2. Load concentrated at mid span.
3. British test.
4. British test - qualified for 6 hour use (Grade "A").
5.

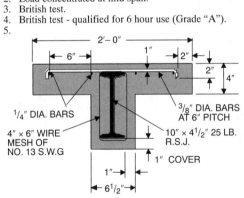

6.

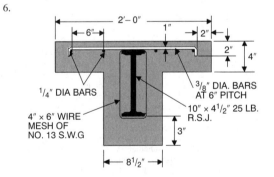

7.

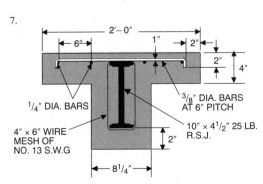

8. See Table 4.1.3, Note 5.

9. Hourly rating based upon B-12-RC-2 above.

TABLE 4.1.3—REINFORCED CONCRETE BEAMS
DEPTH 14″ TO LESS THAN 16″

ITEM CODE	DEPTH	CONSTRUCTION DETAILS	PERFORMANCE		REFERENCE NUMBER			NOTES	REC. HOURS
			LOAD	TIME	PRE-BMS-92	BMS-92	POST-BMS-92		
B-15-RC-1	15″	Concrete flange: 4″ deep × 2′ wide (3290 psi) concrete; Concrete beam: 10″ deep x 8¹/₂″ wide; "I" beam reinforcement: 10″ × 4¹/₂″ × 25 lbs. R.S.J.; 4″ cover on bottom flange; 1″ cover on top flange; Flange reinforcement: ³/₈″ diameter bars at 6″ pitch parallel to "T"; ¹/₄″ diameter bars perpendicular to "T"; Beam reinforcement: 4″ × 6″ wire mesh No. 13 SWG; Span: 11′ restrained.	10 tons	6 hrs.			7	1, 2, 3, 5, 6	4
B-15-RC-2	15″	Concrete flange: 4″ deep × 2′ wide (4820 psi) concrete; Concrete beam: 10″ deep × 8¹/₂″ wide; "I" beam reinforcement: 10″ × 4¹/₂″ × 25 lbs. R.S.J.; 1″ cover over wire mesh on bottom flange; 1″ cover on top flange; Flange reinforcement: ³/₈″ diameter bars at 6″ pitch parallel to "T"; ¹/₄″ diameter bars perpendicular to "T"; Beam reinforcement: 4″ × 6″ wire mesh No. 13 SWG; Span: 11′ restrained.	10 tons	6 hrs.			7	1, 2, 4, 5, 6	4

Notes:
1. Load concentrated at mid span.
2. Achieved 6 hour fire rating (Grade "A," British).
3.

4.

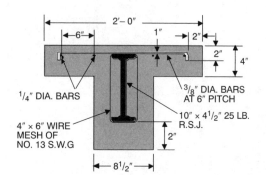

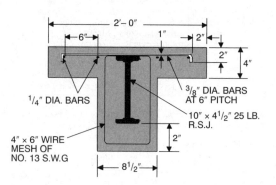

5. Section 43.147 of the 1979 edition of the *Uniform Building Code Standards* provides:
   "A restrained condition in fire tests, as used in this standard, is one in which expansion at the supports of a load-carrying element resulting from the effects of the fire is resisted by forces external to the element. An unrestrained condition is one in which the load-carrying element is free to expand and rotate at its support.
   "(R)estraint in buildings is defined as follows: Floor and roof assemblies and individual beams in buildings shall be considered restrained when the surrounding or supporting structure is capable of resisting the thermal expansion throughout the range of anticipated elevated temperatures. Construction not complying . . . is assumed to be free to rotate and expand and shall be considered as unrestrained.
   "Restraint may be provided by the lateral stiffness of supports for floor and roof assemblies and intermediate beams forming part of the assembly. In order to develop restraint, connections must adequately transfer thermal thrusts to such supports. The rigidity of adjoining panels or structures shall be considered in assessing the capability of a structure to resist therm expansion."
   Because it is difficult to determine whether an existing building's structural system is capable of providing the required restraint, the lower hourly ratings of a similar but unrestrained assembly have been recommended.
6. Hourly rating based upon Table 4.2.1, Item B-12-RC-2.

TABLE 4.2.1—REINFORCED CONCRETE BEAMS—UNPROTECTED
DEPTH 10″ TO LESS THAN 12″

ITEM CODE	DEPTH	CONSTRUCTION DETAILS	PERFORMANCE		REFERENCE NUMBER			NOTES	REC. HOURS
			LOAD	TIME	PRE-BMS-92	BMS-92	POST-BMS-92		
B-SU-1	10″	10″ × 4¹/₂″ × 25 lbs. "I" beam.	10 tons	39 min.			7	1	¹/₃

Notes:
1. Concentrated at mid span.

TABLE 4.2.2—STEEL BEAMS—CONCRETE PROTECTION
DEPTH 10″ TO LESS THAN 12″

ITEM CODE	DEPTH	CONSTRUCTION DETAILS	PERFORMANCE		REFERENCE NUMBER			NOTES	REC. HOURS
			LOAD	TIME	PRE-BMS-92	BMS-92	POST-BMS-92		
B-SC-1	10″	10″ × 8″ rectangle; aggregate concrete (4170 psi) with 1″ top cover and 2″ bottom cover; No. 13 SWG iron wire loosely wrapped at approximately 6″ pitch about 7″ × 4″ × 16 lbs. "I" beam.	3.9 tons	3 hrs. 46 min.			7	1, 2, 3	3³/₄
B-SC-2	10″	10″ × 8″ rectangle; aggregate concrete (3630 psi) with 1″ top cover and 2″ bottom cover; No. 13 SWG iron wire loosely wrapped at approximately 6″ pitch about 7″ × 4″ × 16 lbs. "I" beam.	5.5 tons	5 hrs. 26 min.			7	1, 4, 5, 6, 7	3³/₄

Notes:
1. Load concentrated at mid span.
2. Specimen 10-foot 3-inch clear span simply supported.
3. Passed Grade "C" fire resistance (British) including hose stream and reload.
4. Specimen 11-foot clear span - restrained.
5. Passed Grade "B" fire resistance (British) including hose stream and reload.
6. See Table 4.1.3, Note 5.
7. Hourly rating based upon B-SC-1 above.

SECTION V—DOORS

FIGURE 5.1—RESISTANCE OF DOORS TO FIRE EXPOSURE

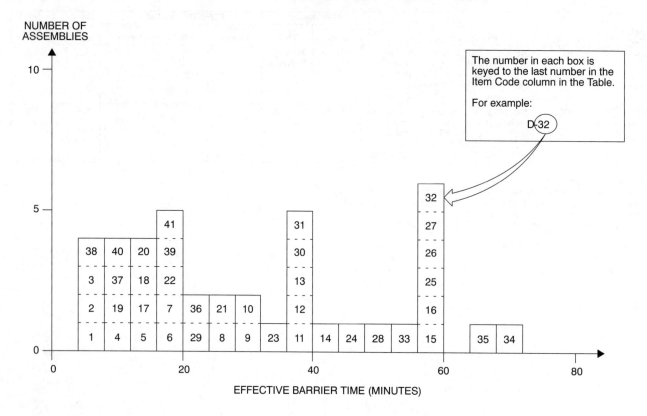

TABLE 5.1—RESISTANCE OF DOORS TO FIRE EXPOSURE

ITEM CODE	DOOR MINIMUM THICKNESS	CONSTRUCTION DETAILS	PERFORMANCE		REFERENCE NUMBER			NOTES	REC. (MIN.)
			EFFECTIVE BARRIER	EDGE FLAMING	PRE-BMS-92	BMS-92	POST-BMS-92		
D-1	$^3/_8''$	Panel door; pine perimeter ($1^3/_8''$); painted (enamel).	5 min. 10 sec.	N/A			90	1, 2	5
D-2	$^3/_8''$	As above, with two coats U.L. listed intumescent coating.	5 min. 30 sec.	5 min.			90	1, 2, 7	5
D-3	$^3/_8''$	As D-1, with standard primer and flat interior paint.	5 min. 55 sec.	N/A			90	1, 3, 4	5
D-4	$2^5/_8''$	As D-1, with panels covered each side with $^1/_2''$ plywood; edge grouted with sawdust filled plaster; door faced with $^1/_8''$ hardboard each side; paint see (5).	11 min. 15 sec.	3 min. 45 sec.			90	1, 2, 5, 7	10
D-5	$^3/_8''$	As D-1, except surface protected with glass fiber reinforced intumescent fire retardant coating.	16 min.	N/A			90	1, 3, 4, 7	15
D-6	$1^5/_8''$	Door detail: As D-4, except with $^1/_8''$ cement asbestos board facings with aluminum foil; door edges protected by sheet metal.	17 min.	10 min. 15 sec.			90	1, 3, 4	15
D-7	$1^5/_8''$	Door detail with $^1/_8''$ hardboard cover each side as facings; glass fiber reinforced intumescent coating applied.	20 min.	N/A			90	1, 3, 4, 7	20
D-8	$1^5/_8''$	Door detail same as D-4; paint was glass reinforced epoxy intumescent.	26 min.	24 min. 45 sec.			90	1, 3, 4, 6, 7	25
D-9	$1^5/_8''$	Door detail same as D-4 with facings of $^1/_8''$ cement asbestos board.	29 min.	3 min. 15 sec.			90	1, 2	5
D-10	$1^5/_8''$	As per D-9.	31 min. 30 sec.	7 min. 20 sec.			90	1, 3, 4	6
D-11	$1^5/_8''$	As per D-7; painted with epoxy intumescent coating including glass fiber roving.	36 min. 25 sec.	N/A			90	1, 3, 4	35

(Continued)

TABLE 5.1—RESISTANCE OF DOORS TO FIRE EXPOSURE—(Continued)

ITEM CODE	DOOR MINIMUM THICKNESS	CONSTRUCTION DETAILS	PERFORMANCE		REFERENCE NUMBER			NOTES	REC. (MIN.)
			EFFECTIVE BARRIER	EDGE FLAMING	PRE-BMS-92	BMS-92	POST-BMS-92		
D-12	$1^5/_8''$	As per D-4 with intumescent fire retardant paint.	37 min. 30 sec.	24 min. 40 sec.			90	1, 3, 4	30
D-13	$1^1/_2''$ (nom.)	As per D-4, except with 24 ga. galvanized sheet metal facings.	39 min.	39 min.			90	1, 3, 4	39
D-14	$1^5/_8''$	As per D-9.	41 min. 30 sec.	17 min. 20 sec.			90	1, 3, 4, 6	20
D-15	—	Class C steel fire door.	60 min.	58 min.			90	7, 8	60
D-16	—	Class B steel fire door.	60 min.	57 min.			90	7, 8	60
D-17	$1^3/_4''$	Solid core flush door; core staves laminated to facings but not each other; Birch plywood facings $1/_2''$ rebate in door frame for door; $3/_{32}''$ clearance between door and wood frame.	15 min.	13 min.			37	11	13
D-18	$1^3/_4''$	As per D-17.	14 min.	13 min.			37	11	13
D-19	$1^3/_4''$	Door same as D-17, except with 16 ga. steel; $3/_{32}''$ door frame clearance.	12 min.	—			37	9, 11	10
D-20	$1^3/_4''$	As per D-19.	16 min.	—			37	10, 11	10
D-21	$1^3/_4''$	Doors as per D-17; intumescent paint applied to top and side edges.	26 min.	—			37	11	25
D-22	$1^3/_4''$	Door as per D-17, except with $1/_2'' \times 1/_8''$ steel strip set into edges of door at top and side facing stops; matching strip on stop.	18 min.	6 min.			37	11	18
D-23	$1^3/_4''$	Solid oak door.	36 min	22 min.			15	13	25
D-24	$1^7/_8''$	Solid oak door.	45 min.	35 min.			15	13	35
D-25	$1^7/_8''$	Solid teak door.	58 min.	34 min.			15	13	35
D-26	$1^7/_8''$	Solid (pitch) pine door.	57 min.	36 min.			15	13	35
D-27	$1^7/_8''$	Solid deal (pine) door.	57 min.	30 min.			15	13	30
D-28	$1^7/_8''$	Solid mahogany door.	49 min.	40 min.			15	13	45
D-29	$1^7/_8''$	Solid poplar door.	24 min.	3 min.			15	13, 14	5
D-30	$1^7/_8''$	Solid oak door.	40 min.	33 min.			15	13	35
D-31	$1^7/_8''$	Solid walnut door.	40 min.	15 min.			15	13	20
D-32	$2^5/_8''$	Solid Quebec pine.	60 min.	60 min.			15	13	60
D-33	$2^5/_8''$	Solid pine door.	55 min.	39 min.			15	13	40
D-34	$2^5/_8''$	Solid oak door.	69 min.	60 min.			15	13	60
D-35	$2^5/_8''$	Solid teak door.	65 min.	17 min.			15	13	60
D-36	$1^1/_2''$	Solid softwood door.	23 min.	8.5 min.			15	13	10
D-37	$3/_4''$	Panel door.	8 min.	7.5 min.			15	13	5
D-38	$5/_{16}''$	Panel door.	5 min.	5 min.			15	13	5
D-39	$3/_4''$	Panel door, fire retardant treated.	$17^1/_2$ min.	13 min.			15	13	8
D-40	$3/_4''$	Panel door, fire retardant treated.	$8^1/_2$ min.	$8^1/_2$ min.			15	13	8
D-41	$3/_4''$	Panel door, fire retardant treated.	$16^3/_4$ min.	$11^1/_2$ min.			15	13	8

Notes:
1. All door frames were of standard lumber construction.
2. Wood door stop protected by asbestos millboard.
3. Wood door stop protected by sheet metal.
4. Door frame protected with sheet metal and weather strip.
5. Surface painted with intumescent coating.
6. Door edge sheet metal protected.
7. Door edge intumescent paint protected.
8. Formal steel frame and door stop.
9. Door opened into furnace at 12 feet.
10. Similar door opened into furnace at 12 feet.
11. The doors reported in these tests represent the type contemporaries used as 20-minute solid-core wood doors. The test results demonstrate the necessity of having wall anchored metal frames, minimum cleaners possible between door, frame and stops. They also indicate the utility of long throw latches and the possible use of intumescent paints to seal doors to frames in event of a fire.
12. Minimum working clearance and good latch closure are absolute necessities for effective containment for all such working door assemblies.
13. Based on British tests.
14. Failure at door - frame interface.

Bibliography

1. Central Housing Committee on Research, Design, and Construction; Subcommittee on Fire Resistance Classifications, "Fire-Resistance Classifications of Building Constructions," <u>Building Materials and Structures</u>, Report BMS 92, National Bureau of Standards, Washington, Oct. 1942. (Available from NTIS No. COM-73-10974)

2. Foster, H. D., Pinkston, E. R., and Ingberg, S. H., "Fire Resistance of Structural Clay Tile Partitions," <u>Building Materials and Structures</u>, Report BMS 113, National Bureau of Standards, Washington, Oct. 1948.

3. Ryan, J. V., and Bender, E. W., "Fire Endurance of Open-Web Steel-Joist Floors with Concrete Slabs and Gypsum Ceilings," <u>Building Materials and Structures</u>, Report BMS 141, National Bureau of Standards, Washington, Aug. 1954.

4. Mitchell, N. D., "Fire Tests of Wood-Framed Walls and Partitions with Asbestos-Cement Facings," <u>Building Materials and Structures</u>, Report BMS 123, National Bureau of Standards, Washington, May 1951.

5. Robinson, H. E., Cosgrove, L. A., and Powell, F. J., "Thermal Resistance of Airspace and Fibrous Insulations Bounded by Reflective Surfaces," <u>Building Materials and Structures</u>, Report BMS 151, National Bureau of Standards, Washington, Nov. 1957.

6. Shoub, H., and Ingberg, S. H., "Fire Resistance of Steel Deck Floor Assemblies," <u>Building Science Series</u>, 11, National Bureau of Standards, Washington, Dec. 1967.

7. Davey, N., and Ashton, L. A., "Investigations on Building Fires, Part V: Fire Tests of Structural Elements," <u>National Building Studies</u>, Research Paper, No. 12, Dept. of Scientific and Industrial Research (Building Research Station), London, 1953.

8. National Board of Fire Underwriters, <u>Fire Resistance Ratings of Beam, Girder, and Truss Protections, Ceiling Constructions, Column Protections, Floor and Ceiling Constructions, Roof Constructions, Walls and Partitions</u>, New York, April 1959.

9. Mitchell, N. D., Bender, E. D., and Ryan, J. V., "Fire Resistance of Shutters for Moving-Stairway Openings," <u>Building Materials and Structures</u>, Report BMS 129, National Bureau of Standards, Washington, March 1952.

10. National Board of Fire Underwriters, <u>National Building Code; an Ordinance Providing for Fire Limits, and Regulations Governing the Construction, Alteration, Equipment, or Removal of Buildings or Structures</u>, New York, 1949.

11. Department of Scientific and Industrial Research and of the Fire Offices' Committee, Joint Committee of the Building Research Board, "Fire Gradings of Buildings, Part I: General Principles and Structural Precautions," <u>Post-War Building Studies</u>, No. 20, Ministry of Works, London, 1946.

12. Lawson, D. I., Webster, C. T., and Ashton, L. A., "Fire Endurance of Timber Beams and Floors," <u>National Building Studies</u>, Bulletin, No. 13, Dept. of Scientific and Industrial Research and Fire Offices' Committee (Joint Fire Research Organization), London, 1951.

13. Parker, T. W., Nurse, R. W., and Bessey, G. E., "Investigations on Building Fires. Part I: The Estimation of the Maximum Temperature Attained in Building Fires from Examination of the Debris, and Part II: The Visible Change in Concrete or Mortar Exposed to High Temperatures," <u>National Building Studies</u>, Technical Paper, No. 4, Dept. of Scientific and Industrial Research (Building Research Station), London, 1950.

14. Bevan, R. C., and Webster, C. T., "Investigations on Building Fires, Part III: Radiation from Building Fires," <u>National Building Studies</u>, Technical Paper, No. 5, Dept. of Scientific and Industrial Research (Building Research Station), London, 1950.

15. Webster, D. J., and Ashton, L. A., "Investigations on Building Fires, Part IV: Fire Resistance of Timber Doors," <u>National Building Studies</u>, Technical Paper, No. 6, Dept. of Scientific and Industrial Research (Building Research Station), London, 1951.

16. Kidder, F. E., <u>Architects' and Builders' Handbook: Data for Architects, Structural Engineers, Contractors, and Draughtsmen</u>, comp. by a Staff of Specialists and H. Parker, editor-in-chief, 18th ed., enl., J. Wiley, New York, 1936.

17. Parker, H., Gay, C. M., and MacGuire, J. W., <u>Materials and Methods of Architectural Construction</u>, 3rd ed., J. Wiley, New York, 1958.

18. Diets, A. G. H., <u>Dwelling House Construction</u>, The MIT Press, Cambridge, 1971.

19. Crosby, E. U., and Fiske, H. A., <u>Handbook of Fire Protection</u>, 5th ed., The Insurance Field Company, Louisville, Ky., 1914.

20. Crosby, E. U., Fiske, H. A., and Forster, H. W., <u>Handbook of Fire Protection</u>, 8th ed., R. S. Moulton, general editor, National Fire Protection Association, Boston, 1936.

21. Kidder, F. E., <u>Building Construction and Superintendence</u>, rev. and enl., by T. Nolan, W. T. Comstock, New York, 1909-1913, 2 vols.

22. National Fire Protection Association, Committee on Fire-Resistive Construction, <u>The Baltimore Conflagration</u>, 2nd ed., Chicago, 1904.

23. Przetak, L., <u>Standard Details for Fire-Resistive Building Construction</u>, McGraw-Hill Book Co., New York, 1977.

24. Hird, D., and Fischl, C. F., "Fire Hazard of Internal Linings," <u>National Building Studies</u>, Special Report, No. 22, Dept. of Scientific and Industrial Research and Fire Offices' Committee (Joint Fire Research Organization), London, 1954.

25. Menzel, C. A., <u>Tests of the Fire-Resistance and Strength of Walls Concrete Masonry Units</u>, Portland Cement Association, Chicago, 1934.

26. Hamilton, S. B., "A Short History of the Structural Fire Protection of Buildings Particularly in England," <u>National Building Studies</u>, Special Report, No. 27, Dept. of Scientific and Industrial Research (Building Research Station), London, 1958.

27. Sachs, E. O., and Marsland, E., "The Fire Resistance of Doors and Shutters being Tabulated Results of Fire Tests Conducted by the Committee," <u>Journal of the British Fire Prevention Committee</u>, No. VII, London, 1912.

28. Egan, M. D., <u>Concepts in Building Firesafety</u>, J. Wiley, New York, 1978.

29. Sachs, E. O., and Marsland, E., "The Fire Resistance of Floors being Tabulated Results of Fire Tests Conducted by the Committee," <u>Journal of the British Fire Prevention Committee</u>, No. VI, London, 1911.

30. Sachs, E. O., and Marsland, E., "The Fire Resistance of Partitions being Tabulated Results of Fire Tests Conducted by the Committee," <u>Journal of the British Fire Prevention Committee</u>, No. IX, London, 1914.

31. Ryan, J. V., and Bender, E. W., "Fire Tests of Precast Cellular Concrete Floors and Roofs," <u>National Bureau of Standards Monograph</u>, 45, Washington, April 1962.

32. Kingberg, S. H., and Foster, H. D., "Fire Resistance of Hollow Load-Bearing Wall Tile," <u>National Bureau of Standards</u> Research Paper, No. 37, (Reprint from <u>NBS Journal of Research</u>, Vol. 2) Washington, 1929.

33. Hull, W. A., and Ingberg, S. H., "Fire Resistance of Concrete Columns," <u>Technologic Papers of the Bureau of Standards</u>, No. 272, Vol. 18, Washington, 1925, pp. 635-708.

34. National Board of Fire Underwriters, <u>Fire Resistance Ratings of Less than One Hour</u>, New York, Aug. 1956.

35. Harmathy, T. Z., "Ten Rules of Fire Endurance Rating," <u>Fire Technology</u>, Vol. 1, May 1965, pp. 93-102.

36. Son, B. C., "Fire Endurance Test on a Steel Tubular Column Protected with Gypsum Board," <u>National Bureau of Standards</u>, NBSIR, 73-165, Washington, 1973.

37. Galbreath, M., "Fire Tests of Wood Door Assemblies," <u>Fire Study</u>, No. 36, Div. of Building Research, National Research Council Canada, Ottawa, May 1975.

38. Morris, W. A., "An Investigation into the Fire Resistance of Timber Doors," <u>Fire Research Note</u>, No. 855, Fire Research Station, Boreham Wood, Jan. 1971.

39. Hall, G. S., "Fire Resistance Tests of Laminated Timber Beams," <u>Timber Association Research Report</u>, WR/RR/1, High Sycombe, July 1968.

40. Goalwin, D. S., "Fire Resistance of Concrete Floors," <u>Building Materials and Structures</u>, Report BMS 134, National Bureau of Standards, Washington, Dec. 1952.

41. Mitchell, N. D., and Ryan, J. V., "Fire Tests of Steel Columns Encased with Gypsum Lath and Plaster," <u>Building Materials and Structures</u>, Report BMS 135, National Bureau of Standards, Washington, April 1953.

42. Ingberg, S. H., "Fire Tests of Brick Walls," <u>Building Materials and Structures</u>, Report BMS 143, National Bureau of Standards, Washington, Nov. 1954.

43. National Bureau of Standards, "Fire Resistance and Sound-Insulation Ratings for Walls, Partitions, and Floors," <u>Technical Report on Building Materials</u>, 44, Washington, 195X.

44. Malhotra, H. L., "Fire Resistance of Brick and Block Walls," <u>Fire Note</u>, No. 6, Ministry of Technology and Fire Offices' Committee Joint Fire Research Organization, London, HMSO, 1966.

45. Mitchell, N. D., "Fire Tests of Steel Columns Protected with Siliceous Aggregate Concrete," <u>Building Materials and Structures</u>, Report BMS 124, National Bureau of Standards, Washington, May 1951.

46. Freitag, J. K., <u>Fire Prevention and Fire Protection as Applied to Building Construction; a Handbook of Theory and Practice</u>, 2nd ed., J. Wiley, New York, 1921.

47. Ingberg, S. H., and Mitchell, N. D., "Fire Tests of Wood and Metal-Framed Partition," <u>Building Materials and Structures</u>, Report BMS 71, National Bureau of Standards, Washington, 1941.

48. Central Housing Committee on Research, Design, and Construction, Subcommittee on Definitions, "A Glossary of Housing Terms," <u>Building Materials and Structures</u>, Report BMS 91, National Bureau of Standards, Washington, Sept. 1942.

49. Crosby, E. U., Fiske, H. A., and Forster, H. W., <u>Handbook of Fire Protection</u>, 7th ed., D. Van Nostrand Co., New York 1924.

50. Bird, E. L., and Docking, S. J., <u>Fire in Buildings</u>, A. & C. Black, London, 1949.

51. American Institute of Steel Construction, <u>Fire Resistant Construction in Modern Steel-Framed Buildings</u>, New York, 1959.

52. Central Dockyard Laboratory, "Fire Retardant Paint Tests - a Critical Review," <u>CDL Technical Memorandum</u>, No. P87/73, H. M. Naval Base, Portsmouth, Dec. 1973.

53. Malhotra, H. L., "Fire Resistance of Structural Concrete Beams," Fire Research Note, No. 741, Fire Research Station, Borehamwood, May 1969.

54. Abrams, M. S., and Gustaferro, A. H., "Fire Tests of Poke-Thru Assemblies," Research and Development Bulletin, 1481-1, Portland Cement Association, Skokie, 1971.

55. Bullen, M. L., "A Note on the Relationship between Scale Fire Experiments and Standard Test Results," Building Research Establishment Note, N51/75, Borehamwood, May 1975.

56. The America Fore Group of Insurance Companies, Research Department, Some Characteristic Fires in Fire Resistive Buildings, Selected from twenty years record in the files of the N.F.P.A. "Quarterly," New York, c. 1933.

57. Spiegelhalter, F., "Guide to Design of Cavity Barriers and Fire Stops," Current Paper, CP 7/77, Building Research Establishment, Borehamwood, Feb. 1977.

58. Wardle, T. M. "Notes on the Fire Resistance of Heavy Timber Construction," Information Series, No. 53, New Zealand Forest Service, Wellington, 1966.

59. Fisher, R. W., and Smart, P. M. T., "Results of Fire Resistance Tests on Elements of Building Construction," Building Research Establishment Report, G R6, London, HMSO, 1975.

60. Serex, E. R., "Fire Resistance of Alta Bates Gypsum Block Non-Load Bearing Wall," Report to Alta Bates Community Hospital, Structural Research Laboratory Report, ES-7000, University of Calif., Berkeley, 1969.

61. Thomas, F. G., and Webster, C. T., "Investigations on Building Fires, Part VI: The Fire Resistance of Reinforced Concrete Columns," National Building Studies, Research Paper, No. 18, Dept. of Scientific and Industrial Research (Building Research Station), London, HMSO, 1953.

62. Building Research Establishment, "Timber Fire Doors," Digest, 220, Borehamwood, Nov. 1978.

63. Massachusetts State Building Code; Recommended Provisions, Article 22: Repairs, Alterations, Additions, and Change of Use of Existing Buildings, Boston, Oct. 23, 1978.

64. Freitag, J. K., Architectural Engineering; with Especial Reference to High Building Construction, Including Many Examples of Prominent Office Buildings, 2nd ed., rewritten, J. Wiley, New York, 1906.

65. Architectural Record, Sweet's Indexed Catalogue of Building Construction for the Year 1906, New York, 1906.

66. Dept. of Commerce, Building Code Committee, "Recommended Minimum Requirements for Fire Resistance in Buildings," Building and Housing, No. 14, National Bureau of Standards, Washington, 1931.

67. British Standards Institution, "Fire Tests on Building Materials and Structures," British Standards, 476, Pt. 1, London, 1953.

68. Lönberg-Holm, K., "Glass," The Architectural Record, Oct. 1930, pp. 345-357.

69. Structural Clay Products Institute, "Fire Resistance," Technical Notes on Brick and Tile Construction, 16 rev., Washington, 1964.

70. Ramsey, C. G., and Sleeper, H. R., Architectural Graphic Standards for Architects, Engineers, Decorators, Builders, and Draftsmen, 3rd ed., J. Wiley, New York, 1941.

71. Underwriters' Laboratories, Fire Protection Equipment List, Chicago, Jan. 1957.

72. Underwriters' Laboratories, Fire Resistance Directory; with Hourly Ratings for Beams, Columns, Floors, Roofs, Walls, and Partitions, Chicago, Jan. 1977.

73. Mitchell, N. D., "Fire Tests of Gunite Slabs and Partitions," Building Materials and Structures, Report BMS 131, National Bureau of Standards, Washington, May 1952.

74. Woolson, I. H., and Miller, R. P., "Fire Tests of Floors in the United States," Proceedings International Association for Testing Materials, VIth Congress, New York, 1912, Section C, pp. 36-41.

75. Underwriters' Laboratories, "An Investigation of the Effects of Fire Exposure upon Hollow Concrete Building Units, Conducted for American Concrete Institute, Concrete Products Association, Portland Cement Association, Joint Submittors," Retardant Report, No. 1555, Chicago, May 1924.

76. Dept. of Scientific & Industrial Research and of the Fire Offices' Committee, Joint Committee of the Building Research Board, "Fire Gradings of Buildings. Part IV: Chimneys and Flues," Post-War Building Studies, No. 29, London, HMSO, 1952.

77. National Research Council of Canada. Associate Committee on the National Building Code, Fire Performance Ratings, Suppl. No. 2 to the National Building Code of Canada, Ottawa, 1965.

78. Associated Factory Mutual Fire Insurance Companies, The National Board of Fire Underwriters, and the Bureau of Standards, Fire Tests of Building Columns; an Experimental Investigation of the Resistance of Columns, Loaded and Exposed to Fire or to Fire and Water, with Record of Characteristic Effects, Jointly Conducted at Underwriters' Laboratories, Chicago, 1917-19.

79. Malhotra, H. L., "Effect of Age on the Fire Resistance of Reinforced Concrete Columns," Fire Research Memorandum, No. 1, Fire Research Station, Borehamwood, April 1970.

80. Bond, H., ed., <u>Research on Fire; a Description of the Facilities, Personnel and Management of Agencies Engaged in Research on Fire</u>, a Staff Report, National Fire Protection Association, Boston, 1957.

81. <u>California State Historical Building Code</u>, Draft, 1978.

82. Fisher, F. L., et al., "A Study of Potential Flashover Fires in Wheeler Hall and the Results from a Full Scale Fire Test of a Modified Wheeler Hall Door Assembly," <u>Fire Research Laboratory Report</u>, UCX 77-3; UCX-2480, University of Calif., Dept. of Civil Eng., Berkeley, 1977.

83. Freitag, J. K., <u>The Fireproofing of Steel Buildings</u>, 1st ed., J. Wiley, New York, 1906.

84. Gross, D., "Field Burnout Tests of Apartment Dwellings Units," <u>Building Science Series</u>, 10, National Bureau of Standards, Washington, 1967.

85. Dunlap, M. E., and Cartwright, F. P., "Standard Fire Tests for Combustible Building Materials," <u>Proceedings of the American Society for Testing Materials</u>, vol. 27, Philadelphia, 1927, pp. 534-546.

86. Menzel, C. A., "Tests of the Fire Resistance and Stability of Walls of Concrete Masonry Units," <u>Proceedings of the American Society for Testing Materials</u>, vol. 31, Philadelphia, 1931, pp. 607-660.

87. Steiner, A. J., "Method of Fire-Hazard Classification of Building Materials," <u>Bulletin of the American Society for Testing and Materials</u>, March 1943, Philadelphia, 1943, pp. 19-22.

88. Heselden, A. J. M., Smith, P. G., and Theobald, C. R., "Fires in a Large Compartment Containing Structural Steelwork; Detailed Measurements of Fire Behavior," <u>Fire Research Note</u>, No. 646, Fire Research Station, Borehamwood, Dec. 1966.

89. Ministry of Technology and Fire Offices' Committee Joint Fire Research Organization, "Fire and Structural Use of Timber in Buildings; Proceedings of the Symposium Held at the Fire Research Station, Borehamwood, Herts on 25th October, 1967," <u>Symposium</u>, No. 3, London, HMSO, 1970.

90. Shoub, H., and Gross, D., "Doors as Barriers to Fire and Smoke," <u>Building Science Series</u>, 3, National Bureau of Standards, Washington, 1966.

91. Ingberg, S. H., "The Fire Resistance of Gypsum Partitions," <u>Proceedings of the American Society for Testing and Materials</u>, vol. 25, Philadelphia, 1925, pp. 299-314.

92. Ingberg, S. H., "Influence of Mineral Composition of Aggregates on Fire Resistance of Concrete," <u>Proceedings of the American Society for Testing and Materials</u>, vol. 29, Philadelphia, 1929, pp. 824-829.

93. Ingberg, S. H., "The Fire Resistive Properties of Gypsum," <u>Proceedings of the American Society for Testing and Materials</u>, vol. 23, Philadelphia, 1923, pp. 254-256.

94. Gottschalk, F. W., "Some Factors in the Interpretation of Small-Scale Tests for Fire-Retardant Wood," <u>Bulletin of the American Society for Testing and Materials</u>, October 1945, pp. 40-43.

95. Ministry of Technology and Fire Offices' Committee Joint Fire Research Organization, "Behaviour of Structural Steel in Fire; Proceedings of the Symposium Held at the Fire Research Station Borehamwood, Herts on 24th January, 1967," <u>Symposium</u>, No. 2, London, HMSO, 1968.

96. Gustaferro, A. H., and Martin, L. D., <u>Design for Fire Resistance of Pre-cast Concrete</u>, prep. for the Prestressed Concrete Institute Fire Committee, 1st ed., Chicago, PCI, 1977.

97. "The Fire Endurance of Concrete; a Special Issue," <u>Concrete Construction</u>, vol. 18, no. 8, Aug. 1974, pp. 345-440.

98. The British Constructional Steelwork Association, "Modern Fire Protection for Structural Steelwork," <u>Publication</u>, No. FP1, London, 1961.

99. Underwriters' Laboratories, "Fire Hazard Classification of Building Materials," <u>Bulletin</u>, No. 32, Sept. 1944, Chicago, 1959.

100. Central Housing Committee on Research, Design, and Construction, Subcommittee on Building Codes, "Recommended Building Code Requirements for New Dwelling Construction with Special Reference to War Housing; Report," <u>Building Materials and Structures</u>, Report BMS 88, National Bureau of Standards, Washington, Sept. 1942.

101. De Coppet Bergh, D., <u>Safe Building Construction; a Treatise Giving in Simplest Forms Possible Practical and Theoretical Rules and Formulae Used in Construction of Buildings and General Instruction</u>, new ed., thoroughly rev. Macmillan Co., New York, 1908.

102. <u>Cyclopedia of Fire Prevention and Insurance; a General Reference Work on Fire and Fire Losses, Fireproof Construction, Building Inspection...</u>, prep. by architects, engineers, underwriters and practical insurance men. American School of Correspondence, Chicago, 1912.

103. Setchkin, N. P., and Ingberg, S. H., "Test Criterion for an Incombustible Material," <u>Proceedings of the American Society for Testing Materials</u>, vol. 45, Philadelphia, 1945, pp. 866-877.

104. Underwriters' Laboratories, "Report on Fire Hazard Classification of Various Species of Lumber," <u>Retardant</u>, 3365, Chicago, 1952.

105. Steingiser, S., "A Philosophy of Fire Testing," <u>Journal of Fire & Flammability</u>, vol. 3, July 1972, pp. 238-253.

106. Yuill, C. H., Bauerschlag, W. H., and Smith, H. M., "An Evaluation of the Comparative Performance of 2.4.1 Plywood and Two-Inch Lumber Roof Decking under Equivalent Fire Exposure," <u>Fire Protection Section, Final Report</u>, Project No. 717A-3-211, Southwest Research Institute, Dept. of Structural Research, San Antonio, Dec. 1962.

107. Ashton, L. A., and Smart, P. M. T., <u>Sponsored Fire-Resistance Tests on Structural Elements</u>, London, Dept. of Scientific and Industrial Research and Fire Offices' Committee, London, 1960.

108. Butcher, E. G., Chitty, T. B., and Ashton, L. A., "The Temperature Attained by Steel in Building Fires," <u>Fire Research Technical Paper</u>, No. 15, Ministry of Technology and Fire Offices' Committee, Joint Fire Research Organization, London, HMSO, 1966.

109. Dept. of the Environment and Fire Offices' Committee, Joint Fire Research Organization, "Fire-Resistance Requirements for Buildings - a New Approach; Proceedings of the Symposium Held at the Connaught Rooms, London, 28 September 1971," <u>Symposium</u>, No. 5, London, HMSO, 1973.

110. Langdon Thomas, G. J., "Roofs and Fire," <u>Fire Note</u>, No. 3, Dept. of Scientific and Industrial Research and Fire Offices' Committee, Joint Fire Research Organization, London, HMSO, 1963.

111. National Fire Protection Association and the National Board of Fire Underwriters, <u>Report on Fire the Edison Phonograph Works</u>, Thomas A. Edison, Inc., West Orange, N.J., December 9, 1914, Boston, 1915.

112. Thompson, J. P., <u>Fire Resistance of Reinforced Concrete Floors</u>, Portland Cement Association, Chicago, 1963.

113. Forest Products Laboratory, "Fire Resistance Tests of Plywood Covered Wall Panels," Information reviewed and reaffirmed, <u>Forest Service Report</u>, No. 1257, Madison, April 1961.

114. Forest Products Laboratory, "Charring Rate of Selected Woods - Transverse to Grain," Forest Service <u>Research Paper</u>, FLP 69, Madison, April 1967.

115. Bird, G. I., "Protection of Structural Steel Against Fire," <u>Fire Note</u>, No. 2, Dept. of Scientific and Industrial Research and Fire Offices' Committee, Joint Fire Research Organization, London, HMSO, 1961.

116. Robinson, W. C., <u>The Parker Building Fire</u>, Underwriters' Laboratories, Chicago, c. 1908.

117. Ferris, J. E., "Fire Hazards of Combustible Wallboards," <u>Commonwealth Experimental Building Station Special Report</u>, No. 18, Sydney, Oct. 1955.

118. Markwardt, L. J., Bruce, H. D., and Freas, A. D., "Brief Description of Some Fire-Test Methods Used for Wood and Wood-Base Materials," <u>Forest Service Report</u>, No. 1976, Forest Products Laboratory, Madison, 1976.

119. Foster, H. D., Pinkston, E. R., and Ingberg, S. H., "Fire Resistance of Walls of Gravel-Aggregate Concrete Masonry Units," <u>Building Materials and Structures</u>, Report, BMS 120, National Bureau of Standards, Washington, March 1951.

120. Foster, H. D., Pinkston, E.R., and Ingberg, S. H., "Fire Resistance of Walls of Lightweight-Aggregate Concrete Masonry Units," <u>Building Materials and Structures</u>, Report BMS 117, National Bureau of Standards, Washington, May 1950.

121. Structural Clay Products Institute, "Structural Clay Tile Fireproofing," <u>Technical Notes on Brick & Tile Construction</u>, vol. 1, no. 11, San Francisco, Nov. 1950.

122. Structural Clay Products Institute, "Fire Resistance Ratings of Clay Masonry Walls - I," <u>Technical Notes on Brick & Tile Construction</u>, vol. 3, no. 12, San Francisco, Dec. 1952.

123. Structural Clay Products Institute, "Estimating the Fire Resistance of Clay Masonry Walls - II," <u>Technical Notes on Brick & Tile Construction</u>, vol. 4, no. 1, San Francisco, Jan. 1953.

124. Building Research Station, "Fire: Materials and Structures," <u>Digest</u>, No. 106, London, HMSO, 1958.

125. Mitchell, N. D., "Fire Hazard Tests with Masonry Chimneys," <u>NFPA Publication</u>, No. Q-43-7, Boston, Oct. 1949.

126. Clinton Wire Cloth Company, <u>Some Test Data on Fireproof Floor Construction Relating to Cinder Concrete, Terra Cotta and Gypsum</u>, Clinton, 1913.

127. Structural Engineers Association of Southern California, Fire Ratings Subcommittee, "Fire Ratings, a Report," part of <u>Annual Report</u>, Los Angeles, 1962, pp. 30-38.

128. Lawson, D. I., Fox, L. L., and Webster, C. T., "The Heating of Panels by Flue Pipes," <u>Fire Research, Special Report</u>, No. 1, Dept. of Scientific and Industrial Research and Fire Offices' Committee, London, HMSO, 1952.

129. Forest Products Laboratory, "Fire Resistance of Wood Construction," Excerpt from 'Wood Handbook - Basic Information on Wood as a Material of Construction with Data for its Use in Design and Specification,' <u>Dept. of Agriculture Handbook</u>, No. 72, Washington, 195X, pp. 337-350.

130. Goalwin, D. S., "Properties of Cavity Walls," <u>Building Materials and Structures</u>, Report BMS 136, National Bureau of Standards, Washington, May 1953.

131. Humphrey, R. L., "The Fire-Resistive Properties of Various Building Materials," <u>Geological Survey Bulletin</u>, 370, Washington, 1909.

132. National Lumber Manufacturers Association, "Comparative Fire Test on Wood and Steel Joists," Technical Report, No. 1, Washington, 1961.

133. National Lumber Manufacturers Association, "Comparative Fire Test of Timber and Steel Beams," Technical Report, No. 3, Washington, 1963.

134. Malhotra, H. L., and Morris, W. A., "Tests on Roof Construction Subjected to External Fire," Fire Note, No. 4, Dept. of Scientific and Industrial Research and Fire Offices' Committee, Joint Fire Research Organization, London, HMSO, 1963.

135. Brown, C. R., "Fire Tests of Treated and Untreated Wood Partitions," Research Paper, RP 1076, part of Journal of Research of the National Bureau of Standards, vol. 20, Washington, Feb. 1938, pp. 217-237.

136. Underwriters' Laboratories, "Report on Investigation of Fire Resistance of Wood Lath and Lime Plaster Interior Finish," Publication, SP. 1. 230, Chicago, Nov. 1922.

137. Underwriters' Laboratories, "Report on Interior Building Construction Consisting of Metal Lath and Gypsum Plaster on Wood Supports," Retardant, No. 1355, Chicago, 1922.

138. Underwriters' Laboratories, "An Investigation of the Effects of Fire Exposure upon Hollow Concrete Building Units," Retardant, No. 1555, Chicago, May 1924.

139. Moran, T. H., "Comparative Fire Resistance Ratings of Douglas Fir Plywood," Douglas Fir Plywood Association Laboratory Bulletin, 57-A, Tacoma, 1957.

140. Gage Babcock & Association, "The Performance of Fire-Protective Materials under Varying Conditions of Fire Severity," Report 6924, Chicago, 1969.

141. International Conference of Building Officials, Uniform Building Code (1979 ed.), Whittier, CA, 1979.

142. Babrauskas, V., and Williamson, R. B., "The Historical Basis of Fire Resistance Testing, Part I and Part II," Fire Technology, vol. 14, no. 3 & 4, Aug. & Nov. 1978, pp. 184-194, 205, 304-316.

143. Underwriters' Laboratories, "Fire Tests of Building Construction and Materials," 8th ed., Standard for Safety, UL263, Chicago, 1971.

144. Hold, H. G., Fire Protection in Buildings, Crosby, Lockwood, London, 1913.

145. Kollbrunner, C. F., "Steel Buildings and Fire Protection in Europe," Journal of the Structural Division, ASCE, vol. 85, no. ST9, Proc. Paper 2264, Nov. 1959, pp. 125-149.

146. Smith, P., "Investigation and Repair of Damage to Concrete Caused by Formwork and Falsework Fire," Journal of the American Concrete Institute, vol. 60, Title no. 60-66, Nov. 1963, pp. 1535-1566.

147. "Repair of Fire Damage," 3 parts, Concrete Construction, March-May, 1972.

148. National Fire Protection Association, National Fire Codes; a Compilation of NFPA Codes, Standards, Recommended Practices and Manuals, 16 vols., Boston, 1978.

149. Ingberg, S. H. "Tests of Severity of Building Fires," NFPA Quarterly, vol. 22, no. 1, July 1928, pp. 43-61.

150. Underwriters' Laboratories, "Fire Exposure Tests of Ordinary Wood Doors," Bulletin of Research, no. 6, Dec. 1938, Chicago, 1942.

151. Parson, H., "The Tall Building under Test of fire," Red Book, no. 17, British Fire Prevention Committee, London, 1899.

152. Sachs, E. O., "The British Fire Prevention Committee Testing Station," Red Book, no. 13, British Fire Prevention Committee, London, 1899.

153. Sachs, E. O., "Fire Tests with Unprotected Columns," Red Book, no. 11, British Fire Prevention Committee, London, 1899.

154. British Fire Prevention Committee, "Fire Tests with Floors a Floor by the Expended Metal Company," Red Book, no. 14, London, 1899.

155. Engineering News, vol. 56, Aug. 9, 1906, pp. 135-140.

156. Engineering News, vol. 36, Aug. 6, 1896, pp. 92-94.

157. Bauschinger, J., Mittheilungen de Mech.-Tech. Lab. der K. Tech. Hochschule, München, vol. 12, 1885.

158. Engineering News, vol. 46, Dec. 26, 1901, pp. 482-486, 489-490.

159. The American Architect and Building News, vol. 31, March 28, 1891, pp. 195-201.

160. British Fire Prevention Committee, First International Fire Prevention Congress, Official Congress Report, London, 1903.

161. American Society for Testing Materials, Standard Specifications for Fire Tests of Materials and Construction (C19-18), Philadelphia, 1918.

162. International Organization for Standardization, Fire Resistance Tests on Elements of Building Construction (R834), London, 1968.

163. <u>Engineering Record</u>, vol. 35, Jan. 2, 1897, pp. 93-94; May 29, 1897, pp. 558-560; vol. 36, Sept. 18, 1897, pp. 337-340; Sept. 25, 1897, pp. 359-363; Oct. 2, 1897, pp. 382-387; Oct. 9, 1897, pp. 402-405.

164. Babrauskas, Vytenis, "Fire Endurance in Buildings," PhD Thesis. <u>Fire Research Group</u>, Report, No. UCB FRG 76-16, University of California, Berkeley, Nov. 1976.

165. The Institution of Structural Engineers and The Concrete Society, <u>Fire Resistance of Concrete Structures</u>, London, Aug. 1975.

UCBC–3 ALLOWABLE STRESSES FOR ARCHAIC MATERIALS

3.10. SCOPE AND INTENT

This guideline provides information on allowable stresses for materials that are no longer in use but may be found in older structures. The values contained herein are based on a review of building codes from approximately 1890 through 1940. Early editions of the *Uniform Building Code*, the *Los Angeles Building Code*, the *New York Building Code* and the *National Building Code* provide the basis for the values presented.

The values contained herein should not substitute for a structural analysis by an engineer experienced in older buildings, a field observation by the building official and laboratory tests as necessary to verify assumptions.

References listed at the end of this guideline will provide additional information for the building official on appropriate investigation and evaluation methods. Early codes of the jurisdiction should also be consulted.

3.20. GENERAL ENGINEERING APPROACH

3.21. STRUCTURAL ANALYSIS

Analysis shall conform to accepted engineering practice or procedure to the extent applicable. A rational approach should be utilized. Additional strengthening of buildings should be provided where a lack of stability is indicated.

3.22. ALLOWABLE STRESSES

Allowable stresses for archaic materials may be assigned, based upon similar conventional codified materials, or tests, as hereinafter indicated. The building official may assign other allowable stresses to archaic materials which represent the conditions, quality and nature of the archaic materials. Designs should provide an adequate resistance to the vertical and lateral forces required under the code. Assigned allowable stresses should not exceed those contained herein without testing and with the approval of the building official.

3.23. BUILDING SUBJECT TO EARTHQUAKE LOADS

When using archaic materials to resist lateral forces, consideration should be given to the past performance record of such materials during actual earthquakes. The general configuration of the building should be considered as to its tendency to generate rotational and non-symmetrical forces which would result in failure of such materials.

3.24. MASONRY AND ADOBE

(a) Existing solid masonry walls of any type, except adobe, may be allowed, under the criteria spelled out in Appendix Chapter l.

(b) Adobe. Unburned clay masonry may be erected or re-erected pursuant to the criteria in Appendix Chapter l.

3.25. WOOD

(a) Lateral-force-resisting element. Existing wood diaphragms or walls of straight or diagonal sheathing shall be assigned shear resistance values appropriate with the fasteners and materials functioning in conjunction with the sheathing. Values for diaphragms and shear-resisting elements should be per Appendix Chapter l.

(b) **Joists and Rafters.** Joists and rafters may be assumed to have an allowable bending stress equal to that of select structural grade lumber. Shear stress may be increased twenty-five percent over that currently permitted. All main timber and framing lumber should be inspected for cracks and damage.

3.26. CONCRETE

Reinforced concrete. The compressive strength (f'_c) of concrete may be determined by core samples. An assumed $f'_c = 900$ psi may be assumed if no data are submitted. Reinforcing steel may be assumed to have an allowable tensile stress of 16,000 psi.

3.27. STEEL AND IRON

Cast Iron: f compression - 16,000 psi
f tension - 3,000 psi
f bending - 3,000 tensile force
12,000 compression force

Steel: f_b = 16,000 psi
f_c = 16,000 psi
f_t = 12,000 psi

3.28. BIBLIOGRAPHY

To aid building officials, owners and architects, a bibliography of old books and periodicals where these archaic methods and materials are documented is appended.

The Architects' and Builders' Handbook. Nolan, T., and Kidder, F., John Wiley & Sons, New York. 1884, 1892, 1897, 1904, 1915, 1921.

Uniform Building Code, 1930 (Pacific Coast Building Officials).

HUD Rehabilitation Guidelines, 1982.

Guideline 9, Guidelines for Structural Assessment.
Guideline 11, Residential Building Systems Inspection.

Building Codes of Major Cities. Examples include:

Los Angeles Building Code.
National Building Code.
Portland (Oregon) Building Code.
New York Building Code (1842 to present).

UCBC–4 ELECTRICAL GUIDELINE

Acknowledgments

The material herein was prepared by the National Institute of Building Sciences on the basis of research performed by Building Technology, Inc. with consultants Melvyn Young, George Schoonover, Eugene Davidson, Richard Lloyd, Larry Gallowin, Heilbron Love, and John McClelland. The guideline was written and arranged by Thomas Ware.

Overall management and production of the *Rehabilitation Guidelines* was directed by William Brenner of the Institute, with David Hattis of Building Technology, Inc. the principal technical consultant. Guideline cover graphics and layouts were designed by the Design Communication Collaborative.

INTRODUCTION

This guideline addresses only those select problem areas most identified with rehabilitation projects. The guideline is not a code, but like an electrical code, it is intended for use by persons knowledgeable about electrical design and installations. The guideline addresses three major subject areas:

- Setting and adopting electrical rehabilitation standards at the state or local level;

- Inspecting existing electrical installations; and

- Problems and solutions for hazardous conditions, inadequate load-carrying capacity, and additions, alterations and extensions to existing electrical installations.

With regard to the problems and solutions, this guideline applies to all types of residential occupancies except hotels, rooming houses, dormitories, and housing for the elderly. It is intended to facilitate the maximal re-use of existing electrical installations in circumstances where, for some reason, code requirements for new construction are being applied to a project undergoing rehabilitation. In general, there are two such circumstances:

- Repair and improvement of existing residential buildings when compliance with the code requirements for new construction is triggered by a 25-50% Rule or similar rule which is in effect in the jurisdiction.

- Change of use or occupancy into a residential occupancy (e.g., from one- and two-family dwelling to apartment building, from hotel to apartment building) when compliance with the code requirements for new construction is triggered by the provisions of the code in effect or some other provision.

For rehabilitation involving a change of use or occupancy, this guideline should be used when it is feasible to reuse some portion of an existing electrical installation.

It has been long recognized that electrical codes pose special problems for rehabilitation projects. Some communities have adopted special electrical codes to be used for rehabilitation. One example, the City of Detroit's electrical code for rehabilitation, is shown as an Appendix to this guideline. Some of the model electrical codes give the code enforcement authority the responsibility for making interpretations of the rules, for granting exceptions to the rules, and for waiving specific requirements of the code. The following sections of the 1978 Edition of the *National Electric Code* (hereinafter NEC) illustrate this "flexible" approach:

"Section 90-2.(c) Special Permission. The authority having jurisdiction for enforcing this Code may grant exception for the installation of conductors and equipment, not under the exclusive control of the electric utilities and used to connect the electric utility supply system to the service entrance conductors of the premises served, provided such installations are outside a building or terminate immediately inside a building wall."

"Section 90-4. Enforcement. This Code is intended to be suitable for mandatory application by governmental bodies exercising legal jurisdiction over electrical installations and for use by insurance inspectors. The authority having jurisdiction of enforcement of the Code will have the responsibility for making interpretations of the rules, for deciding upon the approval of equipment and materials, and for granting the special permission contemplated in a number of the rules."

"Section 90-5. Formal Interpretations. To promote uniformity of interpretation and application of the provisions of this Code, the National Electrical Code Committee has established interpretation procedures."

1
ESTABLISHING STANDARDS FOR ELECTRICAL REHABILITATION

A community using this guideline may also have a need to set standards for rehabilitating electrical installations. A general process for establishing local standards is discussed in detail in the *Guideline for Setting and Adopting Standards for Building Rehabilitation.*

There are a number of other sources of information besides this guideline that a community may use to establish suitable requirements and criteria for electrical rehabilitation. Current electrical codes, such as the NEC, are one such source of rehabilitation standards information. Although these codes principally regulate new construction, and therefore may not adequately address the problems of rehabilitating existing buildings, certain new construction provisions may still be applicable. For example, provisions regulating grounding, feeders, and service ratings can be adopted as electrical rehabilitation standards when a community wishes to maintain a level of performance in rehabilitated buildings equivalent to that for new construction.

In addition, the "alternative materials and methods" provision in new construction codes provides a means by which acceptable solutions to electrical rehabilitation problems can be developed that are different from those prescribed by the current code.

Property maintenance codes, fire prevention codes, and hazard abatement codes could be another basis for setting electrical rehabilitation standards. Though these codes do not contain precise enough information to be useful in setting specific standards, they can still provide a general basis for establishing both a minimum level of performance and a level of performance less than that required by new construction codes.

For example, the BOCA *Basic Property Maintenance Code* states in Section H-602.0, ELECTRICAL FACILITIES:

"H-602.1 Outlets required: Where there is electric service available to a structure, every habitable room of a dwelling unit, and every guest room, shall contain at least two (2) separate and remote outlets, one (l) of which may be a ceiling or wall-type electric light fixture. In a kitchen three (3) separate and remote wall-type electric convenience outlets or two (2) such convenience outlets and one (1) ceiling or wall-type electric light fixture shall be provided. Every public hall, water closet compartment, bathroom, laundry room or furnace room shall contain at least one (1) electric light fixture. In addition to the electric light fixture in every bathroom and laundry room, there shall be provided at least one (1) electric outlet.

"H-602.2 Installation: All electrical equipment, wiring, and appliances shall be installed and maintained in a safe manner in accordance with all applicable laws. All electrical equipment shall be of an approved type.

"H-602.3 Defective system: Where it is found, in the opinion of the building official, that the electrical system in a structure constitutes a hazard to the occupants or the structure by reason of inadequate service, improper fusing, insufficient outlets, improper wiring or installation, deterioration or damage, or for similar reasons, he shall require the defects to be corrected to eliminate the hazard."

Similarly, the BOCA *Basic Fire Prevention Code* states in SECTION F-105.0, ORDERS TO ELIMINATE DANGEROUS OR HAZARDOUS CONDITIONS, F-l05.1 General:

"Whenever the fire official or the code official's designated representative shall find in any structure or upon any premises dangerous or hazardous conditions or materials as follows, the

code official shall order such dangerous conditions or materials to be removed or remedied in accordance with the provisions of this code: ... 7. hazardous conditions arising from defective or improperly used or installed electrical wiring, equipment or appliances"

Past electrical codes for new construction are an especially important source of information for setting electrical rehabilitation standards. The performance levels required by past electrical codes are different from, and may be lower than, the current electrical codes. Past codes, however, are most useful in determining after an on-site inspection whether an existing building currently meets the code under which it was built.

Finally, laws and regulations affecting electrical installations which apply retroactively to existing buildings are by definition mandatory standards for electrical rehabilitation.

2
INSPECTION

An inspection of the existing electrical installation may be necessary to provide the authority having jurisdiction with the information needed to evaluate a proposed electrical rehabilitation project (see the *Guideline for Approval of Building Rehabilitation*). Inspections are also an essential part of enforcing property maintenance, fire prevention, and hazard abatement codes.

This part of the guideline outlines a procedure for conducting inspections of existing electrical installations to determine their physical condition, functional condition, and load-carrying capacity.

Electrical construction drawings and/or specifications of an existing building do not represent the present physical and functional condition of the electrical installation; these conditions can only be determined from an on-site inspection. However, if it is determined that electrical construction drawings accurately and completely represent the present electrical installation in an existing building, they could be used in conjunction with the current electrical code to calculate the installation's load-carrying capacity.

It is recommended that inspections be made by qualified electrical personnel, as determined by each jurisdiction.

STEP 1
PHYSICAL CONDITION

Determine the physical condition of the existing electrical installation, including individual dwelling units and common areas of multi-family dwellings. Inspect the physical condition of the parts of the installation which are normally exposed to view.

Next, turn off the power to the individual dwelling units and common areas of multi-family dwellings, and remove the covers and open the doors of switchboards, panelboards, cabinets, and boxes. Inspect the physical condition of the exposed, internal components and wiring, as well as the surrounding building construction.

If the condition of the conductor insulation cannot be determined by inspection, perform an insulation resistance test. Similarly, if the condition of receptacles cannot be determined by inspection, test them by inserting a standard type flexible cord attachment plug.

Detach fixed utilization equipment such as lighting fixtures, lampholders, and appliances (e.g., built-in electrical space heat-

ers) to inspect the physical condition of their exposed, internal components and wiring, as well as the surrounding building construction. In older buildings, however, detachment may contribute to, or actually cause, defects in equipment, appliances, or wiring.

Therefore, consider detaching fixed utilization equipment only when:

- Such wiring, equipment or appliance is part of a rehabilitation plan;
- Problems are evident from the first inspection of parts which are normally exposed to view; or
- Problems of function are evident from inspection or records, or are identified by owners or tenants.

STEP 2
FUNCTIONAL CONDITION

If the physical condition of the installation seems safe, determine the functional condition with the power on in individual dwelling units and in common areas of multi-family dwellings. Inspecting an installation with the power on is essential to determining its condition.

When a building or dwelling unit is without power because it is unoccupied or an imminent hazard exists, determining functional condition may have to be delayed until rehabilitation has begun, or an exploratory permit may have to be secured by the building owner from an authority having jurisdiction to turn the power on.

Remove the covers and open the doors on equipment to expose circuit breakers, switches, receptacles and other devices, and conductor splices and connections; then:

- Operate circuit breakers, switches, other operable devices and fixed utilization equipment; observe the function of operable devices; and
- Observe the operation and assess the operating temperatures of fixed utilization equipment.

Make inspections to determine the physical and functional conditions of existing electrical installations in accordance with the current code, such as NEC Section 110-3(a). Whenever possible, as an aid in assessing an installation's condition, secure information from owners, tenants, or from the records of all possible authorities having jurisdiction (e.g., health departments, licensing bureaus) about past operating problems that cannot be found easily by inspection, such as the frequency of fuses blowing or short circuits.

STEP 3
LOAD-CARRYING CAPACITY

Determine the load carrying capacity of the existing electrical installation by calculation in accordance with the current code.

3
PROBLEMS AND SOLUTIONS

3.1
HAZARDOUS CONDITIONS

<u>Problem</u>: The existing electrical installation has any one or combination of the following conditions which are contrary to the in-

tent of property maintenance, fire prevention, and hazard abatement codes:

- Equipment or wiring is missing, broken, disconnected, loosely connected, unsupported, not securely fastened in place, corroded, burnt, cracked, split, has evidence of overheating, physical damage, or misuse;

- Equipment is dirty or contains debris;

- Wiring is frayed;

- Labeled or listed equipment or wiring is not installed in accordance with any labeling or listing instructions;

- Circuit breaker, fuse, switch, receptacle, other device, fixed utilization equipment, or wiring is not compatible with the phase, voltage, amperage, or type characteristics of the electricity in use;

- Circuit breaker, switch, or other operable device has visible evidence of arcing or overheating;

- Receptacle contact devices are not firmly in contact with the contact devices of a standard type flexible cord attachment plug when the plug is inserted in the receptacle;

- Bathroom receptacle, garage receptacle, or outdoor receptacle with direct grade level access is without ground fault circuit interruptor protection;

- Neutral is not grounded at the main service entrance equipment location by a properly connected grounding electrode conductor;

- Polarity is reversed in wiring connections to receptacle outlets;

- Fixed utilization equipment, such as a lighting fixture, lampholder, or appliance, operates intermittently;

- Building construction adjacent to wiring, equipment, or appliance is burnt;

- Service, feeder, or branch circuit conductors have evidence of intermittent operation, impaired operation, or cannot otherwise be determined as acceptable when the installation is energized;

- Flexible cord is used as a permanent wiring method;

- Branch circuit, feeder, switchboard, panelboard, or distribution board service rating is inadequate for the load calculated in accordance with the current code; or

- Pull-chain switch or brass shell socket in a wet or damp location is within reach.

Solution: Have all such conditions corrected.

Discussion: These conditions are hazards of varying degree. They are problems associated with defective or improperly used or improperly installed wiring, equipment, or appliances. If any one or combination of these conditions is extensive, severe, or occurs frequently in an installation, an authority having jurisdiction may judge that an imminent hazard exists. In that case, the hazard must be corrected immediately or the installation disconnected.

The use of flexible cord as a permanent wiring method may indicate the need for more receptacle outlets (see Part 3.8 below).

3.2
INCOMPATIBLE CONDUCTORS, DEVICES, AND EQUIPMENT

Problem: Circuit breaker, fuse, switch, receptacle, other device, fixed utilization equipment, raceway, connector, terminal, splicing device, or other fitting is not compatible with the type of conductor used, or the electrical connection does not meet the current code, such as NEC Section 110-14.

Solution: Have all such connections of conductors to terminal parts, conductor splices, or conductors joined with splicing devices corrected to meet the current code, such as NEC Section 110-14(a) and 110-14(b), and have all incompatible conductors, devices, or equipment corrected to meet the current code, such as NEC Section 110-14, by:

- Replacing existing conductors with new conductors which are compatible with the existing devices or equipment; or

- Replacing existing devices or equipment with new devices or equipment which are compatible with the existing conductors; or

- Installing an insulated conductor "pigtail" compatible with the existing device or equipment.

Discussion: Improper connections and splices, and incompatible conductors, devices, and equipment can be hazardous. There are problems associated with defective or improperly installed wiring or equipment. These conditions, depending upon the number and severity of the problems, may be judged an imminent hazard by an authority having jurisdiction. If that is the case, the hazard must be corrected immediately or the installation disconnected.

3.3
GROUNDING OF FIXED APPLIANCE BRANCH CIRCUITS

Problem: An existing fixed appliance branch circuit does not have an equipment grounding means which is required by the current code.

Solution: Permit ungrounded, nonconforming, existing fixed appliance branch circuits to remain, provided:

- Alternative grounding is provided for appliances by the connection of an equipment grounding conductor to a grounded, metallic, cold water pipe;

- Service equipment, service raceways, service grounded conductors, switchboards, and panelboards are grounded in accordance with the current code, such as NEC Article 250, or alternative grounding is provided by the connection of an equipment grounding conductor to a grounded, metallic, cold water pipe;

- Branch circuit equipment grounding conductors are in accordance with the current code, such as NEC Article 250; and

- Ungrounded, nonconforming, existing, general purpose branch circuits conform to Part 3.4 of this guideline.

Discussion: This alternative method of grounding existing fixed appliance branch circuits is not the method usually required by code, but it will provide an equivalent level of safety. And, since this alternative method is relatively simple to install, it is an aid to rehabilitation. But, it's important to make sure in such installations that equipment grounding conductors are connected to cold water pipes which are *metal* and which are *grounded*.

3.4
GROUNDING OF GENERAL PURPOSE BRANCH CIRCUITS OR FEEDERS

Problem: An existing general purpose branch circuit or feeder is without an equipment grounding means which is contrary to the current code.

Solution: Allow ungrounded, nonconforming, existing, general purpose branch circuits, or feeders to remain, provided that:

- No circuit or feeder is overloaded when the load-carrying capacity is calculated as in Part 2.3 of this guideline;
- No general purpose branch circuit serves loads required by the current code to be served by small appliance branch circuits; and
- No receptacle outlet or fixture is located where it will be in reach of grounded surfaces.

Discussion: An existing general purpose branch circuit or feeder without an equipment ground which is inspected, found to be still in acceptable physical and functional condition, and is not overloaded can be considered to have a history of operating safely. Therefore, its safe operation can be expected to continue, and it may be allowed to remain. It is important that such a circuit does not serve as an applicance branch circuit; that load calculations consider both existing loads not affected by rehabilitation and new loads which are a result of rehabilitation; and that the receptacle outlets and fixtures on such a circuit are safely located out of reach of grounded surfaces.

3.5
UNDERSIZED SERVICE

Problem: The size of the service is inadequate for the load as calculated according to the current code.

Solution: Recalculate the size of the service for the actual connected (installed) load and the loads for circuits calculated according to the current code, provided:

- The service disconnecting means has a rating not less than the actual connected load;
- Loads established for branch circuits and feeders are determined with the diversities and calculation methods defined in the current code; and
- All other aspects of the service meet the current code, such as NEC Tables 310-16 to 19 including the notes to these Tables, Article 210, Article 220, Article 240 and Article 230 except Section 230-79(c) for single-family dwellings and Section 230-79(d) for all other occupancies.

Discussion: In determining the actual connected load, include both existing loads not affected by rehabilitation and new loads which are planned as a part of rehabilitation. The probability of the use of room air conditioners should also be considered. The use of energy sources other than electricity can reduce the load. Therefore, consider the use of other energy sources for cooking, heating, and domestic hot water. Determining existing loads and new loads planned as a part of rehabilitation requires judgment. If there is any indication that loads will increase in the future, this should be taken into consideration. Using the actual installed load

is a means to control otherwise unnecessary rehabilitation, while maintaining the standards of safety required by the current code.

3.6
SECOND SERVICE ENTRANCE AND DISCONNECT

Problem: In one- and two-family dwellings, the existing service rating is to be increased by the addition of a second service entrance and a second service disconnect in order to meet the current code or this guideline, but space is limited or there are other, similar constraints.

Solution: Add the second service entrance and the second service disconnect at a location different from the existing service disconnect, provided:

- Both disconnects meet the current code, such as NEC Section 230-44 and 230-72(a) and (c);
- Permanent warning signs are erected at each location indicating separate service disconnects; and
- The combined rating of the separate service disconnects is not less than that required by the current code or recommended by other sections of this guideline for a single service disconnect.

Discussion: These recommendations are intended to eliminate the potential hazard of installing a single, new, service entrance in an inappropriate location, and are a means to control otherwise unnecessary rehabilitation. Any hazard associated with a "split" service is also eliminated by the suggested provisions of the recommendations and the restriction of split service to residences of no more than two families. A split service installed as recommended is an alternative to the current code which may provide an equivalent level of safety.

3.7
EXTENDING GENERAL PURPOSE UNGROUNDED BRANCH CIRCUITS

Problem: An existing general purpose branch circuit that is to be extended conforms to the current code, but doesn't have an equipment grounding means.

Solution: Permit ungrounded, nonconforming, general purpose branch circuits to be extended to all locations except kitchens, baths, basements, garages, and locations within reach of grounded surfaces.

Discussion: Kitchens, baths, basements, garages, and locations within reach of grounded surfaces represent a particular hazard as compared to other locations. This hazard is reduced by equipment grounding means installed according to the current code or this guideline.

3.8
NUMBER OF RECEPTACLE OUTLETS

Problem: The number of existing receptacle outlets is less than required by the current code.

Solution: Permit fewer receptacle outlets than required by the current code.

Discussion: The number and location of receptacle outlets required for the safe and convenient use (as this bears on safety) of rooms and spaces varies and can best be determined by the judgment of communities and jurisdictions individually. Such factors as number of occupants, floor area, room configuration, and window and door locations all affect the number and location of receptacle outlets which meets the intent of the current code. Examples of such reductions in the number of required receptacle outlets are contained in the BOCA *Basic Property Maintenance Code*, Section H-602.0, ELECTRICAL FACILITIES (see Part 1 above) and the *Detroit Electrical Code*, Chapter 10 (see Appendix).

3.9
ACCESS TO ELECTRICAL EQUIPMENT

Problem: The configuration of access space to, and working space around, electric equipment to permit ready and safe operation and maintenance of the equipment is different from that required by the current code, such as NEC Section 110-16.

Solution: Permit such existing space to remain when the intent of the current code can be met.

Discussion: Equipment accessibility and working space are essential to safety. The existing space could be permitted to remain unchanged if it meets the requirements of the code under which it was constructed, additional equipment and/or new equipment of a higher service rating is not to be installed, and the installation has a history of safe operation, maintenance, and repair.

Appendix
Detroit Electrical Code, Chapter 10

Appendix 1—Detroit Electrical Code, Chapter 10

Chapter 10 of the code is added as follows:

1000-1. Minimum standards for existing dwelling units.

If inspection reveals that the wiring system of an existing dwelling type occupancy is inadequate, or if code certification as a habitable dwelling under this section is requested, the following minimum requirements shall be complied with:

(a) **Entrances and Exits:** Where two (2) or more entrances and/or exits exist, at least two (2) entrances and/or exits shall be illuminated by exterior lights. Lighting outlets shall be controlled by interior wall switches, located for convenient and readily accessible use.

(b) **Living Room:** Living room shall be provided with illumination. Lighting outlet shall be controlled by a wall switch, located for convenient and readily accessible use. One of the receptacle outlets controlled by a wall switch in lieu of ceiling lighting outlet is acceptable. Convenient duplex receptacle outlets shall be provided. Receptacle outlets shall be equally spaced around the room with at least one duplex receptacle outlet on each wall.

(c) **Kitchen:** Kitchen shall be provided with illumination. Lighting outlet shall be controlled by a wall switch located for convenient and readily accessible use.

A separate kitchen appliance circuit shall be provided, supplying a minimum of three (3) grounding type duplex receptacle outlets. Two (2) of these receptacles shall be readily accessible for convenient use of portable appliances. New appliance circuits shall be twenty ampere capacity.

(d) **Bathroom:** Bathrooms shall be illuminated. Lighting outlet shall be controlled by a wall switch. A receptacle outlet separate from the light fixtures, shall be provided and shall be located at least thirty (30) and not more than forty-eight (48) inches above the floor adjacent to the wash basin and not more than four (4) feet from the basin.

(e) **All Other Habitable Rooms:** Illumination for each habitable room shall be provided. Lighting outlet shall be controlled by a wall switch. Wall switches shall be located for convenient and readily accessible use. Convenience duplex receptacle outlets shall be provided with a minimum of two (2) receptacle outlets equally spaced around the room. An additional receptacle outlet controlled by a wall switch is acceptable in lieu of a lighting outlet.

(f) **Basement:** Basement shall be wired for a minimum of one lighting outlet in each 200 square feet or major fraction of area for use as general illumination. All enclosed areas that may be walked into, such as toilet rooms, fruit storage rooms, utility rooms, excavated areas under porches, etc., shall be provided with at least one lighting outlet (except coal bins).

Stairwell and laundry area lighting outlets shall not be counted as part of the required basement lighting outlets.

(g) **Laundry Areas:** Laundry areas shall be provided with illumination. Laundry circuit shall be an individual circuit. A wall-mounted grounding type duplex receptacle outlet shall be provided, located near the laundry equipment.

An existing drop cord receptacle outlet on a separate circuit shall be acceptable providing it is a grounding type receptacle outlet not more than five (5) feet six (6) inches above the floor.

(h) **Space Heating System:** Heating equipment requiring electrical energy for operation and/or control shall be provided with an individual circuit. A disconnect switch shall be provided on or adjacent to the heating equipment (exception: thermo-pile controlled furnaces).

(i) **Stairwells:** Stairwells shall be adequately illuminated. Lighting outlets shall be controlled by wall switches. Wall switches shall be located for convenient and readily accessible use. Switches shall not be located where it is necessary to use darkened stair sections for their operation. All stairwells to finished portions of dwelling shall be provided with multiple switch control, one at the head the other at the foot of the stairwell.

(j) **Service and/or Feeder:** Service to existing dwelling unit shall be a minimum of one hundred ampere. three wire capacity, service equipment shall be dead front having no live parts exposed whereby accidental contact could be made. Type "S" fuses shall be installed when fused equipment is used.

Exception: Existing service of fifty-five ampere three wire capacity, and feeders of thirty ampere or larger two or three wire capacity shall be accepted if adequate for the electrical load being served.

(k) **Existing Wiring and Equipment:** Existing wiring and equipment shall be in good repair. Circuit extensions made with flexible cord wiring in lieu of permanent wiring shall be eliminated.

1000-2. **New Work.** All new work shall conform to this ordinance.

1000-3. **Evidence of inadequacy.** Evidence of inadequacy shall be any of the following:

(a) Use of cords in lieu of permanent wiring.

(b) Oversizing of overcurrent protection for circuits, feeders or service.

(c) Illegal extensions to the wiring system in order to provide light, heat or power.

(d) Electrical overload.

(d) Misuse of electrical equipment.

(f) Lack of lighting fixtures in bathroom, laundry room, furnace room, stairway or basement.

UCBC–5 PLUMBING DWV GUIDELINE

Acknowledgments

The material herein was prepared by the National Institute of Building Sciences on the basis of research conducted by the Davidson Laboratory, Stevens Institute of Technology. Technical reviewers for the Institute included Albert Tremari, Robert Wyly, William Tangye, George Schoonover, Wylie Mitchell, Larry Gallowin, and George Jerus.

Overall management and production of the *Rehabilitation Guidelines* was directed by William Brenner of the Institute, with David Hattis of Building Technology, Inc. the principal technical consultant. Guideline cover graphics and layouts were designed by the Design Communication Collaborative.

INTRODUCTION

This guideline is applicable to all types of residential occupancies. The guideline is not a code, but like a plumbing code, it is intended for use by persons knowledgeable about building plumbing design and installation. Its use should facilitate rehabilitation in circumstances where, for some reason, code requirements for new construction are being applied to a project undergoing rehabilitation. In general, there are two such circumstances:

- Repair and improvement of existing residential buildings, when compliance with the code requirements for new construction is triggered by a 25-50% Rule or similar rule which is in effect in the jurisdiction.

- Change of use or occupancy into a residential occupancy (e.g., from one- and two-family dwelling to apartment building, office building to apartment building), when compliance with the code requirements for new construction is triggered by the provisions of the building code in effect or some other provision.

For rehabilitation involving a change of use or occupancy, this guideline should be used when it is feasible to reuse existing drainage, waste and vent (hereinafter DWV) piping in the building, or when existing structural or architectural elements in the building pose physical constraints to the installation of new DWV piping.

New construction building and plumbing code DWV requirements can be a major rehabilitation problem because extensive *additional* structural and finish work may be entailed when either new or existing DWV systems are made to comply fully with current code provisions. There are several aspects to this problem:

- Existing vent systems may not comply with current code provisions for pipe sizing, connections, use of wet venting, and vent location, although they may provide adequate health and safety as installed and used;

- The installation of new vents and drainage lines, even for new fixtures, may be constrained by limited available space and/or the installed configuration of the existing piping system;

- The cost-effective use of existing DWV systems in rehabilitation projects requires judgment and flexibility by building and plumbing officials to a greater extent and in a different manner than is required for new construction.

Code requirements for DWV systems are not always consistent from one state or local jurisdiction to the next. What is permitted by one code may not necessarily be permitted by another. However, the hydraulic principles underlying the functioning of plumbing systems and the potential health and sanitation hazards involved in DWV are universal.

Alternative solutions to various DWV installation problems typically encountered in residential rehabilitation are presented herein. The application of these guidelines is intended to provide a level of health and sanitation which is generally equivalent to the level intended by current DWV requirements, while facilitating the maximal re-use of existing DWV elements.

This guideline is based upon accepted plumbing and hydraulic engineering principles in general practice and the experiences of recognized testing facilities. The synthesis of engineering principle with practical experience provides a sound basis for the judgment and flexibility necessary for successful building rehabilitation.

BASIC DRAINAGE AND HYDRAULIC CONCEPTS

Because the guideline recommends greater flexibility in meeting the health and safety intent of current codes, an understanding of basic drainage and hydraulic concepts is essential to its use.

FUNCTION OF THE DRAINAGE SYSTEM

The function of the DWV system is to collect spent water from the various building fixtures and drains and to convey this waste water to the public sewer or other acceptable point of discharge in a safe and efficient manner.

A "safe manner" means collection and transmission without the emission of sewer gases, foul odors, or suds into the inhabitable area of a building. Traps at the entrances to the DWV system provide water seals which prevent the escape of sewer gases.

Most codes limit the pressure fluctuation within drainage systems to $\pm$ 1 inch of water pressure under design load conditions. A more practical limitation, and the one used in this guideline, is to limit *the trap seal reduction to 1 inch of water under normal conditions of loading*. This concept permits the planning and carrying out of simple field tests on existing systems to determine their condition and provides a basis for approving modified systems in rehabilitated buildings.

An "efficient manner" means the conveyance of waste water and suspended solids without blockage. Efficient transport is a function of both velocity and depth of flow. The generally accepted criteria to ensure efficient performance is to size the horizontal drainage lines such that the velocity of flow is approximately 2 feet per second.

If the depth is not sufficient for a given velocity, solids will settle out. The depth of flow and water velocity are both influenced by the slope or pitch of the drain line. Increasing the slope from $1/8$ inch per foot to $1/4$ inch per foot increases the velocity of the water while it decreases the depth of flow. Knowledge and understanding of these characteristics of flow provides the basis for adjusting the slope of existing building drains, which often determines the capacity of the plumbing drainage system.

HYDRAULIC PRINCIPLES

The rate and volume of spent water discharged from plumbing fixtures and drains, as well as the frequency of fixture use, are important variables to understanding the functioning of a DWV system. Frequency of fixture use is high in public buildings (e.g., stadiums and theaters) and low in residential buildings. Rarely will all fixtures be operated simultaneously, so fixture use in residential buildings can be estimated as the maximum number and combination of fixtures that may discharge simultaneously. In larger buildings, the fixture unit concept is employed. Existing DWV systems are not normally loaded to capacity; therefore, they will usually accept a limited number of additional fixtures without adversely affecting the system's performance.

The rate at which water exits from plumbing fixtures changes continuously. For water closets, the discharge typically begins a few seconds after the flush is started and gradually rises to a peak rate of approximately 30 gallons per minute, remains constant for a few seconds, and then gradually falls to zero. The use of water saving closets does not increase drainage problems since their peak discharge rate is similar to conventional fixtures. The discharge time for a typical lavatory is approximately 12 seconds and the peak flow rate is about 10 gallons per minute. This low flow rate and short duration suggest that lavatories have only a small influence on the functioning of the DWV system. Bathtub discharge is influenced significantly by the geometry of the outlet piping, and may significantly affect the DWV system due to the long duration of the discharge flow. In most outlet arrangements, the rate of discharge rises to approximately 12 gallons per minute almost instantly and thereafter decreases continuously as the tub drains. Water conserving shower heads reduce flow rates, thereby improving the effects of bathtub discharge characteristics on the DWV system.

FLOW IN DRAINS AND STACKS

The flow of spent water in horizontal drainage systems may be described as separated flow since the horizontal drain is generally only partially filled. Water moves through the lower part of the pipe, while air flows through the upper part.

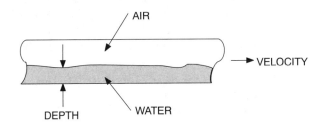

The velocity and depth of the water flow in horizontal drains changes continually. As the volume of water increases, the depth of flow also increases, displacing the air above it. When most of the air space is filled with water, turbulence increases significantly, and even small water pulsations disturb trap seals in the system's plumbing fixtures. Therefore, horizontal drains are designed to flow no more than half full.

The flow in vertical drains or stacks is entirely different. As water enters the stack it attaches itself to the walls of the pipe, forming an annulus. This cylinder of water falls down the pipe, dragging air along with it.

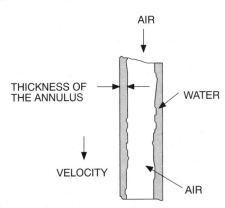

Annular flow is established rapidly within several feet of the point where the water enters the pipe. Increasing the volume of water increases the annulus thickness. When the volume of water occupies approximately $1/3$ of the cross-sectional area of the pipe, the annular flow breaks down, causing extreme turbulence and pulsations which may result in the loss of trap seals. Small diameter vertical pipes close to fixture outlets are susceptible to breakdown of the annular flow which may result in self-siphonage of the fixture. It is for this reason that S traps have been prohibited by codes.

The most critical area in a drainage system is at the base of the stack. In this region the flow must change from the annular flow of the stack to the separated flow of the horizontal drain.

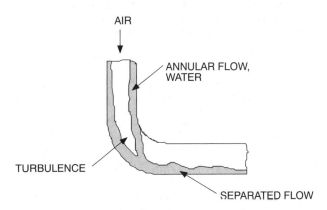

The disturbance at the base of the stack may be large, and significant positive pressures may be generated which, if not relieved, can cause blowback—the reversed passage of water through the trap. If the transition is smooth, much of the air is carried away through the horizontal drain.

Horizontal drains are not able to transport spent water at the same velocity as stacks. This results in a phenomenon called hydraulic jump. The change in velocity from approximately 15 feet per second in the stack to 2 feet per second in the horizontal drain forces an increase in the depth of flow. Recent laboratory tests find that this rise in the water level occurs much further downstream than the generally accepted 10-pipe diameters. What has been observed in the immediate vicinity of the base of the stack is a washing of the sides of the drain which may cause temporary blockage of fixture drains or vents that enter nearby. Fittings rolled up to 45 degrees are effective in avoiding problems in this area.

MODES OF TRAP FAILURE

The traps of a drainage system may fail by one or more of the following means:

- self-siphonage, or reduction of the trap seal as a result of siphonic action by the discharge of the fixture to which the trap is connected;

- induced siphonage, or reduction of the trap seal as a result of siphonic action by discharge of fixtures other than the one to which the trap is connected;

- blowback, or the emission of water, air, sewer gas, or suds into the fixture or the inhabited area of a building through the fixture trap; or

- cross-flow, or the movement of waste water from the trap, trap area, branch drain of an operating fixture to the trap, trap area, or branch drain of an idle fixture.

The first of these modes of failure, self-siphonage, is a function of fixture and branch piping characteristics. Plumbing fixtures which exhibit a sharp fall off in flow (e.g., round bottom lavatories) are more sensitive to self-siphonage than those with more gradual changes in flow. Traps serving bathtubs are rarely subject to self-siphonage. Self-venting trap arms and branch drains can be designed to prevent self-siphonage through knowledge of the fixture discharge characteristics and correct pipe sizing and configuration.

Induced siphonage, blowback, and cross-flow are prevented through correct venting design and installation. Every drainage system has a basic hydraulic capacity which may be increased by the addition of vents. The function of venting is to maintain close to atmospheric pressure in the drainage system so that trap seals will not be disturbed. A sure way to protect the DWV system is to provide individual fixture vents, an obviously expensive approach. Among the more economical alternatives that have been developed, tested, and commonly approved for residential buildings are stack venting and wet venting.

In stack venting, fixture traps are protected by venting provided through the upper portion of the soil or waste stack. Successful installations require that fixtures be connected to the stack independently, in the order of their rate of discharge (those with the highest rate of discharge placed at the lowest point in the module), and at those parts of the stack where pressure fluctuations are small. Most codes allow stack venting of fixture traps on the top floor of a building.

Wet venting is a technique that uses the drain pipe itself for venting of selected fixture traps. In practice, wet vents receive only the spent water from fixtures that have a low rate of discharge. These fixtures need not enter the stack independently, and in many installations, groups of fixtures connect to a single horizontal branch. A variety of wet vented modules have been developed and accepted by various codes over the years.

Progressive plumbing designs incorporate wet vented and stack vented modules as major DWV components, supplemented by individually vented fixtures where required by design restraints.

1
DETERMINATION OF EXISTING CONDITION OF THE DWV SYSTEM

The condition and capacity of the existing DWV system must be determined before any informed decision can be made as to the need for and extent of rehabilitation. This determination may also be necessary to provide the authority having jurisdiction with the information necessary to evaluate a proposed DWV rehabilitation project (see the *Guideline for Approval of Building Rehabilitation*). This part of the guideline discusses inspection procedures, documentation, testing, and methods for estimating system capacity, all of which may be required to determine existing conditions.

1.1
INSPECTION, SYSTEM SCHEMATICS, AND PRELIMINARY EVALUATION

A field inspection of the existing DWV system should be carried out to obtain the following general information:

- Overall physical condition;
- Evidence of impaired structural serviceability and hydraulic integrity
- System configuration and sizing;
- Existence of surcharged sewers; and
- Effects of existing structural and architectural elements, as well as the DWV system, on achieving rehabilitation design objectives (e.g., locating a vent for an island sink).

Based upon this inspection, and in conjunction with data from any available plumbing construction drawings and specifications, a schematic diagram of the DWV system should be prepared.

This diagram will provide information necessary to establish the following:

- Scope of the system and related building elements;
- Nature of specific deviation from code requirements;
- Need for modification or amplification of the functional performance test discussed in Part 1.2 below, and the number of tests to be performed; and
- Calculation of the installed capacity and the code- permitted capacity of the installed DWV system, discussed in Part 1.3 below.

1.2
TESTING THE EXISTING SYSTEM

Structural Serviceability

In most cases, physical testing to determine structural serviceability of the DWV system is unnecessary. Adequate evidence of structural serviceability may be obtained by the following:

- Careful attention to those areas where the DWV system is exposed to view;
- Evidence of exposure to freezing temperatures;
- Evidence of fire damage; and
- Careful attention to the DWV system's attachments to and penetrations of the building structure.

Hydraulic Integrity (Watertightness)

In addition to a visual inspection for hydraulic integrity, one or more of the following three tests, described briefly below, should be performed to determine the watertightness of the DWV system and to locate leaks, if any. Each of these tests will provide evidence on the watertightness of the DWV system. However, if the DWV system has been in recent and continuous use and has not developed any leaks, and if the proposed rehabilitation is not extensive, testing for hydraulic integrity may not be required.

If the DWV system and connected fixtures are intact, perform a Finished Plumbing Test. This test method utilizes a thick pungent smoke so it may be impractical or difficult to perform in a partially occupied building. If a Finished Plumbing Test cannot be performed on an intact system, then perform a Flow Test. If the DWV system is not intact, perform a Rough Plumbing Test.

When available, standard test procedures included in the local plumbing code should be followed for each of the tests briefly specified as follows:

Finished Plumbing Test: The test of the intact DWV system should be performed by filling all traps with water and then introducing a thick pungent smoke into the system near the base of the stack. When the smoke appears at the vent openings, they shall be closed and a pressure equivalent to a 2 inch water column attained. This pressure shall be held for 15 minutes before inspection starts.

Flow Test: The flow test should be performed on all parts of the intact DWV system by filling each fixture within a group to its normal capacity and then discharging the spent water. Where several fixtures are connected to the same branch, the fixtures shall be discharged together.

Rough Plumbing Test: The water or air test conducted on the roughed-in plumbing shall be completed by blocking the lower portion of the system and filling the drain and vent piping with water. In tall buildings, the system should be tested at intervals such that the manufacturer's working pressure for the joints is not exceeded, but no section should be tested with less than 10 feet of water except the uppermost 10 feet of the system. The water shall be kept in the system for at least 15 minutes before the inspection starts. The system shall be tight at all points. When using air as a test media, all inlets and outlets must be sealed except where the air pressure apparatus is connected to the system. Air shall be introduced until a uniform gauge pressure of 5 psi is attained. This pressure shall be held for 15 minutes without the introduction of additional air.

Functional Performance

DWV systems with proven hydraulic integrity (i.e., as described above or repaired in accordance with Part 2.1 below) should be subjected to one or more functional performance tests unless they are in compliance with current codes (see Parts 1.1 above and 1.3 below). Functional performance tests should be carried out to determine the resistance of the DWV system to each of the following modes of failure:

- Self-siphonage;
- Induced siphonage;
- Blowback; and
- Cross-flow.

Tests for self-siphonage, and tests for induced siphonage, blow-back, and cross-flow which may occur on the same floor (i.e., branch pipe testing), should be planned on the basis of analysis of the system schematics discussed in Part 1.1 above. Tests for resistance to induced siphonage and blowback on different floors (i.e., stack testing) should be carried out for each stack.

Performance tests like the one specified below, carried out in the laboratory on full-scale drainage systems, have shown that trap seal reduction by induced siphonage is greatest in those fixtures located 2 and 3 floors below the active fixtures. Blow-back, the most common mode of failure, usually is observed in the ground or first floor water closets. Systems near capacity will show a trap seal reduction of $3/4$ to 1 inch and/or display considerable movement of the water surface in the water closets.

Despite extensive laboratory test experience and the inclusion of performance test guidelines in the Standard Plumbing Code (Ch. XVI), standard test instrumentation and procedures have not been developed for performance testing of plumbing systems. If and when such standard methods are developed, all testing, including the performance testing recommended below, should be carried out in accordance with such methods.

The following clear water test is appropriate for back to back bathroom stacks up to ten stories in height. *

Functional Performance Test for Bathroom Stacks:

Select the required test load from the table below. The test loads are based upon a frequency of use ratio of 0.01. This frequency of use is consistent with data developed at the Davidson Laboratory and the National Bureau of Standards (see Table AS, NBSIR 73-161, *Field Test of Hydraulic Performance of a Single-Stack Drainage System at the OPERATION BREAKTHROUGH Prototype Site in Kings County, Washington*), but is significantly lower than the test loading requirements of Ch. XVI of the *Standard Plumbing Code*, published by the Southern Building Code

Congress International, and British test loading data. For different frequency ratios and related loading requirements, see Table AS referenced above.

Building Type	Test Load
Single family dwelling	One water closet and one bathtub
Multi-family up to four stories	Two water closets
Multi-family four to ten stories	Two water closets and one bathtub

Select fixtures for discharge that are most remote with respect to the building drain in single family homes, and vertically adjacent at the uppermost levels in multi-family dwellings.

Then, fill all fixture traps. Discharge the selected fixtures simultaneously. Observe and record the trap seal reduction in the idle fixture traps. Reduction of more than 1 inch of water is critical and should be recorded. Observe the lower floor water closets for blowback.

1.3
ESTIMATING THE CAPACITY OF THE EXISTING DWV SYSTEM

The installed capacity of the existing DWV system should be estimated for two reasons. First, by comparing it to the code-permitted capacity, potential code-related problems will become evident. Second, the estimated capacity is an indication of the system's potential for accepting additional fixtures to be installed as part of the proposed rehabilitation.

The following procedure should be followed:

Identify and count all fixtures connected to each DWV stack. Translate the fixture count into fixture unit values, based on the following table:

Fixture	Fixture Units
Automatic clothes washer	3
Bathtub (w/ or w/o overhead shower)	2
Bathroom group (incl. tank type w.c.)	6
Bathroom group (incl. flushometer valve w.c.)	8
Dishwasher	2
Floor drain	2
Kitchen sink (w/ or w/o food-waste grinder)	2
Lavatory	1
Laundry tray	2
Shower stall	2
Sink, service type with floor outlet	3
Sink, service type with P-trap	2
Water closet (tank type)	4
Water closet with flushometer valve	8

Based on the system schematic (Part 1.1 above), identify the existing size of the stack and size and slope of the drain, as well as code required sizes.

Based on the system schematic, determine the type of venting. For the purpose of simplification, the type of venting falls into three categories: single stack with no secondary vents, vents of "unknown" condition, and code-compliant vents.

Vents of "unknown" condition are vents which may be partially blocked, or are otherwise of lesser venting than code-compliant vents.

---

* Increased test loads, introduction of solids and/or suds, and other points of observation should be considered for other types of stacks, based on analysis of the system schematic.

215

Based upon the information from the steps above, estimate the fixture unit capacity of the DWV system from the following table (Note: this table applies to back to back vertical stack arrangements only):

Stack size	Building Drain Size @ 1/4" slope* per foot	Allowable number of fixture units		
		Single stack**	Vents of "unknown" condition†	Code-compliant vents
3"	4"	15††	30††	72††
4"	4"	96	150	216
4"	5"			480
5"	5"			480
5"	6"			840

* If slope exceeds 1/4" per foot, capacity will increase.

** Capacity of single stack as found in an existing building. This capacity may be exceeded with engineered single stack systems subjected to final performance tests. Single stack systems are not recommended in locations where building drains are subject to flooding under normal conditions.

† The listed capacities may be exceeded if the system does not fail when subjected to final performance tests.

†† Not more than 3 stories, nor more than 6 water closets.

2
PROBLEMS AND SOLUTIONS (PROPOSED MODIFICATIONS)

2.1
CORRECTING EXISTING DWV SYSTEM STRUCTURAL, HYDRAULIC, AND FUNCTIONAL DEFECTS, AND SURCHARGED SEWERS

2.1.1

Problem: The inspection of the existing DWV system (Part 1.1 above) reveals that the mechanical strength of existing pipes, fittings, and supports is appreciably lower than that required for new construction and/or the DWV system is inadequately attached to the building. These conditions may be evidenced by:

- Extensive corrosion, scale, and other deterioration of wall

- Pipe movement, misalignment, and nonuniform slope;

- Joint separation;

- Other indications of failure;

- Evidence of exposure to freezing temperatures;

- Evidence of excessive thermal expansion and contraction; or

- Evidence of fire damage.

Solution: Removal or repair of the damaged parts.

Discussion: Age alone is not indicative of the condition of a plumbing drainage system. Many systems have been found to be in excellent physical condition after decades of service.

2.1.2

Problem: Reduced clearances in sleeves and supports, pipe deflection, or other like evidence indicates that the DWV system

has been subjected to excessive live or dead loads, above normal service loads.

Solution: Remove such live or dead loads and repair or replace damaged parts.

2.1.3

Problem: The test(s) for hydraulic integrity (see Part 1.2 above) reveals that all or part of the DWV system is not watertight.

Solution: Repair or remove parts of the DWV system as needed to bring it to a condition of watertightness under the subject tests.

2.1.4

Problem: The functional performance tests (see Part 1.2 above) result in a trap seal reduction of more than 1 inch of water (induced siphonage), and/or blowback, self-siphonage, or cross-flow are observed in the DWV system, indicating a functional deficiency.

Solution: Modify the DWV system, in accordance with Part 2.3 of this guideline, to a condition where it meets all the functional performance tests (see also the discussion of Basic Drainage and Hydraulic Concepts above).

2.1.5

Problem: Self-siphonage is observed in an S trap that is subjected to a functional performance test.

Solution: Modify the fixture so that the distance between the trap outlet and the vertical drop is at least two pipe diameters, but only if the size of the vertical pipe is one diameter larger than the trap inlet (see also Appendix B, Figure 1 for additional information on acceptable practices).

Discussion: The concern for self-siphonage of S traps has led to their prohibition by codes. Self-siphonage in S traps can be eliminated by the modification described above, which is consistent with National Standard Plumbing Code §12.8.2, published by the National Association of Plumbing-Heating-Cooling Contractors.

2.1.6

Problem: The drainage system of the building is subject to backflow from the public sewer system.

Solution: Approved suitable means such as sewage ejectors, isolation of basement drainage, and backwater valves should be employed to prevent backflow from entering the building.

2.2
RELOCATING FIXTURES

Problem: The proposed rehabilitation, when the existing DWV system is without structural, hydraulic, or functional defects and has adequate capacity for its installed fixtures (see Part 1.3 above), involves the relocation of fixtures without any additional load being imposed on the system. However, the length of unvented horizontal fixture drain between the proposed fixture and existing vertical drain exceeds that allowed by the local plumbing code.

Solution: For bathroom groups, allow fixture drain lengths having a slope of 1/4 inch per foot up to the maximum indicated in the following table, provided the connection to the stack is with a sanitary tee or a long turn TY:

Maximum Developed Length of Unvented Fixture Drains	
Diameter of Drain	Length
$1^1/_4$"	5'
$1^1/_2$"	7'
2"	10'
3"	12'
4"	20'

For kitchen (flat bottomed) sinks with or without dishwasher and garbage disposer, allow drain lengths having a slope of $^1/_4$ inch per foot up to 12 feet with 2 inch drain (see Appendix B, Figures 2, 3, and 4).

<u>Discussion</u>: The concern for self-siphonage in fixtures has led to limitations on lengths of unvented fixture drains. Existing distances as specified in codes may impose a severe restriction on rehabilitation. The smaller diameter fixture outlets of modern installations have reduced flow rates and suggest the acceptability of longer permissible fixture drains.

The data in the table above is based on the following reports: *Test on Branch Layouts—Investigation of Minimal Tube Diameter*, by O. H. C. Messner, Zurich, Switzerland, April, 1970; and *An Investigation of the Safety and Durability of the Plumbing Systems in Mobile Homes*, Report SIT-DL-79-9-2079, Stevens Institute of Technology, Hoboken, N. J. (to be published).

The recommended kitchen unit drain lengths are based on *Plumbing Manual*, BMS-66, U. S. Government Printing Office, 1940.

2.3
ADDING NEW FIXTURES TO EXISTING DWV SYSTEMS, EXTENDING DWV SYSTEMS, AND/OR INSTALLING NEW DWV SYSTEMS IN EXISTING BUILDINGS

<u>Problem</u>: The proposed rehabilitation, when the existing DWV system is without structural, hydraulic, or functional defects, involves any combination of the following activities:

- Adding new fixtures to the existing DWV system when its capacity exceeds its installed fixtures (see Part 1.3 above);

- Extending the existing DWV system when its capacity exceeds its installed fixtures (see Part 1.3 above); or

- Installing new DWV systems in an existing building (whether or not the existing system will continue in use).

However, full compliance with current plumbing codes requires extensive structural or architectural changes causing unwarranted additional costs and delays to the rehabilitation project.

<u>Solution</u>: All additions and alterations to existing plumbing DWV systems should be designed and installed in accordance with Performance Criteria (see Appendix A) covering the following six attributes of the system:

- Transport of Wastes
- Durability
- Maintainability
- Structural Serviceability
- Hydraulic Integrity
- Functional Performance

Alternative acceptable solutions may be found in the following documents:

- *Standard Plumbing Code*, Chapter XVI, Section 1602—Single Stack Discharge Ventilating Pipe Systems;

- Southern Building Code Congress International (SBCCI) and Building Officials and Code Administrators International (BOCA) research reports for automatic anti-siphon trap vent devices; and

- NBS <u>Building Science Series</u>, No. 60, *Hydraulic Performance of a Full Scale Townhouse System with Reduced-Size Vents*, August 1975, for reduced sized venting design.

Appendix B illustrates typical solutions which will comply with the Performance Criteria under most conditions of operation and use, based upon engineering analysis and interpretation of test results.

<u>Discussion</u>: Single stack DWV systems, even when fully complying with the Performance Criteria, are not recommended in locations where building drains are subject to flooding under normal conditions.

2.4
THROUGH-THE-WALL VENTING

<u>Problem</u>: An existing DWV system, an addition to an existing DWV system, or a new DWV system in an existing building may include through-the-wall rather than roof venting. This condition, which may be determined by inspecting the building or examining existing and/or proposed plans, is likely to be prohibited by the local code.

<u>Solution</u>: Through-the-wall venting should be accepted in the following instances:

- In an historic building where through-roof venting would interfere with the character of the building.

- In rehabilitation projects where conventional venting is impractical. In this case, the vents should be at least 10 feet horizontally from the lot line and should be turned downward. They should be effectively screened with $^1/_4$ inch mesh to avoid trapping and freezing of any condensation. Through-the-wall vent openings should not be located directly below any door, window, or other building opening, nor should any such vent terminal be within 10 feet horizontally of such an opening unless it is 2 feet above the top of such opening.

APPENDIX A
PERFORMANCE CRITERIA

The following Performance Criteria are referenced in Part 2.3 above.

1. Transport Of Wastes

Requirement

Waste water and sewage shall be removed from the building and transported to an acceptable point of disposal without overflowing, accumulating, or backing up into fixtures.

Criteria

(1) Drainage stacks shall carry design loads when flowing less than $1/3$ full at terminal velocity.

(2) Horizontal branch drains and building sewers (except horizontal fixture drains) shall flow no more than approximately $1/2$ full under design loads. Horizontal fixture drains shall be sized to give an optimum balance between scouring velocity, diameter, and carrying capacity.

(3) Maximum lengths of unvented fixture drains having a scope of $1/4$ inch per foot shall be in accordance with the table in Part 2.2 above.

(4) Waste lines likely to carry grease (especially kitchen lines of 2 inch diameter or less) shall not pass through spaces where they may be subjected to temperatures below the ambient temperature of the occupied space, and all waste lines shall not be subjected to freezing temperatures, unless they are adequately protected.

(5) Vents shall not connect to horizontal drains unless the bases of such vent connections are washed by the discharge from one or more small fixtures.

(6) A uniform, continuous grade of the invert of horizontal drain lines shall be provided.

(7) Fittings, devices, connections, and methods of installation shall not obstruct or retard the normal flow of fluids in soil, waste, or vent lines.

(8) Waste water or waterborne solids from an active drain pipe shall not pass through an idle trap to a fixture.

(9) Suitable means shall be provided for handling drainage below sewer level. Where discharge from part(s) of the drainage system cannot drain by gravity into the sewer, it shall be disposed of through a separate drainage and sewage ejector system and discharged into the building gravity drainage system.

Test

Determine conformance by evaluation of calculations, plans, and specifications, inspection of built elements, and conformance to good engineering and trade practices.

Discussion

These criteria have been derived from experience and research on plumbing hydraulics at the Davidson Laboratory, Stevens Institute of Technology, or from standard design practice in general acceptance.

2. Durability

Requirement

The DWV system and its parts shall have a reasonable life expectancy as determined by the local jurisdiction.

Criteria

(1) New DWV equipment and systems shall be made of materials approved for new construction, free from defects, and designed and installed so as to be durable, without need for frequent repairs or major replacements.

(2) Before proceeding with an installation, the installer should consult with the local building department to determine the durability of materials and joints used under local conditions.

(3) The installer should observe the manufacturer's good practice recommendations regarding handling, storage, installation, and adjustment of materials and equipment so that the performance of such products will not be impaired by defects or damage.

Test

Determine conformance by inspection of installation and materials and conformance to good trade practices.

3. Maintainability

Requirement

The design and installation of the DWV system shall provide for cleaning and servicing of the various elements and shall minimize conditions that contribute to soiling, deposition, fouling, clogging, or other maintenance problems.

Criteria

(1) Horizontal drains shall be installed in uniform alignment at a slope in the direction of flow of at least $1/4$ inch per foot for diameters of 4 inches and greater to obtain self-scouring velocities. Where such slopes are not attainable, lesser slopes may be used if a mean velocity of at least 2 feet per second can be computed for open channel steady flow at an assumed depth equal to $1/2$ of the diameter.

(2) Access to permit convenient removal of obstructions and fouling matter in horizontal drain lines shall be provided as follows:

*   Not more than 100 feet apart for larger pipes;
*   At each change of direction of the building drain in excess of 450°;
*   At or near the foot of each vertical soil or waste stack; and
*   Near the junction of the building drain and building sewer.

Test

Determine conformance by evaluation of calculations, plans and specifications, inspection of built elements, and conformance to good engineering and trade practices.

4. Structural Serviceability

Requirement

The DWV system shall be capable of withstanding the physical forces that may reasonably be expected in the building during the rehabilitation process and in subsequent use.

Criteria

(1) The mechanical strength of new pipe, fittings, and supports shall be similar to that of new construction.

(2) The DWV system elements shall be securely attached to the building.

(3) DWV piping shall not be subject to dead or live loads above normal service loads.

Test

Determine compliance by evaluation of the installation.

5. Hydraulic Integrity

Requirement

The DWV system shall be air and water tight under conditions of *normal* use.

Criteria

(1) The major elements of the DWV system (building drains, stacks, and horizontal branches) shall be leak tight when subjected to a pressure of 5 psi.

(2) The completed DWV system shall be leak tight when subjected to a pressure equivalent to a 2 inch water column.

Test

Determine compliance with Criteria (1) by the Rough Plumbing Test and with Criteria (2) by the Finished Plumbing Test (see Part 1.2 above).

6. Functional Performance

Requirement

The DWV system shall accept and transport spent water and liquid in a safe and efficient manner.

Criteria

(1) The DWV system shall not, under conditions of normal use, display any of the following failures:

- Self-siphonage at any fixture trap;

- Trap seal reduction greater than 1 inch, indicating induced siphonage;
- Evidence of blowback at any fixture;
- Ejection of suds at any fixture; or
- Evidence of cross-flow in any branches of back to back fixtures.

(2) Single stack DWV systems shall be deemed to conform to this performance guideline if designed in accordance with the Standard Plumbing Code, Chapter XVI, Section 1602.

(3) Automatic anti-siphon trap vent devices may be used in the DWV system as permitted by the local plumbing code or as detailed in a SBCCI or BOCA research report.

(4) Reduced sized venting may be used in the DWV system of buildings under three stories in height, provided that the entire system shall be designed by a professional engineer familiar with plumbing design in accordance with criteria and guidelines contained in the NBS publication, Building Science Series, No. 60, *Hydraulic Performance of Full Scale Townhouse System with Reduced-Size Vents*, August 1975.

(5) Code-accepted, proprietary, engineered single stack DWV systems shall be designed and installed in accordance with the conditions of their acceptance.

Test

Determine compliance with the criteria above by the following test methods, respectively:

(1) Functional Performance Tests (see Part 1.3 above).

(2) Conformance with *Standard Plumbing Code*, Chapter XVI.

(3) Conformance with local code or SBCCl or BOCA research reports.

(4) Conformance with NBS Building Science Series, No. 60.

(5) Conformance with code requirements.

Discussion

Compliance with this requirement can always be achieved by the addition of supplemental venting in DWV systems failing this test.

APPENDIX B
EXAMPLES OF ACCEPTABLE DWV
PRACTICES FOR BUILDING REHABILITATION

The following illustrated DWV practices have been determined to be adequate in solving problems of the type discussed in this guideline, based on engineering principles and the experience of recognized testing facilities. They do not represent all possible problems, nor do they reflect the most extreme solutions in terms of deviation from the specific requirements of plumbing codes.

Symbols

WC	Water Closet
T	Bathtub
L	Lavatory
KS	Kitchen Sink
————	New Sanitary Piping
———	Existing Sanitary Piping
— — —	Vents

FIGURE 1

CORRECTION OF "S" TRAP SUBJECT TO SELF-SIPHONAGE IN FLAT BOTTOMED SINKS

ILLUSTRATION OF SOLUTION TO PROBLEM 2.1(5).

A = NOT MORE THAN 10 PIPE DIAMETERS
B = NOT MORE THAN 24 PIPE DIAMETERS
C = NOT MORE THAN 72 PIPE DIAMETERS

- ALL PIPE 2 IN. DIAMETER

- 1^1/$_2$ IN. TRAP

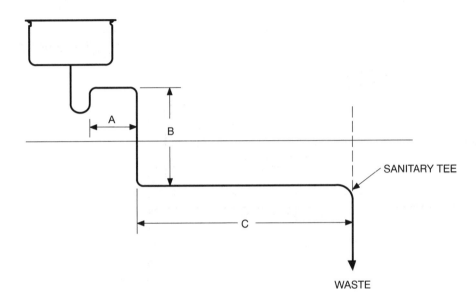

FIGURE 2

ISLAND SINK

EXAMPLE OF SOLUTION TO PROBLEM 2.2.

- ALL PIPE 2 IN. DIAMETER

- 1^1/$_2$ IN. TRAP

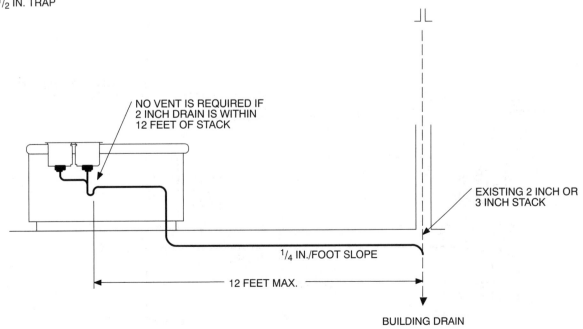

FIGURE 3

ISLAND SINK WITH DISPOSER AND DISHWASHER AT WALL

EXAMPLE OF SOLUTION TO PROBLEM 2.2.

NOTE THAT REQUIRED LOCATION OF DISHWASHER AIR GAP MAY VARY BY LOCAL CODE.

- ALL PIPE 2 IN. DIAMETER
- $1^1/_2$ IN. TRAP

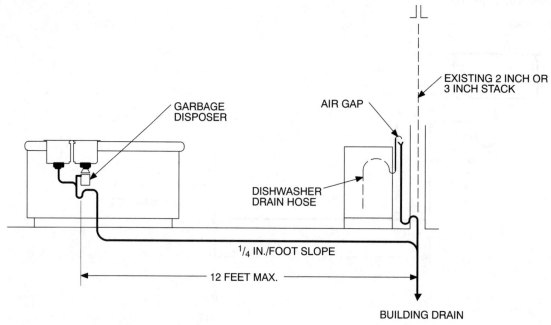

FIGURE 4

ISLAND SINK WITH DISPOSER, DISHWASHERS, AND CLOTHES WASHER AT WALL

EXAMPLE OF SOLUTION TO PROBLEM 2.2.

NOTE THAT REQUIRED LOCATION OF DISHWASHER AIR GAP MAY VARY BY LOCAL CODE.

- ALL PIPE 2 IN. DIAMETER
- $1^1/_2$ IN. TRAP

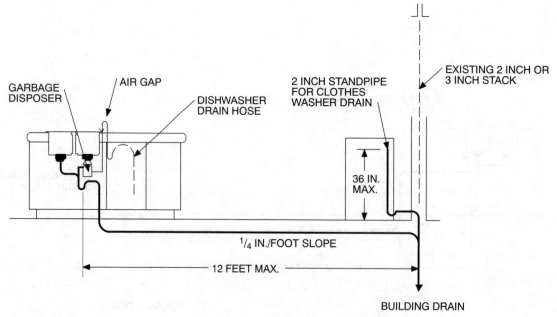

FIGURE 5

ADDITION OF FIRST FLOOR POWDER ROOM OF SINGLE DWELLING UNIT, SLAB ON GRADE

ILLUSTRATION OF USE OF WET VENTING IN SOLVING A PROBLEM OF THE TYPE DISCUSSED UNDER 2.3. FOR POSSIBLE USE OF SINGLE STACK SOLUTIONS, SEE 1.3(4) AND DISCUSSION UNDER 2.3.

NOTE THAT NEW BRANCH DRAIN LINE MAY ENTER BUILDING DRAIN ON STACK.

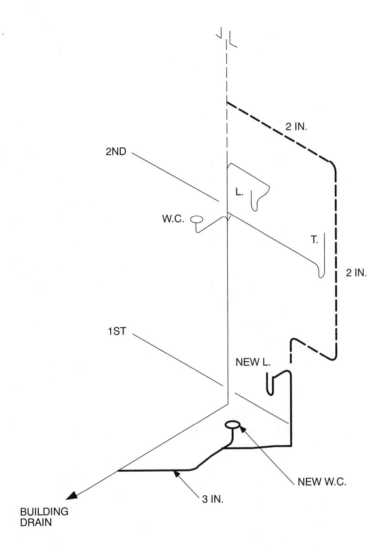

FIGURE 6

ADDITION OF FIRST FLOOR POWDER ROOM OF SINGLE DWELLING UNIT, WITH BASEMENT

ILLUSTRATION OF USE OF WET VENTING IN SOLVING A PROBLEM OF THE TYPE DISCUSSED UNDER 2.3.
FOR POSSIBLE USE OF SINGLE STACK SOLUTIONS, SEE 1.3(4) AND DISCUSSION UNDER 2.3.

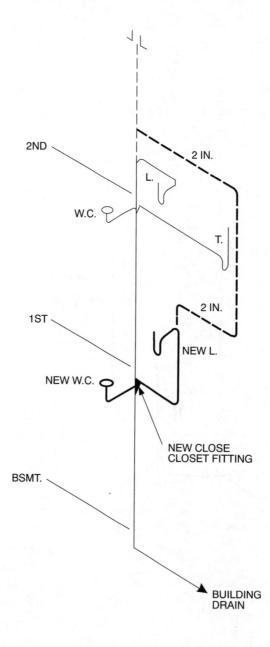

FIGURE 7

ADDITION OF SECOND FLOOR FIXTURE TO EXISTING STACK

A LAVATORY AND BATHTUB MAY BE ADDED TO THE SECOND FLOOR OF A STACK VENTED BATHROOM GROUP. TWO INCH DIAMETER TUB DRAIN MAY RUN 10 FEET MAXIMUM.

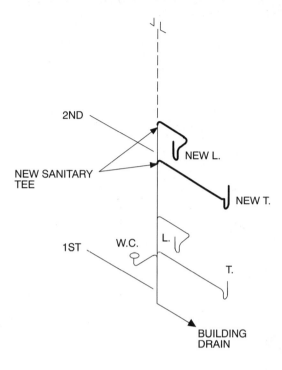

FIGURE 8

ADDITION OF SECOND FLOOR FIXTURE TO EXISTING STACK

A SECOND KITCHEN SINK, WITH OR WITHOUT DISPOSER, MAY BE ADDED TO AN EXISTING 2 INCH WASTE STACK. A $1^1/_2$ INCH FIXTURE DRAIN MAY RUN 7 FEET MAXIMUM.

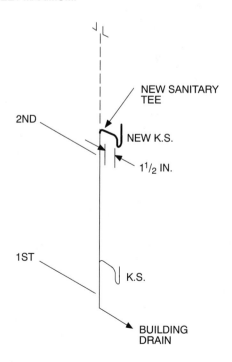

FIGURE 9

ADDITION OF KITCHEN SINK AND BATHROOM GROUP TO EXISTING 3-STORY STACK

ILLUSTRATION OF USE OF STACK VENTING IN SOLVING A PROBLEM OF THE TYPE DISCUSSED UNDER 2.3.

KITCHEN SINKS OR BATHROOM GROUPS MAY BE ADDED TO AN EXISTING WET VENTED STACK
(4 IN. STACK REQUIRED) OF NOT MORE THAN THREE FLOORS IN HEIGHT.

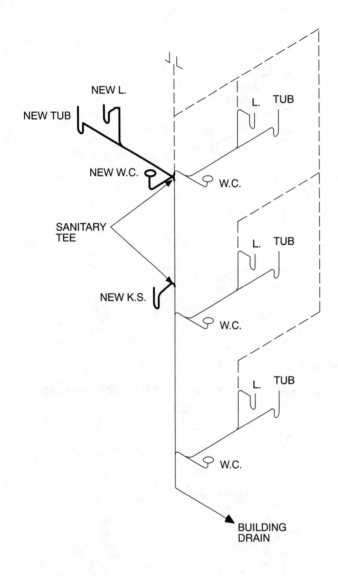

FIGURE 10

ADDITION OF FIRST FLOOR POWDER ROOM TO EXISTING 3-STORY STACK

ILLUSTRATION OF USE OF WET VENTING IN SOLVING A PROBLEM OF
THE TYPE DISCUSSED UNDER 2.3.

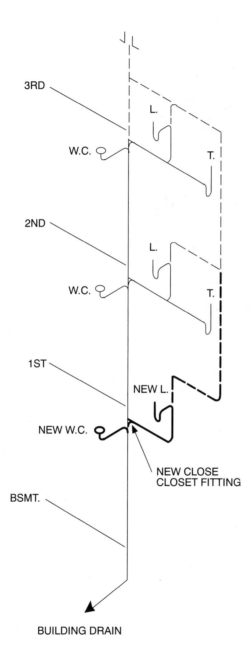

FIGURE 11

ADDITION OF SECOND OR THIRD FLOOR BATHROOM GROUP TO EXISTING 3-STORY STACK

FOR POSSIBLE USE OF SINGLE STACK SOLUTIONS SEE 1.3(4) AND DISCUSSION UNDER 2.3.

NOTE THAT FOR ADDITION OF NEW WATER CLOSET, TUB, AND LAVATORY TO EITHER SECOND OR THIRD FLOOR, SECOND FLOOR MAY BE WET VENTED AND THIRD FLOOR STACK VENTED.

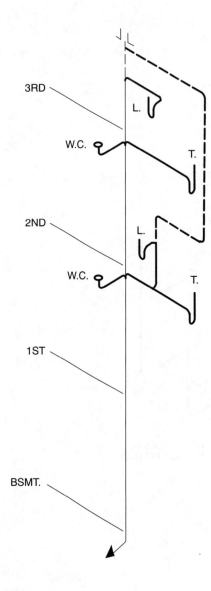

FIGURE 12

TYPICAL FULLY VENTED BACK-TO-BACK BATHROOM STACK WITH ALTERNATE SOLUTION

ILLUSTRATION OF USE OF WET VENTING IN SOLVING A PROBLEM OF
THE TYPE DISCUSSED UNDER 2.3.

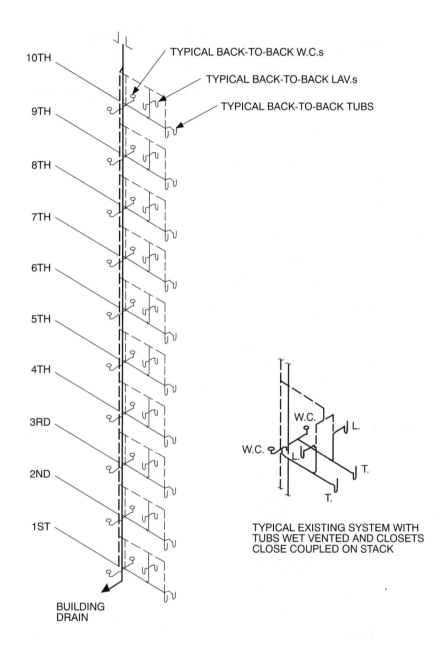

TYPICAL BACK-TO-BACK W.C.s

TYPICAL BACK-TO-BACK LAV.s

TYPICAL BACK-TO-BACK TUBS

10TH
9TH
8TH
7TH
6TH
5TH
4TH
3RD
2ND
1ST

BUILDING
DRAIN

W.C.

W.C.

L.

T.

T.

TYPICAL EXISTING SYSTEM WITH
TUBS WET VENTED AND CLOSETS
CLOSE COUPLED ON STACK

FIGURE 13

WET VENTING OF TUBS AND WATER CLOSETS

ILLUSTRATION OF POSSIBLE SOLUTION TO PROBLEM OF THE TYPE DISCUSSED UNDER 2.3.

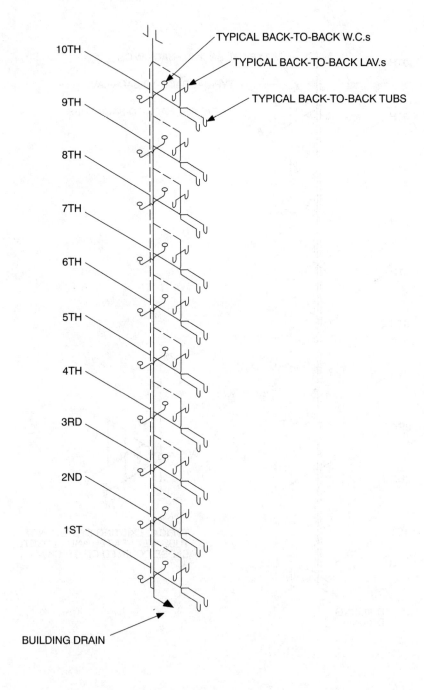

FIGURE 14

ENGINEERED SINGLE STACK SYSTEM SIZED ACCORDING TO PUBLISHED CRITERIA

ILLUSTRATION OF POSSIBLE SOLUTION TO PROBLEM OF THE TYPE DISCUSSED UNDER 2.3.

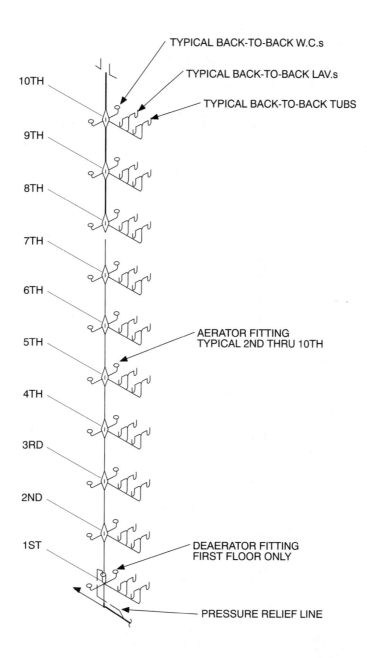

TYPICAL BACK-TO-BACK W.C.s

TYPICAL BACK-TO-BACK LAV.s

TYPICAL BACK-TO-BACK TUBS

AERATOR FITTING
TYPICAL 2ND THRU 10TH

DEAERATOR FITTING
FIRST FLOOR ONLY

PRESSURE RELIEF LINE

FIGURE 15

ADDITION OF DISPOSER AND DISHWASHER TO KITCHEN SINK ON EXISTING STACK

ILLUSTRATION OF ACCEPTABLE ADDITION OF DISPOSER AND DISHWASHER TO A 2 INCH
STACK ON EVERY FLOOR (SEE PROBLEM 2.3).

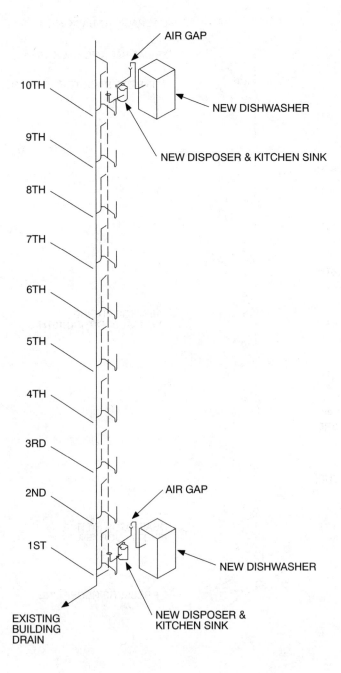